WHO MAKES THE LAWS?

WHO MAKES THE LAWS?

Creativity and Power
in Senate Committees

DAVID E. PRICE

SCHENKMAN PUBLISHING COMPANY
Cambridge, Massachusetts

Distributed by General Learning Press

Schenkman books are distributed by
General Learning Press
250 James Street
Morristown, New Jersey

To my parents

ELNA HARRELL PRICE
ALBERT L. PRICE

with love and gratitude

CONTENTS

FOREWORD

Two major questions lie at the heart of this study. The first has to do with how, in a day of supposed executive-bureaucratic ascendance and parliamentary "decline," specific lawmaking roles are shared within and between the American governmental branches. The second focuses on the sources and conditions of legislative independence and creativity in the American Congress.

The case material is drawn mainly from the 89th Congress (1965-1966), a period of unique interest in light of the purposes of this study. These years of extraordinary legislative productivity, spurred by an "activist" President enjoying large Democratic majorities in both houses, should, according to most indicators, have represented a high point in executive leadership. Displays of congressional independence and initiative during this period thus provide particularly persuasive evidence that Congress remains, in Ralph Huitt's phrase, a "durable partner" in the policy-making process. I offer no pronouncements as to which branch is or should be "dominant"; my aim is rather, by discriminating among various facets of the lawmaking process and examining patterns of action and inaction on a range of measures, to develop a more refined description of the legislative division of labor than those now extant and to begin to trace out its implications and consequences.

The thirteen major bills chosen for analysis all fall within domestic policy areas; despite this limitation, the variations discerned in congressional role and capacity are striking. Closer examination reveals that these variations may often be accounted for in terms of which congressional committees are handling the legislation; this, in turn, suggests that the exploration of my second question — as to the sources and conditions of congressional activism — might well focus on the committee settings in which legislators find themselves. Accordingly, I examine Commerce, Finance, and Labor and Public Welfare, the three committees which handled the thirteen bills in the Senate. My aim is to ascertain what aspects of committee life best help us understand the characteristic patterns of legislative action and inaction, initiative and deference, that emerge.

Foremost among the many debts I have incurred in the course of this project is that I owe the late Senator E. L. "Bob" Bartlett of Alaska. It was work on his staff that awakened my interest in the Commerce Committee and the Senate; I learned much from him, and he opened doors for me all over Washington after this project was begun. Without Senator Bartlett this study would not have been conceived and could not have been carried out.

To many members of Senator Bartlett's staff I am also indebted — to William S. Boesch, John M. Cornman, and Mary Nordale for interesting conversations and fruitful ideas, to Sylvia Curry and Diana Henry for clerical assistance. Administrative Assistant Hugh Gallagher was the source of many helpful suggestions; he read most of an early draft and effectively punctured more than one inflated phrase.

Virtually every page that follows mirrors my debt to the dozens of senators, staff assistants, lobbyists, and agency personnel who invited me into their offices and gave me insights into the legislative process that I could have obtained nowhere else. In almost every case, they were generous with both time and information, patient with my attempts to grasp in a few hours what to them was common knowledge, and helpful not only in giving answers but in leading me to the right questions. Many, besides granting multiple interviews, read and criticized early drafts. Their contributions in most cases must remain anonymous, and certainly I alone can be faulted for what errors of fact or interpretation the study contains. But it was they who furnished the basic data — and who made the gathering of it a pleasant and rewarding experience.

This study had its beginnings in a seminar paper prepared under the guidance of William K. Muir and a doctoral dissertation written under the direction of James David Barber. To several friends and colleagues — Jonathan Casper, Irwin Gertzog, C. E. Lindblom, John Manley, David Mayhew, Nelson Polsby, Richard Simeon, James Sundquist, Stephen Wasby, and H. B. Westerfield — I am indebted for suggestions, criticisms, and reinforcements at various stages of this book's development. Ethel Himberg was accommodating and painstaking in preparing the dissertation manuscript, while Noreen O'Connor and May Sanzone have been unfailingly patient and helpful in seeing me through innumerable subsequent revisions. Peter Maier provided valuable assistance in computing and indexing. And my wife Lisa, besides helping with typing and proofreading, gave more by way of forebearance, encouragement, and good humor than I could ever adequately acknowledge.

Portions of this study earlier appeared, in somewhat different form, in *The Journal of Politics* and *The Review of Politics*.

WHO LEGISLATES?

"Is Congress," asked Senator Mike Monroney as he opened debate on the Legislative Reorganization Act of 1967, "still capable of initiating and enacting its own legislative program? . . . Are we a viable, creative legislative force or are we, as our detractors contend, mere ornamental trappings to legitimize the legislative program of an increasingly powerful federal government?"[1] One respected political scientist, who is by no means atypical, has a ready answer: "The President is now the motor in the system; the Congress applies the brakes."[2] An equally dim view is taken by a colleague: "The congressional role in legislation has largely been reduced to delay and amendment."[3] But a rotund United States Senator, puffing emphatically on a cigar while leaning back in his chair, retorts: "These political scientists don't know a damn thing about Congress. Of course we still write our own bills up here."[4]

Thus is framed one of the more challenging problems facing the student of American government: Who legislates? In one sense, the answer is obvious: no statute becomes a part of the United States Code without being introduced and passed in Congress. But even a hundred years ago, when the American system was generally thought of as a set of independent institutions performing designated tasks, checking and balancing one another, it was often observed that the executive branch bore a heavy responsibility for what finally made its way into the statute books. "In theory," wrote Theodore Roosevelt in his *Autobiography,* "the Executive has nothing to do with legislation. In practice, as things now are, the Executive . . . must take a very active interest in getting the right kind of legislation in addition to performing his Executive duties with an eye single to the public welfare."[5]

Lawmaking today is often viewed as only one, and not necessarily the most important, instance of the allocation of values and mobilization of resources which constitute a society's "political function."[6] Such a view tends to deflect attention from the traditional institutions of government; it also makes questions regarding the interrelationships of the "branches" seem obsolete. Talcott Parsons, for example, abandons traditional distinctions entirely, treating the formulation and achievement of collective goals as the function of *both* executive and legislature, working "intimately in interchange" with one another. Both act as "sponsors of the principal interest groups in the system," and both are directly involved in "the main stream of collective responsibility."[7]

However intertwined the roles may seem from the lofty perspective of the social theorist, the fact remains that the tasks performed by our dual sets of policy-making institutions still can and, for several reasons, should be differentiated. At the very least, differentiation is necessary if one is to specify the components of the "political function" and to relate their performance to existing structures. Beyond that, interesting questions arise as to the relative *quality* of legislative performance in the two branches—the capacity for creativity and innovation, the ability to handle complexity and crisis, the potential for "sponsoring" or resisting various groups and for arbitrating their conflicts, the ability to respond effectively and "responsibly" to public opinion and to focus attention on important problems. What roles do (or could) the two branches and their committees or agencies play in the lawmaking process? How do their capacities and their characteristic modes of performance vary from area to area? What factors best account for the patterns of legislative activity that have developed, and what considerations might serve as a basis for assessment or alteration?

The present study will approach these questions through an examination of the division of labor on thirteen major bills processed during the 89th Congress (1965–66) and an analysis of the operations and environments of the three committees which handled these bills in the Senate. Our first objective will be to ascertain how and to what effect legislative tasks and influence are shared in certain major areas of domestic policy and among various constellations of policy-making forces. We will then attempt to specify various factors which have a bearing on the division of responsibility that emerges in a given area, with particular attention to the conditions of and the potential for an independent and creative role for the congressional committee.

THE QUESTION: LEGISLATIVE RESPONSIBILITY

Six Functions. The initial task is to isolate the crucial actions and actors on thirteen bills. This sort of venture is surprisingly rare in the political science literature. Some 25 years ago, Lawrence Chamberlain examined 90 bills enacted between 1873 and 1940, in an attempt to determine whether they were the result primarily of presidential, congressional, or interest-group influence.[8] Failing, however, adequately to differentiate the facets of the legislative process, he often virtually equated legislative initiative with the initial formulation of a bill. This led him to emphasize the role of Congress:

> *The long germinative period detectable in the genesis of most laws is of the utmost importance: it constitutes one of the most valuable contributions that a legislative body can make. No other agency in a democracy is so well equipped by composition and organization to discharge this function. The accessibility of Congress, coupled with its ever-changing personnel, tends to guarantee a maximum of responsiveness to the varied but always moving currents of thought.*[9]

But Chamberlain acknowledged that, while most proposals had deep "legislative roots," it was often presidential initiative that pushed them through to final passage. Policy initiation was, after all, a multi-faceted phenomenon.[10]

James Robinson strives for greater precision in his recent study of congressional "influence and initiative" in the making of foreign policy. Employing Harold Lasswell's functional breakdown of the decision process (intelligence, recommendation, prescription, invocation, application, appraisal, termination),[11] Robinson estimates the weight, domain, and scope[12] of congressional influence at each stage.

> *Congressional participation in foreign policy decisions is principally in the recommendation and prescription stages of the decision process. Recommendations of important measures frequently are initiated by the executive rather than the legislative branch. Thus in the prescription stage Congress is legitimating, amending, or vetoing executive proposals. The scope of Congressional influence varies with the constitutional provisions governing the making and conduct of foreign relations . . . The domain of Congressional influence, especially when it is initiative, tends to be on marginal and relatively less important matters.*[13]

Robinson's results are a bit disappointing, however. His primary focus remains on *legislation*—Lasswell's "prescription" stage—rather than other aspects of the formulation, execution, and evaluation of foreign policy. He would thus perhaps be better served by categories which subdivide the prescription stage and permit a more specific and precise attribution of roles. In any case it must be asked, as will be seen below, whether Lasswell's categories do not omit certain activities crucial to the development and passage of a piece of legislation.

The present study represents a narrowing of focus and an attempt at greater precision. The focus is on *legislation,* and on legislation of a particular sort: *major* bills which passed the Senate. The bills have been selected according to several, often mutually reinforcing, criteria of "importance": the number of days the committee devoted to hearings, the evaluations of personnel from the relevant committees and executive agencies, and the amount of *New York Times* coverage. When several bills were virtually equal in these respects, those which represented the widest coverage of the issue-areas under the committee's jurisdiction were chosen. In other words, only bills of considerable "scope" and wide "domain" are being considered. A case study format has been adopted to present a coherent view of each episode, a view which encompasses a wide range of potential actors and permits an assessment of what each actor did or failed to do. The narratives, however, have been compressed and summarized so as to focus on the one central question: Who was "responsible" for the bill's enactment?

The notion of "responsibility" is perhaps better suited to our purposes than either "initiative" or "influence."[14] It entails more than the introduction of a bill or the exercise of "power" in its behalf. Assessing responsibility requires a scanning of the bill's history, a mapping of the activities crucial to its development and passage, and an examination of who performed them. One need not become involved in the philosophical tangles surrounding "functionalism" to isolate a series of tasks normally involved in the successful advocacy of a bill and to conceptualize them as "functions" or as logical (sometimes temporal) "stages" of activity. Six such functions emerged from the investigation of the thirteen bills chosen for the present study.

(1) *Instigation and publicizing*—the public or private advocacy of an issue as one worthy of attention and ameliorative action. Typical instigators include the staff man or lower-level bureaucrat who calls a problem to his superior's attention, the congressman who highlights an issue through investigative hearings, or the author who documents and dramatizes a social need.

(2) *Formulation*—devising and advocating a specific legislative remedy for a supposed need. The formulator draws boundaries around an issue and establishes a focal point for its further consideration.

(3) *Information-gathering*—collecting data on the nature of hazards and abuses; the alternative schemes for solving problems and their costs, benefits, and inherent difficulties; the likely political impact of each scheme; and the feasibility of various compromises. Information-gathering is crucial to each of the other functions—to devising a workable proposal, as well as to plotting its political course and building a sense of need and legitimacy.

(4) *Interest-aggregation*—responding to the needs and wishes of individuals or groups affected by a given proposal. In one instance it might mean the championing of one group over or against others, in another the assumption of a mediating, "balancing" role, in yet another the stimulating of latent group sentiments. Such activities may both resolve and exacerbate conflict; they may, on the one hand, contribute to the instigation

and mobilization effort, or, on the other, give rise to attempts at modification or obstruction.

(5) *Mobilization*—the exertion of pressure, persuasion, or control on behalf of a measure by one who is able, often by virtue of his institutional position, to take effective and relatively direct action to secure enactment. Whether an issue goes beyond the publicizing and formulating stages usually depends on the support it receives from individuals, groups, or governmental units that possess authority and legitimacy in the policy area and on the extent of "intra-elite organizing" by key leaders.[15] Mobilizers may become involved in other functions as a part of these efforts, but they may benefit from—or be stimulated by—those who were active at the "earlier" stages as well.

(6) *Modification*—the marginal alteration of a proposal, sometimes "strengthening" it, sometimes granting certain concessions to its opponents in order to facilitate final passage. Modification may or may not complement actions taken at earlier points, but in any case the modifier shares responsibility for a bill's final form.

These six functions, though they display a certain sequential character and complementarity, do not represent simply a logical breakdown of the components the legislative process must "necessarily" include. They point up, for example, quite specific *norms* which govern the process in American legislative assemblies and the activities which legislators and the public *think* should precede approval: the thorough airing of the issue, the attempt to hear and accommodate all interested groups, the buttressing of every major bill by a compendious hearing record. They also point up the thoroughly *political* character of the lawmaking process in America. It is worth noting in this connection that the six functions delineated here differ considerably from those postulated by Lasswell and applied by Robinson to foreign policy-making. They come considerably closer, in fact, to the categories utilized by Gabriel Almond in describing the operation of "political systems as whole systems."[16] This may indicate the inadequacy of Lasswell's rather bloodless portrayal of the decision process and his neglect of interest-aggregation in particular. But it may also demonstrate the difficulty of accommodating a great deal of legislative activity within a decision-making framework.[17] The introduction, publicizing, legitimizing, and processing of a piece of legislation involve a great deal more than the "gentle," rationalistic, problem-solving processes of intelligence, recommendation, and prescription. The process entails gathering "intelligence" and responding to articulated needs and sentiments, but it also requires stimulating those sentiments, activating and mollifying groups, and precipitating and participating in conflict. In the legislative process, ends as well as means are in constant flux, ever the subjects of division and debate. Much is overlooked, then, if the process of a bill becoming a law is seen merely as a prescription being made, a self-evident problem being solved. Congress, indeed, "serves as an excellent laboratory for the study of politics and the [larger] political process."[18]

The six functions delineated above will permit us to break down legislative initiative into its component parts and to isolate the activities that were crucial to the passage of the thirteen bills. In this manner, "responsibility" for their enactment can be fixed more precisely, and a more sophisticated view of legislative activism may result. For the initial problem is not so much to ascertain whether Congress or the executive enjoys a *general* policy-making preeminence as to understand exactly who does what. If such a view challenges current orthodoxy, it also promises to give a more accurate picture of the division of labor that actually prevails.

An Historical Note. Woodrow Wilson in 1885 borrowed some lines from Bagehot to describe what had happened to the constitutional balance between the executive and Congress:

> *"In an ordinary despotism the powers of the despot are limited by his bodily capacity, and by the calls of pleasure; he is but one man; there are but twelve hours in his day, and he is not disposed to employ more than a small part in dull business: he keeps the rest for the court, or the harem, or for society." But Congress "is a despot who has unlimited time,—who has unlimited vanity,—who has, or believes he has, unlimited comprehension,—whose pleasure is in action, whose life is work." Accordingly . . . it has virtually taken into its own hands all the substantial powers of government.*[19]

A frustrated congressman today might well depict the balance in diametrically opposite terms. There can be little doubt that there has been a shift in the Executive-Congress relationship although there is disagreement as to its extent and permanence and the factors that best explain it.[20] Surely the growth of the country and its problems, the proliferation of government and its responsibilities, and the broad reach of mass media have given *every* president what would once have been considered an extraordinarily assertive role in policy formation.[21] Yet fluctuations in the balance of initiative and involvement have continued to occur. Some of this may be explained by the differing role-conceptions and skills of individual presidents. Party factors also come into play; Republican control of the White House, for example, seems to be linked with a less assertive executive, though it can also be argued that congressional assertiveness is linked with periods when different parties control the two branches and that which party is where is of secondary importance.[22]

The present study focuses on a period when, according to most indicators, executive responsibility should have reached something of a peak. The Democratic Party was in the White House and controlled two-thirds of the seats in both houses, and the President was one for whom the conception of a "weak presidency" with which Eisenhower had flirted "had not even a fleeting charm."[23] The 89th Congress, in short, offers an opportunity to study what might well be the extreme case of presidential initiative. Displays of congressional independence and initiative during this period would provide particularly persuasive evidence that Congress is indeed a "durable partner" in the policy-making process.

The study of lawmaking in the 89th Congress, and particularly of the distribution of responsibility within the Senate, promises to shed light on a second historical problem as well: Are the legislative functions becoming more widely shared *within* the legislative branch? During the fifties William S. White popularized the notion that the Senate was run by an "inner club," and Donald Matthews gave the concept some concreteness by describing a set of "folkways" to which "effective" Senators seemed to conform. Legislative influence was generally associated with being from the South, espousing a moderate or conservative ideology, having high seniority, specializing and doing one's homework, showing deference to one's elders, being open to bargains and compromises, and avoiding appearances of "pushiness", headline-grabbing, or ambition.[24] It may, indeed, be questioned whether such criteria ever served to identify an exclusive bloc in the Senate or, if they did, if that bloc had any monopoly of legislative effectiveness.[25] In any case, the circumstances that gave the "club" hypothesis a certain plausibility changed appreciably during the sixties. In certain respects, ironically enough, the way was paved by that archetypal insider, Lyndon Johnson. The effect of his personalized and centralized Majority Leadership during the fifties was to undermine the power of the "informal directorate" and radically to alter Senate organization and procedure.[26] Johnson's departure left a power vacuum which neither his successor nor the Senate elders were able to fill; the result was an increased dispersal of power within the institution and an increased openness to executive leadership (particularly since that leadership fell into Democratic hands) from without. Of particular and lasting importance was the "Johnson Rule," whereby the Majority Leader eased the force of seniority and assured each freshman of a major committee assignment. A device for the consolidation of power and patronage in Johnson's hands, the rule also gave younger, more liberal and activistic senators positions of increased visibility and leverage.

The number of members inclined to take advantage of such dispersals of power increased markedly with the mid-term landslide of 1958 and thereafter. A new breed of younger and relatively liberal senators became increasingly conspicuous; the nature of their constituencies (usually urban and industrial), the requirements of campaigning (increasingly oriented to the mass media and to the image of non-specialized "national leadership"), and their own styles and ambitions militated against an unqualified adherence to the norms that had previously served to keep freshmen "in their place." Their activism created pressures for, and was in turn fostered by, a proliferation of subcommittees, many of them chaired by members who would hardly have spoken up in the Senate of the mid-fifties; by 1971 there were 131 Senate subcommittees and only three Democratic senators who did *not* chair at least one committee or subcommittee. Other developments during the sixties—the breaking of filibusters, the bypassing of intransigent committee chairmen, the increased amenability of the Senate to presidential objectives, the increased frequency of publicizing and other policy initiatives in the lower reaches of the chamber—likewise suggested that the balance of power within the Senate was shifting:

> The Senate of the United States is today a mildly progressive legislative body in which the Old South has lost its grip, in which junior members are playing increasingly important roles, in which the fabled power of the committee chairman has been scattered, and in which the dominant influences are those of urban, industrialized America and the President of the United States.[27]

The present study will permit a more detailed assessment of this trend and of its implications for the policy-making process.

If an historical overview thus heightens interest and provides perspective, it may also convey a warning:

> To decide whether the power of Congress has declined is not as simple as most observers assume. . . . [In a sense] the 'power' of Congress over policy and appointments has declined since its apex in the period after the Civil War . . . [but] the Congress is now a far more active institution, far better equipped to deal with complex matters of public policy, far more deeply involved in an incredible range of important issues that ever it was or could be in the nineteenth century. . . . In the twentieth century, government regulation and control, welfare programs, foreign affairs, military policy, and the taxation and spending measures required for all these purposes have produced a veritable "policy-explosion." . . . In sum, in the post-Civil-War period Congress enjoyed a monopoly control over policies mostly of trivial importance; today Congress shares with the President control over policies of profound consequence. Congress has, then, both lost and acquired power.[28]

It cannot be assumed, in other words, that increases in executive responsibility have meant a proportional decline in congressional responsibility. The legislative activity of *both* branches has increased in absolute terms. There is no fixed and necessary amount of lawmaking activity over which Congress and the President are locked in zero-sum conflict. The increased involvement of one set of actors will not necessarily mean the eclipse of the other; indeed, they may stimulate one another, and their efforts may be cooperative more often than they are competitive. What is of interest is the *relative* distribution of roles and responsibilities, the functions and capacities of various men and institutions in relation to the ever-expanding range and complexity of policy-making tasks and possibilities.

THE FOCUS: THREE SENATE COMMITTEES

If Woodrow Wilson's comments on "congressional government" are of primarily historical interest, his description of congressional committees is still remarkably relevant:

> [The committees] dictate the course to be taken, prescribing the decisions of the House not only, but measuring out, according to their own wills, its opportunities for debate and deliberation as well. The House sits, not for serious discussion, but to sanction the conclusions of its committees as rapidly as possible. It legislates in the committee rooms; not by the determinations of majorities, but by the resolutions of specially-commissioned minorities; so that it is not far from the truth to say that Congress in session is Congress on public exhibition, whilst Congress in its committee-rooms is Congress at work.[29]

Committees are, of course, occasionally rebuffed or bypassed, and the growth of certain "centripetal forces" may promise further reductions of their hegemony. But the committees still enjoy "comparative independence," and their actions are imbued with "relative finality."[30]

Congressional policy-making is largely committee-centered. Most bills are introduced by the chairman or other members of the committee under whose jurisdiction they fall, with the committee staff often responsible for initial and subsequent drafts. The legislative interests of a member are generally shaped by his committee assignments (and *vice-versa*); his own efforts on behalf of a particular project will focus, in turn, on his chairman and on fellow committee members. It is members of the relevant committees who most often speak on the Senate floor or in public about pending bills; often the committees themselves have well-oiled machinery of publication and propaganda. Information-gathering is a prime function of committee staffs, and it is at the committee level, in public hearings and private dealings, that most of Congress' interest-aggregation is carried out. It is the committees, and particularly their chairmen, who determine for the most part which bills in a given area come to the floor and in what form. The committee chairman is often the key congressional figure in setting priorities in a given issue-area and in mobilizing congressional support. The committee room is the most important arena of modification and amendment. Norms of committee deference and reciprocity make for a presumption in favor of the committee's handiwork on the Senate floor, while the chairman's acceptance of a floor amendment normally ensures its success. In short, most of the activities associated with the introduction, processing, and passage of a piece of legislation, insofar as they take place within Congress, are committee-centered. The case studies will, of course, provide further evidence on this point.

If most of Congress' lawmaking activity comes under the rubric of "committee activity," the committee is then a natural, indeed a crucial, focal point for generalization and analysis.[31] It became evident at an early stage in the present research that the case studies would not merely indicate "who legislated" in thirteen policy areas—though each case surely had its own peculiarities. A broader picture emerged: that of three committees in characteristic patterns of action and inaction, patterns which cut across bills and areas of jurisdiction. A fruitful avenue of explanation was thus opened. For while the committees involved—Commerce, Finance, and Labor and Public Welfare—all presided over substantial areas of domestic policy, they differed greatly in composition, organization, orientation, and in their relationships to interest groups and executive agencies. The case studies will point up these differences, and a fuller profile of the committees and their environments will in turn help to explain the patterns of legislative initiative and responsibility that characterized the policy areas over which they had jurisdiction. This focus is by no means narrow: it will permit us to consider factors much more varied than might at first be supposed, and it will enable us to examine quite specifically the reasons for, and the consequences of, the range of legislative capacities and disabilities Congress displays.

THE SEARCH FOR EXPLANATION:
IMAGES OF THE CONGRESSIONAL COMMITTEE

Which aspects of committee life are most relevant to an understanding of the kind of policy initiatives, with what resources and what prospects of success, its members undertake? A committee is a complex pattern of action and interaction, structures and norms, internal and external relationships. Various models have been used for purposes of description and analysis, each of which calls attention to certain aspects of the whole; at least six such images can be gleaned from the current literature of political science. This multiplicity is not necessarily to be despised, especially when one's interest is in generating questions. Sketches of these six images will therefore be drawn and the following question asked of each: Given this picture of committee operations, what factors can plausibly be related to the level and the kind of legislative responsibility assumed by the group and its members? The result will be a heightened sensitivity to factors which can explain the mixes of legislative responsibility the case studies reveal.

The Committee as Personalities. "You people have this congressional reform business all wrong," a presidential press secretary once told a group of political scientists. "What's wrong with Congress is not the rules, seniority, and all those things. What's wrong with Congress is the *people* in it. You're not going to change anything until you change that." There is much truth to this jibe. Although any attempt to explain why a committee behaves as it does cannot rely on personal factors alone, as the discussion below will indicate, it must nevertheless at least start with the traits and purposes of the members themselves.

To categorize and account for the goals and purposes of political actors is a task more difficult than is often assumed; the implications of such difficulties for the "explanation" of policy outcomes will be tentatively explored in Chapter 8. For the present, however, it can simply be noted that legislators do tend to fit into certain "role" patterns, in terms of the activities they undertake and the conceptions of their job they express, and that these individual orientations generally have an impact on the "ethos" and the collective pursuits of the committee.[32] These goals and orientations are not formed in a vacuum; they may in fact be constrained by (as well as have an impact on) "the power position and functions" of the legislature or committee itself.[33] But recent research has highlighted the latitude a legislator enjoys and the variety of roles he may assume: "The issues or answers the congressman chooses to deal with are largely determined by the kind of job he as an individual wishes to do."[34] To appreciate this fact is not to deny the impact of external influences and constraints on a senator's or a committee's behavior, but it is to realize that group and constituency pressures, as well as the entreaties of party, president, and colleagues, are filtered through—and sometimes deflected by—preconceptions and predispositions in the legislator's mind. Indeed, on many matters—particularly in areas which are poorly "covered" by existing law and are thus ripe for policy innovations—external cues and pressures are either weak or ambiguous, so that what a senator attempts or does not attempt will largely be a function of how he sees his job and what he wishes to accomplish. Thus, if a committee contains a number of members who wish to play the role of "inventor,"[35] formulating remedies for troublesome public problems, the behavior of the group will likely differ considerably from that of a committee whose members display more passive orientations.

The extent to which, as well as the way in which, a role conception finds legislative expression might be related to a number of additional "personal" factors. Ideologies, ambitions, identifications, interests—all are relevant to an understanding of the sources and the shape of legislative initiatives. Among these factors ideology is of particular interest: it lends itself to quantification in terms of voting records and can thus be applied to the committee as a group, and there is considerable evidence linking social-welfare "liberalism" not merely with a certain kind of activism but with activism in general.[36] It will thus be important to supplement our inevitably fragmented account of the role conceptions and legislative interests of various senators with a generalized portrayal of the committee's ideological composition. Both should provide clues as to the degree and kind of legislative responsibility the group might assume.

The question of effectiveness must also be considered. The fact that we are interested not merely in the policy-making goals of senators but also in the extent to which their aspirations are translated into effective committee and Senate action makes it necessary to examine, in addition to the personal traits and orientations associated with the assumption of legislative responsibility, those that might influence the initiator's chances of success. One thinks in particular of the studies of Senate "folkways" which point to quite specific and restrictive criteria governing effectiveness in that institution and, in fact, suggest that, at least in the fifties, the very liberalism and activism which led to policy-making endeavors at one point perhaps worked at another point or in other ways to *reduce* the chances for success.[37] It is difficult, of course, to assess the precise impact such traits and abilities have on a given individual's—to say nothing of a committee's—effectiveness in a concrete instance. It is possible, however, to come to some assessment of the personal characteristics which members *feel* are related to legislative success on a particular committee or in the parent chamber. Such information, checked in a rudimentary way against actual performance, will be necessary in order to obtain a fuller understanding of the "personal" factors which are relevant to an individual's or a committee's success in assuming—as contrasted with merely desiring to assume—legislative responsibility.

The Committee as an Organization. To view the committee as an organization is to note that it structures human behavior for the accomplishment of certain objectives. Although this model calls attention to the group's formal anatomy, it may also focus on the "human elements"—purposes, incentives, patterns of legitimacy and deference—and the "linking processes"—communication networks, "equilibrating" and feedback mechanisms, decision processes—which hold the group together, bring forth and coordinate individual efforts, and marshal energies for the tasks at hand.[38] At the outset, however, it should be acknowledged that organization theory is limited in its applicability to the congressional committee. Lawmaking activity is rarely focused on either "accomplishing goals," as the "classical" theorists would have it, or on "offsetting those forces which undermine human collaboration," as stressed in "neoclassical" theory. The committee member who undertakes a legislative project is doing something different from the goal-achievement or problem-solving, even innovative problem-solving, that goes on in most organizations. His primary orientation is ordinarily to the *external* environment, and his main concern relative to that environment is rarely that a stated organizational goal be attained or that the organization successfully "adapt." To a considerable extent he must pose both question and answer. He will often generate an issue for political purposes, and even when he speaks in terms of solving problems, the cues for his diagnosis and remedy will rarely come from the committee as a group.[39]

But if the innovating legislator is neither motivated by clearly articulated group goals nor concerned primarily with the committee's viability as an instrument of human collaboration, his behavior is nonetheless shaped by organizational factors. His proposal of a piece of legislation sets forth a course of action for the committee to pursue; it thus must "gear in" to ongoing group tasks and procedures. Moreover, the senator proposes a bill from a certain place within the organization: he possesses or lacks certain resources and prerogatives, is subject to various rewards and deprivations, and is helped or hindered, encouraged or discouraged, by group structures and norms. It seems likely, then, that organizational factors will be helpful in understanding the incidence, the content, and the success or failure of legislative initiatives within the congressional committee. Three of these factors are of particular importance here; certain maintenance and communication processes will be reserved for later consideration.

(1) "The contributions of personal efforts which constitute the energies of organizations are yielded by individuals because of incentives."[40] If, as stressed above, it is necessary to begin with individual goals, orientations, and abilities in order to understand a committee's performance, it is also important to understand the reciprocal effect the group's "ethos" and reward structure will have on individual perceptions and efforts. "Pushy" activists, for example, may well find their way blocked if the senior members of their committees are strict "folkways" adherents, but their behavior will probably be affected in more subtle ways as well: the frequency and boldness of their lawmaking efforts will themselves be tempered by the anticipated reception of such attempts. Is the development of new policy departures in a given field explicitly or implicitly recognized as a committee goal? Is such assertiveness rewarded or frowned upon? Such questions relate directly to the efforts which individuals "contribute" to the group, and to the role of the group itself in the policy-making process as well.[41]

For the congressional committee, of course, many of the relevant incentives will be found in the policy-making environment; indeed, these "external" incentives may offset or lead to the modification of those associated with the group ethos. How adequately are the areas within the committee's jurisdiction covered by existing law? Does the formulating or publicizing of new departures promise political benefits? Is one area or another a matter of intense group or constituency concern; or, on the other hand, is public opinion either apathetic or sharply divided? Is the area preempted by other policy-making units? Are the problems so intractable as to make it politically dangerous to focus on them? The answer to these questions, too, are essential to an understanding of how the legislative aims of members are developed and expressed.

(2) When one turns from the structure of incentives to the more formal aspects of group organization, numerous hypotheses are available as to the structural requisites of innovation and initiative. Consider, for example, James Q. Wilson's and James D. Barber's speculations as to the general effects of organizational "pluralization."[42] When the number of "organizationally defined sub-units" is great, so the reasoning goes, the system's capacity for innovation will be increased: the interests of the organization's members will become more sharply focused and more intense, sub-units will feel a greater need to justify their existence and to enhance their role, and they will probably enjoy a reduced degree of supervision and less rigidly defined jurisdictions. The result will be not only an increased tendency to generate policy, but also a greater likelihood that the proposals will be "radical," due to the specialization and intensity of concern of those devising them. At this point, the argument continues, a reverse effect may set in. For pluralization will also give rise to malcoordination and conflict, and hence to veto, clearance, and bargaining procedures. The result in the long run may thus be the adoption of a lesser number of proposals, less radical in character.[43]

Such hypotheses are suggestive in relation to an old problem: the consequences for public policy of congressional "pluralization" via the committee system.[44] For present purposes, they are useful in exploring the likely impact of decentralization at the committee level. Of particular interest is the possibility that decentralization, as it is practiced on some committees, might result in an increased capacity for formulation *without* at the same time giving rise to frequent efforts at obstruction or amendment. Some committees, it is true, partially conform to Barber's expectations,[45] but in other cases decentralization might increase the intensity of interest and the "strength" of proposals without leading to harder bargaining or veto attempts at the full committee level. Subcommittees often have jurisdiction over areas which are not competitive or which have little relevance to members on other subcommittees. Norms of deference and reciprocity which grant a subcommittee virtual autonomy often, in fact, prevail. Under certain conditions, then, decentralization might be linked to both the frequent formulation *and* the adoption of "strong" proposals.[46]

(3) A third organizational factor influencing legislative initiative, closely related to the other two, is the distribution of power and authority within the committee. Whether "pluralization" results in the generation of "radical" proposals or whether responses can be made to incentives furnished by the environment will often depend on how prerogatives and resources

are spread through the committee. The mere presence of several subcommittees guarantees very little. "Subcommittees may be symptomatic of the atomization of power within a committee and of loose control by the committee chairman, but they may be used as tools by the committee chairman in an integrated power structure."[47] How much control does the chairman of the full committee exercise over subcommittee appointments, the referral of bills, and the scheduling of hearings? How often are subcommittee bills altered or rejected at the full committee level? Do the subcommittees have their own budgets and staffs? The probability that the subcommittees will play an independent, creative, and successful legislative role depends upon the answers to such questions.

Power and resources, of course, are dispersed not only among subcommittees but among other groups (senior members, minority members, freshmen) and individuals as well. Can various members expect hearings on bills they introduce? Can they obtain staff assistance? Are other members likely to quash or preempt their efforts? Can they expect acceptance, or at least a patient hearing, of their amendments? These questions, too, are related to the incidence and distribution of legislative initiatives on the congressional committee.

But the relationship has its ambiguities. If an "atomization of power" is likely to enhance the role of, say, subcommittee chairmen, it is by no means evident that this will always spell an increase in the potential of the committee as a whole. It is conceivable, for example, that a strong or even autocratic chairman—by unifying and utilizing all the committee's staff resources, seizing the initiative from reluctant or ineffective committee members, holding full committee rather than subcommittee hearings to publicize a proposal, cracking stubborn heads together, or squelching distracting attempts at modification—might enhance not only his own legislative role but that of the committee as a whole. If decentralization increases a committee's capacity for formulation, it might decrease its capacity for mobilization—or, if the subcommittee is less activistic in orientation than the full committee, it might actually reduce both. Considerable evidence suggests that the usual impact of a limited "atomization of power" is to increase a committee's policy-making capacities,[48] but its impact cannot be clearly specified in advance.

The Committee as a Social System. To concentrate on those structures and "human factors" which make for the coordination of effort and the achievement of goals is to see the organization in terms of its output. There is an alternative focus which points up additional aspects of organizational life: the group may be viewed as analogous to an organism, whose primary need is for survival and well-being. Two elemental processes are associated with the fulfillment of this need: the achievement of internal homeostasis and adaptation to the external environment. The organization, in

other words, is viewed as itself a *system*, with certain problems of maintenance and self-integration, and as part of a larger system, with which
it must come to terms. Discrete elements of organizational behavior are
interpreted "by establishing their consequences for larger structures in
which they are implicated. . . . *Functions* are those observed consequences
which make for the adaptation or adjustment of a given system."[49] The
main question asked of the system is how it solves its problems of integration and adaptation; the main question asked of structures, norms, and
procedures is how they serve these basic organizational needs. It is this
approach that guides Richard Fenno's studies of the Appropriations Committees: each group is seen as a "political system—having certain identifiable, interdependent, *internal parts*, existing in an identifiable external
environment, and tending to stabilize both its internal and external relationships over time."[50]

As a subsystem of the Senate, the committee must to some extent meet
the parent chamber's needs and expectations; as a system in its own
right, it must "minimize conflict" and attain "a meshing or mutual support
among its subgroups and roles."[51] The techniques and processes of
integration claim a certain priority: they, after all, enable the committee
to "hold itself together" and are essential to adaptation, among other
things. But their very universality—and the universality of conflict and dis-
sensus as well—make it difficult to use "integrated" precisely as a
descriptive term. There are further problems of form and substance. What
unifies one committee may disrupt another. A committee with an autocratic
chairman, a conservative membership, and a propensity to report as little
legislation as possible may be no less integrated than one democratic in
procedure, liberal in outlook, and activist in orientation, although the mode
of integration—to say nothing of its legislative effects—differs greatly.

It is nonetheless true that committees differ greatly in their capacities
for integration and that various aspects of committee life provide indicators
of the group's success in this respect. Figure 1 provides a summary of the
factors found relevant by Fenno and those who have built on his work.
Although the cause-effect relationships are not clear in every case, an
examination of these components and indicators of integration enables
one to assess the group's relative success in attaining internal equilibrium.

What is the relevance of all this to an assessment of the committee's
lawmaking roles and capacities? The assumption of responsibility at one
stage or another of the legislative process can rarely be understood in the
first instance as integrative or adaptive behavior. While the rubrics of
adaptation and integration are flexible enough to accommodate an extremely wide range of behavior, their inevitable focus on the committee's
structural "equilibrium" and its "capacity to persist" certainly misses the
sources and the purposes of much legislative activity.[53] Nevertheless, such
activity does take place amid ongoing systemic processes, and the way

**FIGURE 1. Committee Characteristics Commonly Associated
with Integration.**[52]

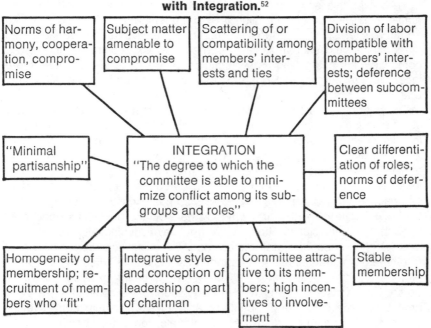

in which, as well as the degree to which, the committee solves its integrative and adaptive problems could have a decisive impact on its legislative role. What, precisely, might that impact be?

In the first place, one would expect to find a general correlation between integration, adaptation, and legislative *success.* "It seems unlikely that a committee consumed by uncontrollable or unpredictable internal conflicts could long retain much respect, confidence, deference, and influence with its parent chamber."[54] Fenno's claim that "of all the actions which promote success on the floor, the committee takes the most important when it creates and maintains an internal structure for integrating its decision-making elements" has received a measure of verification in his own and other studies.[55] However, integration could take place around norms or policy positions considerably divergent from those of the parent chamber, the "other body," or executive agencies; in that case it might make for more, not fewer, adaptive difficulties.

If integration generally facilitates successful mobilization by the committee and its leaders, it is probably associated with the assumption of penultimate legislative responsibilities as well. The prospect of success is a considerable incentive in itself. The integrated committee, moreover, is ordinarily attractive to its members, harmonious in its operations, and stable in its membership. Senators thus stay on the committee long enough to gain expertise and seniority, and become better equipped to play an active role. They enjoy and value their membership and are likely to take an active interest in the group's affairs, finding their participation facilitated by norms of "minimal partisanship," deference, and reciprocity. In short, a committee that has solved its systemic problems generally provides more incentives, resources, and opportunities for the ambitious lawmaker than one that has not.[56]

The possibility must be considered, however, that under certain circumstances adaptation and integration might have dampening effects on legislative activity as well, particularly as regards the chairman. Adaptation and integration are, of course, tremendous resources for the chairman, enhancing his chances for success and making him more likely to undertake legislative efforts. But they are often purchased at a price. Integrative or adaptive concerns might, for example, push the chairman toward a "low-risk" style of leadership, whereby he would avoid offense and perhaps raise his legislative "batting average" by reducing his proposals to lowest-common-denominator dimensions.[57] Similar considerations apply to other committee members. A harmonious and stable "meshing of roles" might open new possibilities to some, but it might exclude others. If potential activists find themselves in opposition to the committee majority, or if committee norms and incentives are stacked against legislative involvement, they might find in the committee's cohesion, consensus, and control a positive hindrance to their efforts.[58] Integration might enhance committee influence and facilitate the assumption of various legislative responsibilities, but under certain circumstances it could discourage innovation, restrict participation, and constrict the committee agenda as well.

The Committee as a Representative Institution. Few would go so far as to assert, with David Truman, that Congress and the executive are in conflict "only in the sense" that they are responsive to and supported by different sets of "organized and unorganized interests."[59] The thrust of recent research, in fact, has been to question the popular image of public policy in either branch as a response to group pressures and of political leaders as ciphers of their constituents; what is often impressive is rather the selectivity of perception and response that is exercised.[60] Yet, it has often been observed that in various policy areas Congress and the President characteristically seem not only to receive their cues from different sources but also to differ greatly in their capacity and propensity to aggregate certain *kinds* of interests and to respond effectively to their demands.[61] Theodore Lowi has recently made a fresh attempt to theorize along these lines, introducing the *type* of policy (i.e. the character of its "impact on society") as an independent variable and hypothesizing that distinctive patterns of political interaction and initiative will hold for different kinds of policies. "Distributive" policies (" 'patronage' in the fullest meaning of the word") dispense benefits to groups and constituencies whose claims are relatively unrelated and undisputed. "Regulatory" policies require more complex choices as to who will be benefited and who deprived but are still generally disaggregable to distinct arenas of "established economic interaction" ("sectors"). "Redistributive" policies directly touch broader segments of society, "approaching social classes," and generally involve a higher degree of conflict, since they are not disaggregable to isolated regions, groups, or economic sectors.

The distributive arena, as Lowi portrays it, displays small, relatively independent and isolated groups, each striving to "get its share." Congress, with its localistic orientations, decentralized operations, and norms sanctioning log-rolling and group accommodation, is generally their most promising point of access on the national level, as dozens of "pork barrel" amendments each session testify. The regulatory arena approximates the pluralist model, composed as it is of a multiplicity of interacting social groupings, shifting their alignments as perceptions of shared interest and conflict develop. Here, too, the interests are likely to be reflected and to find a provisional accommodation and adjustment through congressional operations. But problems of redistribution, Lowi asserts, cannot be handled in this way. In this arena, pluralized interest groupings tend to polarize and to find representation in the more centralized "peak associations" and in the executive branch. Congress is often limited to the ratification or rejection of redistributive measures that "arose out of the bureaucracies and the class agents represented there" or to the appending of a few "distributive" amendments. "A decentralized and bargaining Congress can cumulate but it cannot balance, and redistributive policies require complex balancing on a very large scale."[62]

Lowi's expectations will be re-assessed later in light of our case material.[63] For the present, however, it may be anticipated that his distinctions—particularly between distributive and redistributive measures—will be helpful in understanding a congressional committee's capacity to undertake and sustain legislative initiatives independently. They will be used, accordingly, to analyze the issues the committees under consideration are handling and the demands groups are placing upon them.

If congressional committees are likely to share common disabilities and dependencies with respect to certain kinds of issues, it is nonetheless obvious that committees differ greatly in their degree and mode of responsiveness to the range of interests and entreaties that confront them. Certain of these differences may be traceable to variations in the skill and persistence of the groups themselves; hence some rough comparisons of the committees will be attempted with respect to the number, character, and "strengths" of the groups with which they must deal. A related question is whether the groups that might stimulate the assumption of legislative responsibility in a given area make the committee a prime point of access. Such patterns of access are, of course, contingent on the committee's receptivity to the groups in question and on its ability to have an impact on policy, but there is, nonetheless, a reciprocal effect. Groups often reinforce the policy-making preeminence of the units with which they establish a working relationship, not only through the information and other resources they furnish, but also by virtue of the fact that their policy inputs do *not* give rise to challenges or preemptions from competing policy-making units. Accordingly, an attempt will be made to discern where the committees stand in the "races for representation" that characterize their areas of jurisdiction.[64]

A more decisive determinant of the patterns of interest-aggregation and responsiveness a committee displays is often the predispositions and identifications of the members themselves. Public opinion on many issues is diffuse and inarticulate; groups are often uninformed and ineffectual; messages are often unclear, contradictory, or garbled in transmission. But even when group messages are forceful and clear, the legislator is often free to avoid or hedge commitments, to manipulate perceptions to his own advantage, and to counter the pressures of one group by stimulating or appealing to another. To point up the looseness of "representative" relationships is not to deny that on certain occasions and in some areas, group efforts and constituency attitudes may be determinative of a legislator's vote or even of his more ambitious legislative undertakings. But one must be alerted to additional factors as well: What are the identifications and ideological predispositions of the committee members themselves? To what groups are they likely to respond? Until these questions are answered it will not be possible to understand how a committee stands in the "race for representation" among the policy-making units in its environment and how its members respond to, or even perceive, group efforts and constituency preferences.

The Committee as an "Island of Decision." It is a result both of the diffuse and decentralized character of the American political system and of the natural limits of human coordination and control that neither Congress nor the executive is a unified and hierarchical institution. Congressional committees and executive bureaus often enjoy relative autonomy as the "working units" in a given policy area, and their leaders frequently attain considerable status as "mid-level entrepreneurs of policy."[65] While such a system is not without its benefits and efficiencies as a means for the "rational coordination of governmental decisions,"[66] it also makes for a multiplication of potential checkpoints within and between the branches and places additional burdens on human cooperation. Under such conditions, the character of a congressional committee's coordinate policy-making units and of its relationships with them frequently conditions its legislative potential. The extent to which the committee emerges as a "core group" in the policy areas under its jurisdiction will in large part be dependent on the sorts of interaction and adjustment that take place relative to other "islands of decision."[67]

The preeminence of a committee in a given policy area will in part be indicated by the nature of its "moves"—whether, to use Charles Lindblom's terminology, they take "parametric" and "nonsymmetrical" form.[68] Paradoxically enough, however, one of the group's most important resources is the ties it secures with other groups; such a process will surely necessitate deference and compromise. In portraying inter-group adjustment, as in tracing the history of the legislative-executive "balance," it is important to avoid the zero-sum assumption. On the contrary: various policy-making units will recognize common interests and will find alliance and cooperation to be a means of multiplying the resources and enhancing the role of each—perhaps, but not necessarily, against a common antagonist.[69] Unity, in short, often means strength, while isolation is often associated with a loss of influence and initiative.

Which alliances are likely to prove particularly important to the Senate committee? Patterns of interest group access and support will affect intergovernmental adjustments and will be important in their own right. Among governmental units, relationships with other congressional committees may assume prime importance. Is the authorization committee's leadership, for example, a part of that "interlocking directorate," the Senate Appropriations Committee?[70] Are objectives shared and means of cooperation established between the committee and its House counterpart?[71] Then there are the independent agencies and executive bureaus. The temptation to secure independent alliances with congressional committees is often strong at the cabinet level, to say nothing of the far reaches of the bureaucracy; "it is no secret that some agencies can get far more through their legislative liaison than they can through the Bureau of the Budget."[72] But the agencies are not the only parties that benefit from such arrangements: the power and capacity of Congress—or at least of certain members or committees within Congress—are enhanced as well.

All this is not to deny that the legislative process is characterized by competition and conflict as well as by cooperation. The participants are still "partisans"; they will still "threaten or promise each other, negotiate, seize the advantage of prior decision where possible, build elaborate networks of reciprocity or, where their autonomy permits, simply play a parametric, deferential, or calculated game with the other."[73] Executive unity, while it may make policy changes more likely in a given area, may still represent a threat to committee hegemony; executive disunity or apathy, which may pose certain obstacles to action, can nonetheless be viewed as an opportunity for the formation of a new alliance or the undertaking of new efforts—with the committee closer to the center of things.[74]

Prospects of cooperation and mutual assistance may stimulate committee activity, but so also may a perception of hostility, "usurpation," or deadlock among other units in the field. In any case, relations between the committee and other "islands of decision," both cooperative and conflictful, will provide an indication both of a committee's incentives to undertake legislative leadership and of the role it is likely to play once the processes of manipulation and adjustment are underway.

The Committee as a Communications Center. The legislative process is, among other things, a communications process. Each of the legislative stages, from instigation to amendment, involves the conveyance, reception, and interpretation of information, questions and answers, attempts to persuade and to prescribe. Actors in the process thus form a communications "net," and a person's or group's place in this net provides some indication of his role and his "weight" in the total process. The committee's relationships with interest groups and other decision-making "islands" can be translated into these terms, as can the notions of role and identification. What questions do the committee and its members ask? To whom are communications addressed, and what kind of information is likely to be accepted and acted upon? What sorts of appeals and demands are addressed to the committee, to whom does it listen, and on whom does it depend? Do these communications facilitate independent policy initiatives, or do they predispose the group to some other role? Most of these questions have already been raised in a slightly different form. But the relationship of these patterns to the lawmaking role the committee actually assumes cannot be satisfactorily understood without some knowledge of the capacity and character of the committee *itself* as a communications center. In large part, of course, this calls for an examination of the committee staff.

The first question is one of quality. A committee can hardly expect to match the executive bureaus or even certain interest groups in information and expertise. But it can attain sufficient knowledge and sophistication to make critical use of information received from elsewhere, seek alternative sources where needed, and undertake independent translations into policy proposals. Partisans of a "strong Congress" have often deemed increased expertise essential if the executive's "near-monopoly of the facts and . . . specialized competence" is not to give it "complete dominance."[75] It can, in fact, be shown that staff abilities and other information resources have been crucial to congressional leadership in various policy areas.[76]

A second factor is accessibility. To whom are information and staff assistance available? The distribution of legislative responsibility within the committee, and often the role of the committee as a group, will depend on the distribution of communications resources. On many committees, "the staff is, in effect, the chairman's patronage."[77] Other members some-times find their sources of information and guidance severely restricted. Of particular interest is the situation of the minority. The law establishes in vague terms the minority's right to staff assistance,[78] but specific arrange-ments vary widely from committee to committee.[79] Agreements are often reached whereby a segment of the staff is hired by and solely responsible to the minority, but if the minority staff is spread too thinly or if it is isolated by the majority, such an arrangement may decrease rather than increase the resources the minority would enjoy under a "bipartisan" arrangement.

A third characteristic of the committee as a communications center—the roles and orientations of those performing the information-gathering function—is probably more important, if also more elusive, than the factors of competence and accessibility in influencing the group's lawmaking role. Scattered hints from the literature on communications in organization provide a useful perspective. Anthony Downs, for example, discussing the processes of innovation "inside bureaucracy," stresses the importance of the "search" process in instigating changes both internally and in the organization's performance of its social functions. This em-phasis on the external environment makes Downs' speculations particularly relevant to the processes of information-gathering as they impinge on policy-making in the Senate committee. It is "search," Downs hypothe-sizes, that points up a "performance gap" between perceptions and goals and stimulates the formulation and execution of "strategies of action." Patterns of organizational innovation and change will thus be highly de-pendent on the perspectives of those responsible for the search function. It is not that their expertise and professional ability are unimportant; it is rather that other characteristics of the seekers and transmitters of informa-tion—their inclinations and incentives to undertake "high-intensity searches," the goals they bring to the search and the point at which they perceive a satisfactory "equilibrium" between aspiration and reality, the way they communicate their findings and employ them in devising plans of action—will be equally if not more important.[80]

A second theoretical clue is provided by Karl Deutsch's reflections upon the sources of creativity in decision systems. A capacity to amass or ana-lyze sophisticated data, Deutsch makes clear, is no guarantee of creativity. In fact, information-gathering can be "pathological" in this respect, rein-forcing past patterns of thought and action. Moreover, creativity is gener-ally a function not of the quality of information, but of the form in which it is cast. Innovation is a matter of combining already available bits of information in a new way or to new ends. "The ability to produce novelty, and to recognize relevant new solutions once they have been found," Deutsch notes, "seems related to the combinatorial richness of the system by which information is stored, processed, and evaluated."[81] Thus, in looking at information-gatherers within Senate committees, our attention is once again directed to their purposes and orientations, the way they "combine" and utilize information.

It is being assumed, of course, that staff services rendered to congressional committees can and should go beyond the analysis and interpretation of proposals that come from elsewhere. In this light, Downs' and Deutsch's analyses of creativity and change in organizations suggest interesting analogies and useful questions to ask about the appropriateness of various modes of information-gathering. How is information generated, processed, and presented? Whether staff members approach their area of expertise with a view toward perceiving policy gaps or seeking out the needs of certain groups, for example, will surely influence the committee's capacities and propensities to develop new policy departures. Do the information-gatherers have strong policy preferences, and do they feel free to express them in their own reports and recommendations? Do they frame their "findings" in terms of "the policy aspirations and individual philosophies"[82] of committee members or otherwise attempt to lay out a course of action? Do they see it as part of their job to help certain members attain publicity and legislative leadership in specific policy areas? In order to understand how communications variables are related to the committee's potential for legislative responsibility, such questions must be explored; it will not be enough to ask the usual questions about staff competence and accessibility.[83] In fact, it must even be asked whether increased staff "professionalism"—involving as it often does a stress on nonpartisanship and expertness *per se*—might not in fact tend to restrict or inhibit certain kinds of congressional undertakings.

2

THE COMMERCE COMMITTEE IN ACTION

THE FAIR PACKAGING AND LABELING ACT

Hart's Early Efforts. Michigan Senator Philip Hart, so the story goes, opened a new box of cereal at the breakfast table one morning and found it half empty. "Damn it," he said, banging his fist on the table, "we're going to do something about this!" The tale may well be apocryphal, but subsequent events nonetheless justified Senator Hart's reputation as the father of the Fair Packaging and Labeling Act of 1966.[1]

Senator Estes Kefauver had shown some interest in deceptive labeling and packaging practices shortly before his death, and it was as heir to Kefauver's Antitrust and Monopoly Subcommittee that Hart hoped to implement his own interest in packaging legislation. After holding hearings in 1961 and 1962, Hart, with the help of Subcommittee aide Jerry Cohen, formulated an amendment to the Clayton Act prohibiting restraints of trade through deceptive packaging. But the parent Judiciary Committee took no action, and Hart became more and more doubtful that he could ever obtain a favorable majority there. Hart was nonetheless convinced of the merits of his proposal and of its potential political appeal; one of the most attractive aspects of his appointment to the Commerce Committee in 1963 was the likelihood that he could reformulate his bill and have it considered there. Thus was S. 985 introduced in the 89th Congress, not as an amendment to the Clayton Act, but as a prohibition of the deceptive labeling and packaging of goods shipped in interstate commerce.

Hart was anxious to begin hearings in the new setting, and Commerce Committee Chairman Warren Magnuson accommodated him by scheduling them early in the session. For some chairmen, such generosity with junior members would have been a major concession; for Magnuson, it was standard operating procedure. But the scheduling of hearings did not necessarily indicate great interest on Magnuson's part. He was not particularly close to Hart, knew little about his bill, and had slightly negative first impressions. Magnuson was interested in identifying with consumer issues and had a staff that was pushing him in that direction, but Hart's bill initially raised for him images of petty bureaucratic control. Quite willing to let the hearings be Hart's show, Magnuson opened the hearings on April 28, 1965, but barely showed up thereafter.

Senators Hart and Neuberger presided over the hearings most of the time; for ten days they heard from a parade of carbonated beverage executives, perfume manufacturers—and some relatively lower-echelon representatives of the executive branch. The unenthusiastic participation of the downtown agencies was indicative of the level of enthusiasm the proposal had generated there. Presidents Kennedy and Johnson had given vague endorsements to packaging regulation, but no White House bill had ever been sent to Capitol Hill and no Hart Bill had ever been given a specific endorsement.

There had been some consultation from the first between congressional advocates and the agency administrators who were to be responsible for the proposed program. However, as a Food and Drug Administration counsel put it,

> I don't think Hart was in contact with us to any great extent as he drafted the bill . . . Except for giving testimony from time to time, we weren't very actively involved at all until 1966, when the Senate-passed bill was running into trouble over in the House . . . Before that we weren't involved much, even on the question of [who was to have] jurisdiction.

Food and Drug declined to support the first Hart Bill, claiming that the agency already had sufficient authority to handle the problems the bill encompassed. The bill was unfamiliar, it looked questionable from an administrative point of view, and it dealt with matters which the Kennedy Administration held in low priority. By 1963, however, the FDA had shifted, again in response to instructions from above, to a position of cautious support. But the agency's role was by no means an active one. There were some people down through the ranks who welcomed the envisaged authority, but congressional protagonists were able to make few helpful contacts. The agency would cooperate and would not obstruct; Hart could hope for little more.

The administration's leadoff witness in 1965 was Esther Peterson, Special Assistant to the President for Consumer Affairs. Mrs. Peterson's office was genuinely enthusiastic about the legislation, but it was in no position to make its views prevail in administration councils. It lacked, as one of Mrs. Peterson's assistants admitted, "any real power base."

> Its original and basic purpose is political and public-relations oriented. That's the fact you start with, and anything else you do has to

*just go on from there. Probably half the staff [of ten] are tied up with
public-relations type things.*

As it turned out, Mrs. Peterson's staff, by virtue of its expertise, was able
to give considerable help and exert some influence on Capitol Hill as the
proposal was refined; but in its early stages the office was in no position
to undertake policy initiatives. Its main purpose was to bear witness to the
President's concern for consumer-affairs-in-general. Mrs. Peterson could
not give a detailed critique of the bill or testify concretely as to what the
administration would do with the proposed authority; the Committee thus
questioned her gently, politely, and briefly.

The administration's only cabinet-level witness, Secretary of Commerce
John T. Connor, testified on the third day of the hearings. His appearance
was belated and his testimony even more bland than usual; after his statement Senator Cotton feigned doubt as to how the administration really felt
about the bill.[2] As one Commerce Department official admitted:

*This department was cool to the fair packaging bill all along and
never really got behind it until the President wanted to get it out of
the House Committee . . . We're talking mainly here about the people
involved with state programs of standards, those in BDSA [the Business and Defense Services Administration, the Department's main
liaison with industry], Governor [and former Commerce Secretary
Luther] Hodges, and Secretary Connor. I don't think Connor ever
liked the bill. I think it was his honest opinion that the bill would be
bad for the business climate. He also felt that the case had not been
made for "undue proliferation" [of package shapes and sizes] and
that the record had not clearly established that the bill was needed.
. . . Now Connor had not publicly opposed the bill; he had given it
nominal support. But his manner was such as to let it be known that
he didn't really care whether it passed or not.*

The Department was not heavily lobbied, but it did not need to be; most
Commerce officials were instinctively cool to the bill, which they felt might
harass or unduly restrict the business community.[3]

The apathy of the Commerce Department, however, was not monolithic.
An independent and active role was played by the Department's Office of
Science and Technology—or, more precisely, by the Office's Chief, Assistant Secretary J. Herbert Holloman, and by an Assistant General Counsel
with whom he worked closely, Gordon Christenson. On fair packaging,
and to an even greater extent on automobile safety, these men demonstrated their ability to take positions at variance with those of the Department and to serve congressional advocates as a vital source of information,
ideas, and support. They were fortunate in the newness and relative independence of their positions within the bureaucracy, but the role they
assumed was the result primarily of their own interests and abilities. Armed

with doctors' degrees, a philosophical interest in problems of regulation and standardization, and a conviction that both government and the business community must assume increased responsibility for the protection of the consumer, these men hardly succeeded in transforming the Department's role. They did, however, provide for the articulation of a new point of view and the consideration of new departures in policy within the Department. The initiative they took and the expertise they developed also made it more likely that once the Department, for one reason or another, got behind various consumer bills, its advocacy would involve substantive recommendations and a concrete plan of action. In addition, they offered congressional advocates an invaluable point of access; because of them the Commerce Department was viewed much differently and dialed much more frequently. The wall of apathy and unresponsiveness was breached.

The fact remains, however, that from the time Hart first began his inquiries until the fall of 1966, when the bill was about to be shelved by the House Commerce Committee, the role of the executive branch was for the most part passive. Little interest or initiative came from either the White House or the agencies, and what little activity there was, was largely uncoordinated. A member of Esther Peterson's staff summed it up this way:

> There are important differences between just giving your endorsement to something and deciding that you really want it. This was never high on the President's list until he finally made a push near the end, and even then the idea was more to get a bill than a strong bill. It was easy enough to say, when you were thinking up presidential messages, "Oh, there's the Hart Bill; why not throw that in?" But the executive branch never did really get to work on the proposal or come to grips with the issues involved. That's why all the agencies testified pretty much in their own way. I know when we did our testimony we hardly consulted with anybody. The Bureau of the Budget said, "Sure, send it in." They suggested a couple of minor changes, and we checked with the agencies to make sure we weren't directly contradicting anybody. But nobody was coordinating this thing, and nobody was doing any homework.

Enter Magnuson, with Staff. The hearings came to a close in mid-May with Mrs. Neuberger taking testimony from the Toilet Goods Association, Max Factor, and Charles of the Ritz, and Senators Bass and Pearson "retreating blushing" as the conversation ranged from face masks to bedtime perfume.[4] The bill was still not being taken seriously by either the executive branch or the interest groups involved; it looked as though Hart lacked the support and the resources to succeed. As it happened, however, the staff of the Commerce Committee was looking for issues and for issues of a particular kind: those which would give Warren Magnuson prominence as a national legislative leader. Fair packaging filled the bill, staff interest was kindled, and the Hart Bill moved forward.

The Commerce Committee had not always had a staff with such concerns; even in 1965 there was a staff division (and enduring tensions) between old guard and new, which reflected the changes that had taken place. The key man as far as the new staff role was concerned was Chief Counsel Gerald Grinstein; the key event was Magnuson's near-defeat in 1962. Grinstein, a young, intelligent, and aggressive staff member, had convinced Magnuson of his usefulness, although the Chairman felt more at ease with some of the old-timers around the office. Grinstein's progressive and reformist inclinations harmonized nicely with his conviction that legislative activism and a refurbished image held the key to Magnuson's future, and incidentally to his own. In the aftermath of 1962 Magnuson became somewhat more inclined to accept this diagnosis; he eventually made Grinstein Chief Counsel and left him considerable freedom to hire his own aides and continued on his projected legislative course.

One of Grinstein's first recruits was Michael Pertschuk, formerly a legislative aide to Senator Maurine Neuberger. Pertschuk quickly became the key man in the field of consumer legislation, an area which Magnuson and Grinstein felt held unique potential for legislative innovations and public appeal. Tackling the job with relish, he had strong convictions about the issues involved and enjoyed the idea of engineering a legislative attack. While he was not close to Magnuson personally, Pertschuk was responsive to the idea of enhancing the Chairman's stature and became increasingly confident of Magnuson's willingness to support him.

Pertschuk had been interested in the packaging bill for some time, and as Hart brought the bill to the Commerce Committee, Magnuson and Grinstein became increasingly convinced that it would fit into their scheme of things. At the same time, Magnuson was well aware of the coolness with which the bill had been received downtown and of the business opposition it was likely to stimulate. He was inclined to take critics at their word when they portrayed the bill as poorly drafted and impractical, and he was not impressed with Hart's ability to make adjustments or effectively to mobilize support. Magnuson thus instructed his staff to develop a "workable bill." Pertschuk was searching for ideas when he had breakfast with Christenson in September; the notion of giving the Commerce Department a role in the development of packaging standards was an outgrowth of that meeting.

S. 985 had authorized the Secretary of HEW (for food, drugs, and cosmetics) and the Federal Trade Commission (for all other consumer commodities) to issue regulations requiring that labels include clear and conspicuous information and prohibiting the use of deceptive pictures or promotional phrases. It had also provided for the establishment, where deemed necessary to prevent deception or to facilitate price comparison, of uniform weights, quantities, and shapes of packages. The latter provisions, involving packaging standardization, excited far more alarm in industry than did the labeling requirements. Christenson's answer was to make the packaging provisions partially voluntary. The revised bill thus provided that an industry could utilize machinery existing in the Department of Commerce for the development of "voluntary product standards" following an adverse finding by the promulgating authority. Only after these procedures had been followed could packaging regulations be issued, and then there would be a strong presumption in favor of the standard developed in cooperation with the Department. For Christenson, this change represented administrative good sense as well as practical politics; it took advantage of existing machinery and based the new program on cooperative relationships—without which governmental agencies were sure to lack the means to design and implement an effective program. For Pertschuk, the plan recommended itself as a means of neutralizing or splitting the opposition.

David Swankin, Esther Peterson's Executive Assistant, also became a valuable source of information and advice during this period of reformulation. His influence, like Christenson's, was based not on a position of political strength but on his possession of expertise and on Pertschuk's felt need for allies in the executive branch. A series of alterations were developed that would do minimal harm to the bill while making it less offensive to its opponents in certain particulars. But the changes were not far-reaching ones, and the same interest groups that disliked the Hart Bill disliked the committee draft almost as much. Yet the bill, which a few months before would have been defeated by something like 7-11, was approved by a 14-4 vote on May 13, 1966, with only four Republicans opposed. The explanation lay partially in the "improvements" that had been made, partially in the exertion of counter-pressures by groups favoring the bill (organized labor's representations to Senator Hartke were a conspicuous example), and partially in the White House's belated (and rather feeble) attempts at persuasion. Far more important, however, was one simple fact: S. 985 was now a Magnuson Bill.

Once Magnuson took it upon himself to champion the fair packaging bill, he backed up his staff and stood fast against changes which they felt would damage the legislation. The main tests of his strength in committee came with a Hartke amendment to remove the provisions for mandatory standard-setting after the exhaustion of voluntary procedures and a Cotton amendment to remove the packaging provisions altogether. Magnuson barely won the former contest, and he had to re-fight the latter on the floor. But Magnuson's presentation of S. 985 as a "clean" and "voluntary" bill—

and one he cared a great deal about—had a decisive effect, as Hart attested:

> In fact, Maggie entered the picture at the right moment and in the right way to get the thing passed. A lot of opposition had been created. The Republicans were all opposed and they picked up support on some points from Bass, Monroney, Brewster, and of course from Lausche. So Magnuson's stepping in when he did probably saved the bill. After two or three executive sessions he called everybody together, including some boys from downtown, and hammered out a "substitute" bill. That it was supposedly a substitute and not merely an amended Hart Bill made it a lot easier to get through. We lost some things, but by and large it was a good bill and much the same as mine. You know how Maggie can pull that sort of thing off, with his broad sweeping statements which everybody somehow accepts: "This is a new bill!"

Involved here was usurpation of a sort, but this was something Hart was prepared to accept, recognizing as he did the plight of the bill and the unique resources for mobilization held by committee chairmen, and by this chairman in particular. Besides, Hart noted, Magnuson's involvement did not change one fundamental fact: "Back home, 'Hart' and 'fair packaging' are synonymous."

As the Committee prepared to report the bill, administration concern grew, and executive branch participation became increasingly centered in the White House and the Department of Commerce. Some FDA officials viewed the Christenson-Pertschuk compromise as a worse "administrative monstrosity" than the Hart Bill, but they suffered from not having developed greater expertise or better access to the White House and the Senate Committee at an earlier point. The Commerce Committee staff, for its part, was not accustomed to working with FDA and had unfavorable impressions of the agency's bureaucratic sluggishness. Better communication and greater trust existed between the Committee and the consumer office, but the office's lack of political muscle inevitably led it, too, into eclipse. One of Mrs. Peterson's assistants put it this way:

> We would have liked to say to Larry O'Brien [White House Assistant], "Look, Larry, why don't you just let us handle this one for you?" It wouldn't have hurt things much, but they weren't ready to do it. And as you got further along toward the point of decision, we were farther and farther from the center of things. Mike would ordinarily touch base with us each step of the way, but toward the end nobody was paying any attention to us. . . . White House concern stepped up as the Senate Committee moved into executive session, and there was a flurry of activity the night before it made its final decision. But it was [Joseph] Califano and O'Brien and their people that were in on that, not us. . . . We were more like a pest, out on the sidelines.

Senate and House Action. Magnuson ordinarily got along well with his Republicans. This was partly because they were a relatively moderate and diversified lot, but most members credited the Chairman's personal attributes as well. Affable, compromising, anxious to avoid conflict and to take a united committee to the floor, Magnuson's relationships with the minority were generally cooperative. The fair packaging episode represented in some respects an example of, but in other respects an exception to, this situation.

A number of factors encouraged the minority to take a positive role in the processing of S. 985. The area of consumer protection was one of broad public appeal and, more than most other such fields, it was one which the President and the Democratic Party had not pre-empted legislatively. Moreover, Magnuson's handling of the bill gave the Republicans an opportunity, with an eye to the Chamber of Commerce, to denounce the earlier and "extreme" Hart Bill while giving the clean bill their support and working to "improve" it further. They were encouraged to exercise such initiative by the attitudes and practices of Magnuson and his staff.

The minority staff man assigned to the bill, Jeremiah Kenney, was anxious to see his mentors assume such a role; the extent to which he influenced them is difficult to ascertain, but majority staff members credited him with a significant mediating role. Kenney's position in this and similar episodes was not without its tensions. Although he was regarded a "solid conservative" by most of the majority staff, he nonetheless had more in common with Grinstein and Pertschuk than did the rest of the minority staff. In fact, his position on the minority staff was roughly analogous to that of Grinstein's staff recruits on the majority side: just as they had an old guard to contend with, so did he find himself working with an older and more conservative staff which, among other things, had doubts about the role he was carving out for the minority in consumer affairs. At the same time, the majority staff, anxious to cultivate Kenney and to encourage his efforts, admitted him to their councils and made him a part of their working team.

If Kenney's mediation promoted committee cohesion, it also increased the minority's legislative leverage. This was evident on a number of bills, S. 985 among them. Kenney drew up a substitute bill, in many respects more exacting than the Hart measure. A number of his changes were incorporated into the committee bill, including mandatory requirements regarding the location of content statements, the size of lettering utilized, and the units to be used in specifying quantities. The Republicans, as a result, frequently claimed credit for "strengthening" the proposal.[5]

The minority, however, could only go so far. Even Kenney had little use for the sections providing for uniform weights and sizes in packaging, and the minority members, to a man, were less favorably inclined yet. Industry had focused most of its criticisms on these sections, and the fact that the

Commerce Department had been given administrative authority did little to soften the complaints. Here the Republican approach was not, as Hartke had earlier proposed, to soften the packaging provisions further, but rather to delete them entirely. Magnuson, departing from his usual style, proved adamant; the Republicans, departing from their usual practice, filed a sharply worded minority report and continued their fight as the bill was brought to the floor.

It was a rather mild floor fight compared with some of those involving the Finance and Labor and Public Welfare Committees. But by Commerce Committee standards it was a bruiser, and most members, upon reflection, were struck by its atypicality. "A party split that deep is very rare on this committee." Ranking minority member Norris Cotton spoke frequently on the bill. Recalling that it had come to the Committee in "impossible" condition, he praised Magnuson for working out a proposal that was for the most part "good and constructive."

> *While we were in strong disagreement with regard to some provisions of the bill, we helped strengthen the bill in other particulars. Then we found that the proponents of the bill were absolutely adamant in yielding an inch on some parts of the bill that we considered extremely dangerous legislation.*

The bill as reported, Cotton said, would never be approved by the House, "but it is insisted that we have a 'going' issue rather than a bill." Moving to a discussion of the offensive sections, Cotton reverted to the designation of S. 985 as the "Hart Bill" and likened the "vicious" sections to holding a gun at industry's head.[6] But his proposed deletion was defeated 32-53, and Minority Leader Dirksen's proposal to send the entire measure to the Judiciary Committee was defeated by an even larger margin. Final passage, which had looked so doubtful the year before, proved to be anticlimactic. The vote was 72-9, and Morton was the only Commerce Committee member voting nay.

Trouble awaited in the House. The Committee on Interstate and Foreign Commerce, less liberal and activistic in orientation than its Senate counterpart, had never held hearings on a packaging bill. Nor were conditions in late 1966 likely to stimulate the Committee's interest. Time was short, public interest was not acute, and businesses were lobbying furiously. The Senate Committee was resented for once again having sent over a controversial consumer bill, this one very late in the session, putting the House Committee on the defensive. All the indicators pointed to sure defeat—unless, that is, the executive branch could fill the gap. In case the President and his agencies did not understand the urgency of the situation, it was communicated to them in various ways by Hart, Magnuson, and their staffs.

The executive branch was imperfectly geared for the effort, but its preparation was more adequate and its interest greater than the year before. For this, the activities of the Senate Committee were partly responsible. Also important, however, was the fact that the President, looking for issues with which to garnish the Great Society and—in the face of rising war costs—for inexpensive legislative proposals, had made consumer legislation a more important part of his 1966 program than it had ever been before.[7] Thus, when the House Committee opened hearings on July 26, 1966, a high-level executive panel—including Secretary Connor, Mrs. Peterson, HEW Undersecretary Wilbur Cohen, and FTC Chairman Paul Rand Dixon—appeared in concert, furnishing a nice contrast to the staggered and uncoordinated appearances on the Senate side the year before. The greater public effort was accompanied by intensified liaison work. Executive involvement continued to center in the White House and Commerce Department. Commerce's General Counsel Robert Giles, in fact, surprised a number of participants by the strength of his advocacy, although a number of other Commerce officials disliked the way they had been drawn into the administration of the program and looked askance at those of Christenson's activities about which they knew. The Consumer Office lacked the staff connections it had enjoyed with Pertschuk and felt an increasing frustration as executive branch functions were assumed by those who, in its view, were ready to make unacceptable compromises in order to get a law on the books. But the involvement of the Food and Drug Administration stepped up considerably. FDA officials were accustomed to working with the House Committee (which, unlike Senate Commerce, had jurisdiction over most FDA programs), and they now had a definite mandate from above. FDA established a close liaison with the House Committee and even succeeded in getting some "strengthening" amendments adopted.

Administration officials, however, were unable to prevent the House Committee from removing what many regarded as the key provisions of the bill. How hard they tried, the extent to which they responded to business pressures, and what they might have accomplished with maximum effort are still matters for debate.[8] But the bill as reported did not provide for the setting and enforcement of packaging standards by the promulgating authority after the exhaustion of voluntary procedures. The bill had lost its teeth.

The House Committee's consideration of the bill was hurried and stormy. On September 13 Representative John Bell Williams moved abruptly to table the bill and, because of the large number of absentees, his motion carried. The move was later reversed by a narrow 17-14 vote, but the episode probably alarmed the bill's advocates and made them more open to compromise. With mixed feelings, Commerce Department officials drafted an amended bill which contained no provisions for mandatory packaging requirements. Thus altered, the bill was reported without difficulty and could even be brought to the floor under the suspension-of-the-rules procedure generally reserved for non-controversial legislation. The vote on final passage was 300-8.

The choice confronting the Senate conferees, as Magnuson told his colleagues, was to accept the House version "or to have no bill at all." Time was running out, and the House negotiators were adamant (even those who favored a stronger bill did not think it could pass the House). The House's least-common-denominator version was thus accepted by the conferees, easily approved by both houses, and, on November 3, signed into law. Interestingly enough, it was Hart who expressed pleasure at the outcome and confidence that acceptable standards would be developed, while Magnuson expressed disappointment and pledged the Commerce Committee to the pursuit of the matter until a "comprehensive and meaningful" law was on the books.[9]

The Interests and the Outcome. Mancur Olson, in a book that reverses the conventional wisdom on pressure-group politics at a number of points, shows that small, narrowly-based groups often have distinct advantages over larger groups when it comes to marshalling the energies and resources of their membership for collective ends. The reason, basically, is that at the small-group level the conditions of rational individual action are approximated: the individual's "share" of the collective good is relatively larger, and the likelihood that the benefits of group success will match the individual efforts necessary to ensure success is much greater. Moreover, the individual knows that if he does *not* participate, group success will be imperiled. In the large group, however, the reward is less likely to offset the cost of individual involvement and the individual can usually assume that his contribution is not crucial to the group effort; whether or not he participates will often have no influence either on whether the group succeeds or on whether he will benefit from that success. It follows that large groups will generally not be able to mobilize their membership effectively without either coercion or the offering of some particular incentive, apart from the general prospect of group success, to individual members.[10]

In the political sphere, this suggests that small firms or groups of firms (e.g. perfume and cookie manufacturers) might more quickly and effectively mount a lobbying effort than larger or more broadly-based organizations (e.g. the National Consumers League or the National Association of Manufacturers). The packaging and labeling episode bears out these expectations in some respects and suggests qualifications in others. The consumer groups, notorious for their weakness and general inability to mobilize support, fit Olson's pattern nicely; Hart and Magnuson were stimulating more than they were responding to them. Organized labor's efforts were late and limited. Nor, interestingly enough, were the NAM and the U.S. Chamber of Commerce particularly effective, though they made energetic representations to both committees; congressional participants reported not only a general ineptitude and lack of coordination but, significantly, that their objections were too "general" and "philosophical" to be taken into account. The constituents of these organizations themselves generated little pressure on behalf of such broad recommendations; what the smaller trade associations and local firms were more interested in were narrow and specific exemptions and alterations, and it was at this level that lobbying was most effective.[11] These interests were less successful in the Senate than in the House—perhaps because of the conservative inclinations of many members of the House Commerce Committee, perhaps because the businesses in question wielded less statewide influence than they did in the smaller House districts—but the processes of interest-aggregation and modification as they were undertaken on the Senate side mirrored their influence as well.

While it is clear, then, that Olson's theory sheds some light on the relative impact of various groups on the packaging proposal, it is also clear that the bill was something far different from a mere outgrowth of group pressures or a mirror of group "strengths." The House Committee's more general revisions reflected ideology and long-term identifications more than they did immediate group efforts. More significantly, Hart, in his initial publicizing and formulating efforts, and later Magnuson, demonstrated that political leaders had incentives and motivations that transcended the rewards promised and the sanctions threatened by interest groups.[12] In choosing to appeal "over the heads" of the dominant groups, they obviously expected that the consumer, however unwilling to contribute to formal group efforts, would nonetheless benefit and respond in a politically profitable manner. Pertschuk and Christenson, too, while they were sensitive to industry complaints as they reformulated Hart's bill, were more concerned to develop a "strong" and workable measure. And in the end, most of Magnuson's members found it more politic to stick with him than to yield to industry demands.

The upshot, then, in terms of the legislative functions delineated in Chapter 1 is that *publicizing* and *formulation* in this case represented independent attempts at policy entrepreneurship, primarily in the Senate, and that *interest-aggregation,* coming later, had its main impact at the *modification* stage, particularly in the House Committee. The remaining functions, *information-gathering* and *mobilization,* involved the executive branch more extensively, though the Senate Committee continued, as an executive participant testified, to "take the lead." Executive agencies and actors were involved peripherally, sometimes unwillingly, in the formulation and modification processes, but their information resources were indispensable to Senate advocates, as was their assistance in mobilizing the House Committee. Congressional participants complained that much information was inadequate or not cast in a usable form, and the final mobilization effort was a partial success at best, but Senate initiators were indebted to their executive collaborators for such success as they achieved at both tasks.

If the labeling and packaging episode provides an initial indication of the capacity and propensity of the Senate Commerce Committee to assume legislative responsibility, it also permits a preliminary characterization of the aspects of the group's membership, organization, and environment which contributed to its initiatory role. The mere presence of a member with Hart's interests and orientations was important, but much more crucial was Magnuson's own particular combination of problems and ambitions, which led him to permit, support, and even push forward certain kinds of legislative undertakings. Related but independent variables were an organizational structure that permitted the pursuit of individual policy interests and an activistic staff that facilitated and stimulated such ventures. The integrative character of Magnuson's leadership was also apparent; its main effect in the packaging case was to facilitate the mobilization effort and to bring the Republicans into the formulation process.

That the Committee's environment was filled with interest groups varying greatly in influence and style has already been noted, as has the fact that many members, after making symbolic concilatory gestures, felt safe in casting their lot with the Chairman and presumably the consumer. It remains only to note that the other decision-making groups occupying the environment did not appear at first glance to be particularly unified or energetic in their approach to consumer affairs; this area had not been given high priority by the President, and there was no established center of responsibility. Some agencies were supportive, others apathetic, others internally divided. The situation was flexible enough to permit the Senate Committee to choose freely which agency or which officials within a given agency it could rely on for information, assistance, and support; it thus multiplied its resources while strengthening the hand of executive officials sympathetic to its position.

The three episodes to follow will be related in such a way as to facilitate comparison with S. 985 in terms of executive and congressional responsibility. Here, too, the relation of certain committee characteristics to legislative roles and capacities will receive preliminary analysis, with a view to assessing the typicality and the impact of various factors in Chapter 3.

THE FEDERAL CIGARETTE LABELING AND ADVERTISING ACT

The Gauntlet is Thrown. The Federal Trade Commission does not ordinarily meet on Saturday mornings. In fact, a stroll on almost any day of the week through the dimly-lit corridors of the odd triangular building that is the Commission's home, would hardly give the impression that this is a vital center of activity. Although there have been some hopeful stirrings in the early seventies, the FTC traditionally has had a reputation for timidity, sluggishness, and collusion with the businesses it is supposed to regulate. Its often-touted "independent" status (symbolized by its location midway between Capitol and White House), far from giving it a position from which to exert leverage or to exercise "objective" judgment vis-à-vis the two governmental branches, frequently has meant instead that it was highly dependent on *both* Congress and the President while enjoying the full support of neither.

The Commission was never intended to generate legislation, and in size, budget, self-image, and political stature, it was ill-equipped to do so. Its role in the fair packaging episode was typical of its legislative involvements. The Commission had some interest in who received the bill's administrative authority, but it was not in a position effectively to push its jurisdictional claims over against those of FDA. As one Commissioner wryly put it, about all the Commission could do for Hart was "simply to sit on our butt ends."

> We had authority to pursue a number of cases which were in this fair packaging area, but we didn't do it because we knew that then people would think that if we already had all this authority, then there wasn't any need for legislation.

As for the administrative question, "we lost on that, as we often do."

On Saturday, January 11, 1964, however, the Federal Trade Commission appeared neither cautious nor inactive nor weak. "It hasn't been like that around here before or since. There was excitement in the air." This was the day the long-awaited report of the Surgeon General on smoking and health was to be released. It was a report a number of the Commissioners had anticipated and on which some of them were determined to act; they had received advance word that the report would be a telling one. A release drafted by Philip Elman, a Commissioner for whom tobacco hazards had long been an issue of great concern, was sent out immediately. It committed the FTC to a study of the report and to the issuance of whatever regulations proved to be necessary. What then happened is related by a member of the Commission:

> I read the report over the weekend and so, I know, did [Chairman] Rand Dixon. It really had an effect on him—he took out an old pipe and never touched a cigarette again. It was really a pretty dramatic thing, and on Monday things started to move. . . . We have a reputation, pretty much justified, for being a standpat outfit, never rocking the boat, but on this we moved. It was the Federal Trade Commission's finest hour.[13]

The FTC thus began hearings with the announced intention of determining what rules were necessary to prevent deceptive practices in the marketing of cigarettes. Six months later, the Commission issued a rule requiring that all cigarette package labels (as of January 1, 1965) and all cigarette advertising (as of July 1, 1965) include a warning "that cigarette smoking is dangerous to health and may cause death from cancer and other diseases."[14]

It was this unilateral FTC action that made it virtually certain that a cigarette labeling and advertising measure would be on the agenda of the 89th Congress. There had earlier been only a few scattered efforts in this direction. A House Government Operations Subcommittee had provoked the wrath of the tobacco industry in 1957 with a report challenging the truthfulness of cigarette advertising claims. This was one of the few areas in which Utah's Senator Wallace Bennett, staunch Mormon that he was, favored federal activity, and he had introduced a bill to require a warning label on cigarette packages at about the same time. But Oregon's Maurine Neuberger became the best-known senatorial advocate. Several Neuberger research, labeling, and advertising bills, introduced in the 87th and 88th Congresses, secured for their author a reputation as a specialist in the field and the champion of a particular point of view. But the bills made little progress.

Mrs. Neuberger and her staff found limited grounds for encouragement as they contacted the various federal agencies with a potential interest in the problem. The FDA did not interpret its authority under the Hazardous Substances Labeling Act to extend to the regulation of cigarettes. The FTC had made some preliminary moves in the area—some twenty actions had been brought against individual companies for misleading advertising since the early 1930's, promotional references to the physical effects or health consequences of smoking had been prohibited in 1955, and in 1960 an agreement to discontinue making claims and counterclaims regarding tar and nicotine content had been secured among leading manufacturers—but congressional proponents were told that more decisive FTC action must await more conclusive medical evidence. Meanwhile, medical evidence was already mounting, and certain Public Health Service officials were anxious for the government to synthesize and publish these findings and to step up its own research efforts as well. Interested senators and representatives were getting some headlines, and a few health and consumer groups were beginning to make their voices heard. The American Cancer Society, American Public Health Association, American Heart Association, and National Tuberculosis Association sent a joint letter to the President urging the formation of a commission to study the "widespread implications of the tobacco problem."

The White House, which a Neuberger aide described as "passive, to say the least," thus found it increasingly difficult to ignore the problem.

In such a situation, a frequent and familiar "out" is to turn the entire matter over to an advisory panel for study. In this particular instance, a study happened to be one of the things virtually all of those interested in the issue agreed was needed. So in mid-1962 the Kennedy administration, still fearful of alienating the tobacco-state congressmen whose votes it needed, gave PHS the go-ahead "with instructions to handle with care."[15] The Surgeon General proceeded to pick his panel, clearing his selections not only with various federal agencies and health and medical societies but also with the Tobacco Institute, which represented the major cigarette manufacturers. It was the evidence this group presented, after some fourteen months of work, that gave the FTC a basis for action and brought public and congressional interest to new levels. Twelve bills strengthening federal regulation of cigarette labeling and advertising were soon introduced in the House, while an equal number authorizing additional research were introduced by tobacco state representatives. The House Commerce Committee held five days of hearings on the labeling and advertising proposals, while House Agriculture took three days of testimony on two research bills. Agriculture on February 7, 1964, reported a bill authorizing a research program which Chairman Cooley said would "dispel all the disquiet about smoking and associate good health with the enjoyment of tobacco."[16] No hearings were held in the Senate, but Senators Neuberger and Moss introduced a new set of labeling, advertising, and research bills.

Whether labeling and advertising legislation, which had gotten nowhere before the Surgeon General's report, would have passed during the 89th Congress under the impetus the report provided is an interesting but academic question. For after the FTC made its move, the tobacco industry got into the act and it became clear that some sort of congressional response would be forthcoming. The House Commerce Committee gave immediate and sympathetic attention to several bills designed to head off the FTC regulations, while buying time for the industry with a request to the Commission to defer the effective date of its labeling requirements until July 1, 1965, the same day the advertising regulations were to go into effect. The Committee suggested to the FTC that the enforcement of the ruling would be tied up in the courts for a long period in any case and that it might in the long run save time to wait for congressional authorization.[17] Dixon's response did not accede to this point of view—several Commissioners felt that the courts would speedily approve their ruling and that the Commission should not imply that it needed additional statutory authority in any case—but the FTC nonetheless granted the Committee's request for a postponement of the labeling requirements. Meanwhile, the lines of the legislative battle were drawn.

The Senate Committee Assumes the Lead. The opening weeks of the 89th Congress again saw the introduction of a spate of cigarette labeling bills, but with a difference that was to prove all-important: Included among the proponents now was one Warren G. Magnuson. Magnuson was neither a Mormon, nor a crusading liberal, nor was he one who had quit smoking "and wanted everyone else to stop too."[18] But he was open to a new role as champion of the consumer and he had on his staff Senator Neuberger's former legislative assistant, Mike Pertschuk, for whom tobacco hazards was a "gut issue." Pertschuk was more isolated in this concern than he was on fair packaging: it was not an issue in which Grinstein or Magnuson had previously taken a great interest, there was little support among minority members and staff, and there were a number of Committee members who not only were opposed to a labeling requirement but wanted to enact a preemption of the FTC as well. But Magnuson still chose to introduce a bill, S. 559, which definitely put him on the side of those seeking regulation. He proposed that every package of cigarettes be labeled, "Warning: Continual Cigarette Smoking May be Hazardous to Your Health," and that each package also state the average tar and nicotine yields per cigarette. His bill contained a clause to prevent the issuance of alternative or additional labeling requirements, but it left intact the FTC's authority to regulate advertising.

Senator Neuberger, meanwhile, like Senator Hart, had gladly abandoned the Agriculture Committee for Commerce. She had actively sought the new assignment because of the Committee's increasing involvement in consumer affairs and, in particular, because Commerce was the committee that would be handling cigarette labeling. Early in 1965 she introduced a bill that was much more specific than Magnuson's in the mandate it gave to the FTC to regulate advertising. But Mrs. Neuberger, according to her legislative assistant, "knew that she could never get a bill passed on her own." Formerly quite apprehensive lest Congress simply meet industry demands and preempt FTC action, she was encouraged when Magnuson revealed that he was on the side of the angels. She became resigned to the fact that the Senate's final product would be a "Magnuson Bill" and decided to utilize her position within the Committee to offer strengthening amendments.

One of the few things that can be said with certainty about the United States Senate is that it is a man's world. When a woman comes into the club, she is treated with unfailing politeness, but often virtually excluded from the informal life of the institution and from the day-to-day processes of bargaining and consultation. The role the woman most easily assumes is that of the "spectator,"[19] participating mainly in the formal life of the institution and specializing in the ceremonial aspects of the job. In the 89th Congress Margaret Chase Smith, with her unfailing smile and her perfect attendance record, was the exemplar of this role; to Maurine Neuberger it came much less easily. She had a number of interests that she wanted to pursue, and these frequently involved conflicts with powerful senatorial champions of one group or another. By some members she was patronized or ignored, by others she was regarded as shrill and "out of line" (she was not only a woman, after all, but a junior Senator as well), and some criticized her for trying to play a man's game and not doing it well. One Senator expressed his sentiments this way:

> [Would you say Magnuson "cut out" Mrs. Neuberger on the cigarette bill?] He did it politely. You know how it is with these women in the Senate; you can't say anything against Maurine or Maggie Smith. Sometimes I think we've been a little too polite to Maurine in committee; we've given her a lot of what she wanted. . . . She is too feminine or something, and all of her arguments depend on "human interest" rather than logic.

In any case, Mrs. Neuberger had not been a particularly effective advocate of cigarette labeling and advertising regulation, and it is unlikely that senatorial deference would have extended far enough to counterbalance industry pressures. Magnuson's sponsorship of a labeling bill was, therefore, all-important, though he took pains to give Mrs. Neuberger's amendments fair consideration.

The tobacco manufacturers, who at first had been rather confident that a congressional preemption of the FTC could be secured, were alarmed at Magnuson's stand. Having secured the services of former Senator Earle Clements of Kentucky, the industry began to concentrate a greater amount of effort on the Senate and, in particular, on Commerce Committee members. A firm liaison was established with the members from tobacco states—Morton and Bass—and with other members who it was thought, for one reason or another, might prove sympathetic—Brewster, Lausche, Hartke, and all the minority members. Advocates of regulation, discouraged by developments in the House Commerce and Agriculture Committees, likewise pinned their hopes on the Senate group, and it was during Magnuson's hearings in the spring of 1965 that the range of agencies and interests involved first came into full view.

Senate hearings made unmistakably clear the administration's determination to avoid a substantial commitment. No cabinet-level official appeared. Routine agency reports ranged from HEW's endorsement of both labeling and advertising regulation to Agriculture's suggestion that present knowledge did not justify either.[20] The general coolness displayed by the White House and its conspicuous failure to coordinate agency views was not mainly due to industry pressures or interdepartmental conflict. Much more decisive was the administration's reluctance to offend congressmen or to use credits badly needed on Great Society measures. It was a matter of priorities, and neither the Public Health Service nor the FTC had the political muscle or the external support necessary to reverse those priorities. Surgeon General Luther Terry, the Commerce Committee's first witness, did not mention the President at all, and he mentioned his parent department only by way of noting that "they" felt labeling regulation should be administered by the FDA—with the clear implication, brought out in questioning, that this recommendation was not his own.[21] Terry gave the Magnuson and Neuberger bills strong endorsement, but the very circumstances of his appearance demonstrated how isolated he was in the degree and the direction of his concern.

The testimony of the Federal Trade Commission pointed up more clearly yet the dilemmas encountered by a low-level agency when it chose to pursue an independent course. The Commissioners had come under heavy pressure from various sources—industry, congressional, and executive—ever since their initial response to the Surgeon General's Report. From the apex of the administration came only stony silence, but numerous lesser executive officials, "often claiming," as one Commissioner noted, "to speak for the White House," did not hesitate to take the Commissioners to task. Congressional critics, welcoming a chance to base their arguments on something other than a mere defense of industry interests, fastened on "FTC usurpation of Congressional authority."[22] Industry representatives, of course, had arguments and inducements of their own, but they were also quick to play on this source of congressional resentment:

> If [regulatory] action is to be taken, we believe it should be taken by the Congress—and by no one else. . . . A great diversity of interests is involved in this matter. . . . It is wholly inappropriate, therefore, for a decision of this scope to be made by the FTC or by any other single federal administrative agency whose jurisdiction and expertise are confined to one particular phase of this complex problem.[23]

Dixon took much of this criticism to heart. A unilateral move by the FTC had not been his idea in the first place; although he was finally convinced of its legitimacy and desirability, he came increasingly to feel that the ruling should have an additional statutory buttress. The Commission's original position of necessity had been that the FTC Act's prohibition of deceptive marketing practices provided an adequate statutory base; FTC reports on the Senate bills simply asked that Congress leave the Commission's present regulatory power unchanged.[24] But during the hearings Dixon equivocated on this point. He acknowledged that a law authorizing labeling requirements was probably needed to avoid lengthy litigation, something that he had declined to do seven months earlier in replying to the House Committee's request for a delay in the effective date of the labeling requirements. As regards advertising, Dixon simply told the Senate committee, "The law is on the books." But he later clouded that issue too, as he discussed the various interpretations that might be given to congressional inaction on the advertising question:

> **SENATOR BASS:** If we fail to act in the field of advertising . . . should the fact be stated in the report of the bill that is passed, that the Committee . . . felt that no legislation was needed in this field . . . ?

> **MR. DIXON:** *You would give us more problems, Senator, than if you you said nothing about it. We are not trying to end up with a most complicated of all problems, what do you do about advertising. We do know now that as the law now exists, we have the responsibility to attempt to move against deceptive advertising . . . I am a creature of the Congress. . . . I urge you that if you feel you must legislate on this problem, don't leave us in the dark. . . . The worst thing you can do is leave us hanging in the air.*[25]

One close observer described Dixon's dilemma in these terms:

> *One thing is sure; the President didn't back the Commission up at all. Without that backing, the momentum just couldn't be kept up, and soon the Commission started getting hesitant and timid again. The Chairman was concerned about this, but he's a very political creature, and he doesn't like to have his neck stuck too far out. I think he began to have second thoughts very soon after that first release was issued. . . . To tell you the truth, I think Rand was just as glad to have Congress take it off his hands. It had become too hot an issue politically, and he wasn't comfortable with it. The Commission didn't take a very active part in things once Congress took over.*

A Commerce Committee staff member added a sympathetic note:

> *It's not fair to be too hard on Dixon. He may have shifted his ground some, but he probably wasn't too sure of himself in the first place. I think it was his finest hour. After all, the Chairman is in a pretty hot spot. And anyway you look at it, what the FTC did was pretty unusual for an agency of that type. It was a difficult thing for them to do.*

Mobilization and Compromise. A few senators from time to time came to the FTC's defense;[26] Pertschuk relied heavily on his contacts there, particularly Elman, and sustained them somewhat in their role of advocacy. The Public Health Service also attempted to strengthen its position by joining with two sister HEW agencies—the Office of Education and the Children's Bureau—and thirteen private health and professional organizations to form a unique body for lobbying and publicizing purposes, the National Interagency Council on Smoking and Health.[27] But all this could barely mask the isolation and increasing discomfit of PHS and FTC, nor was it any match for the well-oiled operations of the tobacco lobby.[28] And the industry succeeded in isolating the advocates further, this time from the medical community; early in 1964 the industry gave the American Medical Association a $10 million study grant, and the AMA continued to refrain from joining the Interagency Council or endorsing either the Surgeon General's report or any proposed legislation.

Clements and his lieutenants had many friends in both branches and large amounts of campaign money to spread around. Moreover, they settled early on a strategy that would enable their supporters to make a gesture in the direction of regulation while giving the industry most of what it wanted. They decided they could live with a labeling requirement if it were coupled with a removal of the FTC from the advertising field. Besides being strategically sound, the acceptance of a statutory labeling requirement had the advantage of heading off any more drastic action that might be taken by the FTC or by state and local agencies.

The industry was thus in a strong position. It had a reliable base of support in tobacco-state representatives, well-anchored in both Commerce Committees. It had numerous supporters, ample finances, and skilled insiders running its operation. The agencies opposing the industry seemed weak, nervous, doubtful of their own authority, and they were obviously lacking in White House support. Industry wisely cast its arguments so as to appeal both to Republicans who wanted to strike a blow against government regulation and to Congress-first men who wanted to strike a blow against agency usurpation. And the industry's strategy enabled its supporters to avoid appearances of kowtowing to its demands. They could back what seemed to be a reasonable compromise, endorsing a labeling requirement, voiding FTC's advertising rules, and teaching the Commission a lesson, all in one blow.

It soon became obvious that the industry was going to get exactly what it wanted from the House Committee. "I had no contact at all with them," noted an FTC participant, "and I don't know of anyone over here that did. I think we all regarded them as Industry-dominated." Meanwhile, Morton was proving an extremely effective advocate for the industry in the Senate. A relatively senior and greatly respected member of the Commerce Committee who chose his issues carefully, Morton took a low-key, commonsense approach to the problem that had considerable appeal, particularly in view of the fact that it was Mrs. Neuberger who was doing most of the talking on the other side. On April 27, 1965, the Committee rejected the Neuberger Bill 11-2 and tentatively approved the Magnuson Bill, to which had not yet been added a preemption clause regarding advertising. But such an amendment was to be offered the following week, and the *Times* confidently predicted a "substantial victory for the tobacco industry."[29]

It was Magnuson and Magnuson alone who gave the lie to that prediction. To be sure, Morton won his vote. The Committee approved a permanent moratorium on the regulation of advertising, 9-8. But after the vote Magnuson announced that this was a bill he would not manage on the floor. Morton, obviously surprised, asked the Chairman what it would take to make the bill acceptable. Magnuson then said that he could not accept any more than a three year moratorium—and that is precisely what he got.

In some ways this move represented a deviation from Magnuson's usual pattern of action. "I admit Maggie surprised me on that one," said one member. "I thought he was pretty well going to go along with us and come out with a moderate bill." But Magnuson's proposal, after all, still represented a substantial concession to industry's wishes, and the Committee's response, far from being unusual, displayed with great clarity certain facts about the group. It showed how much deference the Chairman enjoyed and how many credits he had accumulated. It also showed how committee integration—exemplified in this case by bipartisanship, a willingness to compromise, and a desire for unity and cohesion—while it "cost" the Chairman something to maintain, was nonetheless a resource which he could exploit at critical junctures. At certain points a concern for integration prompted him to trim his legislative sails, but in other situations the fact of integration made feasible a certain legislative boldness.

Two additional features of the bill reported by the Committee are worth noting. The dispute over administration was resolved by a provision for direct enforcement by the Department of Justice. In addition the FTC was directed to report annually to Congress on "(1) the effectiveness of cigarette labeling, (2) current information on the health consequences of smoking, (3) current practices and methods of cigarette advertising and promotion, and (4) such recommendations for legislation as it may deem appropriate."[30] The latter provision had been designed by Clements and minority Committee aide Ray Hurley as a substitute for a limitation on the FTC moratorium. In the end, however, their suggestion backfired: it did not forestall a moratorium limitation and in fact proved important in keeping the FTC involved in the area and encouraging continued revisions in the act.[31]

The behavior of the Committee on the floor again demonstrated its cohesion. The arguments in favor of the bill were notable for their reiteration of the theme that the Committee's work was satisfactory because it had adequately aggregated the interests involved, "worked out" the difficulties, and reached an equitable compromise. Mrs. Neuberger proposed unsuccessfully that the moratorium on the regulation of advertising be reduced to one year; Magnuson, characteristically, said that though he would have originally favored the amendment, he would now abide by the Committee's decision.[32] Only five senators opposed the bill on final passage, most of them claiming that it was too favorable to industry, but every member of the Commerce Committee voted yea.

Subsequent Developments. The House Committee, true to predictions, recommended a permanent ban on the regulation of advertising. The Committee had grilled Dixon for three days in early April and ended up proposing that his agency, or any other that might issue advertising regulations, be removed from the picture altogether. In addition, the House bill did not contain the Senate bill's directives to the FTC to come back to the Congress with reports and recommendations. If there was any remaining doubt as to the hostility that existed toward the Commission among members of the House Committee, their pronouncements on the floor soon dispelled it. Representative Walter Rogers scored the FTC for attempting "to write the death penalty for a very strong segment of the economy of this nation" and the Surgeon General for trying to "brainwash the public," while expressing his relief that Commerce Committee Chairman Oren Harris and the Congress had "moved in." Representative Kornegay then arose to link together the sins of the Commission and the Senate Committee; the two together, he charged, had "thrown down the gauntlet" and forced House action.[33]

The House ratified its committee's product, though not without hearing some strident accusations as to the extent of industry influence. In conference, however, the Senate Committee was in a position of strength in some ways analogous to that of the House on the fair packaging bill a year later. For one thing, the Senate bill derived legitimacy from the fact that it appeared to be a more equitable compromise, a better balancing of the interests involved, than the House's rather blatant endorsement of industry objectives. Harris, in fact, was not entirely happy with his committee's performance, and a Drew Pearson column entitled "Steamroller Goes through House" had brought public attention to the lower chamber's action—and presented an image that even the industry was anxious to avoid.[34] More important was the fact that the House Committee, which once before had bought time for the industry, was now anxious to get a law on the books quickly. The Senate Committee could expect some concessions in return for its speedy acceptance of a ban on the regulation of advertising. The conference report thus contained the labeling requirements common to both bills, limited the ban to four years, and continued to provide for an annual FTC report.

The *Times* nonetheless recommended a veto, characterizing the bill as "a green signal to the lobbyists that any regulatory agency is open to invasion and emasculation." A group of eight Democratic senators and representatives (among whom only Representative Moss was a member of either Commerce Committee) likewise publicly asked the President to veto the bill on the grounds that it "protects only the cigarette industry." But Senator Neuberger took issue with this position, noting that the ban on further regulation was only temporary and taking pains to give Magnuson credit for that fact.[35] On July 27, 1965, the President signed the bill without fanfare.

In the development of the Federal Cigarette Labeling and Advertising Act, then, the congressional role was considerably different from that displayed in the packaging episode. Crucial functions were performed outside the Congress, and without them it is doubtful that the isolated efforts that had begun within Congress could have succeeded. Of prime importance was the information-gathering and publicizing undertaken by the Surgeon General; this alone made a congressional response more likely. But its immediate importance was in providing the basis for FTC action. Because they took place within the limits of the Commission's existing authority, the policy moves of the FTC framed the issue in terms of the regulation of labeling and advertising. This largely determined the focus future proposals would assume, and of course it elicited an equally specific industry response. Congressmen and senators came to this issue not primarily as formulators, information-gatherers, or publicizers, though some of them, to be sure, had earlier played these roles. For the most part they came to an issue which had already been framed, researched, and publicized and whose presence or absence on the agenda was beyond their control. They came as proponents or opponents of policies announced and roles assumed by a regulatory agency; they came as self-conscious spokesmen of certain constituencies and interests; and they came preoccupied with the task of adjusting those interests, realizing that some sort of action was required by the fact that a mammoth industry and a federal commission were on a collision course.

The solution that easily could have emerged, however, would not have reflected a balancing of interests, much less a recognition of some broader public or consumer interest, so much as a response to the one interest that by virtue of its resources, the intensity and immediacy of its concern, and its strength in several states and districts, had come to outweigh all the others. But Magnuson's move made the labeling requirement, which the tobacco industry had only been willing to accept in exchange for a long-term advertising immunity, the only permanent feature of the bill, and it furthermore guaranteed that advertising regulation and the role of the FTC would remain live issues. He and his committee thus shifted appreciably the thrust of the legislation, undertaking a counter-mobilization which partially reaffirmed the moves of the FTC and offset some of the efforts of industry and its spokesmen. It was only by virtue of the Senate Committee's eleventh-hour assumption of responsibility that the early initiatives of PHS, FTC, the health associations, and scattered congressional advocates found even partial fruition.

Certain characteristics of the Senate Commerce Committee and its environment were particularly relevant to the roles it and its members initially assumed. The interests impinging upon various members, the effectiveness or ineffectiveness of certain senators, the absence of a widespread crusading sentiment on the Committee, the preeminence of norms of moderation and accommodation, the strengths of certain lobbies and the weaknesses of others, the absence of executive pressure, and the vulnerability of the agencies supporting regulation—all these helped account for the fact that a "strong" bill did not emerge. The compromise Magnuson finally engineered, however, pointed up certain additional aspects of the committee life, variables with a somewhat different impact:

Magnuson's emerging role as champion of the consumer, his increasing willingness to defy certain interests, the activistic proclivities of the staff, Magnuson's power and prestige in his committee, and the cooperative and mutually beneficial ties that the staff and certain members were securing between the Committee and other "islands of decision." It was these latter factors, as the fair packaging story also demonstrates, which in significant respects were transforming the legislative role of the Commerce Committee.

THE TRAFFIC SAFETY ACT

The Issue is Framed. The Johnson Administration in late 1965 was looking for low-cost legislative proposals. Anxious to keep up the pace of the 89th Congress' first session, but faced with inflation and a mounting war budget, White House aides were poring over issues which a year before would have been considered small potatoes—campaign financing, consumer protection, water pollution, the length of House terms, and cabinet reorganization. Another such issue was traffic safety. The President's State of the Union Message of January 12 and his Economic Message two weeks later promised the proposal of a comprehensive safety program. On March 2 the President sent up the Traffic Safety Act of 1966. The bill was introduced as S. 3005 by Senator Magnuson, and an identical bill was presented in the House by Representative Staggers, who had just succeeded Oren Harris as Chairman of the Committee on Interstate and Foreign Commerce.

The Traffic Safety Act thus differed from the fair packaging and cigarette labeling bills: it bore the administration seal. That difference, however, was more apparent than real; it can be argued with considerable plausibility that Senate action in this field in 1966 would have been virtually the same whether or not the administration had sent up a bill. The issue, in fact, had already been framed, its dimensions explored, and solutions considered in Congress and the private sector. The President was already behind the times when his bill was introduced—the White House on February 13 decided to leak the details of the bill in view of the fact that some fifteen traffic safety bills were already on the floor of each house[36]— and he never really caught up.

Some piecemeal legislation had been enacted in the early sixties,[37] largely through the efforts of Kenneth Roberts, a Democratic Representative who was defeated in 1964 as Goldwater Republicanism fell on Alabama. The Department of Commerce was given responsibility for setting and enforcing safety standards for brake fluid and seat belts, and the General Services Administration was given authority to set safety standards for federally purchased automobiles beginning with the 1967 model year.

These bills, rather inconspicuous at first, later proved to be of considerable significance. The brake fluid and seat belt laws got the Commerce Department into the field of vehicle safety, an involvement accepted with extreme reluctance. But the Department's Office of Science and Technology, whose role in fair packaging has already been discussed, was saddled with a good share of the responsibility for developing and administering the standards. This meant that automobile safety became a rather important concern for Holloman and Christenson soon after they took their jobs:

> *We could see that these laws were only piecemeal and were pretty unworkable besides, and we started looking at the problem in a more systematic way.*

The involvement of the GSA was likewise significant. The new authority given to the agency, partly because the Commerce Department did not want it, was exercised with great circumspection and numerous difficulties, due somewhat to GSA's deficiencies in expertise and political muscle. But the 1964 legislation established the principle of standard-setting in the field and, in time, stimulated within GSA the feeling that a federal program involving *all* vehicles and tires was needed.

Meanwhile, Abraham Ribicoff had come to the Senate. Having already achieved national prominence as Representative, Governor, and HEW Secretary, and, as one observer put it, "never objecting to seeing his name in the paper," Ribicoff eschewed the traditional role of the freshman Senator and began almost immediately to make pronouncements and introduce bills on a wide variety of subjects. Both his style and his committee positions suited him better for a publicizing than for a mobilizing role; no issue with which he concerned himself during his early years in the Senate illustrated his relative strengths and weaknesses better than did traffic safety. Having obtained the Chairmanship of the Government Operations Subcommittee on Executive Reorganization after two years in the Senate, Ribicoff in 1965 opened hearings on governmental and industrial safety efforts. Executive branch officials betrayed a lack of knowledge and concern; Ribicoff's successor at HEW, Anthony Celebrezze, seemed particularly confident that the industry was voluntarily developing adequate safety standards. But it was the appearance of the Detroit representatives that did the most to fire congressional interest and attract nationwide headlines. For four days Ribicoff and Robert Kennedy took automobile executives over the coals, accusing them of giving safety considerations a low priority in car design, pointing to laxity in the recall of defective models and parts, and ridiculing the ratio of company profits to the amounts spent on safety research.

One of the more important resources on which the Ribicoff Subcommittee drew was Ralph Nader, a young attorney who had a consuming interest in automobile safety and was gradually mounting a publicity campaign of his own. "A basically sound fanatic," as a Senate staff man described him,[38] Nader had in 1964 moved to Washington for the express purpose of devoting full time to his cause. For a short time he worked in the Labor Department on a study of the federal role in traffic safety, from which, as he indicated, "a slew of memos and recommendations" and not much else resulted.[39] Meanwhile, he conducted an extensive one-man lobbying campaign, talking to anyone in government who would listen and concluding work on his book, *Unsafe at Any Speed.* The book was published in November, 1965, and received considerable press notice, securing for Nader a nationwide reputation and heightening congressional and public awareness of the issue.

Most early congressional efforts at formulation, apart from the three Roberts bills, came from the office of Senator Gaylord Nelson. He proposed, among other things, that all automobiles be required to meet GSA standards, that GSA be authorized to build a prototype automobile incorporating various safety features, and that the Secretary of Commerce be authorized to set and enforce standards for the manufacture of tires. Nelson's position, however, was somewhat analogous to that of Hart on fair packaging and Neuberger on cigarette labeling. He was often regarded as a crusading liberal whose proposals were utopian and unrealistic. He was not equipped, either by expertise and staff resources or by prestige and seniority within the Senate, to undertake the interest-aggregation, information-gathering, and mobilization needed to work out feasible proposals and steer them to passage. Moreover, he lacked even that one advantage which Neuberger and Hart did enjoy, a seat on the Commerce Committee. Thus, Nelson might have been expected to turn, like Ribicoff, to a publicizing role. But here, too, he lacked the crucial resources—nationwide prominence, press interest, a suitable subcommittee chairmanship—which others, like Ribicoff, had.

Magnuson and his aides meanwhile were surveying the safety issue in general, and Nelson's tire bill in particular. After the Ribicoff hearings Magnuson, in a thinly veiled preemption, introduced and scheduled hearings on his own Tire Safety Act, with Nelson as a little-noticed co-sponsor. Magnuson saw the tire safety bill as something of a test case through which he could develop certain regulatory schemes, test the reactions and the potency of certain interests, and see further how a relatively new type of legislative role agreed with him—all with a view to the larger issue of vehicle safety which loomed ahead. But it was important to him also as a means of staking out his committee's jurisdictional claims. This was Commerce Committee territory, and he was irritated that others, particularly Ribicoff, were encroaching upon it. "Magnuson," one of his staff men recalled, "thought Ribicoff had no business nosing around in what he considered to be his area." He resented Ribicoff's headline-grabbing, particularly because his pronouncements implied that the Commerce Committee, along with the rest of the government, had been slow to move. So the tire safety bill served to establish Magnuson's authority and to prefigure his intentions.

Grinstein and Pertschuk had been anxious to get the Chairman into the area of traffic safety "at least as early as the first set of Ribicoff hearings," and they too welcomed the tire safety bill as a trial run. Processing the bill gave them experience which would later be valuable, but even more important was the self-confidence it gave them about Magnuson's dependability in his new role. The Chairman proved surprisingly resistant to industry pressures, seeming to discover, as one of his aides put it, that "he could defy some of these interests and they couldn't do a thing to him; he seemed rather to enjoy it." Grinstein and Pertschuk were subsequently less hesitant to involve Magnuson in the auto safety issue and to commit him to a relatively hard line.

This experience also enabled Grinstein and Pertschuk to establish a firm working relationship with the Commerce Department's Office of Science and Technology. Holloman and Christenson had been at odds with most of their colleagues in welcoming the authority granted them under the Roberts bills and in desiring broader departmental involvement; they considered it a major victory when Commerce reported merely that it "would not object" to being granted discretionary authority to set tire standards. Pertschuk therefore largely bypassed the Department's other liaison officers and worked with Christenson in rewriting Nelson's tire safety bill. It was frankly viewed as a "trial balloon":

> We were anxious to see what kind of reaction we got, and we also saw this as a model for what could follow with regard to auto standards. We both had that in mind.

Ribicoff's and Magnuson's assistants found—apart from these stirrings in Commerce and the standard-setting activities of the GSA—"nothing going on" in the executive branch prior to late 1965, when preparation for the State of the Union message got underway. Some research had been undertaken by Commerce, Labor, and particularly HEW, but there were serious questions as to its practicality and the degree to which it had been transmitted to industry or to state departments of safety. Certainly there seemed to have been, as Nader claimed, "little interpretation and less integration into policy-formation."[40] There existed, in addition, the President's Committee for Traffic Safety, but this group displayed most of the weaknesses and few of the strengths of the President's consumer office. Its functions were advisory and public-relations oriented, and, unlike the consumer office, it had traditionally been industry-dominated. The Committee had been organized by General Motors President Harlow Curtice at the request of President Eisenhower; its membership consisted of representatives of automotive, insurance, and other private and "professional" safety associations, while most of its operating funds came from the Automotive Safety Foundation and the Insurance Institute for Highway Safety, the safety "arms" of their respective industries. To critics like Nader, the Committee represented the apotheosis of the "traffic safety establishment." During the Kennedy administration some governmental representatives were added to the Committee, and there was some talk of downgrading the group in favor of an interdepartmental highway safety board. But the Committee continued, as one of its critics put it, to make "unabashed use of the prestige of the presidential seal to spread the industry gospel."[41]

Such policy development as the executive branch finally undertook was centered in the Department of Commerce. Sympathy with the industry point of view, based more on the predilections and perspectives of the officials involved than on actual lobbying efforts, pervaded the top levels of the Department, fed by distrust of Ribicoff's sensationalistic tactics, doubts about Nader's "soundness," and reluctance to see the Department undertake major new regulatory efforts. But forces without and within were operating to alter this position. Holloman and Christenson were making their voices heard, and Alan S. Boyd, who was soon to be Undersecretary for Transportation, was developing a favorable inclination as well. In mid-1965 Holloman proposed that the Department develop a traffic safety program, including a program of vehicle standards. Boyd, assigned to study the proposal, brought back a favorable report, but by that time intradepartmental pressures had been superseded by a message from above: the President wanted a traffic safety proposal for 1966. It was by no means certain at that point that automobile standards were to be included, although had the Department not come around, a directive to that effect might eventually have been forthcoming. In any case, the decision was made at the departmental level: General Counsel Robert Giles had been converted to the idea of vehicle regulation and, in a November meeting, he and Holloman convinced Connor that such standards should be provided for in the administration bill. The Department then set about formulating a proposal; most of the work on automobile standards fell to Christenson.

Connor was anxious that the bill not appear punitive and that, if possible, extensive departmental involvement in standard-setting be avoided. Thus, he preferred that the Department's authority be discretionary and that the bill's timetable be relaxed enough to permit industry to get its own house in order. Christenson agreed, but for his own reasons: he was convinced that, in vehicle safety as in fair packaging, the Department could not administer a successful program from an adversary position; neither its competence nor its sanctions were adequate. Despite the fears of some presidential advisers that the bill would appear "weak," the Commerce Department viewpoint prevailed and S. 3005, as introduced, permitted but did not require the Secretary of Commerce to issue vehicle standards after two years, if he determined that the industry was not developing adequate standards of its own.

Re-Writing the Bill. The President's bill was immediately denounced by Nader and Ribicoff, and as he opened Commerce Committee hearings on March 16, 1966, Magnuson also insisted that it must be strengthened. Ribicoff was leadoff witness; his appearance before the Committee was characterized, on both sides, by alternating periods of painful politeness and thinly-veiled irritation. But the first day revealed no deep congressional cleavages as to the policy issues involved, and it put the administration on notice as to where the President's bill stood:

> **THE CHAIRMAN:** *I might say here, Senator, that we both have the same idea, that this bill is inadequate. . . .*
>
> **SENATOR RIBICOFF:** *Mr. Chairman, I wish in no way to suggest a lack of concern with traffic safety in the Department of Commerce or an unwillingness . . . to take action against the Nation's largest industry. But according to press reports, so-called administration officials . . . have indicated already that any use of the enforcement provisions in the President's bill is "highly unlikely."*[42]

The administration was thus thrown on the defensive; it became more difficult to maintain a united front within or among executive agencies. Representatives from GSA, the only federal agency which had come before the Committee to endorse the tire safety bill, presented another strong statement in favor of vehicle standards, hinting, in fact, that they took issue with S. 3005's rather leisurely timetable and its provision of only discretionary authority.[43] Secretary Connor appeared in support of the bill, carrying with him to the witness table a detailed defense of the discretionary approach. Much to his surprise, the question was not even broached, so as the first day of hearings drew to a close, he brought the subject up himself and read his argument into the record. In responding, Magnuson revealed that, despite the opening statement he had read, the issue was not yet clearly focused in his own mind; he dismissed the Secretary with the observation that there did not seem to be any "great disagreement" between them.[44] But Magnuson and several other Committee members learned rather quickly, and the reception subsequently given to witnesses who praised present administration efforts or who criticized proposals to "strengthen" the bill was noticeably less cordial.

One reason for the increasingly strident tone of the hearings was the growing involvement of Senator Vance Hartke. Hartke, like Ribicoff, was a senator who often concentrated on the "public" aspects of his job—making frequent policy pronouncements, introducing bills on a wide variety of subjects, and fighting valiantly for amendments on the floor (which he may or may not have bothered to offer in committee); as a publicizer, however, his successes rarely matched those of Ribicoff. Moreover, during the 89th Congress Hartke, for reasons best known to himself, had supported efforts to weaken both the fair packaging and cigarette labeling bills. So it was with great relish, and perhaps with a touch of compensation, that Hartke assumed the role of the exponent of the strongest possible auto safety bill. Magnuson and Hartke were not particularly close, but it was the Chairman's practice to accommodate his members where possible; moreover, he was assured of his own ability to exert decisive control over the processing of the bill, and he had no objection to Hartke's doing a good part of the work and getting some publicity. Thus, many hours of the hearings found Hartke in the chair, asking questions fed to him by Nader, and a number of committee amendments were worked out and presented under his name.

Hartke conducted an exhaustive interrogation of HEW and National Safety Council representatives, and other Committee members joined him in giving the four major automobile manufacturers the kind of reception "traffic cops give when they nail down a speeder."[45] The industry proposed that the development of safety standards be left to a board consisting of the president of each company and a chairman nominated by the industry and approved by the Secretary of Commerce; Mrs. Neuberger's response was, "I say 'ha-ha' for any industry that comes along and wants to 'let us do it.'" And when it was proposed that the Vehicle Equipment Safety Commission, a voluntary and largely inactive association of state safety officials, be beefed up with federal members and given oversight responsibilities, Magnuson himself had a sharp retort:

> **MR. BUGAS:** . . . I think the states . . . appear just as concerned as we are about their being left out of this. . . .
>
> **SENATOR MAGNUSON:** Let's not stir that up. We are not leaving the states out. The states have no control over how you manufacture a car. We are talking about that.[46]

The industry, in fact, misread the seriousness of congressional intentions at virtually every stage of the legislation's development—perhaps because of the smallness and isolation of their Washington offices and the failure of those who sensed the temper of the times to make themselves heard in Detroit.[47] As a result, their testimony, drafted in Detroit by a committee of industry vice-presidents, was largely unresponsive to the Committee's concerns. The prudent course would have been to accept the President's bill as the gentlest among realistic alternatives and to suggest only marginal changes. Instead, the industry presented a proposal which left standard-setting up to the industry and involved federal officials only in an advisory capacity, without even a majority of the votes, on the VESC. The industry, in other words, practically invited the Committee to say "ha-ha"; its members could not have accepted the industry bill without appearing to abandon the cause entirely.

But the incentives to aid the industry were rather low in any case, whatever tactics Detroit might have chosen. The publicity that surrounded the issue made clearly identifiable and extremely vulnerable "bad guys" of the manufacturers, and they were singularly unsuccessful in rehabilitating their image. In fact, their image hit a new low at about the time Magnuson opened his hearings. Nader revealed that he was being trailed and harassed and that detectives hired by General Motors were asking his acquaintances about his personal conduct and political beliefs. The Ribicoff Subcommittee investigated the affair, publicizing GM's culpability and securing a grudging apology to Nader from company President James Roche. "Everybody was so outraged that a great corporation was out to clobber a guy because he wrote critically about them," said one senator, "at that point, everybody said the hell with them."[48] Senators became increasingly wary of coming to the industry's defense; even the minority members of the Commerce Committee became interested in strengthening the President's bill. Minority Aide Jerry Kenney, on traffic safety as on fair packaging, was interested in developing a positive Republican contribution; Pertschuk again cooperated with him to that end.

Ribicoff's publicizing continued into the summer, focusing mainly on industry procedures for recalling and repairing defective models. It was indicative of the success of his press relations, and perhaps also of the myopia of the news media, that as late as May 7 the New York Times featured Ribicoff as its "Man in the News"—"A Fighter for Safety."[49] For by that time the legislative reins were firmly in Magnuson's hands and the staff was well into the task of revising the bill. "Our relations with the Ribicoff people on this were minimal," a staff member recalled, "only what was required by politeness." Nor was Ribicoff or his staff in effective contact with the Commerce Department officials who were working on the bill. There was no question on the part of any of the participants that the center of re-formulation, interest-aggregation, and amendment was the Senate Commerce Committee. "We were in the driver's seat alright."

Nader had developed a working relationship with both Christenson and Pertschuk, and he helped Hartke and his staff prepare their strengthening amendments. On the other side was Lloyd Cutler, an experienced Washington lawyer who in mid-April had been retained by the Automobile Manufacturers Association. He too had a list of amendments. To Pertschuk fell the task of sifting through these proposals, balancing one against the other, and coming up with an equitable compromise. His own sympathies, of course, were more with Nader than with Cutler, but he recognized the legitimacy of certain industry criticisms and was anxious to develop a workable program. In addition, it was necessary to consult with the White House and the Commerce Department, both of whom had a strong interest in the bill. But Pertschuk had a relatively free hand, and his position was immensely strengthened by the backing Magnuson gave him.

The industry's abandonment of its earlier all-or-nothing approach helped it to gain several marginal concessions. "It was a tougher game after Cutler got into it," one advocate admitted.[50] On the central question of mandatory standards, the industry was still too late with too little. Their readiness to accept a modified version of the President's plan was revealed to the House Committee in May, and Commerce Department officials, including Christenson, continued to favor a relaxed timetable and the discretionary approach. Despite this, the Senate Committee moved ahead with a plan to impose "interim standards," based for the most part on GSA specifications, by January of 1967, and more complete requirements one year later. But the industry secured the insertion of language giving the Secretary of Commerce flexibility in determining the effective dates of standards and deadlines for compliance in special cases. Nader's amendments, many of them contained in an alternative draft prepared by Hartke, received favorable consideration as well. Among those adopted were provisions for the development of a prototype vehicle, for on-site plant investigations, and for the examination of industry records to determine compliance.

Amendments such as these were, for the most part, never seen by Committee members. Accommodations were made and agreements reached on the staff level. Pertschuk drew on the expertise of both Nader and Cutler, secured the confidence of both, and occasionally played them off against one another. Only a few issues could not be handled in this way and spilled over into committee meetings. Two of these involved Russell Long, a new member of the Committee, whose duties as Majority Whip and Chairman of the Finance Committee, if they left him little time to concern himself with Commerce Committee affairs, also made Magnuson anxious to accommodate him when he did have something to propose. Long's first traffic safety amendment sought to insure that the results of federally sponsored research would be freely available to the public. This did not greatly concern the large auto manufacturers, since research authorized by the bill would be undertaken mainly by manufacturers of specialized equipment. Moreover, even if the large companies were to become involved, they could reject federal funds and keep their patent rights secure. But there was another amendment which did concern large manufacturers, one on which they had encountered substantial opposition: they wanted whatever collaboration they might undertake in the development of safety devices exempted from the coverage of antitrust law. They went to Long, therefore, with an offer to support his patent amendment in return for his sponsorship of the antitrust provision. Long accepted.

His success, however, was limited. The Committee secured from the Justice Department a letter stating that present antitrust law did not throw doubts on the legitimacy of "any cooperative effort to develop safety devices or to exchange information concerning standards . . . where joint efforts seem necessary and constructive and are not accompanied by unduly restrictive collateral agreements." The reported bill, therefore, simply stated that the act was not meant to alter existing applications and interpretations of the antitrust statutes.[51] Long succeeded, however, in getting his patent amendment adopted, thus prompting a minority report and the only party split that occurred on the bill.

A third amendment considered in committee had to do with the imposition of criminal as well as civil penalties. This was an issue on which Nader focused; the industry had not been concerned with the penalty provisions at first, but with more publicity criminal penalties came to be seen as a reflection on the manufacturers' integrity. The provision was not included in the committee draft, and Hartke offered it unsuccessfully in committee and on the floor.

"Mr. Chairman," Secretary Connor had quipped during the hearings, "you are usually ahead of us."[52] That quip continued to characterize executive-legislative interaction down to the time of final passage. In mid-May the Commerce Department sent, then partially retracted, a letter to the Senate Committee opposing the immediate imposition of mandatory standards; a few days later President Johnson launched a public attack on the industry for its attempts to delay the legislation, and an eighteen-page letter to the Senate Committee from Deputy Attorney General Ramsey Clark—which Commerce Department officials could not help viewing as a preemption and an insult—detailed the administration's objections to most of Cutler's amendments. The Senate Committee, however, was already dealing with Cutler on its own terms: "It was moving under its own steam," Christenson recalled, "and didn't need a push from anywhere."

The Bill is Passed. Senate floor action took only one day, June 24, 1966. Most debate centered on Long's patent amendment; Cotton termed the *Report's* defense of the provision "utterly asinine" and threw in a jibe at the "bright young men . . . on the staff" who must have drafted it.[53] His tongue was in his cheek, however, for he knew that the paragraphs in question had been drafted by Long himself. Cotton picked up the votes of all Committee Republicans, plus Lausche, and lost by a fairly narrow margin, 35-43. Hartke then picked up the votes of four different Committee members, including Magnuson, in favor of criminal penalties, but he lost by 14-62 after Senator Pastore mounted a vociferous opposition. Final passage came quickly and painlessly, 76-0.

The House Committee had been expected to sympathize with the industry's point of view; early indications were that it might do with auto safety what it later did with fair packaging: pass a substantially altered bill, and then only under great administration pressure. The reason it did not behave in this fashion can be summarized in a single word: publicity. Though each of the three measures thus far examined passed through the six "stages" delineated in Chapter 1, the relative importance of these activities varied considerably from bill to bill. The traffic safety episode was notable for the continuing prominence of the publicizing function. A comparison to the fair packaging case is instructive. The publicity Hart was able to generate was important in stimulating Magnuson to champion his bill, and their combined efforts increased the eligibility of their cause for inclusion on the presidential agenda. But it was the commitment of the staff and of some key senators, along with certain disabilities of the opposition, which held the Committee to a strong bill, rather than any feeling that to oppose or to weaken the bill would be politically disastrous or would damage the Committee's prestige. In auto safety, however, publicity had a much more noticeable impact. Nader's and Ribicoff's efforts heightened public awareness and caught the President's eye. They also stimulated congressional interest and guaranteed that Magnuson, even had he not wished to exploit the issue, would have been forced to deal with it, if only to protect his jurisdiction and to retain his prerogatives. Moreover, the publicity was prominent and specific enough to make it politically attractive to try to strengthen the bill (witness Hartke) and to make it politically risky to undertake even seemingly inconspicuous changes. This compounded the industry's difficulties, for the nature of the safety issue—to say nothing of the tactics the manufacturers employed— cast a heavy moral shadow upon them and their defenders. Nader's access to the press, his intimate knowledge of what was transpiring on Capitol Hill, and the willingness of staff people in both branches to leak stories to him and to the press—all this made compromise, in the committee room or on the floor, in the White House or in the upper reaches of the Commerce Department, a very risky business (as Hart, Califano, and Doyd learned to their sorrow).[54] Therefore the Senate passed a strong bill, and from the White House came only praise.

The same factors came into play on the House side. On fair packaging, the publicity the issue had received and the prominence it had belatedly enjoyed on the presidential agenda were partially responsible for the House Committee's decision to report a bill. But a majority of the members were left free to champion industry amendments, and executive branch officials also could make important concessions without losing face. This was not the case on auto safety; such compromises could not go undetected. Moreover, many House Committee members were embarrassed over widespread predictions that the Committee, in contrast to its Senate counterpart, would "sell out." The prestige of the Committee, both within and outside the House, seemed to be at stake.[55] Staggers' panel therefore joined the derby and set out to strengthen the bill.

The House Committee continued to harbor some industry sympathizers; according to an administration official, the White House was unsure of the group and took a more active role than it had with the Senate Committee:

> *I think it's fair to say that had it not been for the President's interest and for all the publicity about their supposedly conservative role, they might well have held things up.*

As it was, the House Committee admitted Christenson and Nader to its counsels, reported a bill similar to S. 3005, and then accepted floor amendments which brought it even closer into line. The Tire Safety Act, which the Senate had passed on March 29, was added to the bill; other amendments authorized the Secretary to set standards for trucks and busses, provided for the establishment of a National Traffic Agency in the Commerce Department to administer the act, and strengthened Senate provisions for the notification of owners of models discovered to be defective.

The Senate conferees accepted most of these amendments and secured House agreement to Long's patent amendment and to various provisions regarding the Secretary's investigatory authority and the manufacturers' responsibility to furnish information. "The final product brought here for consideration today," said Representative Moss as the House approved the conference report, "should lay to rest any . . . charges that the House labored less vigorously or with less good faith than the other body."[56] The conference report passed both houses unanimously and the White House staged an elaborate bill-signing ceremony on September 9.

The functions surrounding the passage of the traffic safety act could rarely be isolated in discrete stages or attributed to single actors; perhaps the most remarkable feature of the episode was the way in which governmental participants continually shared the stage with one extraordinary private citizen, Ralph Nader. Publicizing was a continual process, influencing and often instigating the performance of the other functions. Nader and Ribicoff, and to a lesser extent the President and the Senate Committee, were responsible for the public and congressional attention the issue attracted and for its presence on various agendas. Nader's public activity was coupled with behind-the-scenes instigation as well, as he fed information to Christenson, Nelson, Ribicoff, Magnuson, Hartke—and Drew Pearson. Formulation was likewise a protracted process. Nader himself was important in shaping the issue and possible remedies; other early attempts were the work of Nelson and, to a lesser extent, Ribicoff. Christenson then undertook a great deal of original work, which was modified at the departmental and White House levels and presented as S. 3005. And the Commerce Committee introduced a number of provisions of its own during the bill's mark-up.

If the publicizing stage was of relatively great importance in the auto safety episode, interest-aggregation was of much less importance than it was for fair packaging or cigarette labeling. No one took the floor to assure his colleagues that the traffic safety bill took all the relevant interests into account. The auto bill was punitive in a way that the other bills were not, the problem with which it dealt was thought to be more compelling, and the opposing views were seen as less defensible and certainly as less politically viable. However, it was important that industry be heard and legitimate accommodations be made; this process centered in the Senate Commerce Committee. The industry had some friends in the executive branch, but it was clear that the Committee was writing its own bill; Cutler spent most of his time there.

Both Ribicoff's and Magnuson's hearings were crucial to the gathering of information, though here again it was Nader who demonstrated the importance of translating research into policy proposals and turned sheafs of data into a strong buttress for his cause. Christenson's expertise on administrative problems was likewise critical. Mobilization, however, was largely Magnuson's province: he was in a position to do what neither Nelson nor Ribicoff could do. Had he not acted, the President might have filled the gap; as it was, the President's efforts were of secondary importance. Modification, too, was centered in the Senate committee; Hartke, Long, majority and minority staff members, Nader, Cutler, and administration leaders all were able to affect the outcome. But Pertschuk and Grinstein, as brokers with powerful substantive interests of their own, enjoyed considerable latitude.

Committee characteristics highlighted by this episode include some previously mentioned: the ambitions and interests of the Chairman; his jealousy of his prerogatives; the activist bent of several members and the latitude with which they were able to operate; the competence, reformist sympathies, and entrepreneurial orientation of the staff; committee integration and bipartisanship. A new set of interest groups that inhabited the Committee's environment have been introduced; it has been seen that under certain conditions the Committee found it possible and even profitable to defy, or at least to deflect, their entreaties. That the administration suffered from internal divisions and a lack of coordination in yet another area has been discovered; committee initiative represented the filling of a gap more than a response to executive stimuli and in fact itself stimulated a reordering of the President's priorities.

THE MARINE RESOURCES AND ENGINEERING DEVELOPMENT ACT

The criteria used to choose the more prominent bills processed by the three committees under examination have generally led to proposals ranging widely over committee jurisdictions. This is less true of the Commerce Committee, however, than of the other committees to be examined. The three bills thus far discussed are those which, among all the bills reported by the Committee during the 89th Congress, received the most publicity and absorbed the greatest amounts of hearing time. But while these bills varied considerably as to the interest groups and executive agencies they involved, they all fell generally into the area of consumer protection and barely touched on other major areas of committee jurisdiction—aviation, merchant marine and fisheries, communication, and transportation. This in itself was indicative, as Chapter 3 will show, of variations in the Committee's policy-making role from area to area.

There is one area, however, which is in danger of being overlooked, not because of the absence of legislative activity in the field, but because the Committee's efforts were not concentrated on any *one* proposal. Almost half of the bills reported by the Committee were in the area of shipping-fishing-oceanography; though the popular press gave little coverage to such matters, their cumulative "prominence" met our standards many times over. Moreover, some of the bills were extensive in scope, arising from a felt need to rationalize and upgrade the nation's merchant marine and oceanographic programs and to stimulate executive activity. One such bill has been chosen for analysis; it fell somewhat short according to the criteria applied to other bills, but it did seem to be the most prominent of its type.

It was shortly after the 89th Congress convened that Senator Magnuson introduced S. 944, "a bill to provide for expanded research in the oceans and Great Lakes, to establish a national oceanographic council, and for other purposes." This proposal was the last of a long line of bills, offered over a seven-year period, designed to upgrade and coordinate the federal government's efforts in oceanography. Most of them had failed of enactment. At first there seemed to be little reason to believe that S. 944 would fare any differently, but within seventeen months it was on the statute books.

An Issue Emerges. The Federal budget for oceanography—including research, training, ocean surveys, ship and shore facility construction—rose from less than $10 million in 1953 to $55 million in fiscal 1960 and to $141.6 million by fiscal 1966.[57] If these figures revealed a growing recognition in various quarters of the economic and military importance of oceanographic activities, they also reflected an intense lobbying campaign by elements of the scientific community. A particularly significant step was taken in 1956, when the President of the National Academy of Sciences, acting at the behest of a group of marine scientists from several government agencies, appointed a committee to "provide guidance on needs and opportunities of oceanographic research."[58] The result, in 1959, was a twelve-volume report, rich in both basic data and substantive policy proposals, which served as a rallying point for a wider group of scientists and for politicians who had their own reasons for championing the cause of oceanography. Moreover, the NAS committee did not disband but continued to issue recommendations—one of which advocated annual federal funding of $280 million for the decade 1965-1974.[59]

Though some partisans of stepped up oceanographic activity had their own bailiwicks to protect, others saw in the fragmentary character of the federal "program"—involving six cabinet-level departments and some 22 separate agency requests for funds—a threat to its rationalization and development. A step toward improved coordination was taken in 1959 with the formation of the Interagency Committee on Oceanography as a subcommittee of President Eisenhower's newly formed Federal Council on Science and Technology. But the advocates of accelerated federal efforts, generally pleased with neither the functioning of the ICO nor the pace of program expansion, turned increasingly to Congress, where from the first they had received a hospitable reception. The scientists teamed up with the House Merchant Marine and Fisheries Committee and the Senate Commerce Committee to give oceanography programs a relatively higher priority than the Executive wished to give them.[60] The committees found their ties with scientists in and out of government highly beneficial, but their actions were not best understood as a *response* to pressures mounted or arguments expounded by individuals and agencies involved in research. Scientists and government officials interested in expanded and integrated oceanographic activity were fortunate, not in possessing the resources to become a truly effective lobby, but in coming with the right issue to the right people at the right time.

Senator Magnuson was quick to become a champion of both reorganization and increased funding. His involvement, here and in the merchant marine and fisheries area generally, furnished a nice contrast to the role he was later to assume in consumer affairs—a role which, as seen above, was developed only in face of political difficulties, threatened preemptions, and staff instigation. Shipping and fishing, on the other hand, were areas in which Magnuson had been interested since he first came to Congress in 1937. They were important to Washington, and the groups involved wielded considerable influence there and controlled sizable campaign chests. As Magnuson gained seniority and influence, he was increasingly in a position to champion the interests of American shipping and fishing; his assumption of that role worked to his and industry's mutual advantage. The fact that Magnuson felt the need after 1962 to espouse another kind of cause, one that involved less campaign money but more media coverage, bore witness to the changing character of Washington politics. But Magnuson was anxious to retain his old image as the guardian of a set of his state's most vital interests; he thus pounced on oceanography as soon as the first NASCO report appeared and remained interested in the issue. It had considerable general appeal at home and also involved an unmistakable economic potential. The programs envisioned by NASCO called for extensive ship and shore facility construction and the development of equipment potentially beneficial to the merchant and fishing fleets. And the prospect that an oceanographic program might locate various ocean resources and develop means of tapping them was obviously attractive to fishing, mining, and petroleum interests.

Magnuson enjoyed some scattered legislative successes,[61] but his main proposal, a bill implementing several of the NAS committee's funding recommendations and giving responsibility for overseeing the federal oceanographic effort to the National Science Foundation, ran into opposition from the NSF itself and, though passed by the Senate in 1960 and 1961, never got past the hearing stage in the House. The Kennedy administration opposed both the Magnuson bill and an alternative reorganization proposal developed by Representative George Miller which would have given oceanography its own cabinet-level council. The leaders of the House and Senate committees then agreed to put forward a third approach; late in the 87th Congress both houses passed a bill which gave the President's new Office of Science and Technology—established under Kennedy's Reorganization Plan No. 2 in early 1962—the responsibility for establishing a national program in oceanography. The move was of debatable legality: the OST had a statutory base and was not protected by executive privilege, but it was still an advisory arm of the President and the proposal represented an "attempt to control the organization of the Executive Office of the President, and its inner procedures, to an unprecedented degree."[62] President Kennedy pocket-vetoed the bill. The veto could hardly be taken as an indication of presidential disinterest in oceanography; Kennedy had sent a special message to Congress on natural resources which stressed the need for research in the field, and his supplemental appropriations requests for fiscal 1962 had resulted in a one-year increase of 69 percent in federal expenditures in the area. But the events of the 87th Congress did suggest that the President's scientific and organizational advisers were beginning to look askance at attempts to give special status to oceanography and that the plans put forward to date were too ambitious in their reorganization schemes or in their encroachments upon presidential prerogatives to be acceptable.

New Efforts at Formulation. The 88th Congress saw a renewal of efforts to come up with a workable solution. It also saw the beginnings of a widening split between the two houses as to how the issue should be approached. In general, the House Merchant Marine and Fisheries Committee displayed a willingness to tailor the OST bill to the President's wishes. Chairman Bonner reintroduced the vetoed bill, but the Committee finally reported and the House passed a proposal developed by the Bureau of the Budget and OST and sponsored by Oceanography Subcommittee

Chairman Alton Lennon. This bill simply provided that the President, with OST assistance, should develop goals and coordinate programs and that, at his discretion, he might appoint an advisory committee to assist him in his efforts. Magnuson did not even schedule hearings on Lennon's proposal. Instead, he introduced a revised version of Miller's council bill, which drew no more administration sympathy than it had two years before. Meanwhile, a new approach was developed under the aegis of Congressman Bob Wilson. His idea was to form a National Oceanographic Agency, a "wet NASA" as it came to be called, which would actually assume the administration of oceanographic programs previously scattered among several agencies.

As 1964 drew to a close every indication was that the balkanization of the oceanography program was being matched by the balkanization of congressional efforts. Though some of the proposals that were being circulated, notably Wilson's, were more objectionable to the administration than others, the President felt no compulsion to choose among "lesser evils" or to put forth alternative proposals. The White House's only action was to endorse the Lennon Bill, which was simply a restatement of the President's existing authority. For a time it seemed as though congressional efforts might cancel each other out. Nor could it be said that the scientists who had pushed the program in the first place, or the industries that had come to their support, were very helpful in resolving the dilemma. Coordination and government reorganization had always ranked considerably lower than program expansion among their priorities. Many of the scientists, in fact, were located in government bureaus; they were anxious to see their particular programs strengthened but were apprehensive about tinkering with the organizational charts. In any case, the issue was left with Congress.

The opening weeks of the 89th Congress revealed that more senators and representatives were interested in oceanography than ever before but that legislative activity was more fragmented than ever. This time Chairman Bonner joined Lennon in sponsoring the administration-backed bill; Magnuson reintroduced his interdepartmental council bill as S. 944; Congressman Wilson again offered his agency bill; Senator Bartlett offered a variant which would have set up an agency to carry out a program of marine exploration and development of the resources of the continental shelf; and a new plan appeared: Representative Paul Rogers, a member of the House Subcommittee, called for a temporary study commission which would have no administrative responsibilities but would make a comprehensive investigation of oceanography and recommend policy alterations.

On the Senate side, the increasing involvement of Senator Bartlett calls for some comment. Bartlett had come to the Senate in 1958, immediately after Alaska had become a state, and had received an appointment to the Commerce Committee, his first choice, without delay. The factors which had initially led Magnuson to champion fishing and shipping interests, and hence oceanography, were operative in Bartlett's case as well. But Bartlett's first interest was fishing; the fishing industry was a mainstay of Alaska's economy, and many of the new state's woes could be traced to its decline. Fishing, moreover, was an area to which Magnuson had given much less attention than shipping; the early sixties had seen very few legislative innovations.

The legislative setting can be illuminated by a brief examination of group and agency activity. Neither the fishing nor the shipping industry had mounted a concerted campaign in favor of oceanography; its linkage to their interests was not close enough to make it a high priority item. Thus it was up to Magnuson to publicize the issue, to point up the linkages to his clients, to stimulate their interest and secure their support, and to reap the political benefits. But his involvement with the shipping interests did not generally take this form. Management, maritime labor, and construction interests found themselves in agreement on many legislative matters; their lobbying operations were generally similar and often unified. "It must be the most over-represented interest in Washington," remarked a Commerce Committee aide. "There are dozens of these lobbyists around, and I think they've been here forever. They all seem to be old. They've built up long-standing connections and continue to use them." The shipping industry was one of the first to receive federal assistance, and its lobbying habits were long-standing. One of these habits was to go first of all to Congress, generally with quite specific proposals. Senators and staff members sometimes questioned the efficacy of proposals and pointed to a need for new approaches and fresh ideas, but the industry was generally effective at getting what it wanted; continuing efforts after 1966 to keep the Maritime Administration out of the new Department of Transportation served as an example on both counts.

The tendency of the shipping industry to bring its proposals to Congress was reinforced by the careful attention it got there, by the character of the Maritime Administration, and by a relative absence of presidential solicitude. The shipping industry was localized and specialized; its economic difficulties were severe but of limited public concern. The Maritime Administration was a rather inconspicuous bureau in the Commerce Department; the Executive's difficulties in responding to rising demands for a "national maritime policy" bore witness to the fact that the Maritime Administration had never been organized, staffed, or oriented as a center for the generation of policy proposals. It concentrated on the administration of construction and operation-differential subsidies and was viewed by Congress and the shipping interests alike as a "lackadaisical outfit," neither inclined nor equipped to play a prominent policy role. Moreover, the industry's day-to-day dealings with the agency discouraged the development of a client-advocate relationship. Despite the reorganization of 1961, which entrusted the enforcement of the various Shipping and Merchant Marine Acts to an independent Federal Maritime Commission, the Maritime Administration's subsidy programs continued to involve regulation as well—"right down to specifying the kinds of curtains they use in their cabins," as one Committee counsel put it—and this introduced a certain distance into industry-government relations.

The context in which a senator championed the interests of the fishing industry was different indeed. Fishing involved fewer companies, a much smaller work force, and much less money. The industry was less highly organized for lobbying purposes and, having recently come upon hard times, had only begun to think in terms of large-scale and sustained governmental assistance. A separate governmental bureau had been organized around their interests in 1956, the Department of the Interior's Bureau of Commercial Fisheries. This office saw itself as a promoter of the industry, and several of its officials developed various legislative ideas, but the BCF was small, sparsely funded, and barely able to make its voice heard in administrative councils. As a result, the Bureau itself found it profitable to develop a working relationship with the committees of Congress.[63]

All this meant that a senator could champion fishing interests with a relatively free hand. He would not be subject to compelling pressures from either the industry or the executive branch but still could find it politically profitable to dream up legislation to promote the industry, to publicize his program, and to activate support. And he would find in the BCF an agency amenable to his efforts, willing to establish cooperative ties which, while aiding the senator and increasing his chances of success, would at the same time increase the Bureau's leverage in the executive branch.

Senator Bartlett perceived the opportunities this situation offered, and, with the help of William Foster, his staff attorney and later a Commerce Committee counsel, he moved to take advantage of them. The result, during the 88th and 89th Congresses, was a plethora of legislation relating to the fishing industry: a bill establishing a twelve-mile fishing zone forbidden to foreign vessels; authorizations for BCF research to develop a high-grade "fish protein concentrate" and for pilot plants to undertake experimental production; extensive liberalizations of the construction subsidy program for fishing vessels; provisions for the inclusion of fish products in the Food for Peace program; and the establishment of a new program of matching grants to the states for fishery research and development. The formulation of these proposals for the most part followed a uniform pattern. Fishing interests got behind the bills *after* they were proposed; they did not exert decisive pressures or even come to Congress with specific proposals. "Mostly," recalled Senator Bartlett, "we thought up the bills, the way Bill and I worked up that twelve-mile-limit thing." BCF officials were generally sympathetic and helpful, especially in furnishing statistics and other information, though they balked at first at the fish protein concentrate and twelve-mile-limit proposals. The White House gave the bills very little attention, though the Bureau of the Budget, by its refusal to release funds (in the case of Food for Peace) or to make adequate budget requests (in the case of state research and development) later managed to torpedo some of the programs.[64] Bartlett and Foster, in short, were usually one step ahead of the industry and two steps ahead of the executive branch.

It was in this context, then, that Bartlett proposed the creation of a new agency to carry out a program of marine exploration and continental shelf resource development. The bill was formulated by Foster, working closely with Edward Wenk, who as head of the Science Policy Research Division had led the Library of Congress' Legislative Reference Service into substantial information-gathering efforts. Their concern was not so much to develop yet another organizational scheme as to shift the focus of the projected program "from pure research to resource development." It thus made the relevance of oceanography to industry much more explicit—and, for the fishermen's sake, made clear that continental shelf resources included the species that "clung" to the seabed and not merely the minerals beneath. But the bill was notable for another reason as well: it was the first oceanography bill which any senator besides Magnuson had offered. It seemed as though virtually every member of the House Committee had offered a bill, but Magnuson had monopolized the area on the Senate side. The truth is that Bartlett's bill, to say nothing of his long line of fishing bills, represented something of an encroachment.

It was an encroachment of a rather subtle sort. Magnuson regarded the fisheries as his special interest, but they had always been overshadowed for him by the more pressing and more concrete demands of the merchant marine; his legislative efforts had slacked off since the late fifties. Moreover, Bartlett always took pains to let the Chairman know what he was doing and freely to share the credit with Magnuson for what was accomplished. The result was that an impressive percentage of Bartlett's proposals became law, portrayed by the press as "Magnuson bills." But Magnuson was not entirely comfortable with Bartlett's new role, and he was increasingly sensitive to rumors that he was no longer looking after the interests that had "made" him politically. Grinstein's solution was to offer Foster a spot on the Committee staff, hoping thereby to remove the center of initiative from within Bartlett's office and to place the area once again firmly within Magnuson's control. Bartlett concurred, viewing the shift as a means of increasing his voice in Committee affairs, and Foster changed desks in early 1964. The fact that fishing bills continued to spring from Foster's fertile brain proved Grinstein correct in his estimate of the potential both of the man and of the policy area; but the fact that the bills continued to be worked out in consultation with Bartlett and even to be presented under his name demonstrated that his basic strategy had gone awry. Foster proved tenaciously loyal to his former boss and used his staff position to further Bartlett's involvement in shipping and oceanography as well. Bartlett proceeded circumspectly, ever cautious lest he appear "pushy," but considerably emboldened by the success of his efforts and by Foster's ability.

Magnuson behaved circumspectly as well. His tendency was to be generous with his members, but he was not sure to what extent that liberality should apply to merchant marine and fisheries, an area in which others had not until now dared to tread. Action was less circumspect and displeasure less veiled at the staff level. Some staff members had felt from the first that there was not enough room on any one staff for two men with ambitions and personalities as strong as Foster's and Grinstein's, but the Bartlett-Magnuson question served to exacerbate and give focus to a conflict that perhaps would have arisen in any case. As a third staff man recalled, "Things were pretty tense around here for a while." It was not prudent, of course, for Grinstein to hold up Foster's legislative projects, but working conditions became far from pleasant; as soon as the legislative calendar was relatively clear, Foster left the staff. The result, ironically enough, was that Bartlett perceived that a retrenchment was in order precisely at the time Magnuson was forming a new Consumer Subcommittee and leaving Bartlett with the chairmanship of the Merchant Marine and Fisheries Subcommittee. But the reorganization did not occur until Foster had left and staff men appointed by Magnuson had taken over his duties.

In 1965, then, it was clear that oceanography was an area over which Magnuson was to retain his control. Some witnesses mentioned Bartlett's bill during the hearings on S. 944,[65] but it was never formally considered. Some language was added to the Magnuson bill regarding resource development, but after Bartlett and Foster balked at Grinstein's initial suggestion that the two bills might be combined, its organizational features were largely ignored. Bartlett was invited before the House Committee as leadoff witness; there he stressed the importance of oceanography to the fishing industry, pushed his own bill's approach, and refused to be drawn into a debate with Lennon about Magnuson's refusal to accept the House bill of 1963.[66] But by that time Magnuson had completed his hearings and the Senate had already passed S. 944, thus laying down a challenge to the House Committee and wedding the Senate conferees to the council approach.

The Makings of a Deadlock. The appearance of administration witnesses before Magnuson's committee revealed that official positions had changed little over the course of five years, but it also suggested that the administration was not going to mount a massive effort to defeat the bill. No cabinet-level official testified. Donald Hornig, OST Director and FCST Chairman, was the main witness. The thrust of his testimony was that the Interagency

Committee, on the whole, had "performed well." He pointed out that there was strong support on the ICO for an expanded oceanography program and that the group had prepared a projected ten-year plan which drew heavily on NASCO reports. A letter subsequently submitted to the Committee, however, seemed to suggest that the ICO had partially failed in its efforts to stimulate program expansion. Budget requests for fiscal 1966, Hornig admitted, had been some 25 percent below projected levels.

> *The budget request for each year is determined in the light of [an] entire range of factors. . . . The existence of a long-range plan is one of these factors, but it is not necessarily the governing factor.*[67]

Magnuson's questioning focused on the "prodding" which Congress and the NAS had found necessary to get the executive branch moving:

> *There was a lack of interest in this whole field and a very uncoordinated effort.*
>
> **DR. HORNIG:** *I think that is correct.*
>
> **THE CHAIRMAN:** *Now without a legislative base, would you have an opinion as to the permanence or durability of an oceanography policy? . . . What I mean is that men like you might not be here forever you know.*

To which Hornig rather lamely replied, "But the oceans will remain."[68]

Behind the scenes, however, Budget Bureau and OST officials, convinced now that increased congressional interest might well result in the passage of some sort of bill, were contemplating the desirability of a new White House approach:

> *It was obvious that neither committee was really satisfied with that first administration bill, so we started looking around for the most satisfactory compromise we could make.*

Strongly opposed to the creation of another cabinet-level council, and spurred on by the realization that the Senate Committee was going to move quickly, administration strategists began to suggest that they "would not look with great disfavor" on the establishment of a temporary study commission along the lines of the Rogers proposal. Foster, however, had another idea, which Grinstein accepted mainly for strategic reasons. The Commerce Committee thus left the Magnuson Bill intact, but added to it, layer-cake style, a section giving the President discretionary authority to appoint a study commission and a provision specifying that the council would expire after five years—thus emphasizing that the commission would be free to suggest any reorganization plan it wished. "I guess you could say the Senate Committee responded to us in a way," a BOB official noted, "but in another sense they took a lot of the wind out of our sails."

Magnuson had no trouble getting his bill processed and approved—partly because of his exclusive claim to the area and partly because the proposal was noncontroversial and of low priority for most members. Kenney perused the bill for the Republicans and added some language asserting that federal activity was designed to stimulate the involvement of the private sector. The bill was reported on July 29 and passed by voice vote on August 5. Cotton gave a strong supporting statement, noting that the administration was "drifting aimlessly on an ocean of indecision."[69]

The administration, however, was busy at that very moment making its views known to the House Committee. The House group had always been more willing to listen, and now their willingness was increased by their irritation at the Senate's precipitous action. Lennon scheduled extensive subcommittee hearings, and during August Commerce Department, BOB, OST, Navy, Coast Guard, ICO, and BCF representatives made their way to Capitol Hill. The House group heard the administration described as "open-minded as far as the Commission is concerned," although it was also announced that the President's Science Advisory Committee Panel on Oceanography had itself undertaken a broad study which would be completed by the spring of 1966 and might make a commission study unnecessary. Expressions of administration support were reiterated for a bill of the type the House had passed in 1963, which, as Lennon never tired of noting, "was not even considered by the committee in the Senate."[70]

Proponents of increased oceanographic efforts within the scientific community continued to give little guidance on the organizational question. The Senate Committee had given considerable attention to NASCO, hearing from its chairman and immediate past chairman, and had managed to secure from them a blanket endorsement of the Magnuson bill:

> I am 100 per cent for this bill, Mr. Chairman. I am not one who nit picks words in a thing. . . . The idea of a council will focus attention at the right level on oceanography.[71]

On the House side, however, many government scientists were represented by their bureau or department chiefs, who appeared under administration sponsorship. As an Environmental Science Services Administration officer recalled, "We generally favored the idea of an oceanographic council, but we were overruled and [our Commerce Department superiors] testified against the Magnuson bill." As for NASCO, the House Subcommittee received only a short and enigmatic letter from the chairman, who now refused to take a position on behalf of NASCO regarding any of the pending bills.[72]

The House Committee on September 17 reported a two-layer bill of its own, combining the essence of the old Lennon Bill—spelling out "national policy" and presidential responsibilities—with the commission proposal.

The House passed the bill three days later. And then what one staff member characterized as "a very undignified pissing contest between the two committees" began in earnest.

The House Committee, cultivated by the administration and irritated by Magnuson's independent and unsolicitous course, resolved to reject the council idea and to hold out for settlement on the study commission as the least common denominator. But Lennon was under certain pressures which made it rather difficult for him to hold to such a strategy. He was chairman of a subcommittee devoted exclusively to oceanography, and that group had been conspicuous for its failure to produce a reorganization bill capable of securing congressional approval. For Magnuson, however, oceanography was only one concern among many, and he could always counter appearances of inaction on one front by moving on another. Lennon, moreover, could look on the House calendar and see dozens of other oceanography bills; if he did not succeed, some other committee or some other representative was likely to take the lead. Neither could he be assured that his fellow conferees would remain passive. Magnuson, on the other hand, had an effective monopoly of the area and uncontested control over the Senate conferees. Both committees, of course, were being petitioned by industry and by certain elements of the scientific community to break the deadlock and pass a bill, but these pressures were of relatively low intensity and were not clearly directed toward one bill or the other. It was primarily factors internal to Congress which lessened the House conferees' staying power.

The strategic advantage Magnuson enjoyed, however, could have been eliminated had the administration let it be known that it would veto the council bill. Hornig dropped some hints to that effect, but in the end the word that went out from the White House was exactly the opposite: Magnuson received assurances that the bill would be signed. The administration's stance, it is safe to assume, was largely dictated by the realization that it would be politic to accommodate Magnuson. Of some importance was the fact that a number of lower-level bureaus and personnel were sympathetic to the Magnuson Bill, although, on balance, divisions and pressures internal to the executive branch did not give as much aid and comfort to congressional advocates as might have been expected. In fact, when compared to the agency reports on bills like fair packaging and cigarette labeling, those submitted on Magnuson's council bill were remarkably consistent, despite the fact that the White House was not greatly concerned to present a united front or to fight the bill to the bitter end. As a BOB official put it:

> This wasn't the sort of thing the White House was going to get greatly concerned about—it was way down on their priority list. So there wasn't any high-level decision to which all the agencies had to conform. They just went through routine BOB clearance.

Of course BOB clearance was not exactly "routine" in this case, since it was the Bureau, along with OST, that was handling the substance of the matter for the President. This in itself may help explain why agency reports emerged from clearance displaying a remarkably consistent point of view. More determinative, however, was the fact that most scientists and officials in lower-level agencies involved with oceanography were not concerned primarily with *reorganization* and were, in fact, often apprehensive of it; hence they generally did not agitate strongly for the Magnuson proposal.

Magnuson nonetheless benefitted in the end from the low level of White House concern. His hand was further strengthened quite unexpectedly as the President's own Science Advisory Committee panel, so frequently mentioned during the House hearings, prepared its report. A number of scientists partial to oceanography had worked their way onto this panel, and it soon became evident that this group was likely to recommend the formation, not merely of a commission or even of a council, but of a separate agency, much like the "wet-NASA" Wilson had first proposed.[73] This made for a modification of the BOB's viewpoint:

> *I'm not saying that the administration took the council bill as a means of preempting the PSAC proposal. Their report [which did, in fact, recommend the combination of certain ESSA, BCF, Bureau of Mines, Coast Guard, and Geological Survey functions in a new federal agency] was not even issued until July of 1966. But we knew they, and a lot of other people besides, were thinking favorably about proposals of this type. . . . After all, the council plan had some advantages for us. At least it didn't require massive reorganization.*

So Magnuson secured his White House pledge, and the conference bill included a cabinet-level council. The reported bill was a three-layer affair, including Lennon's administration-approved declaration of presidential responsibility as well as provisions for a commission and a council. The conference report followed the House bill in making the appointment of the commission mandatory, and it moved the council's expiration date up to 120 days following the commission's report.[74] The bill was clearly a triumph for Magnuson, but Lennon could point out that virtually the entire House bill had been included in the conference report and that Magnuson had modified his proposal considerably. Even OST and BOB officials could be relieved that a more drastic reorganization plan had been precluded; as one of them gamely asserted, "a consensus of a sort had been reached."

Summary and Conclusions. The oceanography bill, unlike the consumer proposals, furnished an example of clear and continuing executive opposition—albeit an opposition of a rather low intensity. This made for an almost exclusively congressional performance of the legislative functions, though the simplicity and noncontroversial nature of the proposal, as well as its low priority on most agendas, permitted rather minimal efforts at certain stages. Some instigative efforts on behalf of oceanography-in-general came from the scientific community, often from scientists within government, and the NASCO reports performed an essential information-gathering function. But the scientific community had little to contribute to the formulation of reorganization schemes, though reorganization was sometimes welcomed as an impetus to program expansion. Formulation did not require a great amount of ingenuity, since the models for advisory committees, study commissions, cabinet level councils, agencies, and departments were already available. But early opposition within the executive branch set off a search for a politically acceptable formula, and efforts at formulation proliferated. Most schemes made their first appearance on the House side, though Magnuson soon took over Miller's proposal and Bartlett developed a variant of the agency idea aimed at resource development.

Extensive congressional hearings and efforts in the scientific community continued, year after year, to amass information and to publicize the issue, while the Senate Committee relied increasingly on Wenk (who was later chosen Executive Secretary of the National Council established by S. 944) and his staff at LRS. Interest-aggregation in oceanography, to a much greater extent than in most maritime legislation, cast Magnuson in an entrepreneurial role. He saw oceanography as a promising area and became involved at a time when the only "pressures" he was feeling were the occasional representations of the scientific community. But his involvement and the efforts of his staff men stimulated fishing, shipping, and other industry interests and increased Magnuson's stature among them. The accommodation of the executive branch's organizational interests he left to the House Committee.

Magnuson's successful efforts at mobilization in committee and in conference could be attributed to the low priority of the bill among most members and at the White House, Magnuson's control over his committee, his monopoly over the issue-area, and certain strategic advantages he enjoyed vis-à-vis the administration and the House Committee. Amendment and modification were undertaken by Foster and Bartlett with limited success, on a small scale by Kenney and his mentors, and to a much greater extent by Magnuson himself as, mainly for strategic reasons, he added the commission to his bill and gave the council an expiration date.

The oceanography episode lengthens and alters our list of provisional conclusions regarding the Commerce Committee. It sheds light on an additional area in which the Chairman was involved legislatively, one in which he was unusually jealous of his own prerogatives. This placed obvious limits on his desire to run the kind of committee where members could freely pursue their own legislative interests. It also added a dimension to the staff's role: they were to be independent and innovative but, in certain areas at least, were also to protect Magnuson and to see that their labors redounded to his benefit.

Finally, another area has been discovered where the executive branch's efforts were dispersed and its priorities unclear, this time in a situation where interest group pressures were rarely compelling. But the ocean-ography story has permitted a description of group and agency activity in the closely related areas of fishing and shipping as well. These patterns, though dissimilar in many ways, helped account for the Committee's policy-making preeminence in both areas and will be useful as a more inclusive sketch of its environment is attempted in the chapter to follow.

3

THE COMMERCE COMMITTEE: AN OVERVIEW

The preceding chapter has given some indication of how legislative functions were shared as four major bills made their way through the Commerce Committee and the Senate. The varieties of circumstance and performance were surely impressive, but as the Commerce Committee was observed in action, a picture emerged that was relatively consistent from bill to bill: the Committee's legislative role was characterized by a high degree of independence and policy initiative. There have already been limited attempts at explanation; it now remains to systematize and expand this listing of explanatory factors, to test their typicality, and to assess their impact. Our guide will be the successive images of the congressional committee developed in Chapter 1.

Personal Traits and Orientations. In all four bills examined, a large share of the activity at the mobilization and modification stages could be attributed to Senator Magnuson. For their initial formulation or publicizing, however, he bore little responsibility. This pattern sheds considerable light on the Chairman's interests and ambitions, his strengths and weaknesses. Magnuson's personality and bearing represented in many respects the stuff of which public-relations men's nightmares must be made. He was short and heavy, moody and sometimes gruff, inarticulate and often uninformed on major national issues. On the other hand, in his personal dealings he could be charming, generous, persuasive, and shrewd. His impatience with details and his ineptitude with abstract formulations were matched by an instinctive ability to size up men and situations and to deal with them to his advantage. This meant that by both aptitude and inclination Magnuson specialized in behind-the-scenes bargaining and played down many of the more public aspects of the senatorial role. In Magnuson's case, as in many similar cases, this pattern of activity was combined with a low-key ideology—perhaps, as a staff man described it, "an old-fashioned Western liberalism," nothing more doctrinaire or more specific—and a parochial interest orientation which turned him first of all to the needs of Washington state.

To some extent, this behavior pattern changed after 1962. The growth of the mass media, the changing complexion of state politics, the emerging of certain issues, and Magnuson's position of committee leadership made it politically necessary—with reference both to his constituency and to his Senate colleagues—to become more visible and to champion certain causes in which he previously would have had only a very remote interest. Onto the old Magnuson, interested in fishing, shipping, and Boeing Aircraft, and running a rather sleepy committee, was grafted a new one: the champion of the consumer, the national legislative leader, and the patron of an energetic and innovative legislative staff. That the transformation had not been complete was betrayed by the staff's constant fear that the Chairman would lapse and that the old-guard aides, over whom the "bright young men" now had the ascendancy, would be vindicated. For example, in mid-1967 a staff member was heard to remark that the polls were looking better for Magnuson all the time:

> From the standpoint of the Committee that's one of the worst things that could have happened. . . . His natural tendency when things are going well is to pull back, not to get any new fires started.

During the 89th Congress, Magnuson's staff was able to lead him into new areas with a new assertiveness, but his behavior still displayed certain consistencies with the past. He generally took bills that had been formulated, even publicized, by others. His proposals were not new, nor were they radical, and an important part of his role was often to domesticate the bills further, to make them more acceptable to the interests involved and worthy objects of Committee consensus. "We seldom pass a bill in the Commerce Committee that isn't pretty well agreed on," reported one member.[1] Magnuson could and did display stubbornness, partisanship, and a defiance of certain interests, but his normal pattern was to accommodate or to preempt those who had objections to a bill and to make modification an integral part of his mobilization efforts. He still was not inclined to tackle lost or unfamiliar causes, nor was his success at publicizing, when he made the effort, notable. As a staff man recalled:

> I guess we got some political benefit out of those consumer bills, but not all that much. We put out publicity, but public relations is a small part of our operation here. Magnuson is somewhat concerned about image, but that's something you're not really going to change no matter how hard you try. Look how Hart remained identified with packaging and Ribicoff with auto safety—the fact that Magnuson took those over didn't change that.

Magnuson's comfortable victory in 1968, after a campaign based largely on consumer issues, proved such pessimism unfounded. But he still tended to rely on others at the "early" stages; it was at the interest-aggregation, modification, and mobilization stages that his heightened legislative interests found their full and effective expression.

What of the interests, ideologies, and aptitudes of other Committee members? Some of them displayed an interest in formulating policy in areas of broad national import. Hart and Neuberger were active in the field of consumer protection. Hartke's interest in auto safety, Bartlett's in radiation control, and Monroney's and Pastore's in their subcommittee specialties of aviation and communications were also notable. But the Committee's jurisdiction attracted Senators with parochial interests to serve and focused their attention on such interests after they joined the group. An identification with tobacco interests defined, to a great extent, the legislative concerns of Bass and Morton; the same was true of Bartlett and fishing, Pastore and textiles, Hart and Great Lakes development, Brewster and matters affecting the Port of Baltimore or Friendship Airport, and several Senators for whose constituencies national transportation (Pastore, Lausche, Scott) and aviation (Bartlett, McGee, Cannon, Dominick) policy were particularly important.

Some understanding of the ideological complexion of the Committee can be gained by placing its members on a continuum according to the "liberalism" score given them by the Americans for Democratic Action. Figure 2 permits a comparison of this distribution with that of the total Senate membership. The Commerce Committee was slightly more liberal than the parent chamber (the mean scores were 55 and 50 respectively), but a much greater percentage of its membership was concentrated in the "moderate" category. The standard deviation of the scores of majority members was remarkably low (11.7 with the deviant case, Lausche, removed from computation); the Democrats clustered around the Chairman in the 65-76 range. This homogeneity was largely the result of self-selection; Senators at both extremes of the ideological spectrum tended to seek seats on committees other than Commerce. Magnuson himself, revealed one aide, was "surprisingly passive" about the selection process —but "his control of the Committee has never been threatened in recent years, so he has not had to worry about cultivating controlling votes in the selection of new members."

It might well be supposed that senators with "moderate" scores would be less active legislatively—especially in formulation and publicizing— than those at the extremes, though they might be expected to be more successful at the mobilization stage. Some evidence, in fact, bears this out; Chapter 7 will prove more conclusive in this regard. It was on the liberals at the far end of the spectrum that the Senate relied for a disproportionate

FIGURE 2.   Distributions of Senators According to the Rating Given Them by the Americans for Democratic Action, 1965.[2]

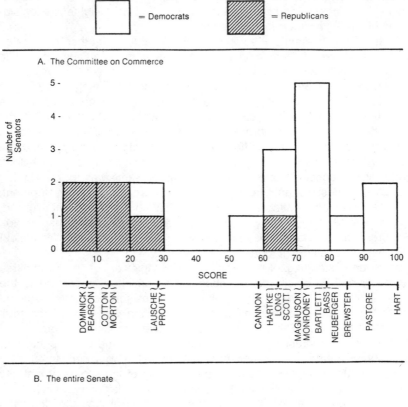

A. The Committee on Commerce

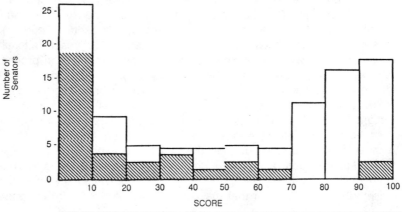

B. The entire Senate

amount of formulation and publicizing in areas of national scope; the absence of such types on Commerce helped explain its shortcomings in this regard. The fact remains, however, that the Commerce Committee, whatever its deficiencies, was an unusually active and independent legislative unit during the 89th Congress. While a good deal of that activity consisted of ratifying the Chairman's initiatives, and while a good number of members hardly lifted a finger legislatively, considerable responsibility for the performance of all the legislative functions was assumed down through the ranks; the activist coterie, moreover, was to expand further with the addition of Frank Moss and Ernest Hollings to the Committee in 1967. And it could in fact be argued that the middling ideological stance of the group *enhanced* its policy role. For one thing, a great many of the bills processed by the Committee were just as likely—sometimes more so—to be sponsored by moderates as by liberals. Even the consumer bills, though they offended certain industries, were middle-class in orientation and did not raise the spectres of massive governmental outlays or extensive redistribution. Committee moderates, therefore, were not necessarily reluctant to participate in policy formulation or to ratify the moves of Magnuson and some of the more active Committee members. At the same time, ideological homogeneity and moderation contributed to the Committee's cohesion and to its reputation with the parent body, thus enhancing Magnuson's powers of mobilization.

Minority members were more widely dispersed ideologically than their Democratic colleagues ($s = 20.9$). This made it more difficult to mount a unified opposition effort. The variations between minority members, the inclination of some of them toward middling viewpoints, and, again, the nature of the Committee's membership and jurisdiction facilitated the overall integration of the group and fostered in the Republicans a cooperative legislative style. Instead of concentrating on countermoves of various descriptions, they often allowed themselves to be co-opted into the processes of interest-aggregation and modification.

If orientation and ideology thus helped explain the initiatives taken by the Commerce Committee, the stage at which and the style in which they were made, "personality" factors also had some bearing on the viability of these efforts. Most members could name colleagues whose legislative efforts were, they thought, substantially enhanced or undermined by various personal traits. The affability and reasonableness of Magnuson, Hart, Bartlett, and Cotton were reckoned as important assets, as were Pastore's incisiveness and Morton's intelligence and persuasiveness. The boorishness of one member was frequently mentioned as a hindrance to success, as were the pettiness and "pushy-ness" of others. Mrs. Neuberger's early efforts in cigarette labeling were not aided by the feelings of some of her colleagues that she was "out of line," both as a woman and as a junior Senator, and Hart's early packaging efforts were made less effective by his weakness at hard bargaining. But in both the Neuberger and Hart cases, the precise impact of personal factors was difficult to assess, since their ideological posture and lack of seniority would have constituted disabilities in any case. Moreover, Committee members generally agreed that Commerce's atmosphere was relatively permissive with respect to deviant or abrasive types: "Bass and Hartke and even Lausche get along better here than they do most places in the Senate." Personal likes and dislikes were thus not to be ignored, but neither was their frequent mention to be taken as an indication of an all-important or systematic impact on the viability of individual or collective legislative efforts.

Committee Organization and Lawmaking Opportunities. The impact which the interests, ideologies, and styles of various members can have on policy depends in large part on the distribution of powers and functions within the committee. It should initially be noted that most members portrayed the Commerce Committee as relatively free and open, especially when compared to the domains of the Southern oligarchs. One new member evaluated Commerce on the basis of his House experience:

> *I found Commerce extremely pleasant; it's a good committee for a freshman member. . . . Never once did I feel the slightest hesitancy to speak out or to try to get an amendment through. [Was your experience on Agriculture different?] Well, the real contrast was with* House *Agriculture. There you don't speak out. I tried it a couple of times, and pretty quickly I got the idea that that was something junior members just didn't do. I think that kind of situation is more prevalent on the House side generally.*

Another member found in Senate Agriculture a more illuminating comparison:

> *I couldn't get off Agriculture fast enough . . . I didn't like the way the committee was run; the Chairman is a humorless man. The Committee is loaded with conservatives and obstructionists. I certainly wasn't getting anywhere on it.*

Another Senator recalled his experiences on Armed Services:

> *I wasn't getting anywhere. [Chairman Richard] Russell sits up at the head of that table and the low men never get anything. . . . And my position made my constituents think I could do impossible things for them with the military. They couldn't understand why I couldn't intervene.*

Senior members, freshmen, and Republicans generally portrayed life on Commerce, by contrast, as open and efficacious and testified to the Chairman's relative permissiveness.

That permissiveness, of course, had its limits: the fair packaging episode provided a particularly illuminating example of those limits and their legislative impact in the case of the Republican minority. The rebuffed and outnumbered Committee members became more assertive, more public and less accommodating in their modification attempts, and, of course, considerably less likely to succeed. How such limitations applied to the majority members is perhaps best understood by an examination of Commerce's subcommittee operations. Subgroup roles do not, of course, necessarily provide a definitive index to organizational permeability and flexibility. In this case, however, examining them will permit greater precision in sorting out the impact of formal and informal "organizational" factors on the Committee's legislative role.

Legislative responsibilities on the Commerce Committee were formally divided among five subcommittees, the fifth (Consumer) being added late in the 89th Congress. Even a casual glance at the calendar, however, shows that the full committee continued to handle many bills on its own. Of the 90 public bills reported by the Committee during the 89th Congress, only 36 had received subcommittee consideration; of the 208 days of legislative hearings, 116, or 56 percent, were held by the full committee.[3]

Subcommittee jurisdictions left major areas uncovered, but even where bills fell under subcommittee rubrics—as in oceanography or traffic safety —they often were kept before the full committee. This not only ensured Magnuson's control over bills with which he wanted to be identified; it also gave him a certain flexibility in dealing with his colleagues. He could reward members by entrusting them with bills regardless of their subcommittee assignments. Lausche and his Surface Transportation Subcommittee were bypassed, for example, when the Committee was considering the proposed merger of the New Haven Railroad, a matter in which Pastore was interested:

> There are ways to do that you know. In this case we made it a full committee hearing and Magnuson simply didn't show up, so, being next in seniority, Pastore naturally presided.

A similar device was used in 1967 when Bartlett wanted to hold hearings on radiation hazards. Since Bartlett was not a member of the Consumer Subcommittee, which ordinarily would have handled the matter, his bill was left before the full committee and he was free to conduct the hearings and to keep the bill under his own care.

There were other indicators of committee centralization. With the exception of a handful of men whom Magnuson allowed his senior members to appoint, committee and subcommittee aides were appointed by the Chairman and regarded themselves as "Magnuson men." During the 89th Congress Lausche did not appear as a prime sponsor[4] of any bill which the Committee reported in his subcommittee's area, and Monroney's

(Aviation) and Pastore's (Communications) names were at the head of only one such bill each. The normal pattern was for both bill and report to carry Magnuson's name, and he often managed the bill on the floor as well. As Chapter 2 indicated, Bartlett deviated from these patterns both before and after he assumed the Merchant Marine and Fisheries Subcommittee Chairmanship; his deviations were limited, and they did not go unnoticed. Still, the tightness of Magnuson's control should not be overestimated. His policy represented something of a mean between the centralization of functions found on committees like Finance and the extreme decentralization of Government Operations and Labor and Public Welfare. There were indications, too, that Commerce was moving toward greater decentralization—a trend prompted by an increased workload, the interests and ambitions of certain members, and currents abroad in the Senate as a whole. As a staff man remarked:

> It's amazing that Magnuson's been able to hold on as long as he has. One reason is that he's so damned benevolent, and extremely well liked. Another is that he's managed to hold on to two central controls—he controls the disbursement of all funds, and all staff hiring. But already you can see some changes—of course the whole Senate is changing. . . . It's Magnuson and Lausche that are doing some of these transportation bills now, and Pastore has some communications things going on his own. Bartlett is restless too. . . . So the Committee is not like it used to be, and Magnuson knows that. He's very good at sensing what the situation is and adjusting to it.

Post-1968 developments bore out this prophecy. With Magnuson safely reelected, Grinstein departed from the staff, and several members seeking greater prominence in anticipation of their own reelection efforts, Magnuson acquiesced in an extensive subcommittee reorganization (by 1971 the five standing subcommittees had multiplied to eight) and increased dispersals of staff resources and legislative responsibilities.

During the 89th Congress it was Pastore and Monroney who enjoyed the greatest freedom of operation. The communications staff counsel, Nicholas Zapple, regarded both Pastore and Magnuson as boss and operated independently of Grinstein's line of command to a greater degree than any other staff man. "Maggie doesn't give a damn about a lot of what Pastore is doing," one member observed "so he lets him go." Behind this was Pastore's ability and assertiveness, Magnuson's prudent style of operation and his increasing preoccupation with other matters, and a cordial relationship between the two men. But Magnuson did not let go easily, as his continuing involvement in the area of educational television demonstrated. A staff man described the situation:

> Sometimes things do get a little tight. Like when we had hearings after the Ford Foundation's [1966] proposal [to develop a satellite system

for educational television.] That involved both educational television and Comsat [a matter ordinarily delegated to Pastore], so we had to strike a pretty delicate balance between Magnuson and Pastore.

Monroney's situation was similar. The Aviation Subcommittee counsel, William Beeks, considered himself responsible to both chairmen, though it was Magnuson who had hired him. Magnuson, of course, continued to have a strong interest in the field, especially where it pertained to Boeing Aircraft and the development of the supersonic transport. A staff man described the impact of this interest on Subcommittee operations:

Magnuson is willing to let Monroney and the Subcommittee operate rather independently. That's pretty much the way he handles the subcommittees across the board. The situation with Bartlett, of course, is a little different right now, but that has nothing at all to do with Bartlett—it's just that Magnuson is sensitive to the charge that he's letting the fishing and shipping interests down, and he has to work to get back his reputation. But there's no principle involved. . . . With Monroney and Pastore there's a great amount of independence. [Can you recall instances when Magnuson by-passed the Aviation Subcommittee?] Like I say, it doesn't happen often. One instance you might point to involves this SST contract that Boeing has had for several years. That's not a perfect example, because Monroney changed his views over the course of time until finally there wasn't any difference of opinion on that. But at first Monroney was interested in holding hearings on the project with the idea of reviewing it and perhaps coming up with a more precise authorization. . . . Well, Magnuson— and the administration was with him on this—just didn't want to rock the boat. You know the risks you run when you bring these things up, no matter how much support you have for them. . . . So let's say the Subcommittee was "discouraged" from holding hearings.

Bartlett's status, according to this aide, was considerably at variance with that enjoyed by Pastore and Monroney—mainly because of Magnuson's unique interest in the MMF area. But the staff man admitted that the Surface Transportation Subcommittee furnished yet another exception to the rule:

[What about Lausche's subcommittee?] Well, that's a different case. Lausche is such a maverick, with crazy views on all sorts of things, that Magnuson simply has to bypass him a good bit of the time. There it is a matter of the personalities involved.

Lausche was indeed a special case. No subcommittee chairman was by-passed or overruled more often, nor any member cited more often by his colleagues as an example of the detrimental effect personal traits could have on legislative effectiveness. If Magnuson's handling of the Surface Transportation Subcommittee was thus not "typical," it nonetheless revealed a role the Chairman could and would assume. As one Senator observed:

> Magnuson doesn't try to run everybody's show, [but] he and Lausche don't get along very well. We haven't had much to do on that subcommittee lately.

Subsequent Congresses revealed certain organizational characteristics of the Committee during the 89th Congress to have been anomalous or transitional; the long-range trend was toward a dispersal of authority, though still within definite limits. After his reelection in 1968, Magnuson assigned the chairmanship of the Consumer Subcommittee to Frank Moss, with Hart as co-chairman, and formed a new Subcommittee on the Environment with Hart as chairman and Moss as co-chairman. These subcommittees were increasingly used to publicize prominent issues—automobile pollution, pesticides, product safety, cigarette advertising, fair packaging amendments, warranty standards, consumer class action—and to develop remedial legislation. Magnuson also proved willing to delegate a great deal of authority to Long, who inherited the Merchant Marine Subcommittee after Bartlett's death in 1968, and to Hollings, under whose care an Oceans and Atmosphere Subcommittee was spun off in 1969. Pastore's niche became even more secure; the processing of major proposals in the areas of political broadcasting and educational television were left largely in his hands. The Surface Transportation Subcommittee remained an industry-dominated underachiever, but Hartke, who inherited the chairmanship in 1969 after Lausche's defeat, was able to gain a measure of leeway and to turn the subcommittee somewhat away from its exclusive preoccupation with industry complaints and the ICC. The overall trend was pointed up by the fact that the portion of the Committee's hearings conducted by subcommittees rose from 44% in the 89th Congress to 80% in the 91st. The only major retrenchment was in aviation: industry interests were wary of Hartke, who was in line for the Aviation Subcommittee Chairmanship after Monroney's 1968 defeat. Magnuson thus, to Hartke's dismay, appointed himself as subcommittee chairman and designated Cannon co-chairman. But in 1971, with a major airport development proposal on the books (1970) and the SST project finally shelved, he turned the subcommittee over to Cannon; for the first time since he became Chairman, Magnuson headed none of the Commerce subcommittees.

The transformation, however, was far from complete: Magnuson retained an *ex officio* membership on each subcommittee, still appointed most staff personnel and maintained a strong full committee staff (of which Pertschuk was now Chief Counsel), frequently co-sponsored and managed bills developed in subcommittee, and continued to handle choice items (e.g. traffic safety and no-fault automobile insurance) at the full committee level. If the trends toward committee decentralization evident during 1965–1966 had advanced, so were the limitations still in evidence. And the question central to our concern remained: What was the impact of Magnuson's peculiar blend of permissiveness and control on the Committee's policy role?

Hart and several other relatively active members had a simple answer that, in its broad outlines, had much to recommend it: Magnuson had achieved, they felt, an ideal "balance" which left them free to formulate and publicize, but also guaranteed that proposals developed in the lower reaches of the committee would obtain the consensual backing and the "push" necessary for final enactment. One crucial question, of course, is whether Magnuson's tendency to preemption and control did avoid dampening the incentives of potentially active members and thus cutting off bills at their source. One staff member proved quite willing to reflect on the problem; while hardly typical, he deserves to be heard at length:

> *I think the committee's tightness has an inhibiting effect. To get at this you have to look at the way Magnuson's staff operates when they take over a bill. The basic question they ask is whether or not the thing is going to pass. If it doesn't look too likely, they're not apt to take it up. If it is going to make it, then they'll get Magnuson on top of it.*

> *[But doesn't some of the staff have gut feeling about these things? And some of these bills weren't such winners before Magnuson got onto them . . .] Well, that may be. I suppose it's true that Pertschuk is really onto some of these things—and some of them were more or less floundering around before Magnuson got hold of them. On the other hand, sometimes I think members don't want Magnuson to get hold of something because, while he'll get it passed, he is likely to compromise it away in the process.*

> *So I think it does inhibit members when they think that whatever they do is going to be taken over, that somebody else is going to get the credit. I know that from the staff point of view it certainly tends to discourage you. I should think a committee run the way Hill does Labor and Public Welfare would be much more congenial.*

> *[Well, perhaps, but there you seem to have a problem too: sometimes the subcommittees get things through so easily that things aren't straightened out in committee, and then the bills run into trouble on the floor. So the members of a "loose" committee might get stifled, too, but at a different point in the process.] That may be. That is certainly one of Magnuson's strong points: he gets these issues resolved in committee, and then takes his members united to the floor. I like that; I think the committee is the right place to legislate. But I would question whether that sort of thing is necessarily combined with the sort of usurpation we were talking about earlier. It seems to me that a chairman can insist that the committee work out its differences in committee, but that doesn't mean he has to take over the*

bills himself and take the credit. I'll admit Magnuson does both, but I don't think it has to be that way.

This aide probably found developments on the Committee subsequent to the 89th Congress promising, but if LPW was his model he also must have concluded that Commerce had quite a distance to go.[5]

There was thus room for doubt as to the optimality of Magnuson's degree of control in terms of his committee's legislative productivity, at least in certain policy areas. But subcommittee performance likewise gave the lie to any simplistic linkage of decentralization with policy generation. One could argue, for example, that the weakness of the Lausche subcommittee and Magnuson's willingness to bypass it probably made for a *more* positive Committee contribution to transportation policy, though still hardly a creative one.[6] Moreover, the two subcommittees enjoying the greatest relative independence during the 89th Congress were far from the most productive legislatively; nor is it clear that increased subcommittee autonomy would have altered the situation appreciably. To be sure, the 89th Congress was atypically quiet in both areas: the Monroney subcommittee had in the past been an important source of airport development legislation,[7] and the Pastore subcommittee's previous and subsequent involvement with educational television, political broadcasting, and communications satellite development has already been noted. Certainly there was room for far-ranging investigations and proposals in both areas, had the chairmen been inclined to pursue them. But there were also certain factors inhibiting policy generation. The Federal Communications Commission, Civil Aeronautics Board, and Federal Aviation Agency functioned more effectively in policy development than did, say, the Maritime Administration, and their relations with industry were relatively cordial, thus lessening the felt need for congressional intervention. The laws on the books were relatively comprehensive; they tended, moreover, to be arcane and of little broad popular interest.

Thus, most of the work of the Communications and Aviation Subcommittees did not consist of legislative projects, and the reasons for this transcended patterns of committee organization. The Communications Subcommittee reported only six bills during the 89th Congress, and all but one of these (a Pastore bill punishing obscene phone calls) were requested by the FCC. The Aviation Subcommittee reported four minor bills, one of which was an FAA request. Budget justifications submitted to the Rules Committee stressed not legislative but oversight activities.[8] Beeks and Zapple spent a great amount of their time simply keeping up with the activities of the administrative agencies and interpreting agency actions and the law to others on Capitol Hill:

There's a great need for expertise. So much of my time is spent simply keeping on top of developments in the field, keeping tabs on the agencies involved, keeping the Subcommittee informed. I also serve as advisor to all senators in the field. . . . I'm not saying that our work doesn't involve important questions of political philosophy. But it is also technical and many of our services are informative and con-sultative. . . . I'm not sure I'd describe myself as an "idea man." I'd like to be, but there's not much time for that.

The fact remains, however, that such dispersals of authority and re-sources as Magnuson was willing to grant, of which subcommittee inde-pendence was an increasingly important component, were positively related to the formulating and publicizing ventures senators like Bartlett, Neuberger, Hart, Moss, and Hollings were able to assume in the 89th and subsequent Congresses. The functional decentralization achieved by virtue of Magnuson's tolerant and accommodating leadership style was also important in dispersing legislative responsibility at the interest-aggregation and modification stages, as suggested by the successes of Hartke, Long, Cotton, and Morton on the bills examined. The impact of such factors on legislative output will come into sharper focus as subsequent chapters examine the organization of two committees in terms of which some Commerce members were inclined to view their own committee as some-thing of a golden mean.

The notion of the structure of incentives furnishes an opportunity for recapitulation and summary. The jurisdiction of the Commerce Committee covered areas of interest and importance to almost any senator, presenting problems to be solved, interests to be serviced, political mileage to be gained. As one senior member expressed it:

The main reason [for the Committee's relative activism] is the subject matter. These commerce powers are specifically delegated to the Congress by the Constitution. . . . And we're talking about areas that have grown fantastically in recent years—aviation, communications, transportation, and now this growth of consumer interest. An ex-tremely wide range. This is the United States?. . . . Other committees can't do as much. How can Foreign Relations really affect foreign policy? And on Appropriations, all you can do is vote it up or down.

Several members, especially those with liberal leanings, perceived a policy gap in some of these areas, particularly consumer affairs, and set out to exploit their potential public appeal.

Other factors, however, while not reducing the desire for a voice and a vote in committee affairs, nonetheless reduced the incentives for direct policy involvement. The fact that certain areas (like aviation and com-munications) were very complex and of limited popular interest, were relatively well covered by existing law, or had active executive agencies working in them often directed interested senators away from policy formu-lation and toward oversight and service functions. Nor were the incentives *within* the Committee uniform from area to area. In general, the Committee was one of the Senate's most open and tolerant, though many members expressed a marked distaste for senators who were "pushy" or unwilling to accept a "reasonable" compromise. But in the areas of merchant marine, fisheries, and consumer affairs, and sometimes in other areas as well, Magnuson and his staff showed a tendency to preempt the legislative moves of other members. While this practice sometimes enhanced the life-chances of a bill, it also posed certain disincentives for members who otherwise would have undertaken publicizing and formulation activities. This, however, was hardly a sufficient explanation for the fact that the legislative efforts of many members were so limited. More important than the structure of incentives, internal or external, were the energies, ambitions, and role-conceptions which the senators brought *to* the structure and *to* their jobs.

Integration and Adaptation. A striking fact about the bills examined in Chapter 2 is the near unanimity with which all were passed and the extent to which the Commerce Committee draft was honored on the floor (Republican amendments were defeated by an average margin of 32 votes). If one looks at the range of roll-calls to which Commerce Committee bills were subjected during the 89th Congress, it becomes clear that such a vote was rarely requested (n = 14) and that both Committee members and the Senate as a whole tended to vote overwhelmingly against proposed modifications of the Committee's handiwork. Commerce members and the parent chamber both registered a mean index of cohesion[10] of 60 on these votes, a very high figure indeed.

Roll-call data suggest, therefore, that the Committee was quite successful both at adaptation to the parent chamber and at internal integration. Several observers corroborated this impression: Commerce was one of the committees least often reversed by the full Senate. This of course gave Committee members, particularly Magnuson, considerable leverage, not only assuring them that their last legislative hurdle would be cleared but also making for a focus of all legislative inputs—political pressures, information, efforts at reformulation and amendment, representations of group and agency interests—at the committee level. The fact that the Committee continued to find itself the court of last resort suggested that most senators were satisfied with its performance. But it also reflected the success of Commerce in solving its second systemic problem, integration. "The Committee is very pleasant and harmonious," said one member, "and that's important to its legislative success. We usually stick together on the floor." Another member added that Magnuson was unusually skillful at smoothing over party and personality differences:

> It's an unusually harmonious committee. Cotton and Magnuson get along well, and Magnuson cultivates that. Of course there's a member

who is always devil's advocate [Lausche], but that doesn't disrupt things much. When these differences come up you just take a vote and go on from there.

Republican testimony provided additional documentation of committee harmony and suggested that an operative norm of minimal partisanship was a crucial ingredient. One minority aide went so far as to suggest that in some ways the Republicans were treated better than the Democrats, though it was the staff and not Magnuson himself whom he charged with occasional disintegrative tactics:

That situation, where members can't get credit for things or get things done—that's something the minority is spared. . . . In some ways our situation is less difficult in the first place. We know that we're not going to get our bills through in our name and so that element of competition is removed. On the other hand, we do draft counter-proposals and are quite successful in offering amendments. . . . Now Gerry does get pretty highhanded at times [but that primarily affects Democratic members]. A lot of that is the fault of the members' own staffs. They ought to stand up and insist on their rights. I know I'd never take them treating the minority that way. In most cases all it would take would be to tell Gerry that perhaps the senator would talk to Maggie about that. That would do it, because Gerry knows that if the senator went to Magnuson, he would tell him, "Sure, go ahead."

Another minority staff man gave an even more benign portrayal of the Chairman:

They say the polls are looking better for Magnuson, and I guess we Republicans should see that as bad news. But I'll tell you, I would have a hard time voting against Warren G. Magnuson. He's a great guy, and he's one of the best for cooperating with Republicans. Often he'll trim down a proposal to meet our objections. [Responding:] Of course that's one reason the Committee is so often united on the floor.

Certain additional indicators buttressed these findings and suggested that the Committee's new activism was making a contribution of its own to the group's integrative capacities. Donald Matthews, studying the 80th through the 84th Congresses, found the mean seniority of Commerce Committee members at appointment to be 1.4 years, less than that of six other committees. As of January 3, 1955, he found the mean continuous service of Commerce Committee members to be 3.1 years, the lowest of any committee in the Senate.[11] An updating of these figures reveals a steady growth in the Committee's attractiveness and stability. It became more sought after; for the period from 1961 to 1965, the mean seniority of committee members at appointment jumped to 3.5 years.[12] The Committee also became more stable: as of January 4, 1965, the mean continuous service of majority members was 6.2 years. The figure was 5.0 even with Magnuson's twenty years not counted—still well above the 1955 figure.

A number of factors helped explain the integration of the Commerce Committee. Chief among them was probably, as one member claimed, "Maggie's personality." The Chairman was liked both as an affable and intriguing person and as a leader who avoided extremes, made reasonable concessions, and usually kept participation open and partisan conflict at a minimum. Also of considerable importance was the Committee's subject-matter. A number of groups were "interested"; though their interests were by no means always compatible with one another or easily adjusted, it could have been much worse. The issues dealt with by the Commerce Committee were for the most part "distributive" or "regulative" rather than "redistributive"; they rarely engendered large-scale group or "class" conflict. Many of the issues were regional, or otherwise selective in their impact, and thus lent themselves to a system of specialization and mutual deference. In addition, these were areas in which the President generally had not become deeply involved; they did not have a deep partisan hue, and the Republicans were left relatively free to add their own shading.

A third factor promoting integration was the Committee's structure of incentives. Senators were finding it increasingly profitable to involve themselves in areas under the Committee's jurisdiction, and they found in the group a generally permissive atmosphere. The results included heightened committee attractiveness and stability, a greater sense of efficacy, and increased inducements to abide by committee norms and thus to gain acceptance and influence. But equally important in fostering integration were the characteristics of the members themselves. As Figure 2 showed, the Committee was made up largely of moderates; neither the Republican nor the Democratic membership was clustered at an ideological pole. The complexion of the group facilitated compromise, adjustment, and partisan cooperation.

The most obvious impact of the Committee's adaptive and integrative capacities was upon the Chairman. For him, these states of equilibrium were resources to be maintained and utilized unless there was some countervailing factor of overriding importance (such as he apparently perceived when he decided to compromise no further on fair packaging). But for other members the Commerce Committee's brand of integration probably had a more variable impact. It often encouraged members like Neuberger, Bartlett, and Hart by providing a permissive and cooperative atmosphere, and by furnishing assurances that bills which made it through the Committee had excellent chances for final passage. It gave viability to attempts at modification as well, such as those undertaken by Hartke and Long on the auto safety bill. Committee integration entailed norms of specialization, reciprocity, and deference, thus stimulating the efforts and increasing the influence of Monroney and Pastore. It also led to an increase in Republican participation in committee deliberations, together with a decrease in their extra-committee legislative efforts. This shift made for a greater, if less visible, minority impact.

But integration, after all, buttressed the Chairman's authority; its legislative impact would thus be expected to partake of the same ambiguity as did the more formal aspects of committee organization. Committee activists were particularly prone to question harmony as an end in itself. Recall the attitudes of the minority and majority aides: the former cited Magnuson's acceptance of qualifying amendments as evidence that he was cooperative and reasonable, a "great guy," while the latter feared that, in taking charge of a bill, Magnuson would "compromise it away." Similarly, Magnuson's refusal to accept further deletions to the fair packaging bill was viewed by the Republicans as threatening "the way this committee usually operates," while Hart and his followers viewed the Chairman's steadfastness as an act of principle, far more praiseworthy than stilling troubled waters.

It seems clear, on balance, that Commerce Committee integration and adaptation were not purchased at the price of making every reported bill a "least common denominator" or a mere patchwork of compromises. Nor did the norms and incentives around which the Committee was integrated make for a stifling atmosphere of the sort that characterized Agriculture and Armed Services. But integrative and adaptive concerns did push Magnuson toward a "low-risk" style of leadership, and members were therefore sometimes prompted to trim their proposals or hold them back. Certainly there was a reduced incentive to offer disruptive or radical ideas. And integration made it less likely that the policy role Magnuson assumed and the deference he demanded would be challenged. On a less integrated committee, independent legislative efforts down through the ranks might have been more frequent. On the Commerce Committee, however, while acquiescence and deference had their frustrations, they also had their rewards.

Interests and Representation. The first thing to be noted about the interest groups we have observed in the Commerce Committee's environment is that "peak associations" seeking "redistributive" measures were not prominent among them. The distributive and regulatory policies with which the Committee characteristically dealt usually involved the large labor and business organizations only peripherally—as advocates of one or another shift in a pluralistic balance of interests rather than as "class" spokesmen or as advocates of a coherent or comprehensive reallocation of national resources. Following Theodore Lowi's lead,[13] it may be suggested that this fact itself contributed to the legislative hegemony of the Senate Committee, making parametric policy moves more viable and less likely to encounter massive opposition. The Committee's dependence on the information resources of the Executive was considerable, and subsequent years were to demonstrate the slippage between legislative fiat and effective bureaucratic implementation, particularly in consumer affairs. But the difficulties and dependence of the Commerce Committee would have been much more acute had the policy areas in which it was operating regularly required the adjustment of zero-sum conflicts between major groups, involved "generalized and ideological demands,"[14] or anticipated massive bureaucratic operations. As it was, the Committee had a relatively free hand to accommodate and adjust the relations among a diversity of interests in both the formulation and modification processes—and sometimes to transcend such "balancing" through response to a poorly organized but politically promising "public interest" as well.

Nonetheless, the groups in the Committee's field of operation did display considerable variety along several dimensions. The tobacco lobby was well organized, well financed, and politically astute. The small companies concerned with the packaging bill were for the most part uncoordinated, poorly informed, and politically naive, while the NAM and USCC had their own problems in maintaining the support of their constituents and developing a unified and practical approach. Consumer groups were weaker and poorer yet. The health societies concerned about tobacco and the scientific groups interested in oceanography ranked high on enthusiasm, information, and expertise, but low on political muscle and experience. The automobile and tire manufacturers were surprisingly disorganized, lacking in information and political realism; they were caught off guard by congressional initiative and never managed fully to recoup their losses. Shipping interests were seasoned at the lobbying game, lacking in imagination and flexibility, but effectively organized and financed. Fishing interests, by contrast, were sporadic in their involvement and scattered and diverse in their concerns.

As Chapter 2 indicated, the strengths and weaknesses of these groups were not unrelated to their effectiveness in stimulating or inhibiting Commerce Committee activity. But the case material also showed that these groups were not as central to the legislative process as one might have imagined, given the Committee's jurisdiction and membership. Only one of the bills, the cigarette labeling act, could with some justification be termed an "interest-group bill," and even there the designation is only partially accurate. Most of the members were contacted by local industries concerning the packaging bill, and several offered or supported modifications designed to ease its impact; yet, in the end, a majority stood with Magnuson in opposition to major deletions. And relatively few concessions were made to the automobile and tire industries, although several members responded to the entreaties of smaller equipment manufacturers threatened by the Long Amendment.

If organized interests were not notably effective in blocking proposals, still less could they be credited with an appreciable positive impact. All of the bills, in fact, represented a sort of political entrepreneurship on the part of Magnuson and other senators. This is not to belittle the role the health societies played in urging executive and congressional action on smoking and health, the early efforts of NASCO in promoting oceanography, or the extraordinary influence wielded by Nader at every stage of the auto safety episode. It is simply to point out that only a fraction of the activity connected with the four bills could accurately be described as a response to lobbying or group representations of any description.

The case studies thus demonstrated the imperfection and flexibility of the linkages between senators and their clients—and that "representative government" was often more a matter of political entrepreneurship than of responsiveness to group entreaties. But they also suggested that Congress was not losing the "race for representation" by as great a margin as was sometimes supposed. In the first place, it was evident that where the interests went was more effect than cause of where legislative responsibility was being assumed. But the fact that various interests—from Nader to the oceanographers—made the Commerce Committee their prime point of access further enhanced its role. This was particularly evident in the MMF area. Fishing and shipping interests were regional in character, firmly based and well-treated in the Commerce Committee, and rather weakly represented in the executive hierarchy. That these interests—and sometimes the BCF as well—went first of all to the Senate had an obvious effect on the role the Commerce Committee assumed vis-à-vis its coordinate policy-making units.

The preponderance of western-state senators on the Committee (one-third of its membership) also made it a promising access point for airport development and air-passenger interests. But the Committee's lead in the race for representation in the aviation area was less marked, and less yet in communications and surface transportation. The interests involved were less exclusively regional than fishing and shipping and less unequivocally represented on the Commerce Committee. They were often less interested in gaining subsidies or other "distributive" benefits than in escaping various sorts of regulation; unquestioning support of their demands was thus somewhat more likely to encounter opposition from guardians of the "public" interest. And these industries generally had more prominent and more friendly points of access in the CAB, FAA, FCC, and ICC than the maritime interests did in their executive agencies. For these reasons, among others, the areas of communications, aviation, and transportation displayed a much more spotty record of congressional policy leadership.

Chapter 2 displayed instances in which neither Senate nor Executive, but the House, became the prime point of access for concerned groups. On all three consumer bills the House Commerce Committee undertook additional interest-aggregation and in at least two of the cases it reported bills conforming more nearly to industry's wishes. Various factors influenced its behavior: some representatives indicated that the "highhandedness" of the Senate group made them more open to industry complaints, while a fear of unfavorable publicity could apparently have the opposite effect. But a glance at the House Committee's membership provides a more concrete indication of why it acted as it did. It contained proportionately more members from southern and tobacco states than the Senate Committee, and one-third of its members had an occupational background in business. While this was only six percentage points above the comparable figure for the Senate group, the Chamber of Commerce's ratings pointed to a much larger difference in orientation. The average score for House Committee members was 53, for Senate Committee members only 34. ADA ratings told a similar story: 36 for the House Committee, 55 for the Senate.[15]

The extent and the location of group efforts, then, were at once cause, effect, and indicator of the policy predispositions of committees and agencies and of the legislative moves they had underway. The points of access chosen by the various groups inhabiting the Commerce Committee's environment often enhanced the group's centrality to the legislative process. Alternatively, however, they could force the Committee to share its prerogatives, and stimulate threats and checks from other units.

"Islands" and Adjustment. The bills examined in Chapter 2, which headed the Commerce Committee's agenda during the 89th Congress, involved for the most part areas which the executive branch was covering inadequately or not at all. In only one case was the White House officially opposed, but in none of the cases was the administration's participation in the legislative process well coordinated, energetic, or sustained. Problems of coordination and control are of course endemic to any large organization, the executive branch included; sub-units are certain to reflect divergent perspectives and sympathies. But the areas of consumer protection, traffic safety, and oceanography were conspicuous in this respect. Executive performance in the latter stages of the fair packaging episode stood out by contrast—and gave some indication of where these matters previously had stood on the President's list of priorities.

The Commerce Committee, however, was not merely filling a policy gap left by the executive branch; it was also countering certain viewpoints and policies perceived there. The Commerce Department's position on all four bills rendered it suspect, the interests of Holloman in consumer affairs and of ESSA in oceanography notwithstanding. The views of the Surgeon General and his staff on tobacco, of GSA on vehicle standards, of the Consumer Office on fair packaging, and of PSAC and other government scientists on oceanography were conspicuous, not only for their closeness to the sentiments of most Committee members, but also for the *lack* of support they had within the administration. These agencies sometimes represented a chink in the administration's armor which congressional advocates could utilize to their advantage. But by virtue of their isolation and lack of success they pointed up the conflict, apathy, and opposition which were immobilizing the executive branch. Congressional advocates realized that if policy moves of a certain sort were to be made, it was they who would have to make them—and that if congressional moves were *not* made, other viewpoints and policies might prevail.

Similar considerations pertained to the Senate Committee's House counterparts. The senators' legislative moves were often influenced by their awareness that these were areas which the House committees could not be relied upon to cover and that House action, when and if it came, was likely to be contradictory to Senate objectives.

Many Senate moves were preemptory in character, "parametric" and "nonsymmetrical."[16] Or as one Senator put it:

> One thing about Senate Agriculture is that it almost always waits on the House to act. It doesn't do much on its own. Commerce isn't like that. It's probably the strongest committee over against its House counterpart in the Senate. What the Commerce Committee wants to do it does, without waiting for anybody.

The pattern observed in Chapter 2 was part of a larger picture: of the 90 bills reported during the 89th Congress only 28 bore House numbers. There were few attempts to tailor bills to meet House objections, as both fair packaging and oceanography (despite Magnuson's claims to have "compromised") demonstrated. In fact, an anticipation of House action in some cases (e.g. cigarette labeling) led to a *strengthening* of the Senate measure as a compensatory move. This nondeferential style of operation often proved successful. In oceanography, for example, the conferees combined two two-layer bills into a three-layer one, but the Senate of course could claim victory. Cigarette labeling was a second Senate triumph. As for traffic safety, no one doubted that, whatever had been the pattern of anticipation and response, the final bill was much closer to the Senate's original intentions than it was to those of the House. It was only on fair packaging, among the bills discussed in Chapter 2, that the Senate could not claim a conference victory—but here it was something of a victory to get the House to agree to any bill at all.

What explained this pattern of successes? Why was the Senate Committee able to emerge as a "core group" in these areas of policymaking? The case studies suggested that in activism itself and in the strategies of preemption and prior commitment a certain legislative preeminence was often to be gained. The Senate group was faced, both in House committees and in executive agencies, not so much with unremitting hostility as with misgivings and apathy. The preferences of the Senate group were more intense than those of the other units and their policy objectives more clearly articulated, but if the issues were forced, House and executive actors could scarcely wish (or afford) to take a purely negative position. Under these circumstances, the Senate Committee could throw down the gauntlet, and other committees and agencies could hardly fail to respond, often taking the Senate bill as their point of departure and proposing only marginal alterations. But the impact and independence of the Senate Committee were nonetheless limited. In two of the four cases, in fact, the Commerce Committee could not have prevailed without the intervention of a third party: the Committee itself did not have the necessary resources. On fair packaging, the House would never have acted at all had not the White House intervened. On oceanography, Magnuson, for all the other advantages he enjoyed, could not have secured approval of his council proposal had not the administration given its tacit consent. And on twenty (23 percent) of the bills the Commerce Committee shepherded through the Senate during the 89th Congress, House committees refused to act.

This leads to the reiteration of a major point made in Chapter 1: for an understanding of a group's preeminence among other islands of decision it is important above all to look at its patterns of *cooperation*. Initiative may be prompted by the apathy, inaction, disorganization, or hostility of other units. Strength may be gained by strategies of preemption and challenge. Committee activism may be stimulated by conflict. But the general principle remains: in a pluralistic political order, isolation ordinarily spells weakness and coalitions generally bring strength.

The Commerce Committee profited from a number of cooperative relationships. One of the most important—though it did not enter directly into our case histories—was with the Senate Appropriations Committees. One-third of the membership of the Commerce Committee was on Appropriations. Magnuson chaired the Independent Offices Appropriations Subcommittee—which handled funds for FTC, FMC, CAB, FAA, FCC, and similar non-departmental boards—and Pastore, Monroney, and Cotton served there with him. Magnuson, Pastore, McGee, and Cotton also served on the subcommittee handling appropriations for the Commerce Department. That such interlocking arrangements enhanced the Committee's, and particularly Magnuson's, legislative leverage was certain. As one minority member put it:

> *That gives him control over appropriations his committee has authorized and gives him power over other committees too. People aren't going to turn Maggie down. Hell, if I wanted to build a gold-plated privy up on top of Fort Knox, and if I was head of the committees which authorized and appropriated for it, of course I could do it. It would give me immense power. A lot of committee chairmen have that arrangement. It's a situation I would like to see changed.*

Magnuson's House counterparts did not have the benefit of any such arrangement. When Senate or executive branch actors were dealing with House committees they could often go independently to those involved in the appropriations process or play the committees off one against the other. Magnuson and the Commerce Committee were not vulnerable in this respect. To those who would manipulate from outside, Commerce and Appropriations represented a united front that could rarely be breached.

Relations with the House Commerce and MMF Committees were more problematic—though the case studies, which happened to focus on areas of particularly strong inter-house disagreement, perhaps overemphasized the conflictful and underemphasized the cooperative modes of adjustment. The picture was much less one-sided with regard to the executive branch. If much of the Commerce Committee's assumption of legislative responsibility was stimulated by executive disorganization, disinterest, or hostility, its successes were at the same time due in no small part to the downtown alliances it was able to secure. The lead which the Committee assumed in fishing legislation, a staff member said explicitly, was "not so much the product of competition [with BCF] as of close cooperation." The same could have been said of the Committee's relationships with FTC, PHS, the President's consumer office, and the Commerce Department's Office of Science and Technology. Numerous benefits were gained: information, ideas, and considerable assistance in the processes of formulation and modification.

These arrangements also gave the Committee increased leverage vis-à-vis other islands of decision. Sometimes they forced confrontations within the executive branch and isolated those who were lukewarm or hostile to the proposals in question. At other times they gave a low-level federal agency a greater policy-making influence than its position in the hierarchy would have warranted. The Committee's success in this respect was mixed (the legislative involvement of the Consumer Office, for example, remained peripheral), but many of its alliances reinforced favorable tendencies and strengthened certain actors within the executive branch.

Information, Expertise, and the Role of the Staff. From one point of view the capacity of the Commerce Committee to generate and gather information did not seem very impressive. The bills discussed in Chapter 2, while simple in comparison with some others on the congressional agenda, still required the gathering of extensive data concerning certain hazards or abuses, the adequacy of existing programs and policies, and the likely impact of proposed changes. In each case most of this information came from outside the Committee. Nader was relied upon to wade through the mass of private and governmental studies on automobile hazards, to make interpretations and policy proposals. The adequacy of the record the Committee compiled was largely the result of his own testimony and the questions he stimulated others to ask. On cigarette labeling and advertising, the Committee, the FTC, and anyone else who desired to act in the area would have been seriously disadvantaged without the Surgeon General's report. On oceanography, the Committee relied initially upon NASCO and later on LRS, but staff members were continually and acutely aware of serious information gaps:

> The staff story on that wasn't the happiest. . . . This is a very complicated area, one where we needed the best in scientific advice. We didn't have it. We had first one man and then another on it.

On fair packaging the Committee relied on FDA and FTC, but in this case *nobody's* resources were very impressive. Hart's difficulties in pushing his bill forward, Magnuson's difficulties in hammering out a workable compromise, and the agencies' later difficulties in developing a meaningful program all stemmed in no small part from deficiencies in knowledge. The Senate Committee, in short, badly needed information; this was one of its main reasons for seeking alliances with the consumer office, Holloman and Christenson, the Surgeon General, FTC, and various bureaus involved in oceanography. Various kinds of currency was exchanged between the allies, and in some species the Committee had a great deal to offer. But the flow of *information* was predominantly in one direction—*toward* the Committee.

If the assumption of an active legislative role, then, demanded that a committee be self-sufficient as an information center, Commerce, like most other committees, would have been relegated to a secondary role. That this did not happen was partly due to the fact that law-making is much more than a matter of information-gathering. But the Commerce Committee's independence and activism were also attributable to its capacities for *utilizing* information. Men like Zapple, Beeks, Foster, Pertschuk, and a growing staff contingent concerned with consumer affairs qualified admirably as "second-level experts," with enough knowledge and sophistication to gain an overview of the areas with which they were involved, to be critical of information and recommendations received from other sources, to request and apply information on their own terms, and to undertake translations into concrete policy proposals. In this respect, the Commerce Committee was one of the best-equipped in the Senate; members, executive branch personnel, and lobbyists agreed that Magnuson and Grinstein had assembled a "damn good staff." From this perspective the Committee's performance on the auto safety and cigarette labeling bills was quite impressive, on fair packaging and oceanography considerably less so.

As important as staff capacities and abilities were, however, they probably did not have as great an impact on the Committee's legislative behavior as did the *orientation* which Grinstein and his recruits Pertschuk and

Foster shared. These were men with considerable expertise and ability; but of crucial importance was *how* they utilized and presented information. It was not entirely fair, insisted Grinstein, when members of more "professional" staffs accused his men of "playing senator," of manipulating their mentors or pushing them into enterprises which they would have been otherwise reluctant to undertake:

> But we certainly don't think of our staff like you would some reference book, to be taken down off the shelf and used occasionally. We see it as part of our job to present alternatives to the senator, to lay out things before him that he might want to do. That doesn't mean that we're telling him every damn move he makes.

All staff members did not describe their job in the same terms. Beeks and Zapple, for example, seemed to regard "keeping up" in their fields and performing functions of consultation and oversight as more central to their jobs than generating policy ideas—an orientation that was both cause and effect of the legislative role assumed by the Committee in communications and aviation. But the approach of Pertschuk, Grinstein, and Foster to the consumer and MMF-oceanography areas was quite different. These men all had a lively interest in several legislative problems—an interest more lively, in some cases, than that of their bosses. They were engaged in a continual "search" operation, seeking both gaps for policy initiatives and fledgling proposals that might be developed and made politically viable. They framed alternative courses of action for the Chairman and sometimes for other members, paying considerable attention to the realities and possibilities of public and group support in the process. They devised hearings so as to realize their maximum potential for publicity, took pains to highlight executive inertia and industry irresponsibility, and often leaked news of rumored defections and opposition efforts to the press. Chapter 2 demonstrated their adeptness at securing mutually profitable liaisons with sympathetic agency officials and individual and group advocates. They also played a considerable role in activating groups—e.g. several consumer organizations and firms with a potential economic stake in oceanography—that in many cases, far from exerting effective pressure, were poorly informed and loosely organized.

Magnuson's desire not to enact "radical" or punitive legislation and the members' determination to report fair and "balanced" bills imposed certain constraints on the staff, but they had considerable room to implement their own preferences and to shape the actions of their mentors. In all four cases, but most conspicuously in the traffic safety episode, they assumed an extraordinary degree of freedom in accepting, rejecting, and altering various amendments and in determining the form in which others came to the Committee for decision. It was clear that most Committee members accepted this staff role and in some cases prescribed it, but it could hardly be doubted that the activities of their aides had an independent impact on their behavior. As one staff man put it:

> *The explanation [for the committee's activism] is the number of concerned senators and a livewire staff. Magnuson believes the Committee ought to be doing these things and is willing to give us free rein so long as we don't get him in trouble. If we get him in trouble, then he'll hold us back. But if not, we can follow our interests.*

Magnuson's acquiescence to such a role for his staff came in the wake of the 1962 election; its legislative impact reached a high point during the 89th Congress and continued thereafter.

It is important to note, however, that such staff activities on the majority side, prior to the 1968 election and to a large extent thereafter, were generally directed toward the enhancement of the role and reputation of Magnuson and Magnuson alone. If the staff eschewed the "reference book" role associated in their minds with "professionalism," so did they not pretend to be nonpartisan or equally accessible to every member. "The Commerce Committee," Grinstein was once heard to remark, "is an extension of the Chairman." A staff member who, like Foster, developed legislation with the idea of building up another member's role breached an inexplicit but well-understood staff norm. Similarly, when the staff fastened upon a bill as one deserving of Committee consideration, they did their work in Magnuson's name rather than in the name of the original sponsor, even if he was on the Committee. In the words of a majority member:

> *Magnuson doesn't one-up his committee members—but you must distinguish between Magnuson and his bright young men. Grinstein and the rest have one aim in mind—to build up Magnuson's prestige and popularity back in the state.*

There was continual speculation among Committee members as to the degree to which Magnuson was cognizant of or responsible for this situation. But the picture of staff exclusiveness was in any case mixed; majority members and their aides often reported adequate accessibility and a "willingness to cooperate." And it would be a mistake to give to personal and partisan loyalty of the sort represented by Grinstein a wholly negative assessment as far as the Committee's productivity is concerned. It could, it is true, lead to the avoidance of areas that did not seem to hold high political potential or which appeared too radical for Magnuson's "low-risk" style (recall the staff man's comment that Magnuson's men applied their talents only to "sure" proposals). It could also mean discouragement or at least a lack of stimulation for other potentially active members; the decentralization of staff operations that followed Magnuson's reelection in 1968 and Grinstein's departure might thus be expected to increase the committee's legislative capacities. On the other hand, personal and partisan ties were—and could continue to be in a decentralized situation—important in reinforcing and giving coherence to the staff's instigative efforts. The fact that the development of policy and the promotion of Magnuson were seen by staff and Chairman alike as two sides of the same coin undoubtedly provided motivation and a focus for effort. Certainly it made Magnuson more willing to see himself and his committee cast as legislative activists in fields of broad national import—a role to which he was still adjusting. The same was true of Bartlett, though his situation also demonstrated the negative impact overly exclusive ties could have when they denied counsel to potential activists. But Bartlett would have gained no more than Magnuson from a neutral or nonpartisan staff orientation; had Foster been less closely tied politically and personally to the Senator, it is doubtful that Foster would have developed the programs that he did or that Bartlett would have felt confident in promoting them.

Many of the relations drawn between the legislative behavior of the majority and the orientation of its staff could be duplicated in a discussion of the minority—as long, that is, as one was speaking of Jerry Kenney. Chapter 2 found him basically in sympathy with the consumer and oceanography efforts, and with several ideas of his own; he thus influenced the initial position of the Republicans, facilitated their involvement in the processes of formulation and amendment, and shifted the locus while increasing the efficacy of their efforts. To do this Kenney needed, and got, the active cooperation of the majority staff:

> I ordinarily have no problem gaining access to the work that the staff has done. Except, of course, in a case like fair packaging where they couldn't include me in on those confabs with the administration and such.

Kenney, however, was in many respects a minority of one on the Republican side. Magnuson had been relatively generous to the Republicans. During the 89th Congress they had four professional aides. Within this group were to be found wide variations in capacity and orientation. Kenney, for example, was bothered very little by the fact that the minority staff could not carefully peruse every proposal that came before the Committee. They should rather survey the possibilities, select those that were particularly interesting or problematic, and apply their creative efforts to those few in depth. And hopefully they could promote some ideas of their own. The views of another minority aide furnished a nice contrast:

> Of course we're badly outnumbered. Just look at the size of that majority staff—and they've added a lot since they got into this consumer business. You'll see what kind of problems we have if you just look at that hearing calendar. Sometimes it's almost all we can do to cover those. [Agreeing:] When you're that rushed you don't have

much time to sit around thinking up new legislation. It's about all you can do to keep tabs on what's going on. . . . All this new legislative activity has complicated our work immensely. . . . The real shift came when Gerry was brought in.

Revealed here was anything but an activistic notion of staff responsibilities. The staff man rather was to know what was going on, to alert his members as to problems and pitfalls; he would see the Committee's spate of activity more as a burden than as an opportunity. Certainly he would feel little rapport with staff members who were promoting this activity and would have little desire to contribute to their efforts.

Republican legislative involvement, then, was influenced in extent and in kind by Kenney's performance. Neither his deviations nor his uniqueness should be exaggerated: the fair packaging episode demonstrated that he had his disagreements with Grinstein and Pertschuk, and when he left the Committee in 1966, his mediating role was to some extent picked up— much to the majority staff's surprise—by Ray Hurley. But Kenney was nonetheless much closer to the sympathies and style of Magnuson's "bright young men" than were his minority colleagues. More conservative in their approach and less concerned to develop "improvements" than to pick out flaws, the bulk of the minority staff could not be expected to instigate much in the way of legislative initiative or innovation among their members. They were more likely to prompt opposition or "weakening" amendments than to encourage the development of alternative proposals or "constructive" changes,[17] and they were neither equipped nor inclined to cultivate the kind of collaborative relationship Kenney developed with majority aides.

THE FINANCE COMMITTEE IN ACTION

THE HOSPITAL INSURANCE, SOCIAL SECURITY, AND PUBLIC ASSISTANCE AMENDMENTS OF 1965

The Legislative Roots. "Historians will mark this year," said Senator Clinton Anderson in introducing the administration's medicare bill on January 6, 1965, "as the turning point in our long struggle to solve . . . what has become one of the most urgent issues of public policy—the problems of financing the costs of hospital care for the aged."[1] His bill was numbered S. 1 to indicate its priority on the congressional agenda, and it had attracted almost half of the Senate as cosponsors before it was introduced. Senator Anderson, looking over his shoulder at the new desks crowded together on the Democratic side of the chamber and thinking as well of the 42 Northern Democrats that had been added to administration ranks in the House, could make this optimistic prediction with some certainty. Within seven months he had been proved correct, although the bill signed by the President on July 31 differed measurably from anything Anderson or anybody else involved with the legislation would have predicted as the 89th Congress got underway.

The medicare idea had undergone an unusually long period of germination. A national program of health insurance was included in the platform of Theodore Roosevelt's Progressive Party in 1912, and model legislation was drafted shortly thereafter by the American Association for Labor Legislation; health insurance bills were soon introduced in sixteen state legislatures. Insurance companies were hostile from the first, while the American Medical Association showed an initial interest. But the proposals were shelved one by one, partly because of the advent of World War I and partly because of the steady growth of opposition within the medical profession. President Roosevelt's Committee on Economic Security, commissioned to formulate the Social Security Act, endorsed the principle of compulsory national health insurance. But Roosevelt, sensitive to charges that he was dominating Congress and alarmed by outcries against the Committee's proposals, backed off. The Social Security Act, as introduced, provided only that the administering board should study the matter, but the House Ways and Means Committee struck even this from the bill. The issue did not reappear on the presidential agenda until 1945, when President Truman, delivering a Health Message which Roosevelt had been planning at the time of his death, asked that a medical insurance plan be added to social security.[2]

Senators Robert Wagner and James Murray and Representative John Dingell, all Democrats, kept the health insurance idea alive in Congress during and after the war. Stimulated and assisted by Wilbur Cohen, I. S. Falk, and other Federal Security Agency officials, they introduced bills making hospitalization benefits available to all families covered by social security. The bills made little headway, even when the Truman administration made a concerted effort to pry them out of committee in 1949. Meanwhile, the AMA was organizing "what became by far the most expensive lobbying campaign in history."[3] The defeat of several congressional supporters of the Truman plan in 1950 was attributed to the efforts of the AMA and its allies, and the Democratic Party backed away from the issue. Adlai Stevenson did not endorse the Truman proposal in the 1952 campaign, while General Eisenhower's rhetoric identified him with the AMA position.

The issue and the need would not die, however; the Republicans were forced to devise alternative proposals, even as health insurance proponents found it politic to regroup around less sweeping plans. By 1952 Cohen and Falk had developed the program that was later to be known as "medicare," providing health insurance for social security *beneficiaries* only. This reformulation had the advantages of focusing on the segment of the population where the need was most apparent, reducing the costs of the projected program substantially, and capitalizing on the increasing potency of the aging as a political force.[4] Cohen and Falk continued to develop the bill while in exile during the Eisenhower years; working with them and helping keep congressional interest alive was Nelson Cruikshank, head of the AFL-CIO's Department of Social Security.

The administration remained adamant in its opposition to any program of "compulsory" insurance for the aging; prior to the development of a proposal for aid to state programs on the eve of the 1960 election, the administration had gone no further than to propose that the government might keep insurance costs down by reinsuring private companies or by permitting small companies and voluntary health insurance groups to pool their resources. Nor did the congressional scene appear much more hopeful: Cruikshank in 1957 could induce no one of higher rank than Aime Forand, fourth-ranking Democrat on Ways and Means, to introduce the medicare bill. Politicians were generally reluctant to commit themselves on the matter, much less to play the kind of entrepreneurial role found among Commerce Committee members in consumer affairs during the sixties. Yet within three years the Forand bill had become a central issue in a presidential campaign, a focal point for controversy within Congress and for pressures from without:

> All this would happen without benefit of any of the circumstances that usually thrust a legislative measure into the national spotlight. No presidential message or television appeal supported it; no crisis compelled attention to it; it had no status as a party measure in Congress; its sponsor there was a little-known Congressman who could not bring national attention to it and, indeed, did not try; its existence was not reported on the front pages of the newspapers until after it had become a major national political issue. Yet many thousands of people managed to learn of the bill's existence and join the "crusade" for its enactment. Support for the Forand bill began as a genuine grass roots movement—surely the most phenomenal such movement of the period.[5]

The AFL-CIO, some fledgling "senior citizens" organizations, some politicians, and, ironically enough, the AMA itself publicized the bill, but a relatively small stimulus was needed to evoke an appreciable public reaction. A responsive chord had been struck.

Prospective presidential candidates could not help but take notice. The belated proposals of the administration were largely made at the urging of Vice-President Nixon, while the three top northern contenders for the Democratic nomination—Kennedy, Symington, and Humphrey—joined in co-sponsoring a revised version of the Forand bill. Lyndon Johnson and Sam Rayburn were also moved to action, by virtue of Johnson's presidential ambitions and the desire of both men to build a strong Democratic legislative record.

The fact that most medicare proposals were linked to social security and were thus revenue measures meant that they must originate in the House; attention and effort had thus been focused on Wilbur Mills, a staunch opponent of the Forand Bill, and his tightly-knit Ways and Means Committee. Speaker Rayburn hitherto had not made strong representations to Mills, but in mid-1960 he urged him to reconsider. The result was what came to be known as the Kerr-Mills plan. Closer to the administration's approach than to Forand's, Mills' bill provided direct aid for persons who were not on public assistance but who could pass a less stringent means test. The federal and state governments would share the costs; it would be left to the states to pass enabling acts and to devise the details of their programs. Mills secured the bill's passage easily as a part of a general liberalization of social security benefits.

It was after both parties had held their national conventions that the bill came to the Senate and the spotlight first fell on the Finance Committee; proponents came to see in it an obstacle almost as formidable as Ways and Means. The Committee was chaired by Harry F. Byrd, an archetypal southern oligarch, and few progressives of any stripe had been admitted to its ranks. Finance had been hostile to social security from the beginning,[6] and certainly to any expansions of the program to include health insurance. For this reason Senate activists had sought their outlet in the more flexible and more liberal Labor and Public Welfare Committee, settling on the holding of field hearings, the generation of publicity, and the gathering of information as the best available strategy.

It made little difference to the Finance Committee that the Democrats had adopted health insurance as a major plank in their platform and that their presidential candidate was a leading proponent of the Forand approach. Only five of its eleven Democrats and none of its Republicans favored amending the House bill in this direction. The party regulars, however, recognized the need to produce some sort of bill before the election, and Senator Robert Kerr, second-ranking Democrat on the Committee and one of Johnson's closest associates, assumed the sponsorship of a bill similar to the one Mills had approved. Kerr convinced Kennedy that he should go along with the bill as the best among realistic options, and he persuaded the AMA that it would be prudent to raise only a minimal protest. Thus the Kerr-Mills program became a reality, and the stage was set for the legislative battles of the sixties. But two additional aspects of the Senate fight of 1960 appear particularly significant in retrospect. A revised version of the Forand plan, offered as an "amendment in the nature of a substitute" for Kerr-Mills, failed by a vote of only 44-51; leading the fight for its enactment was a senator who hitherto had not been prominently associated with the medicare issue, Clinton Anderson of New Mexico.

The Rise and Fall of King-Anderson. Anderson was more interested in medicare before 1960 than most of his colleagues knew; his occupational background was in insurance, and he was well aware of the needs to which the various proposals spoke. One conclusion he reached at an early point, however, was that the Murray-Wagner bills were the equivalent of "backing an empty truck up to the back door of the Treasury." Anderson was a fiscal conservative, anxious that the program pay for itself (this led him to advocate social security financing), but also concerned to keep payroll taxes down (this led him to endorse a limited program, aimed only at older persons and covering only hospitalization costs). If Anderson's approach was rather cautious, he was still the highest-ranking member of the Finance Committee—behind Byrd, Kerr, Frear, Long, and Smathers—with even the slightest positive inclination. Like Forand, he occupied a critical, if not especially promising, position from the standpoint of medicare proponents.

Anderson was Chairman of a committee with many favors to distribute, Interior and Insular Affairs, and was generally well liked in the Senate. He did his legislative work quietly and thoroughly, avoided appearances of "pushiness" and ambition, and proved amenable to the everyday necessities of adjustment and compromise. Moreover, in his very conservatism and circumspection were to be found certain advantages. With Murray and Wagner, medicare had appeared to be the province of liberal mavericks; the efforts of Pat McNamara and John Kennedy on LPW could be dismissed by virtue of the labor ties of the former and the presidential ambitions of the latter. But with Anderson, medicare might get a new image, as well as a slight foothold in the Finance Committee; for the first time the bill would bear the name of a respected member of the Senate "establishment."

In any case, Anderson and Howard Bray of his staff began "serious conversations" with Nelson Cruikshank in 1960, and after the Democratic Convention Anderson cooperated with Kennedy in devising a substitute for Kerr-Mills. Kennedy lost no time in resubmitting the bill after the election; Anderson introduced it in the Senate, and Representative Cecil King, now second-ranking member on Ways and Means, did the honors in the House. There was no change in the positions of the two chairmen, Mills and Byrd, but the opening months of the 87th Congress saw two developments that were to aid medicare proponents decisively. The White House Conference on Aging, organized under Republican aegis, endorsed health insurance under social security, and a large bloc of the delegates gathered at the close of the conference to form an *ad hoc* committee to press for the enactment of the King-Anderson bill. By the end of the year a permanent organization of over half a million members, the National Council of Senior Citizens, had been formed from this nucleus. It was chaired by now-retired Representative Forand and financed primarily by the AFL-CIO and the Democratic National Committee. Equally important was the elevation of McNamara's LPW Subcommittee on the Aging to the status of an independent special committee, with increased financial and staff resources. Field hearings were undertaken on a larger scale, and the staff issued several studies frankly designed to show the total failure of private plans and the Kerr-Mills program to meet the health needs of the elderly.[7] These studies surpassed any information hitherto gathered in Congress and were more effective in their presentation and clearer in their implications than most of the information amassed by the executive agencies. Neither Ways and Means nor Finance had been motivated to collect such data, and Finance—with only one professional staff man—was ill-equipped to undertake such a project in any case.

But the Special Committee, which contained some of the Senate's most vocal medicare proponents, was hardly content with an information-gathering role. Unable to report legislation themselves, a number of its members attempted to recast King-Anderson so as to make possible a referral to Labor and Public Welfare. This was an approach the NCSC came to favor as it became more and more convinced that any bill Mills, Byrd, and Kerr would clear would be a "monstrosity."[8] But such a strategy could hardly get off the ground. The Finance Committee was prestigious, its members high in seniority, and its jurisdiction in social security matters well established. The Special Committee was consigned to a peripheral, though catalytic, role, and congressional responsibility—and obstruction—remained where it always had been: In Finance and in Ways and Means.

Kennedy's first State of the Union message revealed that medicare was an item of high priority on his legislative agenda; several of his appointments gave the same indication. There were some shakeups in the Social Security Administration, normally a relatively "non-political" agency, and Robert Ball, a career man who nonetheless had collaborated actively with Cohen, Falk, and Cruikshank during the fifties, was eventually made Administrator. As one of his associates put it:

> He was very much in the Kennedy image too, so he was a natural. I don't think there was any question that he was looked on as an activist and as a medicare advocate, and that his appointment was designed to push it along.

More conspicuous as a center of executive activity, however, was the office of the HEW Secretary. Here the most obvious indicator of the President's intentions was the appointment of Wilbur J. Cohen as Assistant Secretary, an appointment the AMA tried to block. Paul Douglas once defined a Social Security expert as "a man with Wilbur Cohen's telephone number," and most of the men who had carried the medicare issue forward since the thirties had had that number—not only Murray, Dingell, and Cruikshank, but the designers of the Eisenhower administration and Kerr-Mills measures as well. In fact, Cohen's close identification with the 1960 legislation (which Forand termed "a sham . . . a mirage . . . a watered-down version of a no-good bill that came from the White House."[9]) and his joining with Kerr in urging Senate liberals to support it were indicative of certain characteristics of the man and his approach. No one doubted that Cohen's own goals and preferences included the development of a comprehensive health insurance program under social security, but he was a practical politician, willing to work with those cool to his purposes and to settle for half a loaf. This style, while it made for compatibility with Senate leaders like Johnson, Kerr, and Anderson and gave Cohen a certain leverage even with medicare opponents, at the same time caused certain supporters of the legislation, particularly those working with the Committee on Aging, to develop fears of a "sell-out" and to seek alternate contacts within the Department.

The King-Anderson Bill progressed slowly, despite new blood in the executive branch, increasingly favorable public opinion polls, and the breaking of organized medicine's united front by the American Nurses Association and the American Public Health Association. The only strategy open to the Administration, in light of the intransigence of the revenue committees, was to offer medicare as an amendment on the Senate floor; Anderson agreed to make such an effort. The rider incorporated several provisions from an alternative proposal introduced by Republican Senator Jacob Javits in 1961, but Anderson could not pick up enough minority votes to reverse the 1960 verdict. His 48-52 defeat was a bitter disappointment to him and to the President as well. "Few votes had been changed as the result of two years of some of the most intensive lobbying ever carried out on any measure."[10] But the fight greatly increased the public salience of the medicare issue, and the net effect of the elections of 1962 was to reverse the balance of sentiment in the Senate and to narrow the margin of opposition on the Ways and Means Committee to one vote. The maintenance of that margin was not unrelated to the AMA's agreement not to endorse the Surgeon General's report on smoking and health; the AMA action reportedly stopped the waverings of John C. Watts, representative of a tobacco district in Kentucky.[11] But in the Senate the numbers had definitely shifted in Anderson's favor—if, that is, one looked at the entire chamber and not at the Finance Committee. Anderson was again defeated, 6-11, when he attempted to add health insurance provisions to a social security amendments bill in committee, but he and his allies—Douglas, Gore, McCarthy, Hartke, and Ribicoff—drafted a dissenting report and in mid-1964 prepared to take the battle to the floor.

Russell Long, who as second-ranking Democrat on the Finance Committee had already assumed many of the ailing Chairman's functions, led the opposition with some wily parliamentary maneuvering, but the Senate voted its approval of medicare, 49-44, when Gore offered it as an amendment to the social security revisions then under consideration. Anderson and Gore, however, went to conference under severe disadvantages. Only they among the seven Senate conferees had voted for the Gore amendment, and most of the medicare opponents from both houses were anxious to secure a least-common denominator agreement on the social security increases included in both the House and Senate bills—not only to please their constituents and ease the pain of medicare's defeat, but also to raise payroll taxes to a point that would make medicare appear even more burdensome when next proposed. Anderson, Gore, and the Johnson administration thus decided that their best strategy was to attempt to block agreement, and this they managed to do. Long and Smathers stuck with Anderson, giving him a 4-3 margin among the Senate's representatives. Both Senators justified their action in terms of subordinating their own personal wishes to the "will of the Senate." When asked to further explain his votes, Smathers smiled and said, "Lyndon told me to."[12] With Long, the deciding factor was probably his desire to succeed

Hubert Humphrey as Majority Whip. It was no coincidence that Anderson led Long's campaign for Whip three months later as the 89th Congress got underway.

The conference deadlock came one month before the presidential election. Barry Goldwater accused the administration of blocking needed social security liberalizations in order to "dramatize" the medicare issue. The President countered with the assertion that the matter was now one the people of the country could "pass judgment on. I hope that we get a mandate in November."[13] It was little wonder, then, that the election returns were interpreted as they were—and that as the 89th Congress convened the numbers H.R. 1 and S. 1 were reserved for medicare.

Medicare in the 89th: Mills on Center Stage. There had never been any question on the part of either the supporters or the opponents of medicare that the single most important congressional figure to be reckoned with was Wilbur Mills. In part this was because of the nature of the issue: any bill linked to the social security system was going to be referred to Ways and Means, no questions asked: the jurisdictional precedents were clear. The Committee was second only (and perhaps equal) to Appropriations in seniority and prestige within the House, and its power was doubly secure among Democrats by virtue of the fact that its Democratic members served as the Committee on Committees for the majority. House bills, moreover, were generally brought to the floor under rules that forbade tampering with the Committee's handiwork. Bypassing Mills was thus out of the question. Nor was there any question as to Mills' preeminence over his Senate counterpart. The constitutional requirement that revenue measures originate in the House had been applied by Byrd in a manner that went far beyond the letter of the law. The Senate Committee almost *always* waited on its House counterpart—usually Ways and Means, but often other committees as well—before it acted. This practice accorded well with Byrd's natural preference for governmental inaction and with his distaste for a large or energetic staff. Mills was highly competent and conservative enough in most matters for Byrd's tastes; the Senate Chairman was thus perfectly willing to see the House "act first" and to reserve for himself the perusing of proposals for any minor flaws that might inadvertently have escaped Ways and Means' fine-toothed comb. Anderson and Gore, of course, had utilized the Senate's liberal rules on floor amendments to bypass their committee, and Long himself was already contemplating how he would break out of Byrd's mold when he got the chance. But this did not decisively alter the realities of the situation as far as the proponents of medicare were concerned: in 1965, as in 1962, Wilbur Mills was their key man. When he moved, medicare's future would be secure; until he moved, its prospects would be uncertain.

And move Mills did. HEW Secretary Anthony Celebrezze had a simple explanation: "When the President wants something badly enough, dog's ears aren't the only thing that get pulled."[14] But the differences between 1964 and 1965 had less to do with the intensity of the President's concern or the methods he employed than with alterations in the context. The 1964 Democratic landslide brought 65 new Democrats, most of them medicare supporters, into the House. The shift in party ratios made for the addition of two Democratic seats to Ways and Means, which the leadership managed to fill with medicare proponents. Mills showed little resistance and instead boarded the bandwagon. When one of his associates was asked to explain the Chairman's shift he replied "mene, mene, tekel"—the words King Belschazzer saw handwritten on the wall.[15] Mills saw that the balance in the House and perhaps even on his own committee had shifted against him. Rather than risk the possibility of losing control of his committee, losing face in the House, and decisively breaking with the President, Mills "anticipated the inevitable . . . cooperated with the inevitable . . . and then capitalized on the inevitable."[16] Besides, as Mills himself pointed out, H.R. 1 had been tailored to meet some of his earlier objections and could be tailored further.[17]

So Mills promised quick action, and Vice-President Humphrey assured the legislative conference of the AFL-CIO that medicare would be passed "before the first flower of the spring."[18] Meanwhile, congressional Republicans began devising alternatives—and quarreling among themselves. Thomas Curtis joined with Florida Democrat Sydney Herlong in introducing an "eldercare" bill, drafted by the AMA, to assist the states when and if they decided to subsidize private insurance coverage for needy individuals. The Republican leadership fastened upon a plan midway between H.R. 1 and the AMA proposal, a bill reportedly drafted by a leading insurance company.[19] Like eldercare, it was voluntary, subsidized private insurance policies, and covered doctors fees as well as hospitalization expenses. It retained a means test by making the size of a participant's premiums dependent on his income. But the minority plan, introduced by John Byrnes, ranking Republican on Ways and Means, would not have been dependent on state enabling acts and would have been administered by the federal government.

The split in Republican ranks revealed, among other things, a growing disaffection with the AMA. The Association's tactics had met with measurable success in 1950, 1960, and even 1962, but after the ominous returns of 1964 were in, the AMA embarked upon a course which made the automobile industry's response to the traffic safety issue look ingenious by comparison. Their advertising became more sensationalistic than ever; it was "revealed" that medicare would bankrupt the social security program within ten years, and claims were made for the eldercare bill which even Representative Herlong felt compelled to modify publicly. When they were called before an executive session of the Ways and Means Committee on

February 8, AMA representatives refused to discuss the bill at hand or to recommend marginal changes—the only kind that might conceivably have been accepted. "The AMA people had absolutely *nothing* constructive to offer," a member of the Committee remarked after the meeting:

> *They spouted the usual nonsense, as if we were conducting a propaganda forum rather than a serious meeting. Then, when we indicated that we weren't interested, they got rude and ungentlemanly. Even Herlong and Curtis were annoyed. The behavior of the AMA witnesses was the greatest favor that could have been done for the medicare cause. Their refusal to cooperate relieved us of any obligation to them.*

"It's amazing," Mills remarked as the AMA witnesses left the room. "They haven't learned a thing."[20]

Mills insisted that the hospital insurance funds be kept separate from other social security funds: the worker should know how much he was paying into each program, and depletions in medicare funds should not threaten the fiscal soundness of the basic OASDI program. Mills was also anxious to see any insurance program covering the services of doctors or other *personnel* put on a voluntary basis. The drafters of H.R. 1 had anticipated some of Mills' pet concerns and could have predicted some of the other changes he would make. But they were caught completely off guard by his main move. Mills, taking the Republicans more seriously than they took themselves, added the Byrnes Bill, layer-cake style, to the administration's hospital insurance plan. One observer recalled what took place in the committee room:

> *The Social Security people were caught off guard, and I suspect Cohen was too. Mills had just finished mopping up the floor with Curtis; Mills can do that, and with a lot brighter men than Curtis. Anyway, with that, Herlong just withdrew. But then came Byrnes, and Byrnes is pretty sharp. In fact, he made a very convincing case for how disappointed all these people were going to be to find that medicare didn't cover all these expenses. Well, Mills listened intently, and then he popped his layer-cake idea. . . . We assumed he was calling Byrnes' bluff, because often with these Republican bills you suspect they're not really serious about them. I would still guess that Byrnes wasn't serious in wanting to see all those things covered, though of course I'm not sure. I think Mills really thought he could bring along some Republicans by adding this to the basic bill, though of course he was partly cynical. But Mills is a consensus man and I think he was after Republican votes. Anyway, hc told the [Committee and HEW] staff people to work up an "add on" bill of this sort.*

Mills had managed something of a coup, neutralizing those critics who argued against medicare because it promised more than it could deliver and in fact turning their arguments to the support of a more comprehensive bill. The new bill, reported on March 29, gave enrollees the option of paying an additional $3 a month for coverage of doctors fees and of other professional services, tests, and treatments not included in the "mandatory" hospitalization plan. The bill also made for a seven percent across-the-board increase in OASDI benefits, extended and broadened the Kerr-Mills program, and provided additional federal support for state public assistance programs for the needy aged, blind, and disabled. Social security tax rates were raised, an increment was added to cover hospitalization insurance, and the taxable wage base was increased.

President Johnson reportedly was highly amused by Mills' coup, and Cohen, too, had nothing but praise for the Chairman's strategy:

> *Like everyone else in the room, I was stunned . . . It was the most brilliant legislative move I'd seen in thirty years. The doctors couldn't complain, because they had been carping about medicare's shortcomings and about its being compulsory. And the Republicans couldn't complain, because it was their own idea. In effect, Mills had taken the AMA's ammunition, put it in the Republicans' gun, and blown both of them off the map.[21]*

Some administration strategists had more serious misgivings about "Part B," as the voluntary plan was designated, though most of their criticism had to do with administrative details and financing methods more than with the thrust of the supplementary program. As a Social Security official put it:

> *In the short run I think we generally saw Mills' plan as a way to add needed benefits to the program. In the long run we would have preferred an integrated program with uniform financing procedures . . . I personally thought that we ought to defer the start of Part B by six months, but I didn't get anywhere with that view within the agency.*

The administration, in any case, found it politic to cooperate with Mills in reformulating the bill and to give him full backing in the changes he had made.

The administration publicly expressed opposition to only one of Mills' amendments, a provision that shifted from Part A to Part B, and thus rendered "voluntary" the coverage of services rendered to hospital patients by certain specialists. Of the same opinion were members of the Senate Aging Committee staff; they assisted Senator Paul Douglas in preparing an amendment to return the hospital services to Part A and in stimulating a show of support on the part of hospital administrators and associations across the country. But medicare proponents in the Senate did not limit their criticism to this provision; they were more skeptical about the entire layer-cake scheme than administration representatives were (or could afford to be). Even the members and staff of the Aging Committee became concerned "that we not bite off more than we could chew." Such misgivings were compounded in the case of Anderson, who found himself in basic disagreement with Mills' layer-cake idea. "Anderson's approach was conservative," one of his aides explained, "and he wanted to keep the program limited in scope and cost. He didn't want to overload the program and he could see this Part B leading to all sorts of bureaucratic tangles." But Anderson limited himself to a proposal that the beginning of the supplementary program be deferred by six months. "I bellyached about the bill at the time," he recalled, "but I wasn't going to campaign against it! My main thought at the time was how glad I was finally to get my medicare bill passed." Mills' work was not to be undone.

And then Long . . . On March 26, 1965, as the House was preparing to pass the Mills Bill, President Johnson assembled a number of congressional leaders for a television appearance. Each participant in turn praised the bill (even Smathers said he was "delighted") until only one remained to be heard from: Harry Flood Byrd. The President turned to the failing but still ruddy-cheeked Chairman: "I know that you will take an interest in the orderly scheduling of this matter and give it a thorough hearing." Byrd looked at him blankly. Johnson continued: "Would you care to make an observation?" The Chairman mustered up his best senatorial reply: "There is no observation I can make now, because the bill hasn't come before the Senate. Naturally, I'm not familiar with it." "And you have nothing that you know of," the President went on obliviously, "that would prevent [hearings] coming about in reasonable time, not anything ahead of it in the Committee?" Byrd shifted uneasily: "Nothing in the Committee now." Johnson leaned forward intently: "So when the House acts and it is referred to the Senate Finance Committee, you will arrange for prompt hearings and thorough hearings?" Byrd, barely audible, murmured "yes." At which Johnson smiled broadly, banged his fist on the table, and stared straight into the camera: "Good!"[22]

Finance Committee hearings got underway on April 29; Anderson presided most of the time and Byrd did not interfere. The major unknown factor was Russell Long, who, as de facto Committee Chairman and Majority Whip, was to manage the bill. Long served notice as Senate hearings began that he was dissatisfied with the bill's failure to cover long-term "catastrophic" illnesses; Secretary Celebrezze balked at his suggestion that the 60 days of hospital care provided in the House bill should be extended.[23] It was widely assumed that Long did not expect his criticisms to be taken seriously and that he was making them by way of saving face and coming around to a position of support.[24] But on June 17 it became clear that Long was taking himself very seriously indeed, as he took advantage of confusion and absenteeism on the Committee to secure approval of two major amendments, one providing hospitalization coverage of unlimited duration and another instituting a "dynamic deductible" to make the portion of expenses for which the patient himself was responsible dependent on his income. Cohen, Ball, and Cruikshank went to work immediately to obtain a reversal, arguing that the amendments reinstituted a means test, made it impossible for an individual to estimate his coverage more than a few months in advance, promised to make the program an "administrative monstrosity," and made cost estimates impossible. As the suspicion grew that Long in reality was out to derail the entire bill, liberal Committee members became more responsive to Anderson's pleas for reconsideration, while, by the same token, the Republicans began to line up behind Long. In the end the Committee reversed itself in two extraordinary 10-7 votes, which saw only three committee members voting exactly as they had the week before. On June 24 the bill was sent to the floor by a 12-5 vote, with only Byrd and four Republicans voting "nay."

The Committee, while rejecting Long's major modifications, did not leave the bill unchanged; some 100 amendments, most of them minor in scope, were adopted. A compromise amendment presented by Senator Hartke, which the administration chose not to oppose, took care in some measure of the "catastrophic illnesses" problem by providing for some supplementary coverage on a cost-sharing basis. The amendment offered by Douglas and the administration was accepted, thus bringing the services of certain specialists under the mandatory plan when billed through a hospital, and Anderson's amendment deferring the start of the Part B program by six months was also adopted. Further liberalizations were made in the OASDI, Kerr-Mills, and public assistance amendments, and the tax rate and wage base increases contained in the House bill were raised sufficiently to cover the Senate's program expansions.

The Finance Committee's six Republicans organized no efforts comparable to those led by Byrnes and Curtis on Ways and Means, although all of them were former medicare opponents and voted for at least one of the Long amendments. Carl Curtis, formerly a member of the House Committee, was a veteran of many medicare battles and had built up close connections with the AMA. Thinking of himself "to some extent" as a minority spokesman, he proposed dozens of major and minor alterations and cosponsored the eldercare bill introduced by Senator John Tower for the AMA. But the Finance Committee's ranking Republican, John Williams, while no friend of medicare, could not see much profit in identifying himself with Curtis' fulminations or in precipitating a long and acrimonious committee battle—and most of the other minority members shared his views. Minority Leader Dirksen may have been partly responsible for Williams' unusual display of passivity; in any case, Dirksen and Carlson went so far as to vote to report the bill, though they continued to criticize it vigorously. Senator Wallace Bennett, with Long's support, enjoyed a minor committee victory in a matter that was not as simple or inconsequential as it first appeared: an amendment was approved which designated tips as "self-employment" income for the purposes of social security (thus raising the employee's tax rate and exempting the employer from a matching contribution). But on the whole, the reported bill did not bear the stamp of the Senate minority (except for the concessions made to Javits in 1962 and 1964 and never rescinded). Long was not inclined to seek the Republicans' support except in the one instance when the majority turned against him, and Anderson and his allies, not needing Republican votes, were not inclined to solicit their views. Even if the Finance Committee minority had shared Javits' perspectives and concerns (which by and large they did not), they would not have been in a position to gain marginal concessions of the sort Javits had obtained in previous years. The medicare bill, as reported, was largely the product of majority consensus. It reflected the pet concerns of key Democratic members, but, more importantly, it reflected a decision *not* to tamper inordinately with the handiwork of Mills and the administration.

Senate hearings found the United States Chamber of Commerce and various insurance representatives lining up with the AMA. The Association itself, while exercising more tact with Finance than with Ways and Means and enjoying some success in its backstage maneuvering with Long, Curtis, and other Republicans, still found it difficult to suggest incremental changes; the AMA rather continued to recommend simply that both the basic and supplementary plans be rejected and that the Tower Bill be substituted in their place.[25] Cruikshank's statement, together with those of Celebrezze and several renegade medical and insurance representatives, highlighted the positive testimony taken by the Committee, but relatively few of labor's recommendations for added liberalizations were accepted. Cruikshank's primary role rather involved keeping the Mills Bill intact and, in particular, helping marshall the forces necessary to defeat the Long amendments.[26]

Administration, as well as AFL-CIO, strategists were willing to mute their misgivings about the House bill for the sake of mobilizing the Senate. Some executive participants were "bothered" by compromises which they or others had made, but the differences in approach which some Senate liberals had sensed among Cohen and his colleagues in the early sixties were much less discernible now. As Senate debate got underway on July 7, it looked as though vigilance and unanimity among the protagonists were very much in order; Long, while offering no amendments himself, seemed to be encouraging others to load the bill down. "My God, Mike," Anderson said at one point to Majority Leader Mansfield, "we've got a floor manager who's against the bill!"[27] But in the end, the outcome was much to the administration's liking. As Table 1 shows, while scores of amendments were offered, only two were passed which the administration openly and strongly opposed, and only one inconsequential[28] amendment

TABLE 1. Disposition of Amendments Offered During Floor Consideration of H.R. 6675, United States Senate, July 7-9, 1965.[29]

	Accepted	Rejected or Withdrawn
Opposed by Long and administration	1	13
Approved or accepted by Long and administration	28	1
Approved by Long, opposed by administration	1	3

was rejected to which the administration had given its approval. Long and the administration parted company on only four proposals, and on three of these—though not without some difficulty—administration forces carried the day.[30]

The administration's crucial test came on the first full day of debate, as Ribicoff, a long-time medicare supporter, offered a slightly modified version of Long's first committee amendment (for hospitalization benefits of unlimited duration). Douglas and Anderson begged Ribicoff not to offer it, and Cruikshank coupled his efforts at persuasion with the stimulation of a letter-writing campaign among union members in Connecticut. But Ribicoff persisted, and the Majority Leader himself delivered a rebuttal drafted by Cruikshank.[31] Long, despite an earlier promise to remain neutral, could not refrain from noting that there was a "division of opinion" among the managers of the bill and expressed his personal agreement with Ribicoff. The result was widespread confusion and a curious roll-call alignment which found the administration prevailing by only four votes. But the lines were more clearly drawn and the administration's margin of victory more secure as Curtis offered two slightly different versions of Long's second committee amendment (tying the size of the deductible to income), with Long speaking from his "own desk" in support but Ribicoff speaking for the leadership and the administration in opposition. All committee Republicans except Dirksen (who was absent) supported Curtis, plus Long, Talmadge, and Byrd. The other eight Democrats (Anderson's "hard core" of 1964, plus Smathers and Fulbright) stuck with the administration.[32]

The remaining deviant case—the amendment accepted over the objections of both Long and the administration—was introduced by Hartke. The amendment liberalized in various ways the disability insurance program for the blind and loosened the legal definition of blindness. It was a proposal which senators found difficult to oppose. Administration representatives, as a Social Security official admitted, disliked appearing pecuniary and heartless but nonetheless felt constrained to resist the changes:

That Hartke amendment is one that is often brought up, and we always have to say that the blind are not entitled to assistance out of proportion to that given to other handicapped persons, paraplegics, for example. But they have a good lobby, and there are always those who will propose that they be given special status.

Hartke's amendment was easily passed; only eleven Senators—of whom five were Finance Committee Democrats—voted against it.

The bill's final passage came on July 9 by a lopsided 68-21 margin. This time all Finance Committee Democrats, plus Carlson and Dirksen from the Republican side, were voting or paired in the affirmative. Despite the dozens of revisions that had been tacked on to the bill in committee and on the floor, it was a bill which Wilbur Mills could still justifiably claim as his own. The conference brought the measure even more closely into line. The services of hospital specialists were returned to Part B, where Mills had wanted them, the conferees rejected Anderson's proposal for a six-month delay in the start of the supplementary program, and Hartke's amendment regarding programs for the blind was dropped. The House delegation partially accepted the supplementary coverage provided by the Senate on a cost-sharing basis, but very few Senate amendments remained intact and a long list was rejected outright.[33] The Ways and Means Committee, having given the bill its broad outlines in the first place, also clearly prevailed in the amendment process.

"I can assure you," Mills told his colleagues on July 27, "anyone who voted for this bill as it passed the House can feel perfectly safe in voting for this conference report." The conference, he added, had been "very harmonious."[34] But the next day Russell Long presented a quite different picture to the Senate. As senator after senator rose to complain that his pet amendment had been deleted, Long insisted that his colleagues had "no idea how determined some of the House committee chairmen can be."

Frankly, I have sometimes gained the impression in conference with some of the senior House members that they would be opposed, if they had the opportunity, to the great compromise, even, that brought this Union into being and created the U.S. Senate.[35]

Some questions subsequently were raised about the validity of Long's portrayal of himself as the valiant defender of the Senate's handiwork, especially with respect to the Douglas amendment.[36] But most senators accepted the conference outcome as simply another reflection of the House's traditional dominance in revenue matters.

The Senate passed the conference report by a vote of 70-24, with the Finance Committee aligning itself exactly as it had on final passage. On July 30 President Johnson flew to Independence, Missouri, and signed the bill in the presence of Harry S. Truman, who twenty years before had made the first presidential request for the enactment of health insurance legislation. "We marvel not simply at the passage of this bill," said the President, "but what we marvel at is that it took so many years to pass it."[37]

Summary and Conclusions. Few proposals that came to the 89th Congress were more "mature" than was medicare; few legislative battles were more anticlimactic. All of the legislative functions either had already been performed or had been decisively underway for some time. It was partly because of this long history, the interest the proposal aroused and the difficulties it encountered, that it had become in many respects a joint executive-legislative-interest-group product.

Federal Security Agency officials primarily were responsible for the formulation of the first Murray-Wagner-Dingell bills and for the important reformulations of the early fifties which focused on the aged and gave the broad outlines to medicare in its present form. But reformulation in large and small particulars continued year after year, and the number of participants putting forward refinements and alternatives became unusually large—Anderson, Javits, Committee on Aging members and their staffs; Mills, with his remarkable "combinatorial"[38] effort of 1965; Cruikshank and his counterparts in organized medicine and insurance. Instigation and publicizing likewise took place in various forms on various levels— from the backstage maneuvering of Cohen, Falk, and Cruikshank, to the stimulation of grass-roots support by NCSC and the Committee on Aging, to the promptings of Forand, King, Anderson, and Douglas in the halls of Congress. But the most decisive publicizing moves came as Truman, Kennedy, and Johnson took up the cause; this function, like formulation, was in the end dominated, though hardly monopolized, by the executive branch.

Partly because of the interest and involvement of executive officials and partly by virtue of the uniqueness of its own resources, the executive branch dominated the processes of information-gathering as well. All participants, from Cruikshank to Curtis to Douglas were dependent on the statistics and the counsel of the Social Security Administration, and executive participants like Cohen and Ball who wished to shape the legislation found in their own resources and expertise an indispensable buttress. But congressional and group strategists like Cruikshank, Mills, and Anderson developed considerable information resources of their own, and the Committee on Aging in particular, blocked from direct legislative involvement, used its information resources to good advantage in making a new and compelling case for medicare.

When one turns to the peculiar kind of "information" comprised by the sentiments of various interest groups—and to the accommodation of those groups' preferences and the utilization of their energies—the picture becomes much more pluralistic and diverse, though the executive branch still looms very prominently. Organized labor went first of all to HEW and the White House; no one doubted that the "aggregation" of labor's interests was to be defined in terms far more of preserving the administration's draft intact than of securing marginal expansions in committee and on the floor. This represented a complete reversal of the patterns of interest-aggregation of the fifties, as did the fact that it was now the AMA that was forced to turn to Congress. But most other groups as well found Capitol Hill the more promising point of access, including those who favored the bill and desired to expand it for the benefit of one group or another. Cohen and his collaborators had continually sought to alter the draft as little as possible between and within congressional sessions, but congressional participants, particularly senators, rarely shared this defensiveness.

Mobilization, at one level, was the work of Mills, Anderson, and even Long. All championed the bill with some vigor and used their influence to bring reluctant members into line. But the two floor managers had themselves been in need of mobilization for some years; they were moved only by impressive displays of public and congressional sentiment and an unmistakable expression of the President's priorities. The Democratic leadership assumed a considerable role, and Dirksen's decision not to attempt a counter-mobilization was also important. Presidential mobilization was effected not only through agenda-setting and the election returns; its impact could be direct and compelling, as the rejection of the Ribicoff amendment demonstrated. Interest groups were also partially responsible for the mobilization of members on both sides, but the 1962 episode clearly demonstrated not only that group efforts might cancel one another out, but also that interest groups, no matter how skillful or active, had certain limitations as mobilizing agents.

The modification process, finally, was notable for the number and diversity of congressional participants and interest groups that got into the act—but also for the relative *absence* of executive involvement. Democratic, pro-medicare administrations generally presented their bills as finished products, however they might have been modified from their *past* forms, and entered the process of amendment only in a negative fashion, if at all, thereafter. In 1965, for example, the administration suggested only one amendment to Mills' bill, gave only the blandest endorsement to additional Senate amendments, and reserved its energy for an all-out fight against the Ribicoff proposal. The modification process, therefore, was on the whole left to Congress and the interest groups. Labor, as previously noted, did *not* expend a great amount of energy trying to "strengthen" the bill, primarily because of Cruikshank's close collaboration with the administration and his conviction that the first draft was worth defending. But the hand of medical, insurance, and "senior citizen" groups, of associations of the blind and disabled, and of hospitals, nursing homes, and various professional associations was obvious in many attempts at modification, particularly in the Finance Committee and on the Senate floor.

Medicare furnishes an initial glimpse of the Finance Committee which will be embellished in the case histories to follow. The episode points up Harry Byrd's legacy of conservatism and tight committee control and permits some anticipation of the changes and difficulties that were to result from Long's ascendance to the chairmanship. It provides a nodding acquaintance with the members, few of whom could be termed liberals or activists but a number of whom were willing to help a wide range of interest groups obtain marginal benefits. The Committee's subject matter emerges as partisan and controversial, and its setting as replete with interest groups enjoying considerable access and influence in both branches but finding Senate rules and Finance Committee norms particularly congenial. Perhaps most striking, however, are two additional environmental factors seen clearly in this case history: the executive branch executing a complex and coordinated legislative effort, mobilizing both the Finance Committee and its parent chamber; and the House Committee on Ways and Means continually casting a shadow on the operations of its Senate counterpart.

THE SUGAR ACT AMENDMENTS OF 1965

Sugar and the Law. Medicare was not the only matter that concerned the Finance Committee during the first session of the 89th Congress, though it often seemed to overshadow everything else. Among the other bills processed as the session drew to a close was one revising and extending the Sugar Act. This bill took less time and energy than medicare, though not as much less as one might suppose. It had to do with a different area of Committee jurisdiction, a different set of lobbyists, a different House committee, and different executive agencies. Instead of momentous policy innovations, it for the most part proposed the continuation of a going program. Yet the Sugar Act of 1965 was, in many ways, handled in the same fashion as medicare; certainly the Committee, in processing the legislation, displayed many of the same characteristics.

The sugar program began, as a veteran lobbyist put it, "back during the Depression, when the industry was really flat on its ass." Since the early days of the Republic, domestic sugar producers had been protected by tariffs, but low-cost competition from the Caribbean had often been staved off only to be replaced by domestic overproduction as a factor in depressing prices. Then came the general economic collapse. The Jones-Costigan Act of 1934 introduced a system of quotas whereby certain portions of the market were reserved for various domestic and foreign producers.

By limiting the total amount of sugar that could be marketed, the quota system stabilized prices. But it also pegged sugar prices in the United States considerably above those prevailing in most other countries and thus made the possession of a generous quota highly profitable. The result was constant jockeying among various classes of producers, domestic and foreign, for an increased share of the market. Changes in the law were frequent and congressional battles often stormy; the Sugar Act revisions of 1965 represented the eighth time the quotas had been revamped since their temporary suspension during World War II.[39]

Prior to the war, domestic producers had been allowed to supply approximately 55 percent of the overall marketing quota, a quantity determined at the beginning of each year by the Secretary of Agriculture. The Sugar Act of 1948 gave various domestic areas (mainland beet, mainland cane, Hawaii, Puerto Rico, and the Virgin Islands) and the newly independent Republic of the Philippines fixed tonnage quotas instead of fixed percentages of the overall quota. Sugar needed over and above these fixed tonnages would be purchased from foreign producers; 98.6 percent of the difference between the fixed quotas and the overall quota was reserved for Cuba. The effect of these revisions was to increase domestic producers' share of the market. Mainland refineries were protected by limitations on the shipment of "direct-consumption" sugar into the United States from offshore or foreign processors; quotas were to be filled mainly with raw sugar.

Subsequent legislation further improved the position of domestic producers, both increasing their fixed tonnage quotas and giving them a percentage share of each year's supplementary quota. Various Latin American nations were also given increased shares of the supplementary quota. Cuba's percentage share of the market had thus diminished somewhat before 1959, though its quota remained large and its sugar industry, largely U.S.-built and owned, continued to benefit from the inflated American market price and preferential tariff treatment.[40] But when the revolutionary regime of Fidel Castro began seizing property owned by United States citizens, the Eisenhower administration requested discretionary power to cancel and reassign the Cuban quota. The authority was granted, but not until Chairman Harold D. Cooley and his House Agriculture Committee had given the administration precise guidelines as to which domestic and foreign producers were to benefit from the redistribution of the Cuban quota.

On both the Cuban bill and the administration's later attempt to reassign the quota of one of the bills' chief beneficiaries, the Dominican Republic,[41] the Senate Finance Committee supported the President's request for broad discretion. While there was some feeling that the House Committee was attempting inordinately to tie the President's hands in the conduct of foreign policy, a more important consideration for most senators was Cooley's apparent desire to give foreign rather than domestic producers the benefits of quota reassignments. The Finance Committee contained several members from areas that were or wanted to be heavily engaged in sugar production, but "the House Agriculture Committee," Senator Russell Long charged in a Senate speech, contained "few members who [were] very interested in domestic production."[42] In addition, a group of senators, for whom Senator Paul Douglas emerged as spokesman, were becoming increasingly resentful at the way foreign governments and industries were benefiting from inflated U.S. prices at the expense of American consumers. Therefore, when the House in 1961 finally approved a bill allowing the President to cut back the Dominican quota, the Senate Finance Committee added a Douglas amendment imposing an import fee equal to the difference between the domestic and world prices on foreign producers filling the Cuban quota, while an Anderson amendment providing that the Cuban quota should be reallocated to domestic producers before foreign producers was accepted on the floor. Both amendments were subsequently dropped, but Cooley promised action on a long-range bill designed to improve the position of domestic producers and the administration went to work in devising its own import fee proposal.

In 1962 President Kennedy sent a request for extensive revisions of the Sugar Act to Capitol Hill. He proposed substantial increases in the quotas of domestic mainland producers. He also asked for several revisions of the foreign quota system, including a variant of the import fee scheme Douglas had put forward the year before. A substantial quota, albeit a reduced one, was to be "reserved" for Cuba, and friendly countries were to be allowed to bid for their share of it. Those filling the Cuban allotment were to pay an import fee equal to the difference between the American and world prices. Importers filling quotas of their own (except for the Philippines) would at first pay a fee equal to only twenty percent of the fee paid on Cuban quota sugar, but stairstep increases would result in their paying the full fee by 1966. The hope was that by the end of this period, the price advantage or "premium" having been eliminated, the country-by-country quota system could be abandoned entirely. Only a "global quota" would be assigned; foreign producers would look on the American market as they did on their other markets and enter into open competition for their share.

Cooley agreed with the administration's recommendations for increased domestic quotas but with little else in the bill. The Agriculture Committee reported the measure only after removing the import fee entirely, assigning permanent quotas to thirty countries, reducing the Cuban quota still further, and specifying the eleven countries to whom it was to be reallocated. The Committee was widely accused of pandering to foreign sugar interests, whose lobbyists, Senator Fulbright observed, were "as thick as flies."[43] The Finance Committee secured Senate approval of the administration bill with few amendments and managed to secure some important concessions in conference: it was determined that friendly countries would compete for their share of the Cuban quota and pay the full import fee. But the House conferees secured guaranteed quotas for 28 foreign countries, and the administration's proposed five-step application of the full import fee to regular quota imports was scaled down drastically. A termination date of 1966 was set for the relatively noncontroversial domestic quota provisions, but the foreign quotas were given an expiration date of 1964. No one doubted that the entire matter would at that point be re-opened.

Certain crucial aspects of the politics of sugar are already evident from this sketch of postwar developments. The sugar program was designed to benefit certain domestic interests and to stimulate and stabilize the economies of certain foreign nations. It was therefore virtually certain that domestic growers and refiners and various foreign governments would become actively involved in policy-making. It was also certain that the relations between these participants would be competitive and conflictful. There was no once-and-for-all "solution" to be reached. Almost every producer wanted a greater share of the market than he had; what was a gain for one was a loss for another. Although the absolute growth of the market softened the impact of shifts in quotas, the fact remained that an increase in the quota of domestic cane producers took a share of the market that might have gone to domestic beet producers, that Brazil's gain could be seen as Peru's loss, and so forth. Pressures were constantly exerted, and the responses of policy-makers to them, far from making for any final resolution or adjustment, resulted in constant fluctuations in the law.

Furthermore, this was a policy area which neither the executive nor the legislative branch could easily dominate to the exclusion of the other. The sugar program required an extensive administrative apparatus. It required large-scale statistical and information services. It called for an overview and an equilibrating of the interests of conflicting groups and regions. It involved the coordination of policies related to domestic agriculture, foreign affairs, tariffs, taxation, and trade. It required, in short, the resources and the perspectives of the President and the federal bureaucracy. Yet sugar policy was political through and through. The interests involved were powerful in a number of states and congressional districts, and they always wanted more than they had. The way the program was devised and administered was a matter of vital concern; attacks on the system were inevitable, and their location was most often the decentralized and locally-oriented Congress. All of the participants had a stake in the going program; a return to the pre-1934 state of nature would have been a victory for none. But the contemplation of a hypothetical *bellum omnium in omnes* was ordinarily not sufficient to compel common acquiescence to the *status quo.*

"The Necessity of Action." The Johnson administration in 1964 was faced with the necessity of securing an extension of the foreign quota provisions of the Sugar Act. But a number of administration officials were becoming increasingly disillusioned with the operation of the global quota and import fee provisions adopted in 1962 and thus probably welcomed the early expiration date. One problem was technical, but it had very tangible policy consequences—the elusive and fluctuating character of the "world price." Most sugar was not sold on the open market but was exchanged between nations on a quota or treaty basis; the "world price" applied to only about ten percent of the world supply. The price was applicable mainly to sugar traded at the margins; it was subject to wild fluctuations and often had little relation to the actual rates at which most sugar was exchanged.

A second problem was related to the *political* difficulties involved in imposing an import fee based on this ephemeral standard. The administration's proposal of 1962 had made for a sharp differentiation between nations filling regular quotas and those competing for the Cuban quota. The House bill—increasing the list of nations holding regular quotas and reducing the fees to be imposed upon them—had accentuated this disparity. Those filling the hypothetical Cuban quota, "reserved" only in name, thus apparently were being discriminated against; the imposition on them of an import fee became increasingly problematic. As an Agriculture Department official related, the import fee idea, "never very firmly established" in the first place, fell increasingly into disrepute.

> The original argument rested on the need to keep the Cuban quota available [as an incentive for Cuba to "rejoin" the West] and to keep any nation from making a lot of money on it and getting a vested interest in seeing Cuba stay out. But as five, six years went by, keeping that Cuban quota available seemed less important. And there was always a strong argument on the other side: the need for us to encourage trade with all these countries and help their economies.

Certain developments in the world sugar market in 1963 made the administration's difficulties much more severe but gave rise to disputes that blocked all prospects for change. Cuba's decision to diversify her economy and poor beet sugar crops in Europe resulted in plummeting world inventories. The world price, always mercurial, increased from 2.5 cents per pound in mid-1962 to 12 cents per pound a year later. The United States price also rose, but not as drastically; for 15 months, until June, 1964, the world price was *above* the domestic price.[44] It thus became profitable for foreign suppliers to sell their sugar on the world market and to neglect their U.S. quotas. Some of them did so, though others considered it politic to forego immediate gain and fill their allotment. There was, of course, little incentive to compete for the Cuban quota. Domestic growers, meanwhile, had a strong economic incentive to plant larger crops and the Department of Agriculture, uncertain of the intentions of foreign suppliers, chose not to impose crop limitations. Therefore, as the crisis receded, domestic cane and beet growers, still restricted by marketing quotas, found themselves with unusually large inventories on hand.

The events of 1963 thus made for an increasing disillusionment within the administration with the global quota-import fee scheme and a strong feeling that quotas should be revised so as to reward the foreign suppliers who had met their quotas during times when it would have been profitable to sell elsewhere. More pressing, however, were the problems posed by the bulging warehouses of domestic producers. So the administration proposed unlimited marketing of domestic sugar in 1964, coupled with the withholding of a large portion of the Cuban and other unfilled foreign quotas which otherwise would have been reassigned. As for the foreign quota system, only a six-month stopgap extension was requested, deferring this issue until 1965.

The administration, however, got no legislation at all from the 88th Congress. The reason, basically, was a split within the domestic sugar industry which found expression in Congress. The beet growers, who had the largest inventories on hand, were strongly in favor of the President's proposal. While domestic cane growers, whose quotas and inventories were smaller, were less enthusiastic, the cane sugar refineries were outspoken in their opposition. Some 60 percent of the sugar which they processed was of foreign origin; they could hardly back a proposal that would take quotas ordinarily filled by foreign cane growers and hand them over to domestic beet growers. The summer of 1964 found beet and cane interests and refiners meeting with each other, with Cooley, and with Agriculture Department officials, drafting and redrafting proposals but failing to find a basis for agreement. The beet growers had to find a market for their inventories; the refiners feared that if domestic quotas were increased, even temporarily, the result would be an expansion of the beet sugar industry that would make the future reduction of the beet quota in favor of foreign suppliers virtually impossible. Cooley objected to what he regarded as favoritism toward the beet interests on the part of the administration, announcing on September 8 that there was "no possibility of enactment of a sugar bill, which is opposed by either one of these influential groups." This prompted two of his junior committee members to protest "the influences of refiners of foreign cane sugar on the committee leadership"; but the Chairman was master of the situation and did not budge.[45]

The Department of Agriculture then took administrative measures to continue the sugar program despite the expiration of the foreign quotas, but was careful to preserve the incentives Congress had to pass legislation the following year. The overall national quota was set below expected consumption levels, with the reduction coming mainly at the expense of foreign suppliers. This made it possible to contemplate assigning additional quotas to domestic producers without glutting the market, but it also ensured that each group would continue to have a stake in the passage of legislation. The domestic growers still wanted to market their surpluses. The refiners, besides being unhappy at the reduction of foreign quotas, were still anxious to secure the enactment of a country-by-country quota system, without import fees, which would lower their costs and ensure a steady foreign supply. And all were anxious to get a new basic law on the books, to reduce uncertainty and to stabilize their situation.

By late 1964 the refiners and growers realized, as an Agriculture official put it, that "it was going to have to be a give and take situation. . . . Tempers had cooled off a good bit, and they were ready to talk sense." This time the administration refrained from casting its weight on one side or the other, making it clear that no new appeal to Congress would come prior to industry agreement. Cooley likewise served notice that he would not move until the conflict was resolved. By February of 1965 a compromise had been reached. Industry leaders, significantly enough, took the plan first of all to Cooley and his senior committee members; it was after this group gave its approval that the refiners and growers took their plan to the administration.

Negotiations in the executive branch involved primarily the Departments of Agriculture and State and the Bureau of the Budget. There was little congressional participation or interference in the formulation of the administration bill. One reason for this, of course, was the fact that the interests themselves were actively engaged in the formulation process; there was less need for involvement on the part of their congressional intermediaries. In addition, both of the relevant congressional committees contained representatives of all the competing interests, and all realized that the alternative to compromise was deadlock. Given that fact, both committees were content to have the balancing and adjustment of interests take place in the executive arena; removing the process to Congress could only result in great amounts of work, bruising battles within or between committees, and probably only a slightly different outcome. "I don't think Congress wanted to get too involved," an Agriculture Department official observed. "This is always a hot one for them to handle, and they were just as glad for us to do it. They didn't enter the picture until we sent the bill up, though of course we had them in mind all along." A Finance Committee staff man confirmed this report:

> This whole thing came up to us as a package, all worked out. That is unusual, but it suited the situation. These sugar bills can be awfully tough . . . I'm sure certain senators must have been consulted, but the Committee staff wasn't involved until the bill was sent up and the agreements had been made . . . People like Irvin Hoff and Bob Shields

[refinery and beet lobbyists, respectively] were coming up here arm in arm, and that's really unusual. So we avoided the big fights.

The compromise formula was in legislative form by May. It gave domestic beet and cane growers a chance to dispose of their surplus inventories; their fixed quotas would be permanently raised by 580,000 tons, at the expense of foreign suppliers. However, these domestic producers would then be denied their share of market growth. As the overall marketing quota expanded from its new base figure of 9.7 million tons, *all* of the supplementary sugar required would be purchased from foreign suppliers —until the overall consumption level reached 10.4 million tons annually, at which point the old ratio between domestic and foreign quotas would be reestablished. Market growth beyond that point would again be shared. Domestic producers thus received a short-term quota increase, but they failed to secure a permanent increased share of the market. The refineries accepted a short-term curtailment of their market but managed to hold the line against a permanent erosion of their share. Some congressional partisans felt that the beet growers—faced with a desperate situation in their own warehouses and to some extent abandoned by a formerly partisan administration—had been forced into an unfavorable settlement. But the reaction of an executive participant was revealing:

It doesn't seem to me that any segment got a better deal than any other. [Well, several Committee people seemed to imply that beet . . .] Got the better of the deal? [No, just the opposite.] Well, you see, I didn't know which way it was going to be. You'd expect both sides to say they got the short end of the stick.

A single witness represented all segments of the domestic sugar industry in congressional hearings. That "all of the groups concerned, both industry and . . . executive agencies" had reached agreement on a single bill, he told both committees, was "something of a miracle." Congress, he continued, should find this fact of "great advantage" and should proceed to ratify the settlement before it began to disintegrate.

Failure to achieve sugar legislation this year would so further aggravate frictions within the industry as to make it practically certain that the industry would be unable to achieve unanimity next year.

Hence the "necessity of action:"[46]

Congress was quick to approve the agreement. Some noises were made by partisans of one or another segment of the industry, but the interests themselves could not openly countenance such attacks. When certain representatives from beet-growing districts made it clear that they were "supporting the package only reluctantly," a lobbyist for the refiners recalled, "the beet growers had to say that they stood by the agreement that had been reached. If undercover business had gone on to any great extent it would have undermined everything." The committees were themselves balanced between the interests, anxious to pass a bill, and reluctant to reopen the battle. The provisions of the administration bill having to do with domestic quotas, largely a ratification of agreements reached with the industry, were left intact.

Cooley and the Foreign Quotas. It at first seems strange that the Finance Committee should have jurisdiction over sugar legislation—as various chairmen of the Senate Agriculture and Foreign Relations Committees have from time to time pointed out. But it is no more strange than the fact that matters of social security and health insurance are handled by Finance rather than Labor and Public Welfare. The controlling principle is in both cases clear: any measure involving taxes or tariffs, regardless of its substance, is referred to the Finance Committee. Before 1934 tariffs were the main instrument of national sugar policy, and the Sugar Act itself included an excise or processing tax on domestic manufacturers and an import fee on the small quantities of refined sugar coming from abroad.[47] The addition of the general import fee provisions of 1962 made Finance's jurisdiction even more secure. In fact, it is the involvement of House Agriculture that requires explanation, for the jurisdiction of the House Ways and Means Committee on any matter affecting the tax structure is, if anything, more firmly established than that of Finance. Ways and Means had jurisdiction over the Jones-Costigan Act of 1934. It was only in 1937 that Agriculture entered the picture; a personal deal was struck by the chairmen of the two committees, and Agriculture handled the act's renewal.[48] It is now unlikely that Ways and Means will ever regain jurisdiction, but the involvement of Agriculture is based only on a long-forgotten personal agreement and the force of custom.

While House Agriculture's dominance in sugar policy formation thus has its ironic aspects, the reasons for the failure of the Senate Committee to exercise coordinate control are not difficult to find. Sugar policy is only remotely related to most of the issues being considered by the Finance Committee, while Agriculture is dealing with related matters every day. This—in addition to the general tendency of representatives to specialize more than senators—makes for relatively higher levels of interest and expertise in the House. It also gives the House Committee greater leverage with the administration. As one lobbyist observed in 1967:

> You've got to remember that this is the only agriculture bill Finance is handling. It's one of several for House Agriculture. So Cooley has more leverage over Tom Murphy [Director of Sugar Policy Staff, Department of Agriculture] than Long does. Cooley can say to [Secretary of Agriculture Orville] Freeman, "Well, if you don't give in on sugar, we'll mess you up on those three or four other bills." With Finance, it's a one-shot arrangement.

Agriculture has other advantages over Finance, many of which are similar to those enjoyed by Ways and Means in the area of tax policy. The fact that the Sugar Act contained tax provisions gave the House Agriculture Committee grounds for refusing to receive a sugar bill the Senate had originated in 1960. At that time the House backed Cooley with the passage of a resolution declaring the Senate's action to be unconstitutional. But constitutional strictures rarely had to be forced upon Harry Byrd; in most policy areas he was perfectly willing to let Cooley and Mills, with whom he had few sharp disagreements, assume initial legislative responsibility. One lobbyist insisted that most of Byrd's members "wouldn't have wanted it any other way," at least on matters of sugar policy:

> *Of course they gripe about getting the bill late in the session, about not having the time to work on it, and so forth. But do you think they would want to have days and days of hearings and do all that work that the House Committee does?*

In any case, Byrd led his Committee into a role that reinforced the House's constitutional preeminence and extended the pattern beyond the realm of fiscal policy.

Some Senate Committee members, however, had substantial complaints about Cooley's dominance—usually centering on his indifference to domestic producers and his reponsiveness to refiners and foreign producers —and attempted from time to time to use the Committee as an alternative source of legislation. They usually met with little success, but the 1962 episode and the Senate's passage of a Bennett bill favoring domestic producers during the 1964 deadlock served notice that the Finance Committee was emerging as a force to be reckoned with. These legislative attempts also showed the views of most Finance Committee members, of those from beet- and cane-producing areas alike, to be closer to those of the administration than were the views of the House group, dominated as it was by Cooley. To this natural coincidence of views in 1965 was added the fact that Russell Long, who was in line for the Finance Committee Chairmanship and had already taken over many leadership functions because of Byrd's illness, was also the newly appointed Majority Whip. It was thus not surprising that the Finance Committee emerged as defender of the administration's interests. The need for such defense arose when Cooley, having left the delicate balance between domestic and foreign quotas undisturbed, decided to revamp the foreign quotas themselves.

The administration had been beset by difficulties and delays in formulating the foreign quota provisions, and the process had dragged out over most of the summer. President Johnson heralded the bill's introduction by announcing to a group of Latin American ambassadors on August 17 that the controversial import fee was to be dropped.[49] Besides settling certain administrative and foreign policy dilemmas, the dropping of the fee had the added advantage of pleasing the refineries and Mr. Cooley. Also sure to please them was the decision to drop the concept of an unassigned global quota to be allocated on a competitive basis. The entire foreign quota, including the hypothetical Cuban reserve, was instead to be divided among 30 foreign countries on a percentage basis,[50] and the suppliers were to be paid at the full American price. As for the actual distribution of foreign quotas, the refiners and domestic growers professed indifference. But here Mr. Cooley also had definite ideas, ideas which meant trouble for the administration's plan.

The administration's basic premise was that the quotas should be distributed in such a way as to reward the countries which had continued to supply the U.S. market during the crisis of 1963-64. Not one of their proposed allotments was left intact by the Agriculture Committee, but it was not clear on what basis they were changed. A prominent lobbyist for the refineries defended the reasonableness of Cooley's changes: the House Committee, he claimed, "looked at performance and production over a long period [rather than] the abnormal years of 1963-64" and moved toward the pre-crisis quotas of 1962. Others, including Agriculture Department representatives testifying before the Finance Committee, found the allocations "subjective" and without a consistent rationale.[51] From other sources came more pointed accusations: Representatives Odin Langen and Paul Findley claimed to find direct relationships between the granting of new or increased quotas and the extent of various countries' lobbying activities.[52] Cooley hotly denied "all these vicious insinuations and innuendos," but the impression persisted among a wide range of participants that foreign pressures had had a great deal to do with the House's revisions. "A lot of things probably entered in," an administration official reflected—

> how good a customer of the U.S. a country had been, how an individual member happened to feel about this or that country, and so forth . . . It's hard to pin down the "influence" of the sugar lobbyists on the Committee. Sometimes I think the congressmen themselves don't know when they've been "influenced." [Well, could you approach it by comparing the Agriculture Department, the House Committee, and the Senate Committee as to their responsiveness to these foreign lobbyists?] Yes, I think you can generalize about that. We all give them a hearing and get information from them. I'd say the House Committee is where they get their best reception, though.

Cooley had to cope with an unusual amount of restlessness within his committee.[53] Four Democratic members issued a statement opposing the addition of a Bahamas quota, allegedly for the benefit of a single company, and Findley secured a rule which permitted him to bring two amendments (one reimposing an import fee and the other cancelling the quota of any country which hereafter employed a lobbyist) to a vote on the floor. But the House passed the bill without amendment on October 13 and sent it to the Senate in the midst of the rush for adjournment. Long convened Finance Committee hearings the next day.

It was widely charged that the administration had deferred inordinately to Cooley, possibly by way of rewarding him for his cooperation on the omnibus farm bill earlier in the session.[54] But witnesses from the Departments of Agriculture and State publicly urged the Senate Committee to restore the original bill's "objective" quota system. They were not given a particularly cordial reception: Douglas objected strenuously to the dropping of the import fee, and several Committee members, including Foreign Relations Chairman Fulbright, went on to argue that if the sugar program was to be frankly regarded as an instrument of foreign aid, providing windfalls to various countries, then foreign policy considerations—not the trade patterns of 1963-1964—should govern quota distributions. On foreign policy grounds there was much to complain about: the House, Douglas noted, had lowered the administration's quotas for South Africa, Southern Rhodesia, and various French dependencies; "As between the State Department and Congressman Cooley," he declared, "I am for Congressman Cooley."[55] Fulbright proposed that a decision on foreign quotas be deferred until the next congressional session, at which time "normal hearings" could be held and an alternative distribution could be devised.[56]

While these and other accumulated grievances made for two stormy days of hearings, they did not result in the Finance Committee's turning its back on the administration's requests. Of the 33 foreign quotas which the House Committee had revised or added, the Senate Committee returned 21 to the exact administration figure and moved six more in that direction.[57] The Committee rejected Fulbright's proposed deletion of the foreign quota provisions and Douglas' proposed reimposition of an import fee, prompting the *Times* to observe that Long was "firmly in command,"[58] but a limitation of the foreign quota provisions to a two-year period took care in some measure of Fulbright's concern. This meant that the entire matter would soon be reconsidered and that in the future foreign quotas could be considered separately from domestic quotas (which were not to expire until 1971). The Committee moved the bill further into line with the administration's wishes by removing some, but not all, of the House's "special interest" amendments[59] and by deleting an amendment which, by requiring the Secretary of Agriculture to give preference to suppliers willing to purchase additional U.S. agricultural products, restricted his ability to secure sugar quickly under emergency conditions.

Senators Gore and Douglas appended dissenting views to the Committee *Report*, condemning the entire sugar program for its maintenance of artificially high prices and its provision of windfalls to foreign and domestic producers at the consumer's expense. But the way to passage was indeed, as Douglas complained, "greased," and floor consideration was perfunctory.[60] A second prediction Douglas had made then came true as well:

> We shall probably face, in a few days, the bill agreed upon in conference, which will probably be much closer to the House version than the Senate version, because . . . when a sugar bill comes to conference . . . it is the House which almost always prevails.[61]

On the whole the conference report could fairly be called a "substantial victory" for Cooley.[62] The amendment requiring the Secretary to give preference to countries who were willing to buy U.S. agricultural products was retained. Thirty-one foreign quotas were agreed upon; of these, 12 were exactly equal to the House figure, and two of the three countries which the Senate had added were dropped. In only six cases where the Senate had altered the House quota did the Senate prevail, and in the cases where a compromise figure was reached, the final quota was generally closer to the House figure. But the most important concession Cooley obtained had to do with the expiration date of the legislation. The conference bill, like the House bill, provided that both foreign and domestic quotas would be untouchable for five years, a fact that pleased the refiners and the bill's foreign beneficiaries greatly. Equally important from Cooley's point of view was the fact that foreign and domestic quotas would continue to be considered as a "package," thus permitting him to threaten disruption of the domestic program as a means of securing concessions on foreign allotments.

Sugar: Who Makes the Laws? Recent studies stress the oversimplification implicit in a mere group interaction or "pressure" model of the policy process.[63] While this provides a needed corrective to conspiratorial stereotypes, the present case suggests that, at least in the area of sugar policy, the older view still has considerable applicability. Very few policy areas can be named, in fact, where the major interest groups involved have a freer hand to write their own legislative ticket.[64] The 1965 episode demonstrated this at every turn. The Kennedy administration's original formulation had failed, not because it had left group interests out of account, but because it had supposedly heeded the wishes of beet growers at the expense of domestic refiners dependent on foreign suppliers. The reformulation of 1964-65 thus became essentially a matter of intra-industry negotiation and agreement, partly presided over but hardly directed by the administration. Additional policy-making functions fell to the interests in large measure as well: the gathering and interpretation of relevant information, the instigation of congressional action, the mobilization of support for the compromise measure.

How can this group hegemony be explained? An important clue is to be found in the fact that the domestic growers and refiners represent, to use Theodore Lowi's terminology, a *distributive* interest, i.e. one whose policy preferences can be implemented "more or less in isolation from other [interests] and from any general rule."[65] In short, the sugar lobby has no effective competition. The domestic sugar interests are not without their internal conflicts, of course, but in the end the interests that they share are far more important than those that divide them. And their common interest, while perhaps squaring imperfectly with larger conceptions of the public good, can nonetheless be implemented without coming into direct or frequent conflict with the interests of other well-organized or powerful groups.

Distributive interests are frequently regional in character; this helps explain why they can be dealt with discretely and how policy-making patterns of "mutual noninterference" and logrolling can grow up around them. It also suggests that those interests will often find extraordinarily strong support in Congress.[66] Sugar, no less than fishing, shipping, mining, textiles, and a number of agricultural commodity programs, is a matter of great interest to various states and regions and their representatives. This fact, if it helps prevent one segment of the domestic industry from gaining ascendance over the other, also helps give the refiners and growers collectively a firm anchorage in the policy-making process.

To the advantages accruing from the distributive and localized character of the sugar interests must be added those of a skillful and well-financed lobbying operation. But this "strength" itself calls for explanation, and once again Mancur Olson's discussion of the prerequisites of effective group action can provide helpful insights.[67] If the fair packaging episode demonstrated that "policy entrepreneurs" could to a degree transcend the pressures and demands of highly organized "special interests" on behalf of more poorly organized but more widely shared consumer interests, it must also be acknowledged that the sugar episode bears out Olson's expectations remarkably well. Substantial consumer interests were at stake, as Senators Gore and Douglas strenuously pointed out, but the weakness of consumer group organization and the low visibility of the sugar program as a public issue, coupled with the scale of the sugar lobby's efforts, its effectiveness in mobilizing the energies of its own constituency, and the strength of its support in Congress and the bureaucracy, doomed the protests of the prophets of the public interest to futility.

When we turn from the domestic growers and refiners to the other groups playing a major part in the 1965 drama, the foreign producers, we find interests whose role in the process—appearances to the contrary notwithstanding—was less stable and secure. The successes of the foreign sugar lobbyists in general and of some specific countries in particular could be attributed in part to the support they enjoyed among the domestic refiners whom they supplied. The refiners, of course, fought for an enlarged foreign quota in 1964-65, and, though they professed neutrality in the subsequent battle over how the quota was to be divided, many of them generally approved of Cooley's alterations in the administration plan. But Cooley was responsive not simply to the refiners but to the foreign suppliers themselves, as uncertain and puzzling as the precise reasons for that responsiveness were; if that gave certain foreign suppliers decided advantages in 1965, it provided no sure basis for predicting how the House Committee would respond in the future, even when Cooley's faithful ally, W. R. Poage, succeeded to the Chairmanship.[68] The foreign suppliers had a number of large-scale lobbying operations going, involving several of Washington's more prominent law firms, but the various countries were perpetually in conflict and lacked secure bases of support in Congress and the bureaucracy. This meant that both the administration and the committees of Congress were free to implement their own standards and preferences to a degree that was not possible on the larger question of the balance between the domestic and foreign quotas. It also meant that the equilibration of the interests in this area was less "given"; it might display relatively wide variations, in other words, with a change of administrations or the departure of congressional partisans like Cooley.

While the development of the basic compromise contained in the 1965 legislation reveals the determinative role domestic interests play in this particular area of public policy, the subsidiary battle over the distribution of the foreign quotas provides a fuller picture of the relationships and roles obtaining among the decision-making bodies occupying the field. The importance of the Sugar Policy office—as a gatherer of information on the state of the program and the industry, as an access point for the domestic interests and referee of their negotiations, as informant and peacemaker among congressional partisans—should be given due notice, as should the relatively independent roles of Agriculture and State as formulators of the foreign quota provisions and mobilizers of administration forces in the Senate. But this was an area where Congress retained a certain hegemony; the administration could expect to have its handiwork remain intact only where adequate consultation had been undertaken and attention to congressional preferences given beforehand.

The main force to be reckoned with on Capitol Hill, for reasons already discussed, was the House Agriculture Committee. Its leaders were consulted throughout the formulation process, and on those sections of the bill where their wishes had been ignored—the distribution of the foreign quotas—they opened up a second front of interest-aggregation and mobilized the House in favor of their own alternative formulation. The sugar bill, however, like medicare, found the Senate Finance Committee taking notable steps away from the patterns of action (and inaction) established under Byrd's leadership. A professional staff was for the first time being assembled, with the result that Finance Committee members had an independent, if hardly comprehensive, store of information on which to base their responses to House and administration proposals. On several questions the Senate Committee developed a third alternative, though it could not fairly be said that the Committee had yet emerged as an independent or innovative source of legislative initiative in the area. More significant, both as a deviation from the Byrd pattern and as a foretaste of what was to come in other policy areas, was the increasing willingness of the Finance Committee to champion the position of the administration in the Senate and in conference. This growing responsiveness to the White House, partially concealed in the medicare episode by the fact that Ways and Means itself took up the administration banner and by Long's persistence in championing hostile amendments, was to be demonstrated several more times before the 89th Congress adjourned.

THE UNEMPLOYMENT INSURANCE AMENDMENTS OF 1966

"Long Overdue." "We're great on social legislation," AFL-CIO lobbyists began wryly to tell one another as 1966 wore on, "but we're surely not much when it comes to *labor* bills!" There was a great deal of truth in the jibe. In 1965 labor had given medicare and social security revisions priority over more narrowly focused labor bills. The AFL-CIO had also refused to cooperate with Senator Dirksen when he offered to drop his plans to filibuster against the repeal of section 14(b) of the Taft-Hartley Act in exchange for labor's support of his efforts to modify the Supreme Court's reapportionment ruling; as a reward for this "principled" stand, labor took a severe beating on 14(b). Another long-standing legislative goal, the "common-site" picketing bill, was a victim of House Education and Labor Chairman Adam Clayton Powell's quarrels with the AFL-CIO and the House leadership. Labor did manage to secure a modest increase of the minimum wage and an extension of its coverage, but this was the only legislative triumph of 1966. Labor's major remaining objective, the revision of the unemployment compensation program, was approved only in the Senate—and that was not enough.

The federal-state unemployment insurance program dates from the passage in 1935 of the Social Security Act. For some twenty years prior to that time, various labor and reform groups had advocated the establishment of government-sponsored unemployment insurance, but no response was forthcoming at the federal level until the Depression. When President Roosevelt's Committee on Economic Security was convened in late 1934, it regarded the devising of an unemployment insurance program as its first order of business. And in this area, unlike that of health insurance, the

President and then the Congress proved largely willing to follow the Committee's recommendations.[69]

A major reason for this congressional receptivity was the fact that the Committee plan left administrative responsibility with the states and gave them great flexibility in designing their programs. A three percent federal payroll tax was to be levied against all employers unless they were already making payments into a state program, in which case the federal rate could go as low as 0.3 percent. So within two years every state had instituted some sort of program. But the programs could and did vary widely. Employers were encouraged to avoid layoffs by a provision that a state could lower its rate below the 2.7 percent level only by instituting a tax scale which varied according to a given employer's record of employment stability. By 1948 all of the states had responded to this incentive and established an "experience rating" system. But program coverage, eligibility, and the levels and duration of benefits remained largely up to state discretion, and many programs were always rather minimal. Coverage often paralleled that of federal statute, including only those firms which were liable to the federal tax and which thus stood to benefit from paying into a state program instead. Low unemployment and increased payrolls during World War II enabled many states to accumulate funds and to lower their tax rates considerably. After the war, employers resisted attempts to restore their former tax rates, although state reserves were being reduced by a series of recessions. State legislatures, even when faced with the prospect of bankrupt programs, often heeded the employers' pleas. By 1965, firms were still making annual contributions averaging 2.0 percent or less in 36 states, and the average state tax rate was actually showing a slight decline. The nationwide percentage of jobs covered had leveled off at around 77 per cent, while weekly checks for unemployment averaged barely one-third of the "normal" wage in most states. It was in this context of financial difficulty and "state foot-dragging" that all postwar Presidents from Truman to Johnson proposed various modifications of the unemployment insurance program.[70]

The Wagner-Murray-Dingell bills of the forties had proposed not only the addition of health insurance to social security, but the complete federalization of the unemployment insurance program as well. The latter proposal, like the former, represented such a deviation from existing programs as to discourage its serious consideration. President Truman's postwar proposals, though more incremental in approach, fared little better. Each year Truman requested that coverage be extended, that the federal government assist or reinsure state programs, and that minimum standards of eligibility, benefit amount, and duration be established; but Congress, and the Ways and Means and Finance Committees in particular, proved reluctant. The Eisenhower administration, seeking even more modest changes, was somewhat more successful: in the Republican-controlled 83rd Congress, Ways and Means Chairman Daniel Reed worked with the administration in developing a plan whereby unemployment taxes collected by the federal government and not needed by the states for administrative costs would, instead of reverting to the Treasury, be used to build up a fund from which states could borrow when their reserves were near depletion.

Organized labor, hardly satisfied with the Eisenhower administration's efforts, increasingly took its proposals to friendly Democrats in Congress. During the 1954 debates Representatives Forand and Dingell and Senator John F. Kennedy emerged as labor's most prominent spokesman; they saw the Reed Bill as a stopgap remedy at best and continued to urge the adoption of minimum standards for state programs. A similar role was played by Kennedy and Representative Eugene McCarthy during the recession of 1957–1958: the Eisenhower administration's proposal for a temporary loan program was countered by a proposal that the federal share of the tax be systematically redistributed to hard-pressed states. This so-called "pooling principle" was not to be adopted until the recession of 1961, however, and then only on a temporary basis, under strong pressure from the Kennedy administration, and over the determined opposition of Byrd and all but two (Gore and Douglas) members of the Finance Committee. Meanwhile, McCarthy went to the Senate, and in 1959, by virtue of his ties with organized labor, his previous work on unemployment matters in the House, and his cordial relationship with Majority Leader Johnson, he was appointed to head the Senate's Special Committee on Unemployment Problems. The Committee held extensive field hearings and on the eve of the presidential campaign issued a report urging increased federal funding of state programs and the imposition of standards. But the Kennedy administration could not secure an extension of the 1961 assistance to the states, much less such long-term program changes. Mills opposed the idea of federal benefit standards; as with medicare, it was left to Representative King to sponsor the President's bill. McCarthy did the honors in the Senate, partly because of his past identification with the issue, but also because none of the senior members of the Finance Committee were interested. From 1961 to 1964 Kennedy's requested long-term revisions, proposed anew by President Johnson in his Manpower Message of 1964, did not even reach the hearing stage.

The executive branch thus once again became labor's most promising point of access. There were still sizable contingents in both houses for whom long-term improvements were a matter of high priority, and problems peculiar to certain states—such as Reed Fund repayment requirements—continued to receive congressional attention. But while the balance of sentiment on the federal standards question had shifted only slightly in Congress since 1960, the administration's disposition was different indeed. Eisenhower had never gone beyond proposals for modest increases in coverage and federal loans to hard-pressed states. In Kennedy and Johnson, however, labor found champions of supplementary, federally-financed programs in times of high unemployment, and of minimum eligibility and benefit requirements for all programs. The problem, moreover, was one—like medicare and sugar—which required the resources and the perspectives of the executive branch. The Kennedy and McCarthy bills had lacked plausibility in view of the administrative machinery they purported to establish in the Labor Department by legislative fiat. The bills had displayed technical weaknesses and their sponsors had rarely been armed with sufficient information to make a convincing case. It was thus not simply the policy leanings of the executive branch, but also the complexity of the issue and the administrative and data-gathering capacities the program would require that caused advocates of UC revisions in Congress and the labor movement alike to turn to the President for legislative leadership in the sixties.

The interesting question, then, as President Johnson prepared his 1965 legislative program, was not whether unemployment revisions would be requested; a standards bill similar to those introduced by Kennedy and McCarthy in 1958 and requested by Presidents Kennedy and Johnson thereafter would certainly be offered. The interesting question was one of priorities. The unemployment bill was near the top of labor's list and undoubtedly somewhat farther down on the President's. Yet medicare was number one on *both* lists, and it, like UC, was under the jurisdiction of Ways and Means and Finance. It was therefore agreed not to push both projects at once. The President served notice in his State of the Union Message that proposals to "modernize" the UC system would soon be forthcoming. It was not until May, however, that the bill was ready. Mills introduced it "by request" in the House and McCarthy presented it (S. 1991) in the Senate. Describing the legislation as "long overdue," McCarthy expressed the view that its germination period had been quite sufficient: "During this seven-year period [since the proposal was first broached] there has been extensive discussion but no action."[7] But the extent of the administration's sense of urgency—to say nothing of the direction of congressional sentiment—remained to be established.

The Initial Setback. The Labor Department had been actively engaged since 1961 in gathering information and in formulating and reformulating various proposals. "You might say," a Bureau of Employment Security official acknowledged,

> that in these bills—1961, 1963, 1965—there wasn't much that was really "new." It had been proposed before. But it was new in the sense that it had never really been worked over. Nobody had really known

what these earlier proposals would entail or had worked out very precise language.

Formulation and information-gathering, it is interesting to note, were viewed by BES participants as something quite different from interest-aggregation. This is not to say that they did not see themselves as championing labor's point of view. But they did regard themselves first of all as *experts*—and their methods and procedures reflected this self-image:

> *We assembled a kind of task force, at our own [Labor Department] initiative, as we were drawing up the 1963 bill. It included a number of Department people, but several outside experts as well, mostly university people. No representative of either labor or management were included. A similar group was convened, though with less formality, in 1965, under the joint chairmanship of [Assistant Secretary for Policy Planning Daniel P.] Moynihan and [Executive Assistant to the Secretary John C.] Donovan. This time it was mostly Department people. There was no attempt to get a "cross section" of views. Again, labor and management weren't represented, and neither were the state administrators. These were groups of experts. As experts, you could assume that they would tend to be sympathetic with the UC program and would be looking for ways to upgrade it. . . .*

This approach was a function not only of the technical complexity of the subject matter, but also of the fact that UC was an issue on which the main lines of administration policy were already set. If the issue had been less "mature," if the administration had been less committed to labor's position, or if there had been serious differences of opinion within the executive branch, UC would undoubtedly have been handled far differently—as the Fair Labor Standards episode will demonstrate. As it was, however, much of the responsibility for formulation devolved to the bureau level. Organized labor, reported an AFL-CIO lobbyist, suffered not at all from its formal exclusion from the formulation process:

> *We had no significant disagreement with the Labor Department on this; they were with us. We didn't do as much actual drafting and planning as, say, Cruikshank did on medicare, but we did all we needed to. The Labor Department did most of the technical work, and they did it well.*

It is interesting to note that Bureau officials mentioned "state administrators" in the same breath with management and labor, obviously regarding them as an interest group among other interest groups, and one largely to be ignored. The Bureau, of course, worked closely with state officials on program administration, but by 1965 it had abandoned the idea of reaching any accommodation with the majority of them on the legislative question of federal benefit standards:

The state administrators, frankly, tend to give a very predictable reac-
tion to anything they might interpret as an attempt to "federalize" the
system, so often we just forget about going to them.

"We were excluded," state representatives later told the Finance Committee, "from the discussions and deliberations which produced the original proposal."[72]

If administration officials could approach UC as "experts" within their
own councils, they could rest assured that moving Congress was to be
no mere technical matter. Strategic planning was centered not in BES
but in the office of Samuel Merrick, Special Assistant to the Secretary
for Legislative Affairs. The main question mark was naturally Wilbur Mills.
Merrick's doubts about Mills' and the House's dispositions led him to
contemplate the unorthodox scheme of seeking Senate action first—all
the more because of Long's friendliness to the proposal. But he not only
ran up against the Finance Committee's "custom problem;" he also found
himself disagreeing with Andrew Biemiller of the Legislative Department of
the AFL-CIO, who thought not only that it would be strategically wise to
clear the House hurdle first but that there was a good chance to gain
Mills' cooperation. Ways and Means hearings, held late in 1965, showed
skepticism to be widespread on the Committee, but labor leaders and
administration officials obtained what they thought was a commitment from
Mills to clear a bill containing minimum benefit standards. Another glimmer
of hope came from the Interstate Conference of State Employment Security
Agencies in January, 1966, where a group of liberal state administrators
secured a narrow vote in favor of a modest minimum benefit standard. But
as the Committee began a long series of executive sessions, it became
clear that, whatever were Mills' personal preferences, he was not going
to push for approval of the President's bill. "Federal standards," he finally
announced on May 12, "are out." Mills went on to acknowledge that the
Committee was writing a bill that probably would please neither the administration nor labor.[73] In that perception he was entirely correct.

The administration bill had proposed the adoption of standards for
minimum benefit amounts (50 percent of the worker's wages), their duration (at least 26 weeks), and disqualification (no more than 20 weeks of
work per one-year "base period" could be required for UC eligibility). The
Ways and Means Committee deleted all three standards. The administration
bill had prohibited a state from disqualifying a worker for more than six
weeks following a "disqualifying act" such as quitting or refusing a job
without good cause. The Committee bill omitted this prohibition. The administration bill, while imposing these additional standards, had dropped
the venerable but increasingly disputed experience rating standard; states
were to be allowed to alter their tax rates without respect to an employer's
record of employment stability. The House Committee chose to leave the

experience rating standard intact. The administration bill had proposed a new program of federal grants to aid states where the ratio of benefits claimed to taxable wages was particularly high. This provision likewise was omitted from the Committee bill.

Some of the administration's other recommendations fared better, though almost none remained intact. The administration bill had asked for the coverage of 4.7 million additional workers. The Ways and Means Committee reduced this to 3.5 million, refusing to include hired farm labor and cutting back proposed extensions to employees of small businesses and nonprofit organizations. The administration bill had established a federally financed "extended benefits" program, under which all workers who had a long work history but exhausted their state benefits would be eligible for 26 weeks of additional benefits. The Ways and Means Committee accepted this program but modified it so as to provide that the states would pay half of the cost; the program, moreover, would only go into effect when "triggered" by specified indicators of high unemployment, and its benefits would extend for only 13 weeks. The administration bill had provided for an increase of 0.15 percent in the federal tax rate and an eventual doubling of the taxable wage base. The Committee reduced the wage base increases but raised the tax increase to 0.2 percent, specifying that the new extended benefits program was to be financed entirely from this increase with no reliance on general revenues.

Eleven Ways and Means Democrats (including Mills) voted for federal standards, but thirteen members were opposed. That question settled, the truncated bill was reported by a voice vote. Byrnes joined Mills on the floor in presenting a picture of Committee diligence and bipartisan good will—and in stressing that this bill was indeed different from the President's bill in "many, many respects." Administration partisans on the Ways and Means Committee did not even bother to file a minority report, and though a few scattered members objected to the bill's limitations, passage came effortlessly on June 22 by a vote of 374-10. It was a major defeat for the administration, but Labor Department officials, who had considered dropping the entire matter after the Ways and Means report, continued to get positive readings from Mills:

> Mills encouraged us to get standards approved in the Senate and said he would be favorably disposed [in conference].

Thus did the administration and the AFL-CIO pin their hopes on a group which in the past they would have regarded a very unlikely prospect: the Senate Committee on Finance.

A Second Chance? There had been many reasons to predict favorable action on S. 1991 when it was first introduced. Four postwar recessions and a series of emergency bills had demonstrated the weakness and instability of many state programs, and the figures showed that these programs were being upgraded slowly, if at all. The balance of sentiment in Congress and on the Ways and Means and Finance Committees was more favorable toward UC revisions than it had ever been before. The President was in the process of building an impressive legislative record, and organized labor seemed certain to benefit from his successes. The time, in many ways, seemed ripe.

But there were ominous signs from the first, and they multiplied as time went on. Unemployment was at a nine-year low, and grass-roots concern, both inside and outside the labor movement, was not intense. Labor, moreover, found itself occupied on many legislative fronts at once. The campaign for the repeal of 14(b) was particularly absorbing. AFL-CIO lobbyists hotly denied the accusation that they became preoccupied with the largely symbolic issue of 14(b) to the detriment of more substantive proposals.[74] The fact remained, however, that labor was seeking a great deal and that her energies and those of her supporters were necessarily divided. As one administration official put it, "they went to the well too often."[75] This fact, in addition to the absence of any indications of strong grass-roots interest, undoubtedly affected the sense of urgency about UC in both branches. As the 89th Congress wore on, executive officials found themselves increasingly confronted with an ill-defined but growing feeling in Congress that the administration itself was going to the well too often. Democrats from marginal districts were pulling back, particularly on labor issues, with an eye to the fall elections.[76] All of this helps explain why, although the administration did not waver from its position, various participants sensed that UC was being given reduced priority. Certainly it helps explain Congress' lack of receptivity.

Also of some importance were the efforts of the bill's opponents. Lobbying by the USCC, the NAM, and hundreds of local businesses, though energetic and effective in prompting dozens of marginal amendments, probably changed few votes on the basic standards question. More important, however, were the efforts of state administrators. Many senators and representatives prone to ignore the fulminations of the NAM took a second look when they received a letter from their state Governor or UC Director. The President of the Administrators' Interstate Conference, testifying before the Finance Committee on July 15, reported that the Ways and Means Committee, unlike the Labor Department, had solicited the views of state officials. He went on to minimize the significance of the Conference's earlier vote in favor of a minimum benefit standard; that vote had been narrow, he said, and a subsequent poll had revealed that 41 state administrators favored the House-passed bill.[77] Most legislators were therefore cross-pressured, not only by labor and management, but by the administration and by state officials as well. The result was a general dampening of enthusiasm for the bill and a plethora of amendments purporting to deal with circumstances peculiar to various states.

Whether Wilbur Mills could have shepherded the bill to passage under these circumstances is perhaps doubtful; without his strong backing, however, there was scant hope for success. An exemplar of leadership by "followmanship," Mills was reluctant to move on an issue until he was certain of a supportive consensus in committee and in the House.[78] Thus, while the Ways and Means vote on federal standards furnished a rare example of Mills voting on the losing side of a question, he praised the truncated bill which the Committee finally reported with a vigor that dismayed labor and administration strategists. More puzzling was the fact, however, that Mills continued to give them sufficiently positive assurances to make a massive Senate effort seem worthwhile—assurances on which, they felt, he later reneged. "Mills, in short, lied," was the way a labor lobbyist put it; only slightly more charitable was an administration official's assessment: "He was less straightforward than usual."

AFL-CIO President George Meany left no doubt that he regarded the "token measure" passed by the House as worse than no bill at all:

> Rather than [take] a completely unsatisfactory measure, we would be willing to wait for another go-around. We have waited pretty long anyway. . . . If you take an unsatisfactory bill you more or less close the door, at least for a few years. . . . We gambled on this [on medicare] a year and a half ago and we have done quite well, as you recall.[79]

The crux of the matter, as one lobbyist put it, "was to get the federal standards put back in. We really didn't give a damn about all those other amendments." The Labor Department's priorities were not dissimilar: the earlier requests for federal grants to states with high benefit costs and for the discontinuation of the experience rating requirement were dropped, and the idea of a "triggered" extended benefits program was accepted—though with full federal financing. It did not greatly disturb even the BES formulators of the administration bill to make these strategic compromises. "We would have liked to get a permanent extended benefits program," one of them recalled, "but there wasn't as much concern about that as there had been, given the economic situation." Moreover, even the House bill would have precluded the need for stopgap legislation of the 1958 and 1961 variety. On the question of federal-state financing, the Bureau was more concerned:

> That was going to be a real administrative tangle the way the House left it. A lot of Chamber of Commerce and state people looked on that 50-50 provision as a means of holding off the "federalization" of the program. It meant that the extended benefits program in each

state would depend on the action of the state legislature. Then there would be questions as to whether programs met our standards. We felt very much like we needed to clean it up.

The role of BES relative to other executive branch participants was more prominent in the Senate than it had been in the House, partly because Merrick sensed that Finance Committee staff members—Long had by now hired a staff of four on a nonpartisan, "professional" basis—preferred to think of their job in technical, apolitical terms. But the tasks of pressure and persuasion remained, and here the administration and organized labor emerged with the narrowest of victories: the vote on the three basic standards was 9-8, with Talmadge and Smathers joining the six Republicans in opposition. The Finance Committee standards differed from those prepared by the administration only in setting the upper limit for benefits at 50 (rather than 66.7) percent of the average statewide weekly wage. The Committee also took care of the administration's second main item of concern: full federal financing was provided for the "triggered" extended benefits program. On matters of lesser importance, the Committee left the House bill intact.

On one matter the Committee went even further than Ways and Means. It not only refused to cover hired farm workers; it cut out the coverage the House had provided for workers in businesses of between one and four employees as well. Two diverse groups on the Committee found themselves in agreement on this point. One was a group of liberals, led by Gore, who were concerned about the *small* businessman; another was a group of conservatives, led by Dirksen, concerned about businessmen in general. Long, who had a certain kinship with both groups, was sympathetic, and the deletion was approved by voice vote. The Labor Department did not like the amendment but decided to "let Dirksen have his way" rather than risk delaying the bill further or provoking a filibuster. Besides, it was thought that the House position would prevail in conference.

AFL-CIO representatives, though maintaining their long-standing ties with McCarthy and Douglas, found Finance's new Chairman "totally sympathetic" on this issue and came increasingly to trust him. Long largely dominated Senate operations. If he had altered his predecessor's staffing practices and his relationships with the administration, Long showed few signs of reducing the committee centralization Byrd had maintained. A scattering of responsibility had taken place on medicare by virtue of Long's ambivalence toward the bill, but on UC, McCarthy, whose role had been roughly analogous to that played by Anderson on medicare during the fifties, was not required (or asked) to assume major responsibilities. About this he claimed to have few regrets:

In some committees the chairman is willing to let subcommittee chairmen or other members manage bills, but Russell doesn't do that. The reason is probably that he's new and a little insecure in the chairmanship. He probably will change. But in this case I was satisfied that we finally got the bill passed. I'm sure that the fact that Russell was managing the bill gained some votes for it, probably two or three, that I couldn't have gotten had I been in charge.

Nor was McCarthy interested in asserting himself: administration officials found him "reluctant to get involved" in mobilization efforts.

The Finance Committee tended to attract Republicans with a pro-business orientation; these members had found the leadership of Byrd and the conservative views of the senior Democrats very compatible. But with the retirement of Byrd, gradual shifts in Committee membership and sentiment, Long's increasing responsiveness to labor and to the White House, and the more frequent defections of ideologically marginal members like Fulbright, Talmadge, Anderson, and Smathers, the Republicans came more and more to think of themselves as a beleaguered minority. The UC episode was particularly threatening to them: The fact that Russell Long was using the Committee to overturn a House decision and save an administration bill drafted unapologetically for labor's benefit left the minority with few doubts that the Committee and their status on it were changing. The Republicans issued a strongly worded report characterizing the adoption of benefit standards as a "precipitous action taken by the majority" and, under Morton's leadership, took their battle to the floor.

Long, fearful that ordinarily loyal Democrats might defect to the opposition because of problems the bill posed for their states, decided to ask for a separate vote on each of the benefit standards. This method of voting, the strength, bitterness, and persistence of the opposition, and the technical complexity of the measure made for two chaotic days of floor debate —separated by a weekend in which administration and labor forces tried frantically to get senators to reconsider their initial rejection of two of the benefit standards.[80] In the end, Long was forced to make only one major compromise—allowing the states to continue offering less than 26 weeks of benefits to workers with less than 39 weeks of employment to their credit—and labor reluctantly decided that the prudent course was to go along. There was, however, no shortage of piecemeal amendments offered and, after committee and BES aides reworked them and made certain they did not destroy the sense of the whole, accepted on the floor. Such amendment derbies were fast becoming a hallmark of Long's floor management, but in this case such an openness to marginal modifications was of considerable strategic importance; in many instances it enabled senators to vote with the administration but at the same time to assure state officials and businessmen that they had succeeded in easing their particular problems. Final approval came on August 8 by a 22-vote margin.

McCarthy at one point urged his colleagues to "face up to the question whether or not in a case of this kind we are going to surrender completely to the House of Representatives."[81] The decision finally made, in committee and on the floor, was not to "surrender." But Mills held the high cards in conference, and it soon became clear that, whatever impressions he had left with administration and labor leaders, he was not going to play them in favor of benefit standards. His advantages went considerably beyond the traditional deference paid the House in revenue matters. Mills' bill, like the House's fair packaging bill, was a least-common-denominator proposal, and both the lateness of the session and the controversy surrounding Senate action militated in favor of settling for it. Besides, Mills could argue with some plausibility that the House would defeat the conference report if it contained benefit standards. In any case, Mills did nothing to expedite the calling of a conference and let it be known that he would rather let the bill die than alter the House version in any significant respect. If a bill were to be approved, it would be up to the Senate to take the initiative *and* make the compromise. The choice was between the House bill and no bill at all. It was, as Meany had anticipated, a rerun of the 1964 medicare scenario, and the strategy Meany had counseled was adopted. Organized labor, the administration, and Long's delegation agreed that it was better to block agreement than to approve a weak bill that might preclude reopening the subject for several years. Thus it was announced on October 21 that the conferees had failed to agree and that the bill was dead.

Concluding Observations. Of all the bills examined thus far, none were as exclusively responsive to the interests of a single group as was UC. Yet the development and passage of the bill were dominated to a large extent by the executive branch. The anomaly was only apparent, for UC was one area in which the administration championed labor's interests with few reservations. Labor representatives did not proceed independently, but in fact did less independent bill-drafting and information-gathering than they had on medicare, a matter in which they had a much less exclusive interest.

It had not always been thus; when the Republicans had been in the White House, formulation and information-gathering had been the province of the unions and their congressional sympathizers. But during the sixties labor's cause was taken up at the top levels of the administration, and BES officials developed ambitious plans to upgrade their programs. There were other interests involved: state officials alternatively seeking federal assistance for their hard-pressed programs and resisting "federalization," employers and businessmen fighting to keep tax rates down and coverage restricted. But the Labor Department under Kennedy and Johnson deliberately eschewed any inclusive sort of interest-aggregation. Senators and representatives, on the other hand, took it up with a vengeance. State officials as well as business representatives took their complaints and their proposals to Congress; their efforts helped build up what was probably majority sentiment against the bill in the House and encouraged scores of Senators to attempt, if not to wreck the bill, at least to secure marginal modifications.

The Senate Committee, on UC as on sugar, became involved late in the game, acting primarily in response to the administration's efforts to salvage a badly damaged bill. The Labor Department had established contact with the Committee staff and with McCarthy's office at an early date, but Senate actors exerted little independent influence until the bill was sent over to them. The decision to exempt small business, the debate over the new administration draft, and the adoption of various marginal amendments showed that several Committee members, not merely the Republicans, were undertaking interest-aggregation and modification on their own terms. But the main thrust of Finance Committee action, unlike that of Ways and Means, was not to reformulate or to strike a new balance of interests but rather to *restore* benefit standards and the federal financing of extended benefits. The role assumed was thus similar to that taken the year before in relation to Cooley's sugar quotas. But UC was much more salient to the Senate than sugar had been, and there was a much sharper division of opinion as to whether the reversal of House action was justified. Mobilization, therefore, was more difficult. Long's performance was anything but smooth, but he nonetheless bore considerable responsibility for committee and floor successes, shored up though his efforts were by administration officials, the party leadership, and union representatives.

The bill, nonetheless, ultimately did not make it, and any analysis of its defeat must turn not merely to the counter-pressures of UC opponents but to the more subtle question of what was *not* done, particularly at the publicizing and mobilization stages. Of inescapable importance is the simple fact that the man with the greatest potential capacity to mobilize, Wilbur Mills, chose not to do so. But other circumstances—reduced unemployment, the press of other legislative concerns—helped explain the failure of executive and labor advocates to give a more exclusive or more effective push to the UC measure. This, in turn, reinforced public and congressional lethargy. And, as it turned out, the repeat of the 1964 medicare scenario for which Meany had hoped was not to materialize; 1966 turned out to be the last chance for substantial UC revisions for many years to come.[82]

The UC episode points up several aspects of Finance Committee life which the fourth bill to be considered will illuminate further: Long's erratic leadership style, his preference for centralized committee operations, the growing role of the staff and its "technical" orientation, the general conservatism of the minority bloc and its increasing disaffection with committee operations, the growing amenability of the majority to the administration's interests, and the increasing willingness of Long to deviate from the text of House-passed bills. The legislative dominance of the Ways and Means Committee has again been demonstrated, as has the presence of large and active "peak associations" in the Finance Committee's environment, exerting a selective and divisive influence on the membership. Finally, a third area of committee jurisdiction has been viewed, one of great complexity, involving massive bureaucracies and extensive programs. If and when legislators attempted to take independent initiatives in these areas, they would find themselves greatly hampered without the cooperation of the agencies and some access to their skills and resources.

THE FOREIGN INVESTORS TAX ACT OF 1966 AND THE PRESIDENTIAL ELECTION CAMPAIGN FUND AMENDMENTS

The Dollar Drain. . . . The revenue committees of Congress, by virtue of their responsibility for medicare, were on center stage as the 89th Congress began. They occupied the same position as the Congress drew to a close 21 months later. This time, however, it was the Finance Committee's —or, to be more specific, Russell Long's—show. Because he pressed an issue which until 1966 had been the concern only of a few academics and reform-minded congressmen, the 89th Congress ended in maximum controversy and confusion. A further result, and one equally important from our point of view, was that the Finance Committee showed signs of assuming a new policy role.

The cause of all the excitement, Long's Presidential Election Campaign Fund Act, was appended to a much less controversial measure, but one on which the administration was nonetheless anxious to get action—a bill modifying the tax laws so as to encourage foreign investment in the United States. The balance-of-payments deficit had taken a sudden turn downward in 1963; among President Kennedy's responses had been the appointment of a task force, chaired by Undersecretary of the Treasury Henry H. Fowler and including finance, business, State Department, and Treasury representatives, to design "a new and positive program . . . to promote overseas sales of securities of U.S. companies."[83] A broad-gauged report was issued within a year, and in mid-1964 Treasury officials began translating some of the task force recommendations into legislative proposals. President Johnson served notice in his 1965 State of the Union message that a bill was on the way, and on March 8 the administration proposal was introduced.

Dozens of bills purporting to deal with the dollar drain had been introduced since the problem had reached major proportions in the late fifties. Their pattern of adoption was generally uniform: formulation, publicizing, and information-gathering were centered in the executive branch; congressional committees sometimes amended the bills to accommodate domestic interests but usually left their main lines intact. But congressional action was to be slower and more painstaking on the bill concerning foreign investment. The measure itself was complex, "rationalizing" the tax treatment of foreigners in ways that were not in every case directly relevant to the balance-of-payments problem. Mills and Byrnes suspected, moreover, that some of the provisions designed to attract foreign capital might make the U.S., in effect, a "tax haven" or place domestic investors at a disadvantage. The Ways and Means Committee therefore resolved to give the measure thorough consideration and took it through two sets of hearings and three redraftings before finally reporting a clean bill on April 26, 1966.

Mills' staff resources greatly enhanced his competence to undertake such a review. The Ways and Means staff seldom played a prominent role in shaping legislation; it was competent but small, and very much eclipsed by Mills' preference for doing business personally. On internal revenue matters, however, Mills needed and utilized a much more extensive staff operation—the twenty professionals employed by the Joint Committee on Internal Revenue Taxation. This committee, composed of senior members of Finance and Ways and Means, was formed in 1926 to investigate large and questionable tax refunds, and many of its staff members continued to perform this function. But since the mid-thirties the staff had been heavily involved in legislative affairs, "the first genuinely professional staff maintained by a congressional committee." The Committee itself met infrequently and had no legislative authority, but its select membership and its concentration of staff resources both reflected and enhanced the control exercised by senior members of the revenue committees over tax policy.[84]

The capacities of the JCIRT staff made it possible for Mills to undertake the kind of review of tax laws applying to foreigners that he thought was desirable. It could be asked, of course, why the staff arrangement did not facilitate executive-legislative collaboration at an *earlier* stage and thus preclude the need for a thorough and independent congressional review; in fact, a Treasury Department official confirmed, such collaboration often did take place:[85]

> We ordinarily go to considerable lengths to check things out, even at the drafting stage. The key man there is [Chief of Staff Laurence] Woodworth. Our relations are good with him, but he has ideas of his own, and he certainly is loyal to that committee . . . It's always to our advantage to work things out with him. We try at all costs to avoid disputes with him in front of the members.

This official and Woodworth agreed, however, that there was "less consultation at the early stages on that foreign investment bill than is usually the case." Though Mills showed no particular resentment at this fact, it undoubtedly contributed to his conviction that this was a bill that should be perused rather carefully. The patterns of cooperation established in the past again came into play as the staff worked up a clean bill, and the administration in the end recommended that the Senate accept the House revisions.

These cooperative efforts necessitated striking a balance between the Treasury's desire to attract foreign investments and the determination of Ways and Means members that foreigners should not get inequitable tax breaks. Mills was willing to accept several supposed inducements to investment: broadened exemptions for foreigners from capital gains taxes, the exemption of certain foreign individuals or corporations from income tax rates of over 30 percent on all or part of their American earnings, and reduced tax rates on the U.S. estates of foreign decedents. But he wanted to couple these liberalizations with a tightening of alleged loopholes which Treasury feared would more than offset the effect of the liberalizations on the balance of payments. Bankers concerned about losing foreign deposits and the National Foreign Trade Council, fearful of foreign retaliation, also protested strongly. An accommodation was worked out on many of the items, but on certain types of income the Committee continued to insist on "tax equity." The clean bill subjected foreign insurance companies to the same tax treatment as domestic companies on their U.S. investments. It provided for the immediate imposition of an estate tax on the bank deposits of deceased foreigners. It also terminated the exemption foreigners enjoyed from paying income taxes on the interest from their bank deposits. But the effective date of the latter provision was deferred until 1972, and in the interim the exemption was *broadened* to include interest and dividends paid on share deposits by savings and loan associations and interest paid by insurance companies, as the administration had requested. The House passed the bill without debate on June 15, 1966.

The administration was "talked into going along" with Mills' scaled-down modifications, according to a congressional participant, "though the bankers continued to howl." Treasury officials were by nature sympathetic to the Chairman's aversion to tax loopholes; in any case they recognized that the prudent course was to support the new bill. "It did most of what we wanted," one of them explained:

> We actually didn't care much one way or the other on those amendments that put estate taxes and income taxes on foreign deposits . . . We decided to support the House version. Often we do that. For one thing, the House Committee is a pretty good committee from our point of view; they almost always tighten up tax bills . . . Also, you consider which battles you can win and which you can't. It's a tough thing to beat the Ways and Means Committee, and even if you get the Finance Committee to reverse them, you've still got to contend with them in conference, and they're always strong there. So sometimes the prudent thing to do, if the changes aren't too bad, is to go along with them.

The Commerce Department, although Secretary Connor was reportedly disturbed with Treasury's low-key approach to the entire balance-of-payments problem, brought its views into line on the Mills amendments; General Counsel Giles' report to the Finance Committee simply recommended the consideration of possible "adverse effects," which admittedly were "difficult to determine."[86]

Long opened Finance Committee hearings on August 8 with an announcement that the House had shifted the focus of the legislation:

> *Rather than having as its purpose the encouragement of foreign investment in the United States . . . the bill passed by the House is concerned with providing taxation of nonresident aliens and foreign corporations comparable to that of U.S. individuals and corporations.*[87]

A number of banking and business representatives told the Committee in no uncertain terms that the House had destroyed the original proposal, but Treasury Secretary Fowler pleaded neutrality on the income tax and estate tax provisions, acknowledging that they might have balance-of-payments "implications" but that "as a matter solely of tax equity . . . the Ways and Means conclusions appear to be correct."[88] After three days of hearings, and amidst Williams' familiar complaints that the Committee was being pressured and did not have the "time really to study and understand exactly what is proposed," Long set out to get the bill reported and passed before adjournment. Woodworth continued to work through the bill and to suggest numerous technical revisions. A few members were impressed by the bankers' opposition to the House amendments regarding the taxation of deposits, but there were no members except Anderson from the border states where the opposition was strongest. Since the majority was indifferent and some members, especially Williams, were ready to fight for the House provisions, the idea of deleting them was dropped. It was provided, however, that the estate tax, like the income tax, should not become effective until 1972. The "tax haven" concern found further expression in an amendment tightening House provisions for the retention of regular tax rates for Americans who abandoned their citizenship with the intention of avoiding U.S. taxation. The Committee also responded to widespread misgivings in the business community at home and abroad—misgivings which the Treasury apparently shared[89]—about the vagueness of the House's definition of instances where income could be described as "effectively connected" with the conduct of a trade or business within the U.S. Tightened specifications were adopted which narrowed the range of cases in which foreigners might be subjected to full domestic rates.

By this time, however, such alterations—as well as Williams' concern about being rushed on a complex tax bill—had been overshadowed by the announced intention, first of Long and then of several other Committee members, to make the Foreign Investors Tax Act a vehicle for various other proposals that might have a better-than-usual chance for enactment in the rush for adjournment. Chief among these was a bill which Long had quietly introduced on June 15: the Presidential Campaign Fund Act.

. . . and the "Costs of Democracy". Medicare proponents were not the only ones who could look to Theodore Roosevelt as their prophet: he was also the first major American political figure to recommend governmental subsidies for political campaigns. In this area too, however, Roosevelt was considerably ahead of his time. He was not alone in his recognition that the need for campaign funds could seriously compromise public officials and could give large contributors undue influence. But his "positive" remedy of subsidization, as opposed to merely limiting contributions and expenditures or requiring public disclosure, was to lay dormant for many years.[90] It was not, in fact, until the sixties that proposals for the public financing of campaigns received serious presidential and congressional consideration.

The federal regulations adopted in 1910 and supplemented from time to time thereafter rarely proved effective or enforceable.[91] Senators and representatives adopted practices which, though evasive in principle, had long been sanctioned by practice and by the flexible interpretation of statutory loopholes. A less frequent response was to urge a closing of the gap between theory and practice. A House committee appointed to investigate the 1950 elections, for example, called present ceilings "an invitation to criminal violation" and recommended that they be either substantially increased or repealed altogether. The Elections Subcommittee of the Senate Rules Committee made similar recommendations in 1953, and in 1955 the Rules Committee reported the first of several bills raising spending limits and tightening reporting requirements. The Senate finally voted its approval in 1960, but the House Administration Committee refused to consider the bill. It was in hopes of securing House approval that the Elections Subcommittee steered a bill making less extensive revisions and leaving primaries uncovered to Senate passage the next year. It was also evident that the Subcommittee's new Chairman, Howard Cannon, was considerably more prone to compromise than Thomas Hennings, deceased Chairman of the full committee and sponsor of the 1953-1960 bills. But the House was still unresponsive. Meanwhile, members from one-party states in both houses, including Russell Long, continued to oppose the extension of regulation to primary campaigns.

Formulators of the early regulatory statutes had not had the benefit of any comprehensive information regarding campaign costs and financing procedures—and the reports filed under the Corrupt Practices Act were often flawed, incomplete, and not publicly accessible. Following the 1956 election, however, the Elections Subcommittee, chaired by Albert Gore, undertook a comprehensive study of campaign spending. This investigation dovetailed nicely with research political scientist Alexander Heard already had underway. Heard served the Gore Subcommittee as a consultant and drew heavily on its work for his book, *The Costs of Democracy*, first published in 1960. Heard's book was the first comprehensive treatment of political finance, and it gained for its author a nationwide reputation. Heard also took a leading role in the establishment of the Citizens' Research Foundation, an organization set up in 1958 to do research in money and politics and financed in large part by the Ford Foundation. Therefore, when President Kennedy appointed a Commission on Campaign Costs in 1961, it was natural that Heard should be named its Chairman. Selected as the Commission's Executive Director was Citizens' Research Foundation director Herbert Alexander.

President Kennedy's "attention to the subject was notable because of its novelty in a President, not because he gave it any place in his first legislative recommendations, which he did not."[92] It was also notable because of his openness to some sort of subsidy plan. The Gore Subcommittee had called for "incentives for mass contributions or *perhaps* governmental assumption of the cost and responsibility for the conduct of federal election campaigns."[93] But when a proposal of this type—providing a tax credit of up to $10 for political contributions—finally reached the Senate floor in 1961, the floor manager, Senator Cannon, bowed to objections that it was a revenue item and should originate in the House. Meanwhile, Senator Magnuson and the Commerce Committee were confronted with the desire of both parties to stage nationwide television debates in 1960 without imposing "equal time" requirements on the networks. Magnuson devised a proposal which *required* each network to furnish eight hour-long programs to each major candidate in presidential campaign years. He enlisted 22 of his colleagues as co-sponsors and took favorable testimony from an impressive list of witnesses.[94] But the legislation emerged only as a temporary suspension of the equal-time requirement in instances where the networks voluntarily donated time to the major candidates. Therefore, at the time of the Heard Commission's appointment, neither house had approved any proposal designed to stimulate contributions, to make free broadcasting time available, or to furnish direct subsidies. Some members, notably Senator Richard Neuberger,[95] had long been advocating such action, but most members showed little interest. The Senate Rules Committee was interested only in revising existent regulatory measures, and the House Administration Committee was interested in no revisions whatsoever. President Kennedy was thus considerably ahead of the pack when he expressed his hope that

> before we get into another presidential campaign we can work out
> some system by which the major burdens of presidential campaigns
> on both sides would be sustained by the National Government, as sug-

gested by Theodore Roosevelt, as suggested by Dick Neuberger when he was here.[96]

The President's Commission, while recommending extensive disclosure requirements, the abolition of ceilings on contributions and expenditures, and a system of tax credits or deductions for small contributors, shied away from proposals for direct subsidies.[97] The presidential bills based on the Commission's recommendations stirred little interest in Congress, and with Kennedy's death the spark of initiative in the executive branch was likewise extinguished. President Johnson cancelled a White House conference on campaign financing which Kennedy had planned and showed no interest in the area until the search for items for the 1966 legislative program began. At that point campaign reforms took on a new appeal for Johnson's White House staff, not only because they were inexpensive but also because of their appeal in academic and reform circles, two places where the President's image badly needed refurbishing. There had been virtually no agitation within the administration for action on this front; at the time of the State of the Union message, concrete details had not been worked out and, according to a Treasury official, little consultation had taken place within the executive branch, much less with outside experts:

> *The first I knew of the proposal was in the State of the Union message. I'm virtually sure Treasury wasn't in on the preparation of that, that it was almost entirely a White House operation. Now we had been involved before, with the Kennedy Commission, going over various plans. But the word was that Johnson wasn't nearly as interested . . . Anyway, we were caught somewhat by surprise in 1966. This isn't the sort of thing you would expect Treasury to push for though. The presumption, as far as we are concerned, is against further holes in the tax structure. There's a kind of institutional bias there. . . . But when the administration decides it wants something, of course, we're good soldiers and cooperate fully. So after the State of the Union message we were quite involved, right up until the time the bill was sent up in May.*

It was an indication of the proposal's low priority that its development was left largely to Treasury Department technicians and that, consequently, little consultation took place and little groundwork was laid on Capitol Hill. The bill was in most respects an adaptation of the earlier Kennedy proposals, with no new departures in terms of subsidization. Cannon, alienated both because the bill was more extensive than his own proposal and because Joseph Clark, one of his more critical subcommittee members, had been invited to sponsor it, decided to report his own bill without further hearings. The House Subcommittee on Elections, unlike its Senate counterpart, held extensive hearings on the administration bill, called in Alexander and other experts, and on October 3 produced a clean bill designed to upgrade the President's disclosure and reporting requirements. But there was still no hope of favorable action by the parent Administration Committee. As far as the President's bill was concerned, Clark was right on August 4: "Campaign reform is dead for the year."[98]

At that very moment, however, Long was making plans to hold hearings on a proposal he had introduced on June 15, a plan whereby the Treasury would provide funds to the political parties for presidential campaign purposes through direct grants computed on the basis of popular vote. "As far as I know," a staff man said, "the thing was hatched in Long's fertile brain. He had to tie it to taxation to get it to his committee, and it was his idea to tie it to the number of votes the party got in the previous election." Long's proposal was notable for its reliance on direct governmental subsidies—to "cast out the present system of financing political campaigns through large contributions from only a relatively few rich people."[99] Senator Mansfield in 1961 had suggested that the federal government pay $1 million to each party in presidential election years to cover broadcasting costs. Mrs. Neuberger and the Heard Commission had suggested that the federal government might match small private contributions, but Kennedy had gone no further than to ask Congress to "study" this "original and imaginative approach."[100] The states had done no more than provide limited tax incentives or publish pamphlets on candidates, and in only scattered instances at that, though Puerto Rico had provided subsidies to parties since 1957. Long, therefore, was breaking new ground, and the long-time proponents of reform through *regulation* hardly knew whether he was friend or foe. Certainly he caught the Treasury Department by surprise:

> We didn't think much about his bill at first—there were so many proposals floating around, especially on the Senate side. But we did take him seriously by the time hearings were held in August, and we gave him a rather cautious endorsement. [Responding:] As for my own opinion, I didn't think the scheme was "harebrained," like some did, though I certainly would call it novel.

Undersecretary of the Treasury Joseph Barr, testifying on August 18, recognized the need for an "affirmative approach . . . to insure that political parties and candidates will have adequate financial resources derived from large segments of the population." But he expressed a cautious preference for a tax incentive scheme and stated that the provision of revenues should be coupled with an "invigoration" of disclosure requirements.[101]

By September few observers doubted that Long was serious about his proposal, but fewer still supposed that he could get it past the Committee, the Senate, or, all else failing, Wilbur Mills. Long, however, continued to work on the bill. With the help of JCIRT aides he developed a scheme that tied the proposal more closely to the taxing power, separated the campaign fund from general revenues, and retained the voluntary aspect of political contributions: each taxpayer was to have the opportunity to designate on his tax return whether $1 of his tax liability was to be applied to a special presidential election campaign fund. Douglas convinced Long that both parties should be given equal access to the fund, regardless of their previous presidential vote. But Long's bill caused little discussion or controversy in the Committee, and when he proposed that it be added as a rider to the foreign investors bill he prevailed by a vote of 12-5. Few members, the *Times* reported, supposed that the Long Amendment could become law "this year, if ever."[102]

The "Grab Bag." "I am well aware," said Long as he opened floor debate on October 12, "that the Constitution provides that revenue measures must originate in the House. I do not believe, however, that this constitutional provision was intended to prevent Senators from bringing important matters before the Congress when it is clear they would not otherwise be considered."[103] The bill which Long presented left little doubt that a number of Senators had "important matters" on their minds or that Long was willing to use the nongermane amendment as a vehicle for Senate initiative on revenue matters. It also touched off an acrimonious and extended end-of-session debate which provoked the usually restrained George Aiken to remark that "in the 26 years that I have been here I do not believe I have seen any time when the Senate appeared more irresponsible than it does now."[104]

Two amendments dealt with what Long termed "serious defects" in medicare. One, sponsored by Douglas, provided for the coverage of drug costs under "Plan B." The second, sponsored by Smathers, revoked a clause in the medicare bill which was going to deny persons over 65 the right to claim all of their medical expenses as a tax deduction after 1966. The Committee also adopted three amendments revising depletion allowances for clam and oyster shells (Long), alumina-bearing clay (Talmadge and Fulbright), and shale and slate (Carlson); the sponsors were in each case responding to home-state interests. Also approved were a Hartke amendment defining hearses as automobiles rather than trucks for excise tax purposes; a liberalized investment tax credit provision, also sponsored by Hartke and designed for the benefit of the Harvey Aluminum Company; a Dirksen amendment providing various exemptions from the interest equalization tax; and a provision, sponsored by McCarthy and backed by investment companies disadvantaged by a 1966 Internal Revenue Service decision, exempting appreciated securities "swapped" for shares in an investment fund from capital gains taxation. Finally, the Committee approved an amendment, proposed by Williams at Saltonstall's request, providing for an annual report by the Treasury on the status of the national debt. Saltonstall, his Legislative Assistant recalled, "had been interested in this for some time. His son [who was his Administrative Assistant] pushed it . . . He was interested in seeing it passed before he retired."

Into this mix were thrown several equally nongermane amendments which had already been independently acted on in the House. Chief among these was a provision identical to H.R. 10, which had passed the House unanimously on June 6, giving full (instead of existing law's 50 percent) income tax deductibility for the retirement fund contributions of self-employed persons. A perennial on the calendars of both houses, and one long opposed by both Mills and Long, this measure had finally received Ways and Means approval, reportedly because Mills wanted to honor its long-time sponsor, Representative Eugene Keogh, on his retirement. But the Finance Committee had delayed action. The Treasury objected to the bill because of its discrimination in favor of upper-income professionals and a projected revenue loss of $60 million. Hartke, on an 8-8 vote, failed to get H.R. 10 added to the foreign investors bill in committee. But the Committee added two other amendments increasing the amounts on which certain classes of self-employed persons could claim the existing 50 per-cent deduction, and Hartke later obtained a reversal of the Committee's original decision on the floor. Lobbying by the American Medical Associa-tion, American Bar Association, American Dental Association, American Association of Public Accountants, National Society of Professional Engi-neers, and other groups was intense. "They may have talked to my staff," Hartke told a reporter with a bit of ill-advised caginess. His Administrative Assistant was more straightforward: "I'd say every damn one of 'em came in."[105] When the amendment was offered on the floor, Smathers, Morton, and Carlson joined Hartke as co-sponsors.

"What has the depletion allowance on clam or oyster shells or the financing of presidential campaigns to do with [the Foreign Investors Tax Act]?" Williams asked as floor debate got underway. "Perhaps the title of the act should be amended to read 'Grab Bag Act of 1966'."[106] The answer he got was not fewer amendments but more—only one of which was ger-mane to the bill under consideration.[107] The hostility of Williams and Gore (Douglas would undoubtedly have joined them had he not been in Illinois fighting for his political life) to subsidies or tax breaks for "special inter-ests," prefigured in the Sugar Act debate and generally finding its prime target in depletion allowances, was expressed in a number of unsuccess-ful attempts to reverse the Committee's generosity on the floor—including a 33-39 vote against deleting the campaign fund title. Long, meanwhile, defended his Committee vigorously and continued to invite senators with special projects to get in on the act. By October 13, a number of members had a direct stake in the passage of the bill, which came easily, 58-18.[108]

Mills had been looking dubiously at Long's antics and at one point had threatened not to call a conference. But he was anxious to salvage the foreign investors bill and was under considerable pressure to get H.R. 10 approved. The administration, confident that Mills would delete most of the Senate amendments, urged positive action. Treasury officials were particularly anxious to see H.R. 10, the medicare and swap fund amendments, and the depletion allowance liberalizations (except Long's, which JCIRT aides had drafted with special care) deleted. On campaign finances, their view was more ambivalent. They had been surprised when Long appended his proposal to the foreign investors bill and even more surprised when the Committee and the Senate upheld his action. Many of them viewed the costs of his bill and its absence of regulatory safeguards with disfavor. But Long, after all, had secured action in an area where the President had expressed great concern (albeit with far different concrete proposals), and the administration was committed to Long by virtue of his services as Majority Whip and the tentative encouragement Barr had given during the August hearings. And this was a proposal, it was becoming increasingly obvious, in which Long had a great personal stake. As a Treasury official explained:

> We were completely off guard. I think the GAO [General Accounting Office] was, too; they thought there was absolutely nothing to worry about. [Do you think you would have supported Long to the extent you did had you known that the bill would finally pass—or that it would cause such an uproar?] Well, that's hard to say. I do think the administration was doing more than just humoring Long on something they thought didn't have a chance. I think there was a genuine belief that this could be an important first step. On the floor, though, our policy was pretty much hands off. We were just going to wait and see what happened. Our attitude was on the positive side, but we certainly weren't helping him round up votes. . . . The important thing was that we didn't oppose.

Senator Gore, meanwhile, was also blinking his eyes in disbelief. He had voted for the campaign fund proposal in committee and, though becoming increasingly skeptical, had been content to let Williams lead the opposition on the floor. "To tell you the truth, I didn't pay much attention to the thing at first. Then I was astonished to find that it might actually pass, and I went after it." Gore had in the past displayed a greater interest in campaign financing than Long; some observers detected in his opposition a note of resentment that "his own proposals hadn't made it." But Gore's interest had always been in regulation and disclosure, and it was precisely on these grounds that he opposed Long:

> [I know you've had a longstanding interest in election reform. How about the idea of some sort of subsidy or indirect assistance to candidates?] Of course, this is an immensely complicated area, but I would say in general on the matter of subsidies that it's just as important, or

perhaps more important, that we make sure it's clean *money and* regulate *how it's to be spent.*

It soon became clear that Gore was going to have difficulty. He was not included on the conference committee, Williams was tied up with another conference, and campaign finance turned out to be the issue on which Long's feelings were most intense and Mills' least. Mills, like the Treasury, was especially concerned about revenue losses. Thus the medicare amendments were deleted, the depletion allowances on clay and shale were reduced to token dimensions, and provision was made for the eventual imposition of the IRS ruling on swap funds which McCarthy had sought to repeal. "From the revenue standpoint," a Treasury official noted, "the House prevailed as usual. The only serious problem that remained was H.R. 10." H.R. 10 and the other amendments which Ways and Means had already approved naturally stayed in the bill. But Long secured more concessions than usual, thanks to time pressures, his own assertiveness, and the concern of House conferees to get H.R. 10 and the foreign investors bill on the statute books. The windfalls Hartke had provided for Harvey Aluminum and the hearse manufacturers were retained, as were Long's depletion allowance increases and the interest equalization and public debt amendments. And to Gore's and the Treasury's "astonishment," the presidential campaign fund amendments were retained. The conference committee's revisions made it more difficult for third parties to get a share of the fund and thus made the proposal even more offensive to its critics.

Mills was subdued, even apologetic, as he brought the conference bill to the House floor:

> *It is becoming more difficult with each passing year to have tax bills passed through the House and through the Senate without a great number of amendments being added when the bill is in the other body.*

To which Representative Curtis added:

> *I hope that some day . . . I will see the House of Representatives stand up against . . . the irresponsible operations we have experienced in this instance, and in instance after instance on the part of members of the other body.*[109]

Such comments would hardly have been heard in the days of Harry Byrd! But the fireworks were yet to come. When the Senate gathered to vote on the conference report, the atmosphere was tense and acrimonious. Gore the night before had refused to let the bill come to a vote by threatening to call for a quorum—which, mainly because one-third of the Senate was up for re-election, could not have been produced. The leadership cooperated with Long by delaying the vote on a crucial appropriations bill so as to give the membership an incentive to stay in town and in session. Fowler and Barr tried unsuccessfully to dissuade Gore and Williams, though Long's claim that the administration was "highly enthusiastic" about his campaign financing scheme was still a considerable overstatement.[110] Mansfield held a six-hour meeting which failed to produce a compromise; arrangements were finally made to fly seven campaigning senators (not including Douglas) to Washington via Air Force jets. On October 22 a quorum was present.

The Senate had rarely ended a session on a more turbulent note. Williams condemned the Treasury for "flipflopping" on the Harvey Aluminum amendment and not pressing for an earlier tightening of swap fund regulations. Gore concentrated on the campaign fund proposal and H.R. 10. Lausche's remarks on Long's depletion allowance amendment, the most personal and bitter of all, took note of the fact that his predecessor in the chairmanship had died the day before.

> *Tomorrow the nation will be honoring the late Harry Byrd . . . Not one implication will be made that he used his chairmanship to promote what was of interest to his state and of unconcern to the people of the country . . .*
>
> **MR. LONG:** *I am not going to return these insults in kind . . . As much as I want the bill, as hard as I have worked on it, and as hard as the House, the Senate, the President, and the Secretary of the Treasury have worked on the bill, which is a good bill, I do not think enough of the bill to have a mutual heart attack with anybody.*[111]

Long continually stressed the fact that the administration supported the entire conference report except for H.R. 10, which "we could not modify drastically [because it had been] adopted unanimously by the House." He reported that he had been willing to compromise, even on campaign financing, but that his opponents had escalated their demands and had insisted that a report be brought back that did not even contain H.R. 10. "I am through bending the knee. We can vote one way or the other on it." The outcome was never in doubt: Long and the leadership prevailed, 31-22.[112] Among Finance Committee members, only Gore, Williams, and Fulbright voted "nay." The President signed the bill three weeks later, criticizing the "tax windfalls" it provided, but praising both the foreign investment and campaign fund proposals.

Summary and Conclusions. The Foreign Investors Tax Act and the campaign financing rider contrasted with each other in several respects. The first was formulated, researched, and refined in the executive branch. Private business leaders participated in the process at certain points, but the measure was basically a governmental response to a national economic predicament. The situation itself furnished a degree of "instigation," but the Treasury provided the immediate impetus. This meant coopting relevant interest groups, as on the Fowler task force; it also meant presidential messages to interpret this and other balance-of-payments proposals.

Congress had the staff resources necessary to examine and refine the bill. The interests of certain domestic businesses suffering from foreign competition were accommodated, but these changes were generally consistent with Mills' determination not to let balance-of-payments considerations undermine "tax equity." By the same token, the entreaties of banking interests were sometimes deflected or ignored. In the Senate, however, the foreign investors bill was, as Long put it, "the last train out of the station." For that reason it served as a vehicle for the aggregation of a variety of interests having tax concerns and for the presentation of a long list of nongermane amendments.

The campaign finance proposal, by contrast, demonstrated what the efforts of a single "determined and powerful advocate" could sometimes accomplish; Long's bill was "unique" in significant respects and it was pushed to passage in what was "surely one of the shortest Congressional gestation periods on record."[113] But whatever new ground the proposal broke, it nonetheless built upon a number of successful and unsuccessful measures that had been offered in Congress and in state legislatures over the course of 75 years. Groups like the Gore Subcommittee had gathered information and pointed up the ineffectuality of existing statutes, but it was only with the work of Heard, Alexander, and the President's Commission that an adequate informational base was laid, appreciable governmental and public interest stimulated, and policy recommendations taken beyond the regulatory approach. The fact that formulation, information-gathering, and publicizing had been carried as far as they had—in addition, of course, to the deepening of the problem itself and President Johnson's need for issues — was crucial in gaining a place on the President's agenda in 1966, albeit not a very prominent place, for campaign financing. All this was hardly irrelevant to Long's success in building a case and generating support.

It was Cannon whose role most closely approximated that of the interest-aggregator; from 1961 through 1966 his bills reflected the viewpoint of politicians who wanted to raise troublesome ceilings and stimulate small contributors but not to introduce extensive reporting requirements or public financing. But while Cannon's preemption of the President's bill could be partially explained in these terms, Gore's and Williams' opposition to Long could not. Gore was not pleased with the status quo, but he regarded Long's plan as a mistaken way of dealing with what he agreed was a serious problem. This is not to deny, of course, that many members voted with Gore for the same reason they supported Cannon, any more than it is to deny that many went along with Long not on the merits of his proposal but out of personal and party loyalty—and a desire to hasten adjournment.

Mobilization, once the "grab bag" was assembled, was Long's task. He was aided by the lateness of the session, by Gore's delay in mounting his opposition, and by the stake many members had in one or another of the amendments. He was also aided by the resources he commanded as Committee Chairman and Party Whip, by the leadership's cooperation, and by the administration's willingness to accept the campaign fund and other amendments. But the foreign investors-campaign fund bill was probably more reflective of Long's interests and style than any other major bill produced by his committee during the 89th Congress, and it was clear that his success in committee, on the floor, and in conference was in large measure dependent on his own perseverance and assertiveness and the credits he was able to redeem.

The greatest value of the episode for our purposes might well be the insight it provides into Long's leadership style, his notion of his own and the Committee's potential legislative role, and his conviction that sooner or later he must (and should) say to his colleagues and to various interests, "Alright, fellas, here's a bill we can amend."[114] This in turn had important implications for the Committee's accessibility to various groups, for the policy initiative members down through the ranks could assume, and for the way policy-making functions were shared with the House Committee. In other words, this case study, more than the three which preceded it, revealed trends toward a kind of legislative activism and functional (if not formal) decentralization on the Finance Committee.

The foreign investors-campaign fund episode, like medicare and UC before it, involved a turbulent floor fight fed by intracommittee divisions. The representational roles of several members were evident, as were the inclinations of the "public interest" bloc. The highly competent JCIRT staff came into view, oriented more to review and refinement than to the stimulation of policy initiatives, but equally essential to the quite different kinds of initiatives undertaken by the two revenue committees. The propensity and capacity of Ways and Means for extensive reformulation were again demonstrated, though its dominance over the Senate Committee was less marked than in previous cases. And it was evident that the Finance Committee's increasing fealty to the executive branch involved, at least for the Chairman, certain reciprocal benefits. It will be the task of the next chapter to examine and expand upon these and other generalizations to which the case studies have led—and then to compare them to the modes of organization and operation which influenced the role of the Commerce Committee.

FINANCE AND COMMERCE: COMPARISON AND CONTRAST

The eight case studies thus far developed have permitted a detailed examination of the way the Commerce and Finance Committees handled the bills which headed their agendas during the 89th Congress. Each of the bills displayed its own peculiarities, but certain differences in *committee* behavior at each of the six legislative stages stood out as well (see Table 2). It should not be supposed that the committees represented polar opposites. The differences in their assumption and performance of functions were in some instances quite pronounced, but in others, much less so. Nor could generalizations easily be made concerning the behavior of either group. The "activist" portrayal of the Commerce Committee, for example, was not accurate with respect to its handling of aviation and communications matters. Campaign financing likewise cast doubt on many generalizations commonly made about the Finance Committee. Nonetheless, certain relatively uniform patterns of action emerged, and several distinct differences between the two groups were apparent. In Chapter 3 the Commerce Committee's modes of legislative operation were related to various characteristics of the group and its environment. The present chapter will do the same for the Finance Committee, utilizing in addition a comparative framework.

Leaders and Members. Long and Magnuson resembled each other somewhat in stature and in their jowly features, but there, in many respects, the resemblance ended. Magnuson was from a two-party state, and population growth, the emergence of new issues, and the growth of the mass media motivated him to undertake policy efforts and permit committee activities designed to refurbish his lackluster image and enhance his popular appeal. Long had a safe seat, and his electoral situation did not force him to become legislatively more active or more liberal. He did, however, have a streak of populism in him, and he had ambitions to rise to party leader-

TABLE 2. Patterns of behavior in handling major legislation, Commerce and Finance Committees, 89th Congress.

Function:	Formulation	Instigation-Publicizing	Information-Gathering	Interest-Aggregation	Mobilization	Modification
Commerce Committee	Frequently the work of individual members or the staff.	Committee often weak in publicizing, dependent on others. Members sometimes instigate action in other ways. Chairman rarely instigates, but often takes up proposals developed by others. Staff often stimulates action.	Dependent on executive resources, but staff often makes independent use of them and is able to tap other sources.	Frequently undertaken. Accommodations often made, but "toughness" and selectivity sometimes displayed. Notable for "entrepreneurial" orientation toward supportive groups.	Chairman often assumes the burden successfully.	Frequently undertaken. Largely centered within committee. Many members involved.
Finance Committee	Much more extensive reliance on executive, House committees, private groups. Innovative efforts generally limited to amendment.	Usually performed by executive branch or private groups.	Dependent on executive resources. Finance staff increasingly capable and involved. Committee shares highly competent and critical (but not particularly innovative) JCIRT staff.	Frequently undertaken and frequently productive of conflict. Sometimes restrained on majority side because of responsiveness to executive branch.	Chairman active, but often dependent on party and administration leadership.	Very frequently undertaken. Chairman exerts less effective control. Takes place frequently on floor. Many members involved. More partisan motivation.

168

ship in the Senate. Like Magnuson, therefore, Long had incentives to in-crease his legislative involvement. But where Magnuson was led to develop proposals in areas where the executive branch was not wholeheartedly involved, Long's situation led him to put his weight behind legislation that largely was being initiated elsewhere.

Long's role, however, was not easily stereotyped. He could faithfully defend the administration's proposals, as on UC and sugar, or he could use devious means to undermine them, as on medicare. And he did have his own ideas. "Russell has his prejudices alright," one of his colleagues testified, "but most of them are in favor of the common man"; another colleague added, however, that Long "was never one to die for a principle." His distaste for monopolies, high interest rates, exclusive patents, and Wall Street bankers' were seldom disguised; yet he coupled his patent amendment to the auto safety bill with a championship of industry's desire for antitrust exemptions. If, as his rhetoric indicated, his proposed "liberal-izations" of medicare were undertaken on behalf of the "common man," they at the same time pleased the AMA and others who wanted to kill the bill by loading it down. When Gore and Douglas attacked industries seek-ing larger depletion allowances, Long could be relied upon to stick by the Louisiana interests. His often-touted populism was thus coupled with and sometimes compromised by an apparent belief that the servicing or ac-commodation of particular interests was an important aspect of the legis-lative process in general and of his own role in particular.

Long's various and sometimes contradictory roles and orientations—the party leader, the flamboyant individualist, the populist "tribune," the guardian and accommodator of interests—thus explained a good deal of his legislative behavior. But where Magnuson's personal interests and ambitions found a relatively open field for expression and implementation, Long found the field quite crowded. The executive branch was heavily committed in his policy areas and the Ways and Means Committee was effective and active, if also cautious and conservative, and possessed important constitutional and traditional prerogatives. Long's predecessor had reinforced the prominence of both institutions—by default in the case of the executive branch and by design with regard to the House Committee. Long professed a desire to move the Senate Committee into a new, posi-tive, independent lawmaking role; the present chapter can be read in large part as an explanation of why his successes were so limited. Of considerable importance were Long's aspirations themselves. For one thing, his projected role as party leader, given the involvement of the executive in his issue-areas, moved him away from independent or far-ranging legislative moves. More important, however, was the constricted nature of his policy outlook itself, an outlook that was more likely to lead to piecemeal amendments than to initiatives of other sorts.

To put this last point in perspective, one of the Finance Committee's more thoughtful members may be called upon for an evaluation of the group's policy role:

> We're in a period of transition now in the way we think about tax policy, moving from a consideration of the treatment that should be given to certain individuals and groups to an overall view of what we're trying to do with the economy. . . . It seems to me that the Senate Finance Committee might play a very constructive role in this regard. . . . It should try to step back and take a broader view, evaluating tax policy in light of its impact on the economy and its social consequences. Instead of adding a Ribicoff rider [to the Tax Adjustment Act of 1966] for tax credits for college expenses . . . we might consider the whole tax credit structure. But we didn't think that way on the Ribicoff rider. . . . We send bills back to the House loaded down with amendments, but they're special-interest or technical amendments. We don't do much really to shape policy.
>
> Now the way Long handles legislation is . . . a far cry from what I'm talking about. He'll load on amendment after amendment, but this doesn't indicate that the Committee is being active legislatively in the way I'm advocating. It's the same old kind of piecemeal tax legislation.

However the possibility and desirability of such a shift to synoptic modes of policy formation might be evaluated, the member's comments do emphasize the narrowness of Long's focus; recall that it was in relation to the "grab bag" that Long chose to deliver his declamation on the Senate's right to "originate . . . important matters." Without somewhat broader goals, Long was unlikely to undertake far-reaching or original policy moves.

In the evolution of Magnuson's role, the outlooks and activities of his members were of considerable importance. Were Long's members pushing him in the same direction? Were they vying for policy roles of their own? Some of them seemed to be, but very few played roles of the sort Hart, Neuberger, and Bartlett assumed on the Commerce Committee. Of the seventeen members of the Finance Committee, only Douglas, Gore, and Williams seemed to have serious misgivings about using their committee position to promote home-state or other interests, and even the misgivings of these three were by no means absolute. But in very few cases did this representational role lead to the kind of policy innovations Bartlett and Magnuson undertook on behalf of the fishing and shipping industries. Rather, it usually led to piecemeal amendments or to the support or opposition of administration proposals.

In a few cases there was an attempt at more substantial policy involvement. Anderson's role in shaping the medicare bill comes immediately to mind. Ribicoff implemented his interests in auto safety, education, and welfare policy mainly through publicizing efforts, but he also formulated various tax proposals and social security modifications to these ends.

Hartke's extraordinary responsiveness to a legion of interests together with occasional original formulations added up to a substantial, if not particularly coherent, legislative program; among his proposals were a bill to provide pensions for World War I veterans and their widows; various liberalizations of OASDI programs, especially pertaining to blind persons; and proposals for in-depth studies of the domestic steel industry by both the Committee and the Department of Commerce. Talmadge and Smathers, opposed by both the administration and the House Veterans' Affairs Committee but assisted by Long, developed a proposal to provide special indemnity insurance for servicemen in combat zones, a bill which eventually was approved in compromise form.

These examples obviously fail to document a thoroughgoing or far-reaching legislative activism, even on the part of those directly involved. Among other members even less innovation and initiative was generally to be found. McCarthy and Metcalf, both of whom had achieved prominence as leaders of the Democratic Study Group, a caucus of House liberals, undertook surprisingly few legislative projects. Metcalf came to the committee reluctantly in 1966, only at Mansfield's and Long's insistence; his legislative efforts were focused on the Interior Committee, where Montana had a more direct stake. McCarthy's policy involvement was likewise minimal, though he professed a great interest in bringing social-welfare considerations to bear on tax policy; even his role as the administration's spokesman on UC had little independence or energy about it.

The cases of Gore and Douglas were somewhat more complex. Both featured themselves as activist senators, informed and involved on a number of fronts. The names of both were associated with tax reform and with medicare and social security liberalizations, associations Gore was to strengthen in subsequent Congresses. On his second committee, Douglas had undertaken a number of legislative projects in housing and area redevelopment, and his persistent championing of "truth-in-lending" legislation was reminiscent of Hart's role in the truth-in-packaging cause. But both Gore and Douglas, when it came to their involvement in Finance Committee affairs, conceived of their roles first of all in terms of *defending* the public weal against special privilege. "He and I stood against the interests in fight after fight." Depletion allowances, windfalls to sugar manufacturers or other industries, and tax loopholes of any description were their targets. Douglas felt a great affection for Long, which he attributed in part to their shared "populism," but the fact that he and Gore found themselves most often aligned in their "lonely" battles with Williams rather than with their majority colleagues was indicative of the direction of their efforts. Gore had no doubt, reflecting in 1971 on his and Douglas' defeats and Williams' retirement, that the absence of the reform bloc would have an impact on Committee operations: "There's no one on that Committee now who will really kick the snouts." But their absence was not primarily to be reflected in the Committee's level of programmatic innovation.

There was thus a much lower level of "policy entrepreneurship" on Finance than on Commerce, although Commerce also contained a great many members who rarely developed major legislative projects. One Finance member discussed his own passivity in these terms:

> *We're dealing with such large and complex problems—tax, social security, medicare. It's all you can do to keep up with them. . . . If I have any special interests on the committee, I guess they are the deficit and the gold drain. But I don't introduce bills in these areas. What kind of a bill could I introduce? You've got to let the executive take the lead. He's got the help, the power, the press. I don't like that situation, but I don't see any remedy for it.*

This statement—unique in its bluntness though not in sentiment—revealed a sense of inefficacy rooted, perhaps, in a lack of social and informational support as well as in executive predominance. But it hardly represented the view of one who strongly *desired* to assume policy leadership. There would have been difficulties enough for Finance Committee members who wished to break new ground, but few displayed the basic impulse.

A variable of considerable importance was ideology. Figure 3 permits an analysis of the distributions of Commerce and Finance Committee members according to their ADA scores. In the first place, *both* committees had relatively few members from the urban industrial states which would be likely to breed liberalism, a desire to "strengthen" the President's programs, or a "public" legislative style (i.e., formulating and publicizing). On the Finance Committee, much more than on Commerce, this was in large part a result of recruitment practices. Finance's high prestige and low turnover loaded its membership in favor of senior senators with safe constituencies. And, at least under Byrd, this process of natural selection was reinforced by the conscious manipulation of seats by the Chairman and the party leadership. Gore and Douglas were kept off the Committee as long as possible, not only because Byrd did not like their liberal leanings but also because Johnson, Kerr, and Long did not like their position on depletion allowances. "Nobody got on Finance that wasn't right on oil." Nor were Byrd's powers of gatekeeping limited to the majority side, as Dirksen's appointment in 1963 documented:

> *I got on Finance at Byrd's request. He liked to have a membership that didn't get too far from his views. He called me up out in Illinois and said he would sure like for me to fill that Republican seat. Well, I didn't particularly want on Finance—it's a working committee and I didn't have any time to spare—but I told him I would. So that explains why I'm there. I certainly didn't seek it.*

Recruitment broadened somewhat in the late fifties. The Johnson Rule resulted in the appointment of low-seniority and relatively progressive members like McCarthy, Hartke, and Ribicoff. The members added during Long's first two years in the chair, Metcalf and Fred Harris, were of a different stripe than Byrd would have chosen. Long took an active hand in their selection, though his control over the process hardly approximated Byrd's. But it was not at all evident that Long would use what control he did have to build an activistic majority of the Labor and Public Welfare variety. "I think it's safe to say," a knowledgeable observer reflected, "that he would try to keep either of the Kennedys off." There were thus appreciable forces, personal and impersonal, still keeping liberals off of the Finance Committee.

Figure 3 also shows that the ideological dispersal of Finance members exceeded that of Commerce. While Magnuson was buttressed in his legislative endeavors by a homogeneous and moderate majority, Long's support was less reliable, as was that of any other member who wished to mobilize the Committee behind a particular project. Commerce Committee Democrats displayed a mean index of cohesion of 81 for roll calls on bills reported by their committee, while the comparable figure for the Finance majority was 57.[2] Chapter 4 pointed up the independence and deviances of senators like Long, Ribicoff, Hartke, Douglas, Fulbright, and Gore. Figure 3 suggests that the majority's low cohesion was attributable not only to such individual peculiarities but also to ideological heterogeneity. Democrats on the Finance Committee displayed a standard deviation of 24.6 from a mean ADA score of 64; the comparable figure for the Commerce Committee majority was 17.2 from a mean of 72. Both committees had one atypically conservative majority member; with Talmadge's and Lausche's scores removed from computation, the standard deviations for Finance and Commerce Committee Democrats were 19.1 and 11.7 respectively.

Finally, Figure 3 points up the conservatism and the homogeneity of Finance Committee Republicans. Minority members displayed a standard deviation of only 1.4 from a mean score of 8, while the deviation for Commerce Republicans was 20.9 from a mean of 22. Both figures suggest that Finance Committee Republicans, to a much greater extent than their Commerce Committee brethren, were likely to oppose many majority moves and to resist co-optation. Were they, on the other hand, likely to develop proposals of their own? Here, while the requisite cohesion was present, the mean score suggests that the will might often have been lacking. This was in fact the case. Minority members often voted as a bloc (index of cohesion = 64) on bills reported by their committee—and many of the roll calls were on minority amendments. But there were few alternative formulations put forward. As one Republican member expressed it:

FIGURE 3. Distributions of Senators according to the rating given them by the Americans for Democratic Action, 1965.[3]

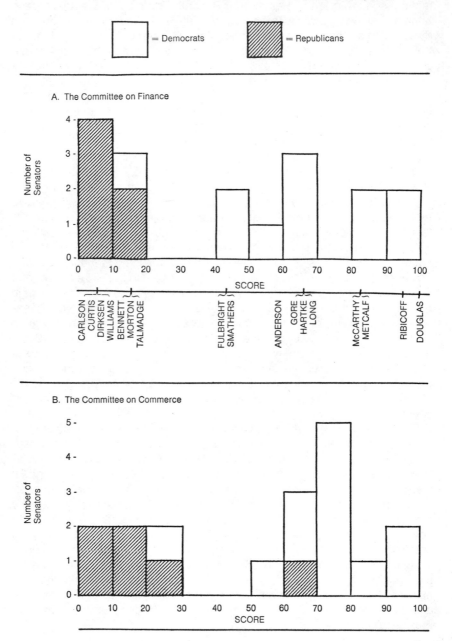

When you talk about this matter of legislative alternatives, you have a problem if you think that a proposal is fundamentally mistaken in the first place. You don't develop an alternative to something you totally disagree with; you oppose it. That's the way I feel about a lot of these things we're doing—the government shouldn't be in them at all, or they should be left to the states.

Two additional factors discouraged unified minority countermoves on occasion. One was Dirksen's position as Minority Leader, which occasionally (recall medicare) led him to refrain from opposing or offering alternatives to popular proposals which appeared certain to pass or upon which he had made some sort of agreement. Another was Williams' devotion to his version of fiscal integrity and the public interest, as displayed on the sugar and foreign investors bills. This posture led him to occasional alliances with Gore and Douglas and to a critical stance toward some of the business-oriented proposals of his minority colleagues.

The Finance Committee's ideological complexion thus helped explain the difference between its policy role and that of the Commerce Committee. The Finance Committee majority was somewhat less liberal and considerably less amenable to legislative mobilization than were Commerce Democrats, while Finance Republicans were less sympathetic to Democratic proposals and more united in that sentiment than their Commerce counterparts. The typical minority legislative move was thus not the development of a "constructive" alternative or a behind-the-scenes adjustment, but a "weakening" amendment which, failing in committee, would probably be taken to the floor.

Other differences could be partially explained by reference to the "personality" variables normally associated with legislative effectiveness. Magnuson's practical and political wisdom, his skills of persuasion and compromise, were often mentioned as reasons for his and the Committee's success. Of Long, on the other hand, it was often said that impatience and a lack of tact compromised his effectiveness. Some complained of a lack of candor and consistency, though others found in his intelligence and ability to comprehend issues substantial legislative assets. The style and aptitude of other Finance Committee members were also often evaluated in negative terms, with the notable exception of Anderson, whose grasp of his specialties and bargaining ability were often singled out for praise. But Finance Committee members were not apt to portray their colleagues as shrewd or effective legislative advocates. The fact that would-be activists Hartke and Ribicoff received more than their share of criticism along these lines might be interpreted as indicating a prior disapproval of their deviant orientations, which probably had little independent effect on the rejection of specific projects. But most members agreed that a native ability to "get people to go along with you" was of crucial importance in determining the legislative successes of a senator and his committee—and that Finance's

Chairman and many of its members fell considerably below the chamber norm in this respect.

If many Finance members evaluated the approach or the ability of their colleagues in negative terms, their assessments regarding the more general traits associated with popularity or respect were often more unfavorable yet. What was striking, especially in comparison to the Commerce Committee, was the frequency of negative personal references. "I just have to restrain myself when I start talking about him." "He's narrow and wooden." "He's the kind that tends to hold grudges." "He was hard to get along with too—very sarcastic and caustic." "He always hoists a flag." "He talks too much." Some members were much more castigated than others, and dislike or distrust was hardly the mode of all or even most interpersonal relationships within the group. But negative feelings were common, and in certain instances they apparently led to an increased reluctance to ratify one another's legislative moves.

Organization and Incentives. In 1970 George Goodwin, while pointing to its new "informality" and "openness," could still describe Finance as "clearly the most centralized committee in the Senate."[4] The Commerce Committee, which was by no means a paragon of decentralization, held 208 days of public hearings on legislation during the 89th Congress, of which 56 percent were held before the full committee. The Finance Committee held only 63 days of hearings, all before the full committee. This figure not only demonstrated the absence of subcommittees. It also pointed to a dearth of legislative activity, at least at the stages (formulation, publicizing, information-gathering) which hearings would reflect. One reason for the Commerce Committee's full schedule was Magnuson's willingness to let his members hold hearings as a means of developing their own projects. A glance down the Finance Committee Calendar, on the other hand, revealed few enterprises of this sort.[5] Over half of the 63 days were accounted for by the four administration bills treated in Chapter 4 plus the Tax Adjustment Act of 1966. Only a few scattered sessions were devoted to such member-initiated projects as indemnity insurance for servicemen, the study of steel imports, and campaign financing.

Magnuson's desire to enhance his own legislative role was a factor in his encouragement of activism down through the ranks—though certain areas and certain types of activity were still implicitly considered off limits. Did Long's professed desire for an increased Senate role in revenue matters have the same effect? One staff member, speaking early in the 90th Congress, perceived such a trend:

> It's hard to see what way the Committee is going to move [as regards legislative initiatives]. I know Long wants to do more. For example, some studies in social security might be undertaken. That kind of

thing has been very significant for some other committees, you know. It might not be practical [for us] though. One handicap we have is the absence of subcommittees; to carry out this sort of thing you've almost got to have subcommittees. That's another legacy from the past: all the power in the hands of the chairman. Long has relaxed that a lot. For example, he let Hartke have hearings of his own on this pension bill, and we've taken on a staff man to do an in-depth study of the steel industry. That was a Hartke project too; all he did was come to Long and ask him about it, and Long said sure, he was interested too.

It is significant, in terms of earlier speculations on the effect of "pluralization" on legislative initiative, that this staff member saw committee centralization as a hindrance to far-ranging information-gathering and publicizing efforts. His statement as to Long's intentions in this regard was much less conclusive. It was significant, no doubt, that Long began to allow his members to hold special hearings more or less independently; he even appointed a few *ad hoc* subcommittees to review special problems—medicare administration and utilization in 1970, international trade in 1971. (Finance's first and only standing subcommittee, on Veterans' Legislation, was appointed in the 91st Congress in an unsuccessful attempt to head off the formation of a separate Senate Committee on Veterans' Affairs.) Furthermore, Long's view that the Committee should be an open arena for attempts at interest-aggregation and amendment made for a considerable dispersal of legislative function and initiative. But both the medicare and UC battles showed Long to be jealous of his leadership prerogatives and little inclined to delegate responsibility. One member further testified that Long not only resented Gore's intrusion into campaign finance but discouraged his own more positive efforts as well:

He didn't like my getting involved in campaign finance at first. But as he got into trouble on the thing [at the beginning of the 90th Congress] he was grasping at straws and glad for anybody who could back him up at all.[6]

While his building up of the staff enabled and encouraged more members to play an active legislative role, Long still controlled all staff appointments and showed himself to be in no hurry to appoint subcommittees or otherwise to disperse his formal authority.

Many Finance Committee members were much more active legislatively on their second committees than they were on Finance. Douglas, Metcalf, Ribicoff, Talmadge, Smathers, Fulbright, Dirksen, and even Anderson were cases in point. A partial explanation in the latter four cases were the duties which being chairman or ranking minority member of another committee entailed. But what of the others? One might expect some negative remarks as to the relative permissiveness of Finance and other committees, but, significantly, virtually no complaints of this sort were heard. Some members complained that the committee was "loaded with conservatives;" others felt that their prerogatives were stifled by the House Committee and the executive branch. But comparisons of the sort that Commerce Committee members drew to Agriculture and Armed Services were not applied to Finance's internal operations. There was a general consensus that things were less "tight" under Long than they had been under Byrd and that more permissiveness was on the way. While majority members could sometimes mention specific instances where Long had discouraged their efforts, they leveled no general indictment. Minority members left little doubt that Long was less solicitous of their views than Magnuson was of those of their Commerce counterparts, but they still reported fair and equitable treatment.

On the other hand, few members bore witness to the positive initiatives they had been able to take on the Finance Committee. Compared to Commerce Committee members, who often contrasted their freedom of operation with that prevailing on the more oligarchical committee, Finance members spoke of freedom of action with a certain lack of concreteness. This suggests, in the first place, that Long's leadership was not experienced as stifling or oppressive. If this was partly due to specific accommodations he had made (e.g. accepting amendments), it also bore witness to the lingering of the norms and expectations that had prevailed during the Byrd regime. But the limits of Long's tolerance had not been tested. The main reason that many members had so little to say about their freedom to maneuver on the Finance Committee was that they had undertaken so few legislative projects.

It could not be said, then, that the membership was pressing for a dispersal of authority or even that full advantage was being taken (except perhaps at the modification stage) of the degree of permissiveness that already prevailed. There was little indication, in other words, that a decentralizing move such as the formation of subcommittees would immediately result in greatly accelerated legislative activity on the part of a number of members, though a few members were obviously ready to take advantage of such a dispersal of resources and functions and others undoubtedly would do so in time. Nor was it clear that Long himself would lose by such a move. Extreme centralization, functional for his predecessor, was perhaps dysfunctional in light of his own objectives—if indeed Long was genuinely interested in carving out a creative legislative role for himself and the Committee. Decentralization would increase the Committee's capacity for formulation and information-gathering, and while Long would lose some of his control over these processes, he could undoubtedly use the groundwork laid by others to enhance his own role. The areas with which the Finance Committee dealt were so complex and so fully covered by executive and House units that great investments of time and thought would be necessary if the Finance Committee was to play an independent, creative role; Long had neither time, resources, nor perspective to develop such a role alone. Subcommittees, if the members eventually responded to decentralization by stepping up their own involvement, would be a source of increased knowledge and broader ideas. Long, like Magnuson, could deepen and broaden his own involvement by providing an improved division of labor and increased incentives to legislative activity—but by maintaining his own prerogatives to oversee the process and to step in at the mobilizing stage. During the 89th Congress and to a large extent thereafter, however, the Committee's centralization, along with the role conceptions of Long and his members, generally militated against the generation of broadly conceived policy innovations.

The notion of the structure of incentives may again be used to summarize and supplement our conclusions to this point. No committee in the Senate affected more citizens more profoundly or was the target of more wealthy, powerful, or politically active interest groups than Finance. Senators with widely differing ideological viewpoints and varying constituency and group ties had a strong incentive to seek membership and a voice in committee affairs. For many members this included perusing legislation and offering amendments with an eye to the welfare of a group or region. For relatively few, however, did it mean an attempt to formulate and develop original or far-reaching policy proposals. The presence of certain disincentives helped explain this fact. In the first place, the groups to which some of the members were responding *preferred* either inaction or piecemeal amendment; they provided incentives to involvement, but not to extensive legislative activity. Secondly, the complexity of many policy areas and the disputes that surrounded them increased the difficulties and costs of involvement. Thirdly, party ties and the activities of House committees and executive agencies militated against independent efforts in some cases and generally made the business of formulating, publicizing, and gathering information seem less urgent.

A fourth disincentive was internal to the committee: the centralization of the organization made for an absence of independent resources and points of leverage and for reduced opportunities to specialize and to promote legislative projects. If this structural characteristic was a legacy from the past, so was a fifth disincentive: a "climate of opinion" that opposed legislative innovation. This factor, like centralization, was changing, but Committee norms still barely sanctioned, much less rewarded, activistic behavior. Recall the disparaging remarks about Hartke's and Ribicoff's efforts. Recall Long's attitude, in three of the four case studies, toward those whose claims to an area in which he was involved equalled or bettered his own. The attitude of Committee Republicans was especially pronounced. Their opposition to subcommittee proliferation and staff expansion was frankly linked to a distaste for accelerated legislative activity. Sometimes their discouragement of "pushy" members took less subtle forms as well; one member noted that his offering of a motion would often be greeted by "conspicuous" remarks and groans on the part of certain minority members.

Shifts in the incentive structure toward the end of the 89th Congress brought forth increased amending activity and suggested that more activism might be on the way. Staff expansion and a degree of functional decentralization gave members improved resources and additional leverage. As a result of Long's leadership, changing norms in the Senate as a whole, and slow alterations in Committee membership and outlook, legislative innovations seemed both less likely to be censured and more likely to succeed. But the atmosphere and the structure were still far from permissive; many external constraints remained; and—perhaps most important—the role conceptions of members often discouraged responsiveness to existing incentives and precluded pressures for further change.

Integration and Adaptation. The Finance Committee was apparently less successful than Commerce in "adapting" to the parent chamber. Five (seven percent) of the bills reported by Finance during the 89th Congress did not clear the Senate, while only one Commerce bill met this fate. And while the bills reported by Finance undoubtedly were inherently more controversial than those reported by Commerce, a failure on the part of the Finance Committee effectively to smooth the way for their passage is also indicated (see Table 3). Fully 74 roll calls were requested. Nor was the Committee generally united as it met these challenges. The Finance Committee's index of cohesion on its own bills was only 38, almost as low as the entire Senate's score on the same bills, and Committee Democrats showed less cohesion than the entire Commerce Committee did on its bills.

According to some indicators, the Finance Committee should have ranked high in both adaptation and integration. It was, for one thing, among the Senate's most *sought-after* committees. Data on transfers of membership from 1947 to 1956 and from 1957 to 1966 show Finance ranking third

TABLE 3.   Indices of cohesion on roll-call votes on bills reported by the Senate Commerce and Finance Committees, 89th Congress.

| | INDICES OF COHESION | | | |
VOTES ON:	Entire Senate	Committee Members	Committee Democrats	Committee Republicans
Commerce Committee Bills (n = 14)	60	60	81	82
Finance Committee Bills (n = 74)	32	38	57	64

and Commerce seventh in both decades.[7] The Finance Committee was also remarkably *stable.* From the beginning of the 87th Congress to the beginning of the 89th, only three new appointments were made, compared to the Commerce Committee's ten. As of January 1, 1965, the average Finance Committee member had served on the committee 8.6 years; the comparable figure for the Commerce Committee was 5.4 years. One would expect members serving such long terms to develop harmonious working relationships with one another; it would also be expected that seniority would be an adaptive asset—bringing the Committee into line with predominant Senate opinion and giving it increased influence in the parent body.

Patterns of *recruitment* could also be expected to foster integration; both Byrd and Long had considerable opportunity to choose "members who fit." The Committee's structure of *incentives*, while it hardly fostered large-scale legislative involvement, nonetheless encouraged members to gain acceptance and influence with their fellows. And the "professionalism," nonpartisanship, and equal accessibility of the *staff* probably had an integrative effect.

In spite of all this, as one member put it, "things on the Finance Committee are stormy and are getting more that way." This is not to say that committee desirability and stability, the presence of incentives to involvement in committee affairs, and uniform patterns of recruitment did not ordinarily foster committee harmony and cohesiveness;[8] but there were additional factors which qualified their impact in the case of Finance. Divisive influences are not difficult to find. Finance's *subject matter*, to a much greater extent than that of Commerce, involved massive expenditures and redistributions of funds. It stimulated competition and conflict between "peak associations" and between various notions of the public weal; it was imbued with distinct ideological overtones and a deep partisan hue. A second factor was the Committee's *membership.* The Republicans, as several members observed and Figure 3 demonstrated, tended "to appoint their most conservative men to this committee;" to this group, clustered at the lower end of the ADA spectrum, was added a highly diversified group of Democrats. Recruitment practices had tended to keep urban-state liberals off the Committee, but even Byrd could not finally block the appointment of mavericks like Gore and Douglas.[9] The Johnson Rule and differences between Byrd's and Long's recruitment preferences made for even more diversity. Some of these differences showed up on the ADA chart, while others were more difficult to categorize. But in any case, as one member expressed it, the result was a committee that often "flew apart":

> *The Republicans tend to vote as a bloc, and sometimes they're immovable. And then look at our side—that's a rather unique lot too.*

Look at Gore. And you never know what Hartke's going to do. Ribicoff isn't noted for his predictability either.

That these cleavages and divergences were accompanied by frequently expressed personal dislikes and conflicts has already been noted. Again, the contrast with Commerce—with its diversified minority, a moderate and relatively cohesive majority, and few apparent personal animosities—was striking.

The third factor militating against committee cohesiveness was the role of the *chairman.* Long's leadership was not entirely divisive by any means. Though his ideology had its peculiarities, his ADA rating, like Magnuson's, was the median score among his committee's majority members. His capacity to mediate between majority liberals and conservatives was demonstrated on both UC and medicare. Each of the case studies found him accommodating his Republican members at the modification stage. Most members found Long personally likable and capable; they rarely described him as solicitous, but still found him to be fair and reasonable:

[Responding:] I can't say he's made much effort to take our [minority] views into account or to trim his sails to get agreement. That's just not his way. But I don't think the minority can say he's been unfair.

At the same time, Long was personally flamboyant and temperamental; he was not an efficient organizer, nor was he particularly skilled at soothing animosity of the sort that characterized the UC and "grab bag" debates. Rather than muting conflicts, he often intensified them. Unlike both Magnuson and Mills, Long often became impatient with efforts to reach a consensus and attempted to work his will by means ill-designed to unify the Committee or to gain the trust of the parent chamber. Sometimes this meant using devious parliamentary tactics, as in the 1964 medicare battle, or giving covert support to opponents of a bill with which he had been entrusted, as with medicare in 1965. On other occasions, as with UC and the "grab bag" amendments, Long would push his colleagues to the limit; where Magnuson would have assured himself of a sizable majority by modifying his proposal, Long would aim for the approval of the proposal that came closest to what he wanted without great concern for the size of the margin. As one of his members put it:

Long isn't like Wilbur Mills. Even if he just has a majority of one on the Committee, he'll take it to the floor and try to push it through. Mills would never do that; he'd have to have a better majority. And Mills never loses floor fights.

A minority member testified that Long often entered these battles as a strong partisan and that his style of operation frequently alienated the Republicans:

Getting along on Finance Committee is more of a problem for Republicans now than it was under Byrd. Byrd ran the Committee as a homogeneous group and party lines didn't matter. That's not to say there weren't party splits on votes. But Byrd was somewhere between the two groups and he stayed in the background acting as Chairman, not as a partisan himself. Long, as you know, is a big partisan. He doesn't stay in the background; he's in there fighting.

Long, then, in his partisanship, his erratic and sometimes pugnacious modes of operation, and his impatience with consensus-building, contrasted nicely with Magnuson, whose integrative role was unmistakable.

Even on the Commerce Committee, where most indicators suggested that integrative and adaptive problems had been solved with unusual success, it was difficult to link systemic characteristics precisely with legislative behavior. With the Finance Committee, where the various determinants and indicators of integration were often contradictory, any assessment of policy impact must be even more tentative. Yet both the case studies and the testimony of members indicated that these factors were of considerable importance.

The Finance Committee's systemic failings may have discouraged legislative efforts on the part of the Chairman and some members; they certainly compromised Long's effectiveness on UC and the foreign investors-campaign fund bill. But their negative impact was probably not comparable to the incentives and the leverage which the Commerce Committee's contrasting qualities gave to Magnuson, Bartlett, Neuberger, and Hart. For one thing, few Finance Committee members had inclinations toward independent or extensive policy involvement in the first place. Others, like Long, Gore, Douglas, Ribicoff, Hartke, and Williams seemed less likely than most senators to be encouraged or deterred by the prospects their committee offered them for success. Their involvement was often motivated by a desire for publicity, by determination to take a "principled" stand, or by a quest for an activist image—motivations upon which the consensus-building capacities of the committee were likely to have little impact.

On balance, in fact, the Committee's increasing "storminess" perhaps bade *well* for its legislative potential. To put it more accurately, the breakdown of the cohesiveness achieved under Byrd promised to loosen certain constraints inhibiting legislative activity; certainly it pointed to certain developments—new recruitment patterns, increased partisanship and responsiveness to the President, a more active chairman, and the broaching of new policy questions—which, while threatening integration, also offered new lawmaking opportunities. While failures of integration and adaptation almost defeated Long on UC, a greater concern for consensus on his or the majority's part might have meant that the standards provisions would not have been offered in the first place. Integrative and

adaptive difficulties could stem from, as well as inhibit, legislative productivity. On the Byrd Committee integration itself, not its absence, in-
hibited activity, strengthening norms of legislative inaction and obstruction
and deference to House committees. Byrd's committee victories on the
"pooling principle" in 1961 and on medicare in 1964, both in the face of
Senate opposition, bore witness to his success in maintaining a cohesive
and homogeneous membership—although his ensuing floor defeats on
both questions showed that integration around norms too far deviant from
those of the parent chamber might militate *against* successful adaptation
as well. Byrd generally found in the Committee's integration an important
asset to his legislative endeavors, such as they were. But this could hardly
be said of Anderson, Douglas, McCarthy, Hartke, or Gore. Some of them
were more ready than others to rebel against Byrd's leadership. But all
surely felt somewhat liberated with the breakdown of the old norms and
patterns of deference which had held the majority of the members together. They found more opportunities under Long than they had under
the less disruptive but more stifling leadership of his predecessor.

The Finance Committee case thus shows that there is no simple relationship between integration *per se* and an active or innotative role. Integration under certain conditions and around certain norms may stifle legislative activity; the breakdown of integration can be associated with an
enhanced policy role. The fact remains, on the other hand, that integration
may serve as a positive factor and that a "return" to more cohesive and
harmonious modes of operation might enhance the Finance Committee's
role as well. More patience and less fractiousness on Long's part would
not necessarily entail an appreciable trimming of his legislative sails; it
probably, on balance, would increase his effectiveness. A broader distribution of functions and resources, the development of a harmonious
"meshing of roles,"[10] would probably foster integration as well as policy
involvement. The recruitment of a wider range of Republicans could have
a similar effect. Integration, it seems clear, could furnish the Chairman
and his members with increased legislative resources and with a more
secure niche in the policy process. But its impact would depend on the
character of the norms, structures, and roles it reinforced.

Interest Groups and the Committee's Role. Perhaps the most striking
difference between the interest-group environments of the Commerce
and Finance Committees is that the latter was frequently dealing with
"peak associations" seeking redistributive ends. To respond to the needs
and demands of these groups often required information-gathering and
administrative planning capacities to be found only in the executive branch
—and a greater ability to withstand countervailing pressures and to resist
ancillary, often distributive, demands than congressional committees could
generally muster; hence, the greater prominence of executive agencies

in the arena of policy and power in which the Finance Committee operated as compared to that occupied by Commerce. But the environment of the Finance Committee was distinctive in other respects as well—distinctive in the type and intensity of the demands presented to the Committee, demands traceable in part to the ubiquity and material impact of tax, tariff, and social insurance policy and the concomitant desire of particular groups to seek special benefits or relief. If group pressures, in short, were likely to stimulate and necessitate presidential involvement in the Finance Committee's realm, they were also likely to force the Committee into systematically responding to a certain kind of quite intense particularistic demand.

One should parenthetically note, however, that the case histories in Chapters 2 and 4 likewise revealed a number of striking parallels in group behavior and committee response. The NCSC no less than the consumer and health groups bore out Olson's observations as to the difficulties encountered by large groups seeking broad goals in effectively mobilizing the energies of their constituents, while the sugar lobby, like the shipping lobby, demonstrated the energy and power a highly particularized, relatively small, regionally based group seeking distributive benefits could wield. Nor were accounts of interest-group ineptness lacking: both the AMA and the automobile industry stand out as groups well financed but notably lacking in political knowledge and skill; the perceptions and strategies of both were unresponsive to congressional needs and expectations, and both, when public and congressional opinion turned against them, forfeited opportunities to cut their losses. The Finance Committee cases, like those of Commerce, point up conspicuous failures of strategy and intelligence and otherwise demonstrate the limits of interest group influence.

When one turns, however, from patterns of group behavior to the inclinations and predilections of the recipients of their efforts, differences between the Commerce and Finance Committees again become apparent. The fact that most Finance Committee members, the Chairman chief among them, identified with local and other interests and saw it as part of their job to offer legislation—usually "piecemeal amendments"—in their behalf has been adequately documented, as has the tendency of a number of members, many of them otherwise quite conservative, to sympathize with the particular welfare needs of various disadvantaged groups. The fact that most members had these inclinations and that Long encouraged the offering of amendments resulted in a logrolling situation whereby bills like medicare and the Foreign Investors Tax Act were elaborately embellished and interest group "responsibility" for their final form was greatly increased. Such factors were less important in explaining the legislative behavior of the Commerce Committee; certain indicators suggested, moreover, that the *direction* of group influence was somewhat different. The

South was heavily overrepresented on the Finance Committee (35 percent of the membership before Byrd's retirement, 29 percent thereafter), but New England and the Middle Atlantic states had only one representative between them. This helped explain the responsiveness to sugar and oil interests and suggested a degree of insulation from labor and other urban interests. Other figures suggested a high responsiveness to business interests as well. 35 percent of the membership (compared to 28 percent of the Commerce Committee and 24 percent of the Senate) had an occupational background in banking or business. While the Commerce Committee's U.S. Chamber of Commerce rating was seven points below the average Senate score of 41, the average Finance Committee score was one point above the mean (Democrats 21, Republicans 80). Finance's AFL-CIO rating, on the other hand, was only 45 (Democrats 69, Republicans 1), compared to the Commerce Committee's 54 and the Senate's 51.[11]

Thus a number of factors—the Chairman's role conception and style, the orientations, identifications, and ideologies of his members, and the resources of the groups themselves—combined to make the Finance Committee relatively accessible to various interests, especially business and other groups desiring "breaks" in tax, tariff, and welfare policy. If Chapter 4 demonstrated the relatively greater competence of the executive branch to handle the demands of groups seeking large-scale redistribution or the design of programs requiring extensive bureaucratic management—and if it also suggested that groups seeking distributive benefits were often attracted by the legislative preeminence of the House Ways and Means, Agriculture, and Veterans' Affairs Committees—the evidence was also strong that the Senate Committee frequently won the "race for representation" among the many groups desiring welfare benefits or tax and tariff relief. The initiatives to which group activity spurred the Finance Committee were not to be found in the main lines of any of the four bills examined, but in the "piecemeal," often nongermane, provisions appended to them. As one member noted:

> Most of our work has to do with the special effects of general legislation, what you might call special interest amendments. That's one of the problems—when you pass these huge bills which are so complicated, nobody really knows what the effects will be, and we have to spend a lot of our time taking care of the people who might be hurt. It seems like you are nearly always working on special problems —in tax, social security, and tariffs too, Yesterday, for example, we changed the classification of Chinese gooseberries.

To some extent, then, the situation in which the Commerce Committee found itself—where groups seeking major policy departures often came to the Senate Committee and the more conservative groups seeking deletions or amendments to the House—was reversed, though the Finance Committee's modifications were by no means always "negative" in intent.

What explained the kind of groups that came to Finance and the kind of role they prompted? Of some importance was simply Finance's place in the policymaking sequence: not only did the administration generally formulate bills; House committees always worked on them first. The House thus always supplied the working text—a considerable advantage —and often prevailed in conference as well. Groups would naturally view the Senate Committee as a place for last-ditch attempts at obstruction or amendment, rather than as a likely point for the development of new or alternative proposals. A second factor was the relative responsiveness of the various policymaking "islands." Executive agencies often championed large inclusive interests, with the result that they could afford or were forced to remain aloof to the demands of the opposition or of peripheral groups. Given the resources of the rebuffed groups and the sympathies of congressional committees, this course involved certain risks. The legislative preeminence of the executive branch was threatened, in other words, when the AMA, state UC administrators, groups representing the blind and disabled, foreign sugar lobbyists, and various business interests turned to Congress with the complaint that they had been "excluded from deliberations and discussions."[12]

One would assume, however, that such groups, considering the Ways and Means Committee's place in the policymaking sequence and its traditional legislative dominance, would have generally turned to the House. Voting patterns gave little indication that Ways and Means would differ greatly from Finance in responsiveness; the USCC, ADA, and AFL-CIO all rated them only a few points apart.[13] But the committees differed considerably in other ways, and it was those differences that at once provided Finance with a distinctive interest-aggregating role and determined the limits of that role. As John Manley has demonstrated, Ways and Means was "heavily involved" with pressure groups, and the ability to gain relief for key interests was in fact a prime inducement to Committee membership. But the attitudes of most members nonetheless dictated that the Committee should not become an easy target for the numerous groups interested in "breaks" of one sort or another. Bringing Ways and Means bills to the floor under a closed rule was frequently portrayed as a protection against group demands. Mills, moreover, attuned as he was to House sentiment, frequently mirrored House norms of budget-tightening and fiscal conservatism. His medicare amendments of 1965 and his UC revisions of 1961 and 1966 demonstrated his determination to make programs financially independent and self-sustaining, while his foreign investors "tax equity" amendments, his opposition to Senate liberalizations of OASDI, his distaste for H.R. 10, and his refusal to join with Fulbright in seeking increased depletion allowances for Arkansas aluminum interests as a part of the "Grab Bag" showed his aversion to extravagant tax and welfare breaks. The administration had and would continue to have its difficulties with Mills, but the Treasury Department frequently had reason to applaud Ways and Means' resistance to the interests. It was generally a "pretty good committee," one official reflected:

> We don't often have to go to the Senate with a request to close loopholes or tighten up a [House] bill. . . . The Senate, on the other hand, usually won't tighten up a bill, and they may loosen it. . . . In general, the Senate Committee is less responsible, more influenced by interest groups. You never know what they're going to do. These senators tend to be prima donnas, and they're much more prone to go off on tangents and to propose expensive schemes.

The attitudes and practices of the Finance Committee reinforced House attitudes and often prompted the assumption of a Treasury-guarding role. And what transpired on the Senate floor—the one place in the legislative process where amendments to revenue bills could be adopted without committee approval—frequently confirmed the worst fears of Ways and Means members:

> With all due respect to the Senate, they don't know what they're doing over there. They're so damn irresponsible you can get unanimous consent to an amendment that costs a billion dollars! And the Senate is supposed to be a safety check on the House. We really act as the stabilizing influence, the balance.[14]

At the same time, the Senate's receptivity to the interests made for what from the House's point of view was a functional diverting of pressures, and House members whose projects had been rejected by Ways and Means could often be found among those petitioning the Finance Committee. That Senate bills were rarely brought to the floor under restrictive rules further enhanced the prospects of would-be modifiers, as Hartke's success with his amendments on behalf of the self-employed and the blind demonstrated. And the fact that Long was frequently receptive both as Chairman and as floor manager provided added encouragement.

The Finance Committee's norms and the orientations of its members, then, its place in the sequence of policy development, and Senate procedures as well, made Finance the natural point of access for interests seeking certain marginal ends. Interest groups could wield decisive influence at various points—as the administration's development of UC and the sugar quotas, Ways and Means' rejection of UC standards, House Agriculture's revamping of the foreign quotas, and Finance's adoption of the "grab bag" testified. But various groups often found one or another policymaking unit particularly receptive to their interests. Where they focused their efforts helped determine not only their chances of success but, reciprocally, the policy role which the unit in question was likely to assume.

Coordinate Centers of Decision. The Commerce and Finance Committees differed from one another in membership characteristics, leadership styles, organization, degrees and modes of integration and adaptation, and in their responsiveness and relationships to various kinds of interest groups. All of these differences were related to the lawmaking roles the two committees assumed during the 89th Congress. But no differences were more striking or more salient than the contrasts between the other policy-making units that occupied their respective environments. The executive agencies and House committees with which Commerce was dealing were often legislatively apathetic and uninvolved. Finance Committee bills, on the other hand, frequently found the Senate group overshadowed by active and assertive administration and House units. The Commerce Committee found the executive divided and uncoordinated; Finance found it united and determined. The divisions that appeared in administration ranks over the years on medicare were rarely available for Committee exploitation, and other bills demonstrated an even more flawless united front. The Labor Department was given complete charge of UC; Agriculture and State muted whatever differences they had on the sugar program; and Treasury, Commerce, and State did the same on foreign investment. Of the major Finance Committee proposals examined, only the campaign fund amendment was reminiscent of the Commerce Committee's situation. Long made a proposal in an area where the administration was only halfheartedly involved. His way was smoothed because of the administration's previous interest and subsequent cooperation, but it was partly because of Treasury's hesitancy that he was able to remain so completely in control.

The reasons for the administration's legislative efforts were apparent: many areas under Finance Committee jurisdiction were vital to the President's "national constituency;" the proposals had to do with problems or programs which involved large numbers of people, massive bureaucracies, and the redistribution of national resources; the perspectives and resources of the executive branch were thus needed. Without executive involvement, the content and probably the volume of federal legislation in the Finance Committee's policy areas would have been altered considerably. There might have been a proliferation of tax statutes, with the largesse being directed in rather predictable ways. But lesser executive involvement on most fronts would have left gaps in formulation, publication, information-gathering, and mobilization which could have been filled only with difficulty and undoubtedly would have been filled quite differently on the congressional level.

The case studies demonstrated not only the extent of executive activity but also the degree to which the Finance Committee was constrained to share lawmaking responsibility with the House Ways and Means and Agriculture Committees (and the same could have been demonstrated for House Veterans' Affairs). All four bills originated in the House, and in each case the House committee had thoroughly reworked the administration's draft. Aggregate data told the same story. Only five (seven percent) of the 72 bills reported by the Finance Committee during the 89th Congress bore Senate numbers; the rest had originated in the House. All five eventually became law in some form, but only one—the Talmadge-Smathers indemnity insurance proposal—represented an independent initiative taken within the Finance Committee.[15] The Commerce Committee, on the other hand, reported 90 public bills, of which 62 (69 percent) bore Senate numbers. All but one of these Senate-initiated bills were approved by the parent chamber, but on 20 of them the House failed to act. The Finance Committee had less success with the parent chamber (five rejected out of 72 reported), but only one of its bills which passed the Senate failed to become law (the amended UC bill). Of course this was to be expected, since 93 percent of the bills Finance reported had received House approval before the Committee touched them. The figure still shows, however, that the type of situation witnessed on UC—where the Senate Committee radically changed the House bill and/or stuck by its version in conference—was relatively rare.

The most convincing explanation for the preeminence of the House was the constitutional provision that the lower chamber must originate revenue bills, which Byrd had not only interpreted conservatively but had also applied to all areas under his jurisdiction. The Finance Committee was to assume a negative, checking role. If this did not breed in every member a willing deference to House committees, it did at least contribute to patterns of inaction and negative thinking regarding policy innovations. Finance's tradition of "waiting on the House" also gave House units definite advantages in conflict situations. They gained the strategic advantages that came from prior commitment, and they were able in most instances to set the agenda, to frame the issue, and to set the terms of debate. The fact that the House acted first often made for conference situations in which a "return" to the House bill as a least common denominator could be urged; certainly it led to a widespread feeling that extensive or innovative Senate revisions were unconstitutional or illegitimate. "The House," as a veteran senator put it, "got used to the idea;" Mills and Cooley could often claim that the attitudes and likely reactions of House members compelled them to rebuff Senate initiatives.[16]

House committees had several advantages in addition to their place in the policymaking sequence and the norms and expectations which surrounded it. Most House committees were better informed and more highly specialized than their Senate counterparts; House members generally had only one major assignment and focused their attention and involvement much more precisely. Finance was doubly disadvantaged in this regard with respect to the Agriculture and Veterans' Affairs Committees. Sugar was the only agriculture matter Finance handled, and its jurisdiction over veterans' affairs was shared with Labor and Public Welfare. Both of the House committees, on the other hand, were dealing with a range of closely related issues with much greater interest and expertise; the results included gains in information-gathering and interest-aggregating capacities, leverage with the agencies, and centrality to the flow of communication. The particular advantages enjoyed by the Ways and Means Committee have been duly elaborated in Chapter 4. Its assertive leadership and tradition of preeminence, its specialization and expertise, and its power and prestige within the House gave strengths to the Committee that went far beyond its constitutional and procedural advantages.

What about the other factor which the "islands of decision" idea and observation of the Commerce Committee suggest, the patterns of cooperation and alliance that *linked* Finance and the other decision-making units in its environment? Such ties both reflected and helped determine patterns of legislative dominance. The Treasury Department's general affinity for Ways and Means was evident; it was both a recognition of this affinity and a prudential calculation of the Committee's power that led to cooperation on the foreign investors and other tax bills. But even if Finance had been closer to Treasury's viewpoint, one official reflected, the Department would have been extremely reluctant to break its ties and offend House sensibilities:

> [With all those recent changes in the Finance Committee membership and staff, would you anticipate going to them more with legislative ideas, bypassing Ways and Means?]. . . . We're reluctant to take a back door approach to things. That requirement that things start in the House applies, after all, to everything we're dealing with, and I think we'd always hesitate to send a nongermane amendment for the first time to the Senate Committee. That's not to say we might not go along with a nongermane amendment they proposed, like last year on that foreign investors bill. . . . But that's no different now than it's ever been. After all, we've got relations with Mills to worry about too, and he's very jealous of his prerogatives.

An HEW official echoed many of these sentiments: his particular agency was frequently at odds with Mills but nonetheless found it necessary to maintain cooperative ties:

> We considered the House Committee the center of power . . . and had good relations built up there. . . . We knew that the House Committee and legislative counsel would consult with us—there's a trust built up there.

His attitude toward new patterns of cooperation, however, was considerably more flexible than that of his Treasury counterpart:

> *Now with these changes with the Senate Committee and staff, things are going to be different. Actually, I think the Senate staff is better than the Ways and Means staff now, and I think this is going to make a difference as to where we go for legislation. Already I'm working on some changes which I'm going to propose that the Senate Committee make in this year's bill.*

Patterns of interaction thus often militated in favor of House committees and executive agencies and left the Finance Committee without appreciable leverage in the early stages of policy formation. Treasury cooperated with Mills and the JCIRT staff in formulating tax bills, Agriculture called in Cooley on the domestic sugar quotas, HEW formed a united front with Mills on his medicare reformulation, and, as Chapter 6 will show, the Veterans' Administration worked closely with the Veterans' Affairs Committee. A number of senators—Anderson, trying to delay the start of Part B; Hartke and Long, attempting to secure social security and welfare liberalizations; McCarthy and Talmadge, attempting to reverse IRS rulings and broaden depletion allowances; Douglas, attempting to liberalize medicare —learned anew what Finance Committee members could hardly help knowing: isolation meant weakness, especially when one's protagonists were the administration and the Ways and Means Committee operating in tandem. But the 89th Congress retaught a more positive lesson as well: that cooperation could mean strength—and both the Finance Committee and certain executive agencies began to reassess their positions and their alignments in light of that fact. Douglas and Gore had long ago learned that alliance with the Treasury Department, particularly with the Office of Tax Analysis, could both help the Department resist "pressures" and strengthen their own hand:

> *You've simply got to have the administration with you in these fights. If the administration and the interests [i.e. other members or committees] are against you, you're sunk. If you've got the administration with you, you might succeed.*

Long displayed the principle in securing approval of depletion allowances on shellfish and in his campaign financing proposal. And the entire committee found that radical departures from the House's sacred text—as on sugar and UC—were best undertaken with executive support.

Figure 4 provides both a broader view and a partial explanation. When the "presidential support" scores of Democrats on Ways and Means and Finance from the 87th through the 89th Congresses are averaged, slight increases in Senate responsiveness and decreases in House responsiveness become evident. Ways and Means' score, however, was consistently

FIGURE 4. **"Presidential Support" scores: Wilbur Mills, Russell Long, and Average Majority Members of the Finance and Ways and Means Committees, 87th through 89th Congresses.**[17]

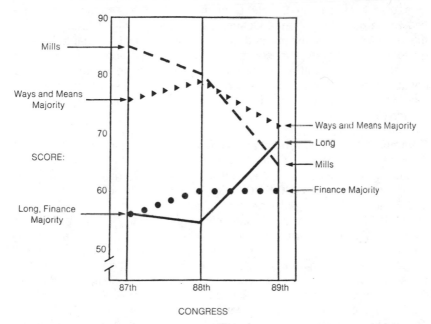

higher than that of Finance. This reflects in part the higher degree of party control in the House and the fact that marginal amendments were more often the subject of roll-call votes in the Senate. It also warns against overgeneralization from the case material; it would be too much to suggest that the liaison or the community of interest between Ways and Means and the executive branch were "breaking down." The divergent trends of the two committees become more significant and more understandable, however, when they are viewed alongside the scores of their respective chairmen. Long's and Mills' ratings both made significant jumps —and in opposite directions. As Long became Committee Chairman and Majority Whip, his record of presidential support noticeably improved; Mills, on the other hand, apparently responded to the administration's legislative boldness with increasing opposition and resistance. It was thus quite natural that committees and agencies were found reassessing their past patterns of cooperation and deference.

It should not be supposed that emerging patterns of group interaction promised to end the policymaking hegemony of the Ways and Means Committee; the hospital services amendment and the UC deadlock demonstrated that, and the tax battles of the 90th Congress were to remove all doubt. Nor was the Finance Committee incapable of teaming up with House units *against* executive agencies, as H.R. 10 and some of the foreign sugar quotas demonstrated. But new cooperative ties were being cemented between the Senate Committee and the executive branch— ties which gave the Finance Committee a more prominent policy role in matters of both presidential and congressional initiative. Chapter 3 suggested that a congressional committee must develop certain resources and outlooks if its cooperative ties are to facilitate not mere subordination but collaboration and an independent policy role. But it seems equally clear that for the Finance Committee, "independence" of this sort could seldom be achieved in splendid isolation.

Communications Resources and Roles. References to the staff of the Finance Committee are still likely to bring grimaces to the faces of many Senators, staff members, and executive officials. Two names are likely to be recalled: Colin Stam, JCIRT Chief of Staff for the 26 years prior to 1964, and Elizabeth Springer, who became Chief Clerk of the Finance Committee in 1949 and departed with the retirement of Harry Byrd. Stam made maximum use of his own resources—a central and exclusive place in the flow of information, his own expertise, and the unfailing support of Harry Byrd—to achieve a high degree of influence and prestige for himself and his staff. Stam professed to keep his operation "out of politics;" in reality, this self-imposed "professionalism" often left him free to implement his and his mentors' decidedly conservative preferences. Mrs. Springer, in her own way, also became legendary. "With Byrd and Elizabeth Springer," a Social Security official recalled, "that committee always meant trouble for us. That woman was simply impossible." Few indeed were the congressional staff, bureaucratic, or even senatorial heads that did not get bitten off at one time or another by Mrs. Springer; supposedly with Byrd's blessing, she restricted access to information, barred staff members and executive officials from meetings, and rendered the Committee practically useless as a source of assistance.

Committee quarters resembled nothing so much as the Tax Assessor's office in a southern county courthouse. During most of the Byrd years the staff was the smallest in the Senate, containing only one legislative expert. When Tom Vail came to the Committee from the JCIRT in 1964, he was the only professional staff member. Byrd got some help on social security matters from the Library of Congress and on revenue matters from the JCIRT, but he generally found a small and loyal staff useful in keeping committee action at a low key and discouraging members who otherwise might have gone off on legislative tangents. His legislative stance, one counsel noted, generally required little independent information:

> *[Since Byrd opposed the administration so often, wouldn't an independent source of information have been to his advantage?] Well,*

you'd think so, but in a lot of cases it was just a matter of being philosophically opposed to an entire program.

The 89th Congress saw appreciable changes. With Stam's and Byrd's retirements the JCIRT staff became more impartial and less tightly controlled. The new Chief of Staff, Laurence Woodworth, held strictly to Stam's professed standard of professionalism ("I don't ask a prospective employee his party, and if he starts to tell me I don't let him") but attempted to broaden his accessibility.[18] Douglas, for one, thought he had succeeded:

The staff situation is better now. . . . I like this guy Woodworth. He's very able and fair, whereas Stam was impossible. The liberals just couldn't get to him.

Changes on the Finance Committee were even more striking, and they were to continue. Mid-1966 found Vail Chief Counsel, assisted by a social security-veterans' affairs specialist, a tax expert, a medicare specialist, and shortly thereafter, an economist working on tariff problems and Hartke's steel study. By 1972 this contingent of subject-matter specialists numbered nine. One of the early appointments, that of medicare man Jay Constantine, was particularly significant in light of the Committee's past performance. Constantine had directed a number of studies for the Committee on Aging and was totally sympathetic to the new health insurance program; he became a key staff man, producing in 1970 an extensive study of the medicare and medicaid programs which served as the basis of ten days of investigative hearings.[19] Staff expansion thus reflected both the Committee's emerging policy interests and its shifting policy views; certainly it created a resource which senators wishing to assume a more active legislative role would find indispensable. Some of Byrd's old cohorts on the majority side voted for the changes only reluctantly:

I voted for the staff changes; we have a lot of complicated things to deal with, and we need a staff that can handle them. We had an excellent staff before though. It was small. . . . Most of these committees are way overstaffed. I look around and I sure do see a lot of people hanging around, and I don't think most of them know what they're doing.

Most majority members agreed, however, that the staff situation had greatly improved. "Russell's getting a good staff built up," reported one of the more liberal members. "Before, there was none."

The new Finance Committee staff was hired according to JCIRT precedent, on a non-partisan and "professional" basis. "It was agreed by both the Democrats and the Republicans," Long reported, "that instead of fragmenting the staff into majority and minority, the staff would be simply a professional staff of a nonpartisan nature whose services would be available to any member of the Committee or . . . of the Senate."[20] Minority members generally felt that the nonpartisan arrangement made for a high degree of staff accessibility; they made their case against staff expansion on the basis of economy rather than complaints about the services they had received. Of course, it had not been the Republicans but the majority liberals who had felt most disadvantaged by Byrd's staffing practices, and they continued to have their complaints—focusing mainly on the need for more personnel and on the extent to which staff time was increasingly pre-empted by Long's various projects. But the liberals, too, generally praised the staff's impartiality and reported vastly improved services.

In some ways, then, the staffs of the Commerce and Finance Committees contrasted less when the 89th Congress ended than they had when it began. Finance aides were still spread rather thinly, but, man for man, they compared favorably with Magnuson's "bright young men" in ability and "second-level" expertise. But the differences in the legislative *orientations* of the two staffs and in the ways they defined their jobs were deep and significant. The "professional" orientation of Finance and JCIRT aides approximated what Herbert Kaufman has termed the norm of "neutral competence"—performance "according to explicit, objective standards rather than . . . personal or party or other obligations and loyalties."[21] The impact of this "non-political" role definition on the Finance Committee's integrative capacities and on the accessibility of its resources has already been noted, but even more direct was its effect on the way information was collected and on the number and kind of legislative proposals which the staff presented to their mentors. It was here that the contrast with the Commerce Committee was most apparent, and it was a contrast of which the Finance staff was well aware:

> *It's not part of our job to sit around dreaming up bills and then to go to the senator and tell him, "Here's something you ought to introduce." Sometimes we may find a problem in a bill, and then we might say, "You have a problem here and here's how you might take care of it," but whether the senator does it or not is up to him. Sometimes too we'll take an idea which a senator has barely developed and help him make something out of it. . . . But the idea always comes from the senator. Don't put us down as one of those staffs that manipulate their senators like a bunch of marionettes. We don't act; we react. . . .*

"Reacting" on the Finance Committee, he might have added, did not mean helping a senator work out a legislative idea as often as it meant helping him understand, or perhaps amend, a House or administration or interest group proposal. But another aide used one of the few legislative ideas that could claim Finance Committee parentage to point up the staff's role further and to link "professionalism" more directly to a role free of advocacy:

[Campaign finance] wasn't a matter of the staff putting a bug in Long's ear; I worked on that, but it was at his direction. Nobody puts a bug in Long's ear. . . . We're a staff that re-acts. Partly that's the result of Tom Vail's philosophy of how the staff should operate . . . but I would assume that Long agrees. He never gets us involved in politics, uses us in Louisiana, etc. . . . Being a professional staff keeps you from taking much initiative. You're there for all the senators to use, and you'd get into trouble if you were feeding ideas to one senator or another. Of course we're nonpartisan too. . . .

The Labor Department learned in the course of the unemployment insurance episode that this aversion to "manipulation" and partisanship made Finance aides reluctant to participate in efforts to sway or even to poll the Committee; they were interested rather in working with bureau officials on the technical details of the legislation. On the sugar bill, both members and aides felt that the Committee made its decisions on the basis of more adequate information than it had possessed in past instances, but staff services were seen mainly in terms of analyzing the differences between the administration's bill and the changes in the country-by-country quota system proposed by the House Agriculture Committee—rather than in terms of developing new alternatives or accommodating the various interests involved. JCIRT aides likewise tended to regard themselves as "above politics;" they stressed their collaborative role in formulating and perfecting major tax bills but insisted that "the nature of our subject matter almost requires that the executive take the initiative." Congressionally initiated projects like the "grab-bag" often displayed staff ingenuity, but aides could rarely be credited with their instigation.

What accounted for this staff orientation? Surely the complexity of the Finance Committee's subject matter, the extent of bureaucratic operations in the field, and the preoccupation of the Committee with simply understanding and reviewing executive proposals militated in favor of a professional staff devoted to these tasks. But the norm of neutral competence had a life of its own among most members and aides, whatever the specific matter in question or the character of the Committee's involvement in the area. Many valued staff "professionalism" as a means of guaranteeing staff accessibility and avoiding partisan disputes. Conservatives found reassurance in the expectation that aides would render "technical" assistance rather than stir up individual legislative projects. But liberals likewise generally favored staff neutrality. This undoubtedly had something to do with the particular kind of staff partisanship they had experienced in the past: anything was better than a return to the days of Springer and Stam. But if past experiences had something to do with the grounds on which staff operations were prescribed and evaluated, so did the present orientations and expectations of the membership. If, in other words, Finance Committee members praised a staff role that would have failed to satisfy a number of their Commerce Committee counterparts, that fact said something about the Committee's place in the legislative process and the lawmaking ambitions of the members themselves.

All of this is not to deny that a high level of staff competence, whether "neutral" or not, is a considerable legislative asset—particularly when it is as formidable as that of the JCIRT. As Chapter 4 demonstrated, the revenue staff's expertise in fact enabled the Ways and Means Committee to rewrite most major tax bills that came its way and to get its concerns taken into account by the Treasury Department at the formulation stage. And the continuing development of Finance's own staff gave the Committee newly found legislative independence and leverage with respect to Ways and Means and the JCIRT professionals; executive formulators and advocates likewise were constrained to step up their consultations on the Senate side. But it is important to recognize what kind of legislative activities the "professional" staff, no matter how proficient, does *not* ordinarily encourage or facilitate. This kind of staff, in short, rarely instigates legislative creativity on a broad scale, to say nothing of that kind of issue generation and development that have gained for the Senate its latter-day reputation as a "publicity machine."[22] One analyst has stressed the importance of the JCIRT staff as a conduit between group and constituent interests and the revenue committees, but his evidence also suggests that Woodworth and his aides rarely independently undertook to write or promote group proposals.[23] The groups that received a hearing during the 89th Congress were generally those who were sent to the staff by, or otherwise enjoyed the support of, a Ways and Means or Finance member. The staff's job was not to promote the proposal, much less to stir up new business, but rather to cast the request in workable language and to advise members as to its implications. Here, as on executive requests, the staff had considerable influence and importance, providing Congress as it did with an independent check on the expertise of the policy-formulators and with the means of evaluating and modifying their proposals. But it was more than mere modesty that made the JCIRT and Finance staffs so self-effacing, so anxious to deny that they "manipulated" or "took sides." What was revealed was a pervasive role-orientation, sometimes prescribed and generally approved by their mentors but strongly internalized as well, which helped explain the kind (and the dearth) of legislative initiatives undertaken by the Finance Committee.

THE LABOR AND PUBLIC WELFARE COMMITTEE IN ACTION

THE ELEMENTARY AND SECONDARY EDUCATION ACT OF 1965

Germination and Failure. If there was little doubt as the 89th Congress convened that medicare was the top item on the President's agenda, neither was there any doubt that aid to education ranked a close second. But education bills were second to none in the complexity of their legislative history or in the controversy they had stirred. While it seemed certain that the new Democratic majorities in both houses would pass the old King-Anderson bill with few changes, proponents of education aid had no such assurance: reformulation as well as party mobilization was needed to assure success. Thus the 89th Congress saw the passage of the first broad-gauged aid to education bill in the nation's history, but it was a bill substantially different from those over which so many bitter legislative battles had previously been fought.

The earliest proposals for federal aid to education were made as public school systems expanded after the Civil War. The first major bill was introduced by Representative George Hoar in 1870, and the next two decades saw the passage of five less sweeping bills—one in the House and four in the Senate. The same bill was never passed by both houses during the same Congress, however, and it was not until after World War I that bills providing aid to elementary and secondary schools again received serious congressional consideration. The Smith-Hughes Act of 1917 represented the culmination of a growing interest in vocational education, and after the war several legislators, alarmed at illiteracy rates discovered by draft boards and concerned for the "Americanization" of immigrants, sponsored bills providing for the establishment of a cabinet-level Department of Education and for federal support of literacy, Americanization, physical education, and teacher-training programs. None of these latter proposals reached the floor of either house, but important legislative seeds were sown. The interest and support of the National Education Association, the national congress of Parent-Teacher Associations, and various labor, women's, and church groups were stimulated, while future conflicts were prefigured by the opposition of the National Association for the Advancement of Colored People, the U.S. Chamber of Commerce and other business groups, and religious denominations operating parochial schools.

The Depression and the near-collapse of public school systems in many states led to a number of bills to provide federal aid of one sort or another, usually on a temporary basis, but these proposals were passed over in favor of the earmarking of general relief funds for unemployed or unpaid teachers. Federal aid proponents, disappointed in their hope that emergency programs might provide a foot in the door, returned in 1936 to the strategy of seeking a permanent program of grants to the states. This time a foothold was gained in the Senate Committee on Education and Labor. The committee's successive chairmen, Hugo Black and Elbert Thomas, were friendly to federal aid, and bills were reported in the 75th and succeeding Congresses. None were considered on the floor until 1943, when a bill introduced by Thomas and Lister Hill (who had been elected in 1938 to fill Black's seat and had immediately been appointed to the Education and Labor Committee) was debated for four days only to be recommitted; the bill's southern supporters abandoned it when it was amended to require an equitable distribution of state funds between "separate but equal" schools. The House Education and Labor Committee, meanwhile, had reported no bill providing for a permanent aid program since the 51st Congress and would not do so until the 84th.

Interest and action stepped up in the Senate after World War II. Republican Senator Robert Taft, one of the principal opponents of the 1943 bill, changed his position, supposedly on the basis of testimony taken by the Education and Labor Committee (reconstituted "Labor and Public Welfare" by the Reorganization Act of 1946). In 1946 Taft joined with Thomas and Hill in sponsoring a bipartisan general aid bill. The Senate voted its approval in 1948 and again in 1949, with the Committee providing "a stable, cohesive bipartisan spearhead of support."[1] The religious and race questions were disposed of by providing that the states could spend the federal money as they did their own and that segregated schools must be provided for "equally". But Representative Graham Barden's subcommittee reported a bill which explicitly prohibited any aid to private schools and thus stimulated the bitter opposition of the Catholic hierarchy. The full House Committee became mired in debate and ultimately voted to kill the bill. Federal aid proponents then either backed away from the issue entirely or began to devise less controversial proposals.

Congressional efforts were neither sustained nor supplanted by the executive branch. Presidents Grant and Hayes supported Representative Hoar and Senator Blair in their pioneer efforts, and President Wilson endorsed some of the post-World War I bills. But the initiative always lay with Congress; with the advent of Harding, Coolidge, and Hoover, executive apathy was transformed into hostility and the struggle for federal aid became even more exclusively "a congressional show."[2] The New Deal did not change this situation appreciably. Roosevelt, like Hoover, appointed an Advisory Committee on Education and then declined to endorse its recommendations. In 1939 Thomas based his bill on the recommendations of the President's own committee, but the Budget Bureau recommended against the bill and Roosevelt announced that he would accept a federal aid program only if it limited its assistance to states unable to meet their own needs. The President remained aloof during the congressional battle of 1943, and only in his last year in office began to hint that some sort of executive proposal might be forthcoming. President Truman made explicit proposals for federal aid, campaigned on the issue in 1948, and supported the Thomas-Hill-Taft bills. He never really stressed the issue, however, and executive involvement in the formulation and processing of the legislation remained minimal.

President Eisenhower was elected in 1952 on a platform that opposed federal aid; it was not until 1955 that he finally sent up a bill permitting the federal government to underwrite and assist school-building authorities established by the various states—an approach which the NEA, state education officials, and liberal congressional Democrats (who had generally not been consulted) promptly denounced as a 'bankers' bill" not nearly adequate to "do the job."[3] Meanwhile, the Supreme Court's 1954 school desegregation decision and his own impending campaign for re-election had made education aid a much more politically charged issue for Hill, who had just become Chairman of the Senate Committee. Thus he did not schedule an executive session to consider school construction legislation in 1955; the initiative passed to House Education and Labor, where the balance of sentiment had shifted, albeit rather tentatively, since the late forties. There a core of 15 pro-aid Democrats overcame the resistance of Chairman Barden, and a bill authorizing $1.6 billion in school construction grants, not loans, over a four-year period was reported. The cause was buttressed considerably when the White House Conference on Education, which many had regarded as stacked against federal aid, produced a large majority in favor of it. President Eisenhower, spurred on by his new HEW Secretary Marion Folsom, responded by revising his own bill to include $1.25 billion in construction grants over a five-year period.

As the second session of the 84th Congress got underway, it thus seemed likely that some sort of construction measure would be approved. But the issue that had immobilized Hill and his committee eventually wrecked the bill. Republican opponents of federal aid joined with liberal Democrats to approve a floor amendment proposed by Representative Adam Clayton Powell to bar aid to states which did not comply with the

Supreme Court desegregation ruling. This shattered the fragile coalition that had produced the bill, and conservative Republicans then joined with southern Democrats to block passage. The next year the Democratic leadership, faced with a similar situation, offered to accept the President's bill intact. But many House Republicans wanted no bill at all, with or without a Powell amendment, and the White House remained inactive and noncommital. When Representative Howard Smith, Chairman of the Rules Committee and an avowed opponent of federal aid, moved to strike the enacting clause, he prevailed by a vote of 208-203, and the bill was once again dead.

While the 85th Congress thus saw another defeat for general aid, it also saw the renewal of one special-purpose educational program and the beginning of another. The adoption of these programs, distinguished from general aid in theory but less so in practice, provided assistance on a piecemeal basis, taught aid proponents some strategic lessons, and set some important precedents. The first program, providing assistance for schools in areas "impacted" by military or other federal activities, began with the Lanham Act of 1940 and was greatly expanded in 1950. By the mid-fifties, every state had school districts receiving these grants, and the program was virtually invulnerable politically. The Soviet Union's launching of Sputnik in 1957 gave rise to a second special-purpose measure: the National Defense Education Act. General aid proponents were quick to seize the opportunities afforded by the widely perceived shortage of scientists and engineers; "I said at the time," Senator Hill recalled, "that if Sputnik could go up like that, it could pull education up with it." Hill undoubtedly saw putting education aid under the rubric of defense policy as a means of avoiding his own political problems as well; he told his staff to devise a bill steering "between the Scylla of race and the Charybdis of religion."[4] Aid advocates within the administration, like Folsom, had similar intentions. HEW and the Senate Committee, working separately, both drafted bills which interpreted defense-related assistance very broadly. Loans for college students in scientific and nonscientific fields, grants to public schools for the purchase of equipment used in teaching science and languages, and funds for training language teachers and improving counseling programs were included in the compromise bill which easily passed both houses.

The next Congress found the administration retreating to its 1955 position, but the House, despite a ten-month delay in the Rules Committee and the addition of a Powell Amendment on the floor, in mid-1960 passed its first general aid bill since the Grant Administration. The Senate, meanwhile, passed its own bill. It seemed certain that construction aid would finally be approved, with the House dropping the Powell Amendment and the Senate sacrificing salary aid in conference. But the conference was never called. The immediate cause was the refusal of the Rules Committee to authorize the meeting. But the NEA and its Democratic supporters were by this time lukewarm; some preferred holding out for salary aid to settling for a construction bill that might close the subject for years, some were looking for a campaign issue, and some hoped to use the incident as a justification for reforming the Rules Committee.

"It seems fair to say that in the long history of federal aid to education proposals, John Kennedy was the first President to make aid a major element in his domestic program and to give it vigorous personal support."[5] This fact, in addition to Speaker Rayburn's success in enlarging the Rules Committee to give administration Democrats a majority, once more raised the hopes of aid proponents as the 87th Congress got underway. Representative Powell succeeded Barden as Education and Labor Chairman and "organized his committee for action rather than inaction," establishing permanent subcommittees and a formal set of rules.[6] The pro-aid majority in the Senate remained secure, with LPW still a reliable "vanguard". Hill, who faced another reelection fight in 1962, was no less sensitive to the racial implications of education aid, but by progressively decentralizing his committee and turning over more and more of the leadership on education matters to Wayne Morse, new Chairman of the Education Subcommittee and an administration stalwart (at least in this area), he rendered LPW even more serviceable to aid proponents. Favorable auguries notwithstanding, however, 1961 produced a debacle that was "a worthy successor to those of 1956, 1957, and 1960."[7] This time the problem was not Scylla but, once again, Charybdis.

Kennedy's education bill was sent up one month after his inauguration; it requested $2.3 billion over three years for salary and construction aid and included, for strategic purposes, a renewal of the popular impacted areas program. Catholic leaders objected to the omission of assistance to private schools, though the administration made known its support of a separate bill amending the NDEA to make loans available for private school construction. The LPW Committee, taking up the public school bill first, did not display the bipartisan harmony it had in Taft's day; liberal Republican members like Javits, Case, and Prouty still favored federal aid, but Senators Dirksen and Goldwater, the ranking minority members, filed a dissent to the Committee report. Since the majority side of the Committee was heavily weighted with social-welfare liberals, LPW retained its "vanguard" role; but what had earlier been "a unified bipartisan spearhead . . . became, in the later period, an effective but unmistakably Democratic floor bloc."[8] Morse, promising to bring the private-school NDEA amendments to the floor later in the session, steered clear of both religion and race and secured floor passage on May 25, 1961. But in the House the religious issue once again proved fatal. Rayburn's enlargement of the Rules Committee came to naught as James Delaney, the swing vote on the Committee and a Catholic, denounced the private-school NDEA amendments as a "sop" and voted with Republican and Southern Democratic members to table both them *and* the general aid bill. Subsequent efforts to bring a construction-only bill to the floor via "calendar Wednesday" procedures also failed; aid opponents were not swayed and the NEA remained opposed to accepting half a loaf. School aid, in Rayburn's phrase, was "as dead as slavery," and Kennedy could not afford to press further what he had termed his "most important piece of domestic legislation" without endangering his entire legislative program.[9]

In the twentieth century, then, as in the nineteenth, the Senate passed general aid bills four times and the House once, but final approval was never achieved. Many explanations could be given for these latter-day failures.[10] Executive leadership, partly because of the difficulty of Kennedy's position as the nation's first Catholic president, was hesitant and ineffective, and before 1961 presidential leadership had not even been attempted. Congressional organization and procedures gave great power to certain opponents of federal aid and provided them with multiple check-points for delay and obstruction. Those in favor of federal aid were themselves divided; together, they formed a majority, but many of them wanted their own particular bill or no bill at all. The NEA and its supporters wanted teachers' salaries or nothing, the NAACP wanted a "Powell Amendment" or nothing, Catholics wanted private school aid or nothing; all preferred inaction to compromise, and that is what they got. Nor was public opinion strong or effective enough to move the President or a great many congressmen to more decisive action; even where education aid was a salient issue, public attitudes, like group pressures, were often fragmented and operating at cross-purposes.

By 1961 it was clear that mere persistence was not the answer for aid proponents. Organizational changes were needed; the earlier renovations of the Rules and Education and Labor Committees were belatedly to bear fruit in 1965, reinforced as they were by rules changes reducing the control exercised by the Rules Committee over the flow of legislation to the floor. Shifts in public opinion were needed; by 1965 a variety of factors—liberalizations and ecumenical concerns in both Protestant and Catholic churches, the favorable images of Kennedy and of Pope John, and perhaps the deepening of the need for federal aid and the germination of the idea— had made for a greater willingness on the part of the Protestant majority to see aid go to private as well as public schools.[11] Changes in the ideological and party balance in Congress were needed, and these too were provided in 1965. But what was needed most of all was a fresh approach which would cut through conflicting group positions and make possible a coalition among aid proponents. The 88th Congress, though it did not see general aid get past the hearing stage, provided valuable lessons in this regard, paving the way for new approaches which made success of a sort possible in 1965.

Agencies and Groups. Just as the appointments of Ball and Cohen were indicative of Kennedy's interest in medicare, so was the appointment of Francis Keppel as Commissioner of Education determinative of much of the future course of the aid-to-education struggle. Secretary Ribicoff and Kennedy's White House aides took leading roles in the 1961 effort, but their job was less to formulate or even to "make a case" than to mobilize congressional forces on behalf of a case that had already been made. The situation when Keppel was appointed in 1962 was quite different. The old ideas and strategies had failed and, unlike medicare, education aid seemed farther from enactment than ever. Keppel thus took charge of the Office of Education at a time when new proposals and new energy were called for; "he . . . saw his role as Commissioner of Education largely in terms of achieving major legislative breakthroughs in the field of federal aid. . . . USOE's policy role increased markedly in extent and sophistication."[12]

Kennedy's 1963 education program showed signs of the shift. The President sent up an omnibus bill, presenting it as a departure from the old general aid approach. The idea was to pinpoint areas of special need and also to facilitate congressional bargaining and build the strongest possible base of support. The extension of popular measures such as the Impacted Areas, Library Services, and Vocational Education Acts was requested, along with expansions of the NDEA and new programs of student aid and construction assistance at the college level. Proposals pertaining to elementary and secondary education included, besides the expansion of the NDEA's programs of science, language, and counseling assistance, the earmarking of funds to raise starting and maximum teachers' salaries and to provide construction, salary, and special-project assistance in depressed rural and urban areas. This attempt at greater specificity on the public school level did not gain immediate support (additional assistance for parochial schools was not requested), but the 88th Congress passed enough of Kennedy's other requests to earn designation by President Johnson as the "Education Congress." Enacted by 1964 were broadened NDEA, Impacted areas, library services, and vocational education programs; expanded research and teacher-training programs for the education of the mentally retarded and the handicapped; new loan programs for medical and nursing students; loan and grant programs for college and medical school construction; and new programs of literacy training and adult education. Meanwhile, in prohibiting federal aid to segregated institutions, the Civil Rights Act of 1964 effectively removed "Scylla" as a peril to education legislation.

But the core proposals pertaining to elementary and secondary schools remained. President Johnson, mounting his reelection campaign and developing his legislative program for 1965, chose to focus on education and appointed Carnegie Corporation President (later HEW Secretary) John

Gardner to head a presidential task force which included several distinguished educators. Morse's role as floor manager of the administration's various bills during the 88th Congress had enhanced his expertise and stature in the field, and he was developing some ideas of his own. Hill had kept his committee decentralized and had developed a particularly cordial working relationship with Morse; and the Education Subcommittee was guided by a knowledgeable and imaginative staff member, Charles Lee. In mid-1964 Morse put forth his own proposal for breaking the impasse on elementary and secondary aid; federal assistance, he argued, should be tied to certain indicators of "poverty" and could be pinpointed in a manner analogous to the aid furnished to impacted areas. One aide recalled,

> *Our approach was to tack federal aid onto the impacted areas program, making the illogical inference that you could speak of an area "impacted" by poverty in the same way that you could speak of an area "impacted" by a federal installation. It was admittedly a gimmick.*

It was a "gimmick," however, which was congenial to many aid proponents. Morse's approach could be viewed as a logical extension of the administration's attempts to locate specific areas of need and to link federal aid with the impacted areas program for strategic purposes. But Morse's bill did not take care of the private school problem, its distribution formulas were not sufficiently refined, and it gave only the broadest specifications as to how the money was to be spent. Administration officials, moreover, were anxious to use 1964 to develop a comprehensive and workable proposal and not to get involved in a late-session congressional battle, especially since a detailed compromise had not been worked out on the private school issue. Morse's bill was nonetheless welcomed as a source of ideas and as a means of breaking ground and testing congressional sentiment; "we would have given him more support," a USOE official claimed, "had not the Budget Bureau held us back." But the BOB, motivated by strategic as well as programmatic and fiscal concerns, infuriated Morse by recommending against his bill in anticipation of the President's proposal.

Morse's ideas were championed by Wilbur Cohen and others within executive councils.[13] Title I of the Elementary and Secondary Education Act took shape as an amendment to impacted areas legislation which would provide for the distribution of federal funds to local school districts according to the number of school-age children coming from families with an annual income of less than $2,000. "Gardner, and Keppel too," a USOE aide later reflected,

> *think Morse performed a first-rate service in getting the idea of objective criteria started. . . . With Morse and Lee, though, I think it was primarily a political thing; with us, it was a good idea on the*

merits. We never did like the idea of just handing money over to the states, and this idea of criteria gave us a chance to design an aid program aimed at specific problems.

The President thus requested a $1 billion authorization for fiscal 1966 to improve the "quality of education in schools serving low-income areas."[14] Families whose children attended private schools would be counted in determining a district's federal entitlement, and local districts would be required to furnish some services, like "shared time" classes or educational broadcasts, which would benefit these children.

Keppel presided over the assembling of the administration's package. He "saw himself in a brokerage role—linking the White House (including the President and the Gardner task force) to the bureaucratic interests within USOE, and both of these to the Congress and to key group interests outside."[15] Keppel himself had influenced the deliberations of the task force, and his first draft in turn drew heavily upon their (unpublished) recommendations. But he and Samuel Halperin, USOE's Assistant Commissioner for Legislation, also tested and refined proposals in collaboration with representatives of the NEA and the U.S. Catholic Conference; with Cohen in HEW, Douglass Cater in the White House, and various BOB and executive advisers; and with congressional leaders like Powell, Morse, and Hill. The testimony of one of Morse's aides indicated that consultation had taken place but also that formulation essentially had been in executive hands:

They put us off [in 1964] while they were working on their own bill. . . . The theory seems to be that the State of the Union Message should be a complete surprise and that you should have all of fifteen minutes to work up a speech to introduce the President's bill when it comes up. Of course, if you have any kind of connections at all you learn pretty much what is going to be in the bill, but sometimes the executive branch avoids contact much more scrupulously than you would expect.[16]

In addition to aid for "poverty-impacted" districts, the President proposed a number of additional special-purpose programs: $100 million annually for the purchase of books and library equipment; $100 million for supplementary educational services and centers; the construction of regional education laboratories; and grants to assist state educational agencies. All school districts would be eligible for this "categorical" assistance, and most of the aid would benefit both private and public school children. Unlike previous aid proposals, the ESEA did not provide specifically for salary or construction assistance, though the funds authorized for low-income districts could be used for these purposes. The plan's USOE and task force formulators saw these departures from the old general aid approach not only as strategically and constitutionally sound but also as desirable on the merits. The bill pinpointed areas of special need and services which the federal government could effectively render, they felt, avoiding an indiscriminate granting of funds to the states but providing various options for local school districts. Morse and Lee (and the NEA) viewed the President's proposal in more pragmatic terms; it was not, Morse said as he opened Senate hearings, to be considered "a substitute for the broad-gauge general aid bill."[17] Ironically enough, the exigencies of politics had channeled funds in a manner for which few of the groups interested in aid would have expressed first preference—and in a manner likely to maximize the "federal control" which opponents of the legislation feared. Categorical assistance required far more federal earmarking and oversight than would have salary or construction aid, and it could be argued that its effect in many cases was superficial, imposing "special purpose projects on a foundation fundamentally weak in facilities or staff."[18] But various factions which favored some sort of federal aid found it possible to settle on the President's bill as the "second-best" proposal, and for that reason it succeeded where others had failed.

The NEA, USCC, and other groups accepted the administration's compromise not only because it represented a reasonable accommodation of their interests but also because the groups themselves had become more flexible since 1961. The NEA had worked for federal aid since the founding of the Association in 1857.[19] Its membership and financial resources were considerable and its lobbying operations in Washington and most of the states well established, but its "federal" organization and the absence of sufficient incentives and constraints to guarantee a high level of participation among its members often reduced its ability to generate effective and concentrated pressures. In the early sixties, moreover, the NEA had exhibited what many regarded as a self-defeating rigidity on the question of private school aid. But if the earlier debacles had pointed up the necessity of compromise, the 1964 elections established it beyond all doubt. Not only had the number of administration Democrats been increased, but the elections had also sent eleven additional Catholics to Capitol Hill (making a total of 94 in the House). Some sort of special-purpose program assisting private as well as public school children was a political necessity. The increased probability that aid in some form would be approved made NEA leaders realize that they must cooperate or else "risk being out in the cold when the hard decisions were made."[20]

The second group to which Keppel was particularly attentive, the U.S. Catholic Conference, also displayed greater flexibility. The Catholic hierarchy had generally opposed federal aid until the late forties when, in response to the Thomas-Hill-Taft bills, categorical opposition was replaced by an insistence that private schools share in whatever program was adopted. Since constitutional strictures precluded requests for construction or salary grants, the Catholics focused their attention on special-purpose assistance; private schools thus shared in school lunch, vocational education, and certain NDEA programs. General aid bills were viewed as inherently discriminatory. But the equal-treatment-or-nothing approach reflected by Delaney in 1961 was gradually modified, particularly when the changes in party ratios and House rules after 1964 raised the possibility that the Church might not be able to stop an unfriendly bill as easily as it had in the past. USCC leaders were thus ready to cooperate with Keppel, and in the end they could point to a number of ways in which the compromise bill was responsive to their interests: several titles would make aid available to private schools, and salary and construction assistance to public schools would be provided only on a limited basis and in such a fashion as not to place parochial schools at a competitive disadvantage.

Other important groups, though enjoying less access to the USOE than did the NEA and USCC, also supported the administration bill. The National Council of Churches and the American Jewish Committee, both of whom had opposed aid to private schools in the past, endorsed the legislation—though the American Jewish Congress and the Protestants and Other Americans United for Separation of Church and State remained opposed. The American Federation of Teachers muted its differences with the NEA and supported the bill, and the AFL-CIO, which had previously urged aid to private schools, also found the compromise acceptable. Thus in 1965, for the first time in the history of the education aid struggle, the major groups favoring federal assistance were united on a "second-best" bill. Only one defection was notable, and it was not complete: the Council of Chief State School Officers, an interstate group which was less active and possessed less political muscle than its counterpart in the field of employment security, expressed general support of the bill but broke with the NEA in opposing the library and supplementary services programs on the grounds that they bypassed state authorities and established "federal control."

Executive officials and group representatives had their first opportunity to testify on January 22, 1965, ten days after the President's Education Message. Administration and congressional strategists decided that the House, where education bills traditionally had met with greater difficulty, should act first. Chairman Powell turned the hearings over to his General Subcommittee on Education, and within two weeks a bill was reported to the full committee. An attempt was made to tighten the provisions for aid to private school children: the Subcommittee bill specified that public agencies would retain title to library materials and textbooks purchased under the bill and would control all supplementary education centers. Powell for a time threatened to hold up the bill until the House granted his committee's disputed requests for funds; the Republicans took advantage of the delay to formulate some 32 amendments which promised to slow action further. But Powell, faced with a threat of rebellion within the Committee and with pressures from party and President, brought the bill to a full committee vote on March 2. The only substantial alteration adopted at this stage was an amendment authored by Representative Roman Pucinski, to which the administration, fearful of Northern Democratic defections, eventually acquiesced: all families on relief, even if their income exceeded $2,000, were to be counted in determining a district's Title I allocation. The full committee also accepted the Subcommittee's amendments regarding aid to private school children and its addition of a two-year extension of the impacted areas program to the bill. But major reformulations were not undertaken.

Rayburn's expansion of the Rules Committee belatedly paid off on March 22 as H.R. 2362 was reported by an 8-7 vote. But Rules Committee hearings highlighted the increasingly vocal opposition of Representative Edith Green, Chairman of the Special Subcommittee on Education (often a rival to Representative Perkins' General Subcommittee), to the Title I distribution formula and to the absence of provisions for the judicial review of private school aid. On the floor, she joined with minority members in offering an alternative formula and in attempting to pin down Floor Manager Perkins as to hypothetical situations in which private school assistance could be rendered. But only one minor amendment was approved; all others were "trounced" amid Republican cries of "White House steamroller."[21] On March 26, by a 263-153 vote, the House passed the bill substantially as the President had requested it.

Senate Ratification. Morse's subcommittee gave the administration bill early and cordial hearings. Javits, who had become ranking minority member upon Goldwater's departure, echoed Morse in voicing regrets that a special-purpose bill was necessitated by "the practicalities of congressional support and opposition;" he even secured an admission from Keppel that his proposal was not the "optimum" federal aid bill.[22] Morse never tired of needling administration officials about their delay in coming around to "his approach" on aid to poverty areas:

> I want you to know, Mr. Secretary, how happy I am that we are back joined arm to arm . . . trying to develop the program which was set out in [my bill] last July, but which I feel the administration has very greatly improved.[23]

But the seven days of hearings were generally harmonious and positive in tone, and the appearance of former HEW Secretaries Folsom and Flemming in support of the bill helped defuse partisan criticism. The support of only one Subcommittee member, Dominick, was in doubt, but Morse delayed action until the House passed the bill. What he saw there alarmed him. The close Rules Committee vote brought back memories of 1960, and House debate revealed the fragile nature of the compromise on private school aid. Morse was thus reinforced in the decision he and administration strategists had earlier reached—to seek Senate approval of the bill as passed by the House and thus avoid the perils of a second Rules Committee vote and of a conference.

Under different circumstances Morse himself would undoubtedly have proposed or accepted a number of modifications of the administration bill. He had long believed that legislation should be passed which would guarantee a court test of the constitutionality of various types of private school aid, thus taking the church-state controversy out of the congressional arena and clearing the way for general aid. In 1965, however, he announced that be believed the present bill was clearly constitutional, that cases already in the courts would test other forms of aid, and that a Judicial review provision, if needed, should be a separate bill.[24] Morse was also interested in raising the income figure ($2,000) which defined a district's level of poverty, and he was sympathetic to sparsely populated western states which found their allocations for administrative costs inadequate. But he chose to defer action on the former until 1966 (a $3,000 ceiling was set when the Act was renewed) and on the latter until late 1965 (minimum administrative grants of $75,000 were authorized by an amendment to the School Disaster Aid Act).

Morse and several other Committee members were also disappointed that the administration bill did not do more for the handicapped. Here too the "embargo on amendments" precluded the addition of specific provisions, but the Committee used its report to effect marginal modifications. Committee reports often slant the meaning of a bill, but the report on H.R. 2362 set something of a record in this regard. Item after item of specific interpretation was presented. The provision regarding handicapped children was one of the most striking: letters from Cohen and Keppel were reproduced which stated that HEW regarded the beneficiaries of Title I programs ("educationally deprived children") to include the physically handicapped.[25] A USOE official admitted that the Senate Committee had forced the administration to reverse its interpretation:

> We didn't have the handicapped in mind in Title I; we were thinking of the economically "deprived". But that Senate Committee just can't do enough for the handicapped. They add an amendment for the handicapped on to every bill they pass. It's the mortar that holds that committee together. You just can't suggest to them that maybe a little perspective is in order on this thing. I think most of them really care.

"That letter you'll find in the report," Lee noted, "was a fifth or sixth draft; we wouldn't take it until we get exactly what we wanted." Nor did the report mark the end of the amending impulse: in later bills the Committee authorized Title I aid to schools for the handicapped which were not operated on a school district basis, ordered the establishment of a Bureau for the

Education and Training of Handicapped Children within USOE, and added a new title to the ESEA to assist the states in programs for the mentally and physically handicapped. Morse, however, managed to hold off all of this until the basic statute was on the books.

The minority's reaction to Morse's strategy was hostile but nonetheless adaptive. "The principal issue facing the Senate today," Senator Prouty told his colleagues on the first day of floor debate,

> *is nothing less than the future of the Senate as a coequal partner in the national legislative process. . . . Today each Senator must choose whether he will follow the trail of . . . lofty responsibility that [Clay, Webster, and Calhoun] have blazed—or whether he will follow the trail that leads to a House of Lords, men distinguished and respected, but superfluous to the conduct of national affairs.*[26]

LPW Republicans filed a statement condemning the administration (not Morse) for "commanding" the Senate to speed the bill through "with every flaw intact."[27] Yet all five voted to report the bill, and only Dominick, Fannin, and Murphy opposed it on the floor.

The minority had, in fact, partially returned to the bipartisanship of the Taft days. The departures of Goldwater from the Senate and of Dirksen from the Committee had left Javits and Prouty in the senior Republican positions. Javits' social-welfare liberalism was atypical among his Republican colleagues in the Senate and on the Committee as well, but his leadership position and his control over staff operations gave him an opportunity to influence, if not entirely to determine, the shape of minority legislative activity. Goldwater generally had developed negative positions with which Javits and often Prouty could only disagree; unanimous minority reports had been a rarity. Javits rather generated alternative proposals and "constructive" amendments; Dominick, Fannin, and Murphy could rarely approve all of them, but the minority could generally settle on a minimal set of recommendations, which members then could supplement individually. The presumption, in any case, was in favor of refinement rather than outright opposition.

The question of the "embargo" on amendments to the education bill was one on which the Republicans—both those wishing to "perfect" the bill and those entertaining deeper "reservations"[28]—could easily and without cost unite to political advantage. But it was significant that Javits and Prouty, while decrying the "aggrandizing Executive" and the impossibility of "latching onto the bill in an effective way,"[29] reacted to the situation much as did their majority counterparts. Minority aides Roy Millenson and Stephen Kurzman worked with Lee in developing the "amendments" to be included in the report. Javits and Prouty shared the credit for the inclusion of handicapped children under Title I; additional language in the report clarified the relationship of new programs to existing federal and state activities, required the USOE to consult with state agencies before making library or research grants, and limited the criteria which the USOE might apply to a local district's aid application. All five Republicans signed a statement hailing these positive "minority attainments."[30]

Floor debate began on April 7. The Republicans had joined in the unanimous vote to report the bill, Javits said, because of their confidence that Morse would keep debate "full and fair . . . so we would have a chance with our amendments."[31] There followed a rapid, almost ritualistic, offering of proposals, ranging from Dominick's attempts to revise the Title I distribution formula and absolutely to proscribe salary or construction assistance to institutions providing sectarian instruction, to Senator Ervin's provision for court tests of the constitutionality of disbursements under the act. All were rejected, and Morse was thus vindicated in his strategy. He was generally backed by Committee Democrats, while on only three of the twelve roll calls did Committee Republicans vote as a bloc. Javits voted with the majority eight times, Prouty five times, and Murphy four. Ironically enough, the restriction on amendments probably smoothed the bill's passage in the end. Attention was diverted from the thorny issues that had disrupted House debate; pro-aid Republicans were enabled to discharge their partisan obligations by attacking the administration's strategy rather than by calling into question the bill's delicate compromises, while pro-aid Democrats were enabled to approach each amendment not on the merits but with "larger" questions of long-range objectives and party loyalty in mind. Final passage came on April 9 by a 73-18 vote, and the bill went directly to the President. Johnson staged a signing ceremony at his old one-room school in Stonewall, Texas, and returned to Washington to host a gathering of congressional leaders instrumental in passing the bill. "With all the trouble I have with Wayne Morse on Vietnam," the President exuded, "I don't have any trouble with him on this!"[32]

That the President had found Morse's cooperation indispensable was beyond doubt, but it was even more evident that Morse had needed executive assistance to attain his own objectives. That had been shown in 1964, and It was demonstrated again in 1966. At that time the President requested a renewal of the ESEA which, among other things, raised the poverty ceiling to $3,000. But the Education Subcommittee reported a bill which authorized $1.5 billion more than the President requested for fiscal 1967, permitted a state to use national (rather than state) average per pupil expenditures in applying for Title I aid, and authorized $81 million for aid to state-supported schools for the handicapped. USOE officials, as in 1964, were largely sympathetic but again were constrained to oppose Morse; as one of them explained it:

First and second sessions [of the 89th Congress] were completely different. In 1965 the sky was the limit. We were setting up programs

*left and right. In 1966 the war had been escalated and we had to cut
back. We had to fight that committee, and I hated every minute of it.
[Isn't OE able to work "underground" with these committees like
some bureaus do?] No, we play by the rules. BOB was in control, and
the word was to keep the lid on. Like I say, we didn't like it; it really
hurt to see those programs cut back.*

The Democratic leadership was responsive to White House entreaties, and
Hill, hoping to forestall more drastic cuts on the floor, engineered a compromise at the full committee level. Authorizations were reduced by $500
million, the program for state-supported schools for the handicapped was
deleted, and the use of national per pupil expenditure figures was postponed. Authorizations still exceeded administration requests and major
amendments regarding the handicapped remained intact. But there could
be little doubt that Morse's powers of mobilization were considerably
lessened when the administration opposed him.

A Cooperative Performance, Executive Dominant. The ESEA of 1965
thus demonstrated the ways in which agreement and co-operation between
executive and congressional participants could further the interests and
increase the leverage of both. The various legislative functions, however,
were often not equally shared: the overall picture, reversing patterns
prevalent in previous years, was one of executive predominance. With the
shift from general to categorical aid came shifts in the locus of formulation;
the earlier work of interest groups and their congressional supporters
served in some instances as groundwork and in others as an indication
of perils to be avoided for the new formulators. Few of the ideas contained
in the administration's 1965 bill were new and most of them displayed
mixed parentage, but the influence and creativity of executive formulators
like Cater, Halperin, and particularly Keppel should not be underestimated
—in guiding the Gardner task force; in refining the ideas and accommodating the concerns of agency, congressional, and group partisans; and in
dominating the final "combinatorial" processes. A similar shift in the locus
of publicizing had occurred with Kennedy's accession to the presidency,
but here, too, 1965 presented new tasks. Congressional and group partisans had to be convinced of the merits of a new approach and, often using
these partisans in turn as mouthpieces, the administration had to disasso-
ciate the issue from some of its past implications and dramatize education
aid anew as a top national priority.

Information-gathering also had been centered in Congress and in interest groups in past years, though private experts had occasionally done
their fact-finding under presidential aegis. At times—recall Taft's con-
version in 1946 and the Eisenhower administration's shift in 1955—information-gathering had been crucial to the advancement of the federal aid
cause; but by 1961 the data were in, and the obstacles to action were to

be found in other areas. Deadlock and new formulations, however, brought forth a need for new, and newly focused, information. It also further tele-scoped the processes of information-gathering and interest-aggregation; relevant information often involved the needs and desires of major interest groups. Both functions increasingly became the province of the executive branch. But just as congressional committees would have been hard-put to fill Keppel's brokerage role, so did they fall heir to the needs and de-mands of the groups which were necessarily left out of the executive calculus. One USOE official acknowledged that interest-aggregation had had separate executive and congressional phases and implied that the division of labor proved functional:

> The main interest groups we work with are the big nationwide ones— NEA and The Catholics. The Senate Committee, on the other hand, has important contacts with the smaller, special-interest groups—the National Audio Visual Association, the impacted areas people [an in-formal association of school superintendents], various organizations representing the handicapped, and sometimes the library association people. That's not to say the larger groups don't go to Congress too; they know it's the court of last resort. But in general I think we deal with the large groups that are interested in the outlines of a broad national program.

This pattern was partially obscured by the no-amendment strategy in 1965, but the responsiveness of the House Committee to impacted areas and of the Senate Committee to the handicapped were apparent.[33]

Extensive mobilization efforts were rendered less essential by the size of the Democratic majority, which not only shifted the predispositions of both houses and of key committees within them but also gave concerned groups additional incentives to adopt a cooperative stance. White House and USOE officials were busy, however; on the Senate side they worked mainly with Morse, on the House side with a more diverse group of party and Education and Labor leaders. The main tactic of the mobilizers was to maintain a sense of the urgency of the legislation and of the fragility of the coalition supporting it. That this strategy was ultimately successful of course meant that the sixth legislative function, modification, was per-formed rather sparingly. But the bill passed by the House and the report issued by the Senate Committee revealed that marginal modifications had taken place—some in response to certain groups or constituencies, some stemming from concerns about church-state issues, program coordination, or "federal control." As was often the case with its high-priority items, the administration's role was primarily defensive after the bill started through Congress; modification, such as it was, was a congressional function.

The aid-to-education story provides glimpses of the history of the LPW Committee as well as of its behavior during the 89th Congress. It had long been a bastion of social-welfare liberalism in the Senate; 1965 saw a predominance of urban-state and other liberals on the majority side and some conservatives, but liberal ranking members, on the minority side. The Chairman, a long-time friend of aid to education, was somewhat restrained by the sentiments of his constituency but was willing to decentralize authority and to let activists like Morse work their will through committee machinery. The legislative involvement and capacity of the USOE had reached a high point, though its patterns of interest-aggregation left various groups seeking congressional assistance. And both majority and minority staffs were small but capable, necessarily dependent on executive sources but interested in developing alternative or supplementary proposals. Subsequent cases will elucidate these and other committee characteristics. It is to an episode particularly illustrative of the interests and ties of the Chairman that we next turn.

THE HEART DISEASE, CANCER, AND STROKE AMENDMENTS OF 1965

Mrs. Lasker and Friends. Visitors to the office of Senator Lister Hill were often struck by the relative absence of photographs of Presidents and other politicians; hung there instead were a picture of Helen Keller, a letter from the pen of Sir Joseph Lister, and various mementos from prominent doctors and medical societies. Those walls mirrored the Senator's own preoccupations, and his conversation often revealed his adulation of those on the frontiers of medicine and an intense interest in the breakthroughs currently being achieved. Raised in a doctor's family and named after the pioneer surgeon Lister, Hill devoted much of his political career to upgrading the country's medical capabilities and to promoting federal support of research. This interest became much more exclusive after the Supreme Court's desegregation ruling of 1954 and his own electoral difficulties made his championship of education aid more problematic. Health was the only area in which Hill did not decentralize LPW authority; he retained the chairmanship of the Health Subcommittee. This position, combined with his chairmanship of the subcommittee handling HEW appropriations, put Hill in a uniquely favorable position to initiate or expand health-related programs and to stimulate administration efforts. Best known for the Hill-Burton hospital construction act of 1946, Hill during the twenty years that followed its enactment was instrumental in broadening that basic program and in bringing the federal government increasingly into the areas of medical research, community health, and mental health as well. Hill assumed his Appropriations Subcommittee chairmanship in 1955, and PHS funds displayed a 56 percent increase for the next fiscal year. A similar performance was repeated year after year; by fiscal 1966 PHS appropriations had multiplied more than eight times and had passed the $2 billion point. A disproportionate share of this increase went into research: in the period from fiscal 1955 to 1966, appropriations for the National Institutes of Health multiplied more than twelve times and passed the $1 billion mark.[34]

Hill was not without his collaborators. He found a kindred spirit in Representative John Fogarty, who from 1949 until his death in 1967 was Chairman of the House Labor-HEW Appropriations Subcommittee. During the fifties and early sixties Fogarty's subcommittee systematically raised administration requests for health programs and Hill's subcommittee hiked the figures still further in the Senate. Both chairmen were independently and passionately devoted to their cause, but both had close and mutually beneficial ties with an extraordinary group of private citizens who had a consuming interest in medicine and research. In 1942 Albert and Mary Lasker had left the advertising business and established a foundation to promote federal support for medical research. Joined by the Daniel Mahoneys, owners of the nation's largest Democratic newspaper chain, the Laskers stimulated Congress' first hearings on health research in 1944 and prompted the Truman administration to give increased priority to the programs of the National Institutes of Health. Mike Gorman, an Oklahoma crusader-newspaperman recruited by the Mahoneys, served as Executive Director of Truman's Commission on the Health Needs of the Nation and thereafter directed a Washington office for the Lasker Foundation. Lasker died in 1952, but his widow continued and expanded their work. Her circle came to include prominent surgeons and medical researchers like Edward Dempsey, Michael DeBakey, Sidney Farber, Paul Dudley White, Karl Menninger, and Howard Rusk. These doctors, Gorman once noted, were unique not only in their deviations from AMA conservatism but also in their ability to communicate their interests and to use political means to further them: "The Rusks, Farbers, DeBakeys have the evangelistic pizzazz. Put a tambourine in their hands and they go to work."[35]

The Hill-Fogarty-Lasker coalition concentrated much of its attention on the National Institutes of Health. Created in 1887 as the Hygienic Laboratory of the Public Health Service, NIH received its new name in 1930 and began to assume its modern role with the passage of the National Cancer Act of 1937. That act authorized the establishment of a separate "Institute" for cancer research and permitted NIH to supplement its own efforts by making research grants to outside individuals and institutions. Institutes for mental health, heart, and dental research were authorized in the late forties, and the Research Institutes Act of 1950, introduced by a Lasker ally, Senator Claude Pepper, and cosponsored by every LPW member, established Institutes for metabolic and neurological diseases and authorized the Surgeon General to establish additional Institutes as he saw fit. Meanwhile, Hill and Fogarty provided appropriations increases which not only made possible a rapid growth of NIH activity but also increased the relative prominence of the Institutes within the Public Health Service. By fiscal 1966, NIH claimed 51 percent of the PHS budget, which in turn was some 28 percent of that allotted to HEW.

This situation set up certain strains within the executive branch and gave NIH officials reason to ally themselves with the Laskers and their congressional supporters. Appropriations patterns and increasing fears "that the NIH tail would wag the PHS dog" widened a gap between NIH and its parent agency that probably would have developed in any case. The Public Health Service was sometimes described as "conservative," sometimes as "weak," and the reasons were not far to seek. The PHS administered programs that were decentralized and operated by state agencies which were often resistant to standardization or change. Many of the services it performed were in areas where powerful interests feared a vigorous or expanded federal role. And even where the PHS attempted to instigate new policy departures (recall the Surgeon General's Report on Smoking and Health), it often did not have the benefit of group pressures in its behalf or of strong support at the White House or secretarial level. It was natural that NIH should assert its independence. Its headquarters in Bethesda, Maryland, were physically isolated from the downtown PHS. Its programs and problems were only loosely related to those of PHS; while the parent agency was trammeled by the interests of doctors and state agencies, NIH activities did not meet with such opposition and its officials often found what they regarded as obstacles to a vigorous, truly national effort in the attitudes and inhibitions of their PHS superiors. NIH was often unsure of its support within PHS and, even when the Institutes had Public Health backing, there were doubts as to the effectiveness of PHS advocacy in higher circles.

NIH officials thus had reason to seek their own channels of influence. Certain aspects of their situation made such efforts more feasible. They were not politically and administratively accountable in the way that officials of most other bureaus were. Their appointments were generally made on a nonpolitical basis, and their work by nature required a large measure of discretion and autonomy. Each Institute, in addition, had an independent Advisory Council drawn from the private sector and attached to it by statute. These councils often contained a liberal sprinkling of doctor-politicians associated with the Laskers. Designed to ensure a two-way flow of information between the Institutes and the world of private practice and research, the Councils also emerged as mechanisms through which NIH officials could have their needs expressed and their interests furthered, apart from official channels. "My main source of information," remarked one senator, "is those Councils. These are people who know what is going on, and they don't have to answer to *anybody.* They're not paid by the government, so they can talk freely and they do."

Quite different, then, from USOE and other agencies which found themselves constrained to "play by the rules," NIH had both the motivations and the means to secure independent alliances with its congressional and private supporters. Dr. James Shannon, NIH Director from 1955 to 1968, thus became an important member of the Hill-Fogarty-Lasker team. During the Eisenhower years the four performed as a "highly polished quartet;" Fogarty and Hill each year elicited statements from Shannon and his subordinates as to how HEW and the Budget Bureau had cut their requests, and then a parade of physicians lined up by Gorman and Mrs. Lasker stated the case for more money.[36] NIH recognized its stake, as one of its officials put it, in the "independence" of Congress from the executive and in the power committee chairmen enjoyed within the institution:

> *If the government structure were entirely hierarchical, NIH would be pretty far down the line and would have a hard time making itself heard. Without Congress operating the way it does, it's hard to imagine Shannon doing the things he's done.*

Mrs. Lasker, however, recognized the potential of hierarchy as well as polyarchy for working her will. She and her congressional collaborators boosted Kennedy's and Johnson's budgets just as they had Eisenhower's, but she also took pains to build up her access and influence at the White House. It was this liaison that was to be of primary importance in the initiation of the Heart Disease, Cancer, and Stroke Amendments of 1965.

Mrs. Lasker had always argued for research in terms of the possibility of breakthroughs in the treatment and cure of major diseases; such an emphasis was both good politics and in accord with her penchant for practical results. Gorman got a plank calling for a White House study of heart disease and cancer inserted in the 1960 Democratic platform. A hastily assembled committee produced a study in 1961 which was disparagingly dubbed the "Bay of Pigs Report" ("both because it was presented to President Kennedy on the day of the invasion, and because it was so badly done that it was a bit of a disaster in its own right"[37]) and shelved. But the Lasker forces pushed for another commission and, aware that Kennedy's father had just suffered a stroke, suggested that strokes too might be studied. At the time of his assassination, Kennedy was considering the idea.

Meanwhile, Mrs. Lasker's concern was heightened by a realization that yearly expenditures for medical research were beginning to level off.[38] Her contacts at NIH and in the medical world shared her concern, and though they were sometimes uncomfortable with her impatience with "pure" research, they appreciated the potential of the heart disease-cancer-stroke emphasis for eliciting political and financial support. On this particular project, however, Mrs. Lasker consulted relatively little at NIH; she worked independently and relied on her personal ties with the President. Johnson liked Mrs. Lasker and valued her support, and he found her emphasis on the practical fruits of research congenial. Thus, during his first year in office the President appointed a Commission on Heart Disease, Cancer, and Stroke. Dr. Michael DeBakey of Baylor University, a friend of the President and a longtime Lasker ally, was named Chairman, and Mrs. Mahoney, Dempsey, Farber, Rusk and other doctors often linked with Lasker causes were among its members. "We had a quorum," Gorman said.[39]

Neither the President nor the Lasker forces expected the Commission to turn up new scientific data. What was wanted was a program outline and sufficient information to justify it. This the Commission provided, in a report prepared just in time for utilization by aides preparing the President's 1965 program. The Commission recommended that 60 "regional centers" for clinical investigation, teaching, and patient care be set up "in universities, hospitals and research institutes and other institutions" during the next five years; that 450 "diagnostic and treatment stations" be set up in local communities during the same period; that development grants be made to medical schools; and that "grant support be undertaken to stimulate the formation of medical complexes [30, over five years] whereby university medical schools, hospitals and other health care and research agencies and institutions work in concert."[40] A price tag of almost $3 billion was put on these and other recommendations; it was suggested that the federal government bear all construction costs associated with the stations and centers and that it share in staffing and operating costs as well.

The report reflected the Lasker group's political astuteness; its information was simply and straightforwardly presented, and 35 concrete recommendations were put forward. But the report also reflected the divergent interests of the Commission's membership: some of the recommendations focused on research, others on treatment, some on medical schools, others on hospitals, and still others on state and community health services. It was an ambitious and variegated list of proposals. The process of translation from report to legislation was obviously going to be of great importance in determining which proposals and which concerns would have a policy impact. That task, as it turned out, fell largely to Dempsey. His appointment as Special Assistant to the Secretary of HEW midway in the Commission's deliberations left little doubt that the President planned to offer a heart disease-cancer-stroke bill. It also meant that Dempsey had a unique opportunity to implement his own particular concerns for research and the medical schools (at the time of his appointment he was Dean of Washington University's School of Medicine). "It was often said," one observer recalled, "that everybody else on the Commission went home, but Dempsey stayed. The proposed legislation showed it."

Of the Commission's major recommendations, the President's bill implemented only the one which proposed the establishment of "medical complexes." Some of the features of the proposed centers and stations were incorporated: each complex was to include a center for clinical research and the training of specialists and a "diagnostic and treatment station." But each complex was to contain a medical school and a hospital as well, and Dempsey's testimony left little doubt that universities or medical schools would ordinarily assume the initiative in the "planning and future development" of the complexes.[41]

The administration bill thus borrowed selectively from the Commission's report, stressing categorical research and the strengthening of medical schools and other existing facilities rather than treatment, community health programs, or the construction of new facilities. This emphasis was generally in line with the sentiments of NIH and the Lasker group; the downtown PHS, which had distrusted the DeBakey Commission from the first because of its own exclusion from membership,[42] could find even less comfort in the draft legislation than in the Commission's report. But the projected program was still vague, and numerous questions remained as to who would administer it and what activities it might subsume. Nor was it clear how much it would cost. The administration asked for only $50 million in the first year and "such sums as may be necessary" for the next four years—a request which Secretary Celebrezze explained in terms of the lateness of the Commission's report and the need for additional planning.[43] The administration presented the bill as a high-priority item, but it bore the marks of haste and of its mixed parentage. Details regarding the size, the administration, and even the content of the program were left to congressional discretion.

The Congressional Phase. Hill had little to do with the drafting activities that centered in Dempsey's office. In many ways this was atypical; participants in both branches acknowledged that "ordinarily much more consultation would have taken place." Fully apprised of what was transpiring, Hill did not interfere because he did not need to. He was in contact with his NIH and Lasker allies, and they generally found themselves in agreement with the focus Dempsey was giving to the program.

Senate Subcommittee hearings began on February 9, 1965, one month after the President's Health Message—a document highlighted by a renewed plea for medicare but giving prominent billing to the new regional medical complexes request as well. Hill described the proposed program as "a logical outgrowth and extension" of the clinical research center programs he had been instrumental in instigating through the earmarking of appropriations in 1958.[44] But as sponsor of the President's bill

(S. 596), he did not claim authorship and in fact proved responsive to certain suggestions for change.

One important concern was administration: The bill provided only for general oversight by the Surgeon General. Hill's first question to executive witnesses concerned the precise location of responsibility, and the answer he received showed that the interagency debate had not yet been resolved:

> **DR. DEMPSEY:** *This has not been completely determined. . . . There exists in the Public Health Service, particularly in the NIH, a background of competence and experience in managing a similar kind of program. The bill calls for this determination to be made by the Surgeon General. . . . The [DeBakey] Commission felt that the administrative management of a program had to be left to administrative determination. . . .*
>
> **THE CHAIRMAN:** *But there was much comment about NIH, wasn't there, and reference to the experience and background of NIH?*
>
> **SECRETARY CELEBREZZE:** *There are strong sentiments and strong reasons for putting it in NIH. . . . On the other hand, we have always identified NIH primarily as a research bureau.*[45]

The next day DeBakey expressed his sympathy for NIH control; he subsequently filed a statement claiming that "the vast majority of the Commission" felt the same way. These sentiments reflected a desire for a research-centered program and perhaps an "endemic . . . distrust of the downtown PHS" as well.[46] Commission member and former HEW Secretary Marion Folsom registered a dissent, urging that administrative responsibilities be given to the PHS's Bureau of State Services to ensure a focus on training and treatment.[47] But those who shared this concern actually had no place to turn. As one observer noted:

> There was no way of implementing their concern short of advocating some sort of PHS administration, and that was playing into the hands of those who didn't want to see a national program at all but wanted to go through the same old public health routine of grants to the states.

Strengthened by the support of Hill, Dempsey, most Commission members, and other Lasker allies, the NIH at length prevailed within the executive branch. "The Committee has been advised," declared the Senate Report on June 24, "that if the bill is enacted, responsibility for the administration of the programs it authorizes will be placed in the National Institutes of Health."[48]

Another question was whether the program would involve the construction of new facilities. In choosing to implement the Commission's recommendations regarding complexes rather than those proposing "centers" and "stations," the bill's formulators implied that their primary concern was the coordination and upgrading of existing facilities. But S. 596 still permitted the construction of new buildings as well as the alteration and repair of old ones. The potential breadth of the program led the Executive Director of the Association of American Medical Colleges to express his concern that the proposed research centers be "intimate parts of medical schools or teaching hospitals, staffed by members of the faculty, rather than isloated and independent institutions;" the American Hospital Association put forth an "interpretation" whereby both the research centers and the diagnostic and treatment stations were to be incorporated into existing hospitals.[49] Likewise anxious to give the program a more precise focus and to allay the fears of those who envisioned "huge new federal complexes," Hill deleted the provisions for the construction of new buildings from the bill. To many of those interested in seeing the bill narrowed, including the AAMC, this absolute prohibition seemed to go too far in the opposite direction. The Senate Committee's alterations, Dr. Farber later told the House Committee, "sharpened the definition of the institutions which would comprise the network of regional complexes, centers, and stations." But, he went on, it was nonetheless important to authorize new construction where needed and where recommended by the "appropriate administration and councils of the NIH." Dempsey, speaking for the administration, agreed:

> We have never envisioned this bill as the instrument for a major construction program. Nevertheless, the authority for new construction, deleted in S. 596, is greatly needed in specific situations . . . where new medical schools are presently being formed. Without authority for new construction it may not be possible to provide the new facilities needed to qualify as a medical complex in these situations.[50]

But the Hill Subcommittee's ban on new construction remained, and many NIH officials welcomed the prohibition, according to one of them, as a guarantee that the program would "stick close to its original purposes."

Conspicuous by its absence at Senate hearings was the American Medical Association. Preoccupied with medicare at the time, the AMA had been caught off guard by the quick formulation of the medical complexes bill; it was not until late April that the AMA *Journal* made known its opposition to the DeBakey Report. But Hill made little effort to seek out the Association's rather predictable views. For years Hill had handled the AMA with care; his support of medicare had long been tempered by his desire to stay on good terms with the medical profession. But in 1962 Alabama doctors were prominent among Hill's opponents, accusing him of liberalism in general and of softness on medicare in particular. Hill emerged from his narrow victory in a much less conciliatory mood. He voted for medicare in 1965, and long before that the AMA had found their relations with the Health Subcommittee cooling noticeably. "They've testified only once or twice during the last several years," one observer noted. "They don't come around here much."

In most respects Hill was satisfied with the administration's bill. At both the national and regional levels it provided for advisory councils of the kind that the Lasker forces and their congressional allies had so effectively used to gain information and to exert leverage on NIH programs in the past. The Health Subcommittee, in what one NIH official termed a "standard Hill-Lasker amendment," added a requirement that the Surgeon General not only consult with the National Council but also secure its approval before authorizing grants. With this change, in addition to the deletion of new construction aid, provisions for NIH administration, and the insertion of precise authorization figures ($650 million for the first four years), Hill was ready to report the legislation. Millenson perused the bill for the minority but suggested few alterations; Javits claimed credit for moving the date for the Surgeon General's report on the operation of the program forward by two years. Subcommittee and Committee votes were both unanimous, and on June 25 floor debate began.

The only factor delaying quick and easy passage was an amendment offered by Russell Long to provide that no private citizen or company should acquire exclusive patent rights if his research was financed under the act. A similar effort was to succeed a year later when the Traffic Safety Act reached the Senate floor, but this time Long failed. He claimed HEW support for his amendment and implied that a good part of the opposition was inspired by drug manufacturers. Hill assumed the burden of defense, arguing that the government's present procedures could be relied upon until comprehensive legislation was developed and that the Long amendment might impede "the productivity of research and development."[51] He knew that a number of NIH and HEW officials were wary of Long's proposal, but he could not secure a letter of disapproval because of the administration's fear of offending Long while medicare was in the balance. Nonetheless, a Pastore motion to table the proposal carried, 55–36. After this single roll call, the bill passed by voice vote without further attempts at alteration.

One of the many oddities of congressional committee jurisdiction is that bills involving PHS—the original function of which was to provide health services for merchant seamen—are ordinarily referred to the House Committee on Interstate and Foreign Commerce. The characteristics of that committee, as discussed in Chapters 2 and 3, would lead one to expect a lower degree of receptivity to the medical complexes bill and a greater concern for interest-aggregation than was found on the Senate side. House hearings, in fact, were not convened until the Senate had passed the bill, the AMA was given considerable attention, and the Committee scaled down the Senate bill appreciably. In retrospect, however, one NIH official described the House Committee's action not in terms of obstruction or of overresponsiveness to medical interests but in terms of being "conscientious and responsible," "giving everyone their say," "forcing us to tighten up our plans"—"an example of the congressional process at its best." This should serve as a warning against drawing simple analogies between the Committee's action on medical complexes and what it did, for example, on fair packaging or cigarette labeling. But it also points up the fact that many of the House changes could be seen as extensions of the trends Dempsey and Hill had already established, responsive to NIH, the medical schools, and the hospitals. That the program was to strengthen existing institutions and facilitate cooperation between them was made more certain by strengthening the ban on new construction, substituting the term "regional medical programs" for "complexes," and explicitly providing that the functions envisaged for "diagnostic and treatment stations" would be performed by existing hospitals.

The fact remains, however, that for a time the bill was considered in "deep trouble"[52] and that many of the House Committee's amendments were aimed more at cutting the program back and meeting the AMA's objections than at giving the bill focus. The AMA's testimony, as usual, concentrated on broad objections rather than on specific revisions. But the Association was forced to take a more practical position when President Johnson, feeling conciliatory after his medicare victory, turned down the AMA's request to hold up the bill but directed new HEW Secretary John Gardner to work with the House Committee and the AMA in modifying the legislation. What emerged were provisions to the effect that regional and national advisory councils must include practicing physicians and that no patient could be given care under the program unless he was referred to the facility in question by a practicing physician. The Committee then cut authorizations back to $340 million over three years, a figure which, when compared to the DeBakey Commission's proposal of $3 billion over five years, gave the program the appearance of a pilot project.

Representative Harris brought his committee's bill to the floor almost apologetically, admitting that he had agreed with the AMA's desire to postpone action until some of the "cloud banks" that surrounded the bill "could be penetrated":

> This did not prevail because the White House cannot let Congress do its work in orderly fashion these days and apparently it was ready to settle for anything containing the words heart, stroke, and cancer.[53]

The Committee's revisions, he went on, had laid the fears of "socialized medicine" to rest. As was to be the case on fair packaging a year later, the administration had sacrificed a great deal to mobilize the House Committee. But what had been salvaged contained those elements from the DeBakey Report which Dempsey, Hill, Shannon and other NIH officials, and probably most Commission members themselves, considered of prime importance. The Senate, on Hill's recommendation, accepted the House-passed bill, and the President's signature made it law on October 6.

Summary and Conclusions. The crucial actors on the medical complexes bill can be isolated with greater ease than is the case with most legislation. As always, critical preconditions had been met: HEW had a rich store of information, a precedent of sorts existed in the clinical research center program, and, most important, a working relationship and a community of interest had developed over the years between Hill, the Lasker group, and NIH. But a series of discrete acts nonetheless led to the bill's introduction and passage. Instigation fell to Gorman and Mrs. Lasker. Information-gathering, publicity, and formulation were the work of the DeBakey Commission; in their performance of the latter two functions, as in their general level of political astuteness and involvement, this group far surpassed the ordinary presidential panel. The executive branch's assumption of responsibility began with Dempsey's legislative formulation and with the President's publicizing of the proposal through its inclusion in his 1965 program.

There were interests to be aggregated both within the executive branch and in the private sector. Although the DeBakey Commission found it impossible to accommodate the AMA (the Association's Director of Scientific Activities resigned from the Commission when, after five months, it became "increasingly evident that the direction in which the Commission was moving was not, in my sincere belief, consonant with the best in medical education, medical research, and the health needs of our nation"[54]), it produced a far-ranging report which, while giving each agency and each viewpoint its "share," failed to make priorities clear. Subsequent aggregations, in Dempsey's office and then in the Senate Health Subcommittee, favored NIH, the hospitals, and the medical schools. The House Committee slanted the bill even farther in this direction, though in many of its amendments and cutbacks the accommodation of the AMA was evident as well.

On the Senate side, mobilization and modification were both dominated by Senator Hill; Long's attempt to get into the act was rebuffed. The executive branch played a more prominent role on the House side. Harris and his committee needed stimulation, and the price of mobilization turned out to be HEW acquiescence and cooperation in the amendment process. Modification remained preeminently a congressional function, though it was undertaken with different motivations and out of responsiveness to different groups in the two chambers.

The medical complexes episode furthers our acquaintance with the LPW Committee in several respects. Its prime value is in elucidating the interests and identifications of the Chairman and in highlighting an extraordinary coalition, a cooperative relationship between Hill, NIH, and the Lasker group which maximized the policy impact of each.[55] In some ways the impressions gained from the ESEA story have been qualified: an area of *low* controversy has been discovered within the Committee's jurisdiction; patterns of executive branch organization and liaison contrasting sharply with those of USOE have been found; and an exception has been seen to Hill's preference for decentralizing his committee and delegating authority. That Hill was able so completely to dominate Senate action on S. 596, however, reflected far more than his wish to retain the prerogatives of the chairmanship in the field of health. It also demonstrated the reputation and the deference he enjoyed as the Senate expert on health matters and the strength he gained by virtue of the integration of his committee.

THE VETERANS' READJUSTMENT BENEFITS ACT OF 1966

A Lonely Battle. While much of the legislation passed between 1940 and 1944 to benefit veterans of World War II and their families continued and expanded existing pension, medical care, insurance, and disability compensation programs, there was a new emphasis on "readjustment" programs designed to facilitate the veteran's re-entry into normal civilian life. The most important and innovative of these measures was the Servicemen's Readjustment Act of 1944, popularly known as the "GI Bill of Rights." This bill, which the American Legion had an important hand in drafting, was championed by both the President and congressional leaders. It provided education benefits (federal payment of tuition and living expenses for up to four years of schooling), special job-placement and counseling services, up to a year of federally-financed unemployment compensation, and guaranteed loans for the purchase of a home, farm, or business. Similar benefits were extended to Korean War veterans by the Veterans' Readjustment Assistance Act of 1952.[56]

President Eisenhower declared the Korean War terminated for benefit purposes on January 31, 1955. But the draft did not end, and various cold war outbreaks made peacetime service more hazardous than it had been in the past. Moreover, large-scale education and housing programs were no longer viewed as radical innovations; all indications were that the World War II and Korean GI programs had been highly successful and that the population groups from which most draftees were being drawn were increasingly in need of this type of assistance. Therefore, in the 84th Congress Senators Hubert Humphrey, Richard Neuberger, and others introduced legislation to continue the 1952 GI benefits until conscription was ended. These bills never received serious consideration, but important seeds were sown. Their nurture increasingly became the self-appointed mission of one man, Ralph Yarborough, who came to the Senate after a special election in mid-1957.

Yarborough was liberal, activistic in orientation, and anxious to make a record for himself. He fastened upon the GI issue immediately, and every Congress from the 86th to the 89th saw the introduction of a Yarborough Bill to provide readjustment benefits to post-Korea veterans. Yarborough quickly saw that the best place for him to pursue this and his other legislative interests was the LPW Committee. Securing an appointment in 1958, within a year he was made Chairman of the Veterans' Affairs Subcommittee (at that time, all the majority members, with the exception of two freshmen senators, had their own subcommittees). Hill was sympathetic to the cold war proposal and let Yarborough go his own way; within seven months the full committee had reported a bill providing benefits for cold war veterans with more than six months of service. The bill was cut back somewhat on the floor, but it passed with deceptive ease. It was not to be reported, however, by the House Veterans' Affairs Committee. Similar bills were again reported by the Senate Committee in 1961 and 1963, but in both instances the leadership refused to bring them to a vote.

Yarborough, in fact, found himself fighting against overwhelming odds. His more conservative colleagues, including most Republicans, disapproved of the bills on fiscal grounds, doubted that peacetime veterans were entitled to such benefits, and suspected that the bills represented a backdoor approach to general education and housing aid. But more formidable obstacles were to be found outside the Senate chamber—in the House, in the executive branch, and even in the major veterans' organizations. On the one item in Yarborough's earlier bills to which there was little objection—the authorization of vocational rehabilitation for peacetime veterans with serious service-connected disabilities—the 87th Congress, with the President's blessing, took separate action. But Yarborough and his Senate backers found themselves isolated on their education and housing proposals.

The three most prominent national veterans' organizations, the American Legion, Veterans of Foreign Wars, and Disabled American Veterans, were at first united in opposition. The DAV had a stake in preserving programs aimed at the disabled, and more broadly-based readjustment programs were seen as a threat to their share of the Veterans Administration budget. The Legion and VFW also perceived a stake in the maintenance of the *status quo;* it was feared that the cold war bill would necessitate cutbacks in medical, pension, and insurance programs. The membership practices of both organizations helped explain their positions. The American Legion admitted only those who had served in time of "war" (and hence no post-Korea veterans), while the VFW admitted only those who had been awarded campaign badges or medals (thus including only those post-Korea veterans who had served in such "expeditions" as Lebanon, Quemoy-Matsu, Laos, and Vietnam). Moreover, both organizations tended to promote their officers on the basis of seniority; when Yarborough began his campaign, a number of World War I veterans, the men who had the greatest stake in existing programs, were in leadership positions. When these factors were added to the general ideological conservatism of both organizations and to the often-expressed feeling of combat veterans that their peacetime counterparts were not entitled to comparable benefits, the opposition of the Legion and the VFW to Yarborough's bills became more understandable.

"Since the big veterans' organizations didn't give us much help on this," Yarborough recalled, "we had to organize our own lobby." Just as Hart brought in consumer groups to testify on fair packaging and Magnuson stimulated industry support for oceanography, so did Yarborough rally smaller and more liberal veterans' groups like the AMVETS, the American Veterans Committee, and the Jewish and Catholic War Veterans to his cause. Yarborough went even further, helping organize and finance student and other veterans' groups to promote the legislation. It was an extreme example of a legislator creating his own "pressures" or, as one staff member put it, of "the echo creating the yell."

But Yarborough did not write off the larger organizations, even as he was stimulating counter-pressures. A cautious endorsement from the DAV was eventually won by the inclusion of provisions for the training of disabled veterans not covered by the 1962 rehabilitation act. The VFW story was more complex. This organization had a younger membership and less conservative leadership than the American Legion, and one of its chief Washington representatives, Francis Stover, was lobbying within the group for the support of peacetime benefits. In 1957 Stover testified on behalf of Neuberger's bill to extend the Korean readjustment program, but in 1959 he was constrained to admit that the "mandates" of his National Convention permitted him to endorse only the "limited" education and training sections of Yarborough's proposal.[57] During the 1960 convention a faction led by World War I veterans secured the defeat of a resolution supporting the cold war bill, but a study group was appointed which eventually voted its approval, with the National Commander casting the deciding vote. After this, the testimony of the VFW was more consistently favorable; "Once they came around," one participant recalled, "they were probably the most effective supporters we had." But as late as 1965, VFW representatives were able to endorse only a bill which defined an eligible veteran as "one who had served in an area of hostilities for which a campaign badge or medal was authorized," and Stover admitted that his organization still had an "internal problem" in "giving blanket endorsement to this GI bill."[58] The Legion was far less equivocal. Until 1965 the organization's position was simply that it had nothing to say about legislation that did not benefit "war" veterans. When, in mid-1965, the Legion's executive committee finally decided that a "war" was in progress in Vietnam, the National Convention voted its approval of a "benefits program" comparable to that enjoyed by veterans of other wars. In subsequent congressional testimony, Legion representatives stated that they favored benefits only for those who had served since the Bay of Tonkin incident (August 5, 1964), and they specifically opposed the VFW's "area of hostilities" concept.[59]

If interest groups gave Yarborough little comfort, executive agencies provided him with less. Eisenhower, Kennedy, and Johnson all opposed the cold war bill, though the latter two held to the position Kennedy had developed as a senator in 1959: a program of loans for college students should be developed for all citizens, not just for veterans. "In the administration," surmised one Senate aide, "the root of the problem was the Budget Bureau, and their main concern was simply costs." But Yarborough perceived the main source of opposition to be the Department of Defense, which opposed the bill consistently and for its own reasons. In the Senate Subcommittee's 1965 hearings, the Deputy to the Assistant Secretary of Defense for Manpower ("They rarely send up their top brass when they're testifying *against* something," one counsel noted) expressed his department's disapproval of "legislation which provides the individual military man with an inducement to leave the military service. . . . Any further inducement . . . merely increases the difficulty of achieving and maintaining an adequate military force." Yarborough was by this time familiar with the argument, but a new Subcommittee member, Robert Kennedy, could barely suppress his outrage:

> *I think it is incredible in the United States . . . in this day and age, to say we don't want the young men to be lured outside the service by having the possibility of attending college, or finishing high school. . . . You would like to keep people who are ignorant in the service? . . . General, I tell you . . . having listened to the testimony of the Defense Department, I am far, far more enthusiastic for the bill than I was before I heard the testimony.*[60]

Equally negative, at least in outward appearance, was the Veterans' Administration. In 1965 Deputy Chief Benefits Officer Arthur Farmer ("You are a deputy," Yarborough said to him at one point; "[your superiors] didn't show up, they sent you here to read this paper. I am serving notice on them—they are going to have to face the music in Congress this time.") reminded the Senate Subcommittee of the VA's opposition to this and "all previous" cold war bills. Peacetime service, he insisted, was "essentially different" from service in time of war; not only were hazards and hardships less severe, but the return to civilian life could be achieved with greater ease. Farmer went on to emphasize the training to which a soldier was entitled while he was in the service and the civilian programs he could take advantage of after his discharge; "the post-Korea veteran should be treated like his nonveteran counterpart in terms of education." "What is the purpose of this Veterans' Administration?" Yarborough responded. "Is it created to help the veteran or block his opportunity in life?"[61]

There was, in fact, considerable sympathy within the VA for Yarborough's proposal; one official speculated that "the VA would have taken a positive stand earlier if the administration had allowed it." Administrators John Gleason (1961–1964) and William Driver (1965–1969) both attempted, without success, to persuade the White House and the Budget Bureau to adopt a more flexible position. Other VA officials, including Deputy Assistant General Counsel Charles Johnston, who had served as Veterans' Affairs Subcommittee Counsel until mid-1965, favored the bill and provided the Subcommittee with limited assistance. But while the activities of VA officials were not as tightly bound by their superiors as were those, say, of USOE, their freedom by no means approached that displayed by NIH. A partial explanation lay in the fiscal significance of the cold war question and the consequent determination of BOB and the White House to hold the line. Nor could the Defense Department easily be defied.[62] "It's hard to give encouragement," one VA official pointed out, "when you've been forced into line with your superiors' position and when you know that senators will pounce on any little expression of dissent and blow it up in hearings." The VA thus obviously did not enjoy NIH's immunity from discipline and control. But its potential bases of support in interest groups and in Congress might have made for a greater degree of independence had it not been for certain characteristics of the VA itself. One congressional aide put this point rather strongly:

> They furnished us with facts and figures, but nothing more than what they called "technical assistance." To tell you the truth, I don't think most of the people down there have enough imagination to do much more. They're the kind that think the official position has to be their position, and that's that.

Whether or not such perceptions were fair to Driver and others who were trying to modify the executive's position from within, the fact remained that numerous congressional participants faulted those who imposed controls less than those whose role conceptions counseled unswerving fidelity to the official line.

Factors similar to those influencing the behavior of the Maritime Administration[63] helped explain the VA's lack of independence and assertiveness. "The Veterans' Administration is just that—an *administration*," said one Senate aide. "They're involved in administering benefits, not in thinking up new programs. They're not a creative agency like some of the others." The orientations and day-to-day operations of the agency were not geared to policy-formulation except as it pertained to the smoother functioning of existing programs. The VA's position as a quasi-judicial agency, passing judgments and entering disputes about claims—to say nothing of its responsibility to the Bureau of the Budget—also introduced a certain distance into its relationships with its client groups and made it less promising as a spokesman for their legislative interests. "I'd say," reflected one VA official, "that [the groups] almost invariably find a better reception in Congress." On Yarborough's bill, of course, many interest groups as well as administrators were indifferent at best; the VA's role perhaps would have been negative in any case. But had the agency possessed a greater capacity for interest aggregation and for independent and innovative policy formulation, it might have been able to play a more creative role in breaking the seven-year stalemate that developed on the issue.

A Changed Context. Yarborough introduced his Cold War GI Bill as S. 9 shortly after the 89th Congress began. On February 8, 1965, he opened another round of Subcommittee hearings with a pledge of "new vigor" on behalf of the legislation. The hearings revealed few changes in executive or group positions, but there were measurable increases in Senate interest and support; 41 senators cosponsored the bill, and 21 testified in favor of it before the Subcommittee. Senate passage seemed assured, and certain developments in Vietnam and in the House Committee—not unrelated to one another—for the first time raised the possibility that the bill might get beyond the Senate chamber.

The House Veterans' Affairs Committee, chaired since 1955 by Representative Olin Teague of Texas, was the most prominent source of veterans' legislation on Capitol Hill. In the Senate, the Finance Committee had jurisdiction over the compensation, pension, and insurance programs in which the veterans' organizations were often most interested; Byrd's fiscal conservatism, his preference for leaving legislative initiatives to the House, and the smallness of his staff had made his committee much less promising as a point of access. "On most things," one lobbyist remarked, "we would go straight to the House, because that's where everything starts." To what extent the formation of a separate Veterans' Affairs Committee in the Senate, a long-standing goal of the veterans' organizations finally realized in 1971, might alter that pattern remained an open question.

Educational and medical programs, however, were another matter. It was these areas over which LPW, a committee contrasting with Finance in its liberalism and activism, had jurisdiction prior to 1971; and these were the parts of their jurisdiction which interested Teague and most members of the House Committee least. "We would probably go to the Senate Subcommittee first on a readjustment bill," the lobbyist continued. "In *that* area, the Senate Committee is more receptive than the House. Teague pretty much mirrors the viewpoint of those older veterans who are more interested in pension programs and benefits for the disabled than in things like education and housing benefits." It was thus not surprising that the

House Committee proved to be an obstacle, perhaps the most important one, to the enactment of the cold war bill. Yarborough went to extraordinary ends to move his House colleagues; after the passage of the 1959 bill, he visited every member of the House Committee. "Most of them told me that a senator had never darkened their doorstep before." A majority of the Committee probably favored the bill, but Teague successfully held off action, posing as a champion of the administration's interests. But those who knew Teague and had seen him defy the administration on matters in which he and his clients themselves had an interest, detected a deep-seated personal animus against awarding benefits to non-combat veterans. Teague himself had been hospitalized for two years as a result of combat-incurred wounds, and he was loath to see those rewarded who had only seen peacetime service. Most of the veterans organizations, themselves fearful that the cold war bill would cause reductions in other programs, reinforced him in his views.

In 1965, however, the war in Vietnam, in which one of Teague's sons was fighting, was deepening. The changed status of the "peacetime" veteran was reflected in the American Legion's decision to reopen its membership rolls. Teague's members were more restless than ever. After the bill passed the Senate, therefore, House hearings were scheduled, and Teague told the administration that the wise course would be to develop a compromise proposal.

Yarborough's floor victory was indeed impressive; the bill that had passed by 26 votes in 1959 passed in a much stronger form on July 19, 1965, by 52 votes. Several Republican "alternatives" were offered, including one sponsored by Peter Dominick, ranking Republican on Yarborough's Subcommittee, which limited benefits to Southeast Asia veterans. But they were all handily defeated, and on final passage Dominick found himself the only LPW member from either party voting "nay."[64] House hearings, which opened six weeks later, left little doubt that Teague was coming around. The fact that he had always favored readjustment benefits for the combat veteran enabled him to claim that his position had "not changed in ten years," but he made it clear that he was now ready "to pass a bill that we can live with from now on."[65] The administration proved less flexible. The President, no friend of Yarborough's but nonetheless impressed with the apparent depth of congressional and public support, approved the development of a compromise proposal, and Teague's hearings came just as the process of reappraisal was getting underway. Defense Department and VA officials thus reiterated the arguments they had made six months earlier before the Senate Subcommittee, but they also reported that studies were underway "to determine the need and type of benefits which may be warranted" and to find a method of assistance which did not "interfere with the mission of the Department of Defense."[66] Shortly after second session began, the administration presented a bill providing education benefits only, giving no help to those serving before 1963, and providing different benefits for post-1963 veterans who had served in an area of hostilities and those who had not. It was a bill which even the veterans' organizations and the House Republican Policy Committee rejected as inadequate. Teague, according to one participant, "just laughed." "He was way ahead of them by that time." In early 1966, therefore, the House Committee set out to write its own bill, consulting with administration officials but working relatively independently.

The House bill, like S. 9, made all veterans who had put in more than 180 days of active duty since the official end of the Korean War eligible for educational assistance and for home and farm loans. It reduced S. 9's educational allowances, however, omitted provisions for on-the-job and on-the-farm training, and reduced the educational entitlement from 1.5 to one month of benefits for each month of service. The cost of the Senate bill was reduced by some fifteen percent, but, in accord with Teague's (and the Legion's) view that "wartime" veterans should be awarded the full range of federal benefits, S. 9 was expanded in some respects; counseling and placement services, preferential standing for civil service employment, and VA hospital care for non-service connected disabilities were added to the bill. The Defense Department's argument that such programs represented an inducement to leave the service was met by the institution of a new program to provide active duty personnel serving more than two years with educational and home-loan assistance while they were in the service.

The administration in the end was forced to concentrate not on developing a less ambitious proposal but on heading off amendments which would have made the Committee bill even more extensive. Teague was cooperative in this respect; the bill was brought to the floor under a motion which prohibited the offering of amendments. To critics, many of them Republicans, who pointed to differences between the bill's provisions and the benefits accorded to Korean War veterans, Teague responded with arguments for economy and for the necessity of passing a bill the administration would accept. The bill passed the House unanimously on February 7, 1966.

Yarborough had little to gain and much to lose by insisting on a conference. Teague was unlikely to bend in any case, and the veterans' groups and executive agencies could not be expected to promote the Senate version. The administration favored Teague's bill on fiscal grounds, and the veterans' groups were interested in preserving the job preference and hospital care amendments; "It was our job," said one lobbyist, "to convince Yarborough to accept the House bill." Rather than take further chances, Yarborough asked the Senate to accept S. 9 as amended by the House. Long agreed not to object, although some of Teague's amendments fell under Finance Committee jurisdiction. Dominick let it be known that he resented not being consulted on the decision to accept the House bill, but his and the 16 other opposition votes that had been registered seven months before vanished on the final tally; the House bill was accepted, 99–0. The President signed S. 9 on March 3 and remarked later in the day:

> *I just had my budget busted wide open this morning by my colleagues from Texas, but it was on behalf of soldiers who needed education. If it were going to be busted, it couldn't be busted for a better purpose.*[67]

The Ingredients of Success. Yarborough's persistent championship of the cold war bill was seen by some as evidence of his dedication and his sensitivity to the veterans' plight, by others as evidence of compulsiveness and a one-track mind. In either case, however, S. 9 was cited as an example of "what one man can do." There was much truth in this view; Yarborough was involved at each legislative stage, and his involvement was unusually detailed and extensive. The existence of the 1944 and 1952 Acts made the task of formulation rather perfunctory, but it was Yarborough and his staff who undertook such revisions as were necessary. Instigation and publicizing was also virtually a one-man effort. Yarborough's Senate colleagues were frequently exasperated or bored by his persistence, but a significant number of them identified themselves with his efforts and formed a strong base of support. Yarborough's extraordinary attempts to instigate action in the House and in the executive branch were less successful, nor was he able to get prominent coverage in the media until late in the game. He was continually frustrated by the tendency of the press to concentrate on presidentially-initiated legislation; one small victory was won—and Yarborough's incredible attentiveness to details was demonstrated—when the Congressional Quarterly *Weekly Report* finally included the cold war bill in its "Boxscore" of major legislation.

Yarborough and his staff were dependent on HEW and the VA in their information-gathering efforts, but the hearings demonstrated that they were able to use the figures to their own advantage and to tap independent sources. Interest-aggregation was likewise performed by the Senate Subcommittee: Yarborough attempted to pacify the larger veterans' organizations by excluding six-month veterans from benefits, he made special provisions for the DAV, and he stimulated and activated the more liberal groups as well as responding to them. Moreover, despite severe limitations, Yarborough could claim some credit for mobilization as well. He did not have great seniority or prestige, and his "pushiness" on the cold war bill may actually have provoked resistance to his efforts in some quarters. The leadership rebuffed him with relative ease in 1961 and 1963, and his failure to move Teague was even more conspicuous. But in 1965, favored by events, Yarborough's efforts bore fruit; enough senators had become identified with the issue and interested in it to ensure easy passage and to provide a stimulus to House and executive units.

It was an impressive performance, understandable only by reference to Yarborough's identifications, ambitions, and activist self-image. His rewards were not entirely in the realm of self-satisfaction. His reputation and his leverage in the Senate were, on balance, enhanced. Publicity, in Texas and elsewhere, was generally favorable. And though the Legion opposed him in Texas in 1964 (on general ideological grounds), he finished the course with a solid reputation as a friend of the veteran and with accolades from all major veterans' groups.

The fact that Yarborough finally succeeded, however, and that he reaped these personal benefits from his success, was due not only to his own persistence but also to events beyond his control. The basic factor was the deepening of the war in Vietnam. This led to a change in the sentiments of Teague and the veterans' organizations, which in turn led to altered positions in the executive branch. It was only after these occurrences that Yarborough's bill was passed—and then as a joint product. The labor of others was mixed with that of Yarborough at each of the latter stages: the veterans' organizations publicized, the executive agencies developed alternative schemes, and Teague undertook a modification so extensive as to approach reformulation, aggregating the interests of groups and agencies and mobilizing the House behind his compromise proposal. It was because of Yarborough's efforts that the bill was passed as early as it was and that it provided for all post-1954 veterans; a bill might eventually have been passed in any case, but it almost certainly would have been of lesser scope. But S. 9 was not simply an example of what one man could do; external events played a crucial part in the story, as did the positive efforts of certain policy-makers and the acquiescence of others.

Of particular interest from the point of view of the present study were characteristics of the LPW Committee and its environment which facilitated Yarborough's efforts. The liberalism and activist inclinations of most of the members made LPW a reliable base of support. The Committee's decentralization enabled Yarborough to chair a subcommittee, to hold hearings and mount his own publicity campaigns, and to use staff resources for his own purposes. His way was also smoothed by the absence of sharp partisan cleavages on the Committee, particularly in his area of jurisdiction. Environmental conditions were equally important, though often in a negative sense. Executive agencies were united in their opposition, but they were not equipped or inclined to develop counter-proposals or to mount extensive opposition efforts. Interest groups, though not always enthused about the legislation, were oriented toward Congress and were not likely to form a strong defensive alliance with executive agencies. These groups, moreover, were divided within and among themselves, and Yarborough was able to form cooperative ties which strengthened liberal groups and factions and sustained his own efforts.

THE FAIR LABOR STANDARDS AMENDMENTS OF 1966

A Matter of Cycles. Less than two months after Yarborough's career as a senator and as Chairman of the Subcommittee on Veterans' Affairs had been crowned by the enactment of the cold war bill, Senator Pat Mc-Namara died, leaving vacant the chairmanship of the Subcommittee on Labor. Yarborough, having no more major projects in mind for veterans, was ready for a change, but the Labor Subcommittee was by no means his first preference. Like the Veterans' Affairs Subcommittee, the environment of the Labor Subcommittee was inhabited by interests which, as one aide put it, were "not interested in what you did for them yesterday, or last week, but *today.*" Politically, membership on either subcommittee was often regarded as a mixed blessing: the groups involved were suspicious as well as supportive, even of their friends, and quite demanding; both subcommittees required extensive work, often on matters with little popular appeal and in areas where it was extremely easy to make enemies. Yarborough would have preferred either Education or Senator Clark's Employment, Manpower, and Poverty Subcommittee over Labor. But Morse, who had pulled rank on Yarborough to get the Education Subcommittee chairmanship in 1961, did not want to change, nor did Clark, who had just had the new poverty program added to his subcommittee's jurisdiction. Thus Yarborough took the only advancement that was open to him and became Chairman of the Labor Subcommittee. It was for this reason that the most prominent labor bill, as well as the most prominent veterans' bill, to be reported by the LPW Committee during the 89th Congress fell under Yarborough's care. But the two bills differed sharply in many ways, including Yarborough's relative importance to their formulation and passage.

The 1965 minimum wage bill, like the unemployment compensation revisions requested in the same State of the Union Message, represented the latest in a series of postwar attempts to extend and expand the coverage of a landmark New Deal statute.[68] The Truman Administration had with difficulty overcome opposition on the House Education and Labor and Rules Committees to obtain an increase in the minimum wage (to 75 cents) and strengthened child labor prohibitions in 1949. But the fifties, on wage and hour questions as on UC and medicare, saw a shift in policy initiative toward Capitol Hill. President Eisenhower's request in 1955 that the minimum wage be increased to 90 cents gave organized labor and congressional Democrats an opportunity to push for more extensive revisions. The Senate Labor Subcommittee recommended a $1.00 minimum, failing by only one vote to approve the $1.25 figure sought by the Clothing Workers and other AFL-CIO affiliates. The House Committee followed suit, and the bill was approved with relatively little controversy. 1960 was another story. With elections approaching, the administration renewed the requests it had made intermittently for the coverage of some 3 million additional workers and, after some hesitation, advocated a 15 cent increase in the minimum wage; Senator Kennedy, now Chairman of the Labor Subcommittee, sponsored a labor-backed bill to expand coverage by 8 million and to raise the minimum to $1.25. The House Education and Labor Committee reported a relatively generous measure, but a bill sponsored by a coalition of Republicans and Southern Democrats which provided for an increased coverage of only 1.3 million was substituted on the floor. The Senate, while trimming the LPW bill, nonetheless approved the extension of coverage to some 4 million additional workers, mostly in the retail and service trades. The conferees could not agree; Kennedy concluded that it would be better to "come back and try to do it in January" than to accept the House bill and close the legislative books for years.[69]

Kennedy's strategy paid off: the passage of the Fair Labor Standards Act Amendments of 1961 was one of his administration's earliest and most impressive legislative victories. In many ways the 1960 story was repeated: the House Committee reported a generous bill but was reversed on the floor, while the Senate Committee granted most of Kennedy's requests and was generally upheld by the parent chamber. What made the difference was the fact that the House Committee had a new Chairman. Barden had not been able to prevent his committee's reporting a pro-labor bill in 1960, but by his own vote and through his appointment powers he had prevented the acceptance of the Senate bill in conference. In 1961, the House conferees, led by Powell, defied their parent chamber and largely accepted the Senate bill. Thus was the minimum wage raised to $1.15 and an increase to $1.25 projected for 1963. More significantly, the 1961 bill provided what its predecessors had not: substantial increases in both minimum wage and overtime coverage. Some 3.6 million additional workers were included, mostly in retail, service, construction, and small industrial firms, although a number of the categories Kennedy wished to include were deleted at one point or another in the congressional process. Newly covered firms were allowed to meet the requirements of the act step by step, fully complying with the wage and overtime standards by 1965.

"This business tends to go in cycles," observed one labor lobbyist, and the dates of the major FLSA revisions—1949, 1955, 1961—seemed to bear him out.[70] In 1964, according to past patterns, the offering of extensions and amendments was a bit premature; the 1961 provisions themselves were not yet fully operative. But labor was pressing its demands for an increased minimum, for the coverage of workers excluded from the 1961 bill, and for a 35-hour work week, and the administration, with elections approaching, felt the need to respond. Representatives Powell and James

Roosevelt had continued to champion the coverage of hotel, restaurant, and laundry workers, and Roosevelt's General Subcommittee on Labor had held hearings on the problem in late 1963. But when the President sent up a bill increasing coverage in early 1964, the Education and Labor Committee delayed bringing it to the floor, reportedly because of the shortness of time and the absence of strong administration backing. Labor's other demands—for an increased minimum wage and a shortened work week—were regarded by the Council of Economic Advisers as likely to touch off a wage-price spiral; the administration was thus constrained to develop substitute proposals. The only immediate result was a bill authorizing double-time for overtime in industries where representatives of labor and management agreed that such a rate would increase employment without greatly increasing costs. The intent, as with the original Depression statute, was less to better the situation of the individual worker than to discourage overtime employment and create more jobs. But on this matter, as on extended coverage, the administration seemed content to get its views on record and to postpone action until the 89th Congress. The House Select Subcommittee on Labor held hearings, but no bill was reported.

The Roosevelt and Dent Bills. That the Senate Committee was heard from relatively little after 1961 reflected no major shift in sentiment. Hill, who had been elected in 1938 on a platform that included the minimum wage, found the coverage of small firms and agricultural workers politically problematic, and Goldwater and Dirksen, to a much greater extent than their predecessors on the minority side, frequently dissented from Committee recommendations. But the views of most members were still decidedly pro-labor, and Hill's permissive style of leadership gave McNamara and the Labor Subcommittee free rein. What was changing in the early sixties was rather the posture of the House Committee. The Committee had become more liberal in labor, as in education, matters during the fifties, a trend culminating in the accession of Powell to the chairmanship in 1961. Powell established "General," "Special," and "Select" Subcommittees in both education and labor; if this arrangement sometimes encouraged rivalry and hostility, it also furnished several liberal representatives like Roosevelt with flexible jurisdictions and machinery for the pursuit of policy interests. Decentralization thus helped translate the liberalism of the committee into an increasingly "radical" policy output.[71] It also accentuated, however, another situation which was becoming evident in the late fifties: the House Committee's adaptive failures vis-à-vis the parent chamber. In part this was the function of gaps in ideology and policy goals; in part it reflected the Committee's internal failures at integration and consensus-building.[72] In any case, by 1965 the House Committee seemed slightly more likely than its Senate counterpart to produce a generous minimum wage bill but considerably less likely to preserve its product intact on the floor. For Biemiller and other labor strategists, both facts seemed to militate in favor of sending the FLSA amendments to the House first: the strongest possible bill could be provided for House debate, the toughest battle could be disposed of first, and the LPW Committee could resume its traditional role of restoring House deletions. On this matter, as on UC, Samuel Merrick, the Labor Department's legislative chief, thought it would be wise to reverse past "habits of thought," but his views did not prevail.

The Wage and Hour bill was not sent up during the opening months of the 89th Congress because the committees under whose jurisdictions it fell were preoccupied with the ESEA. From the administration's point of view, however, the delay was not unwelcome, for there was still considerable uncertainty as to precisely what should be requested. The unions reiterated their demands for a 35-hour week and set $2.00 as their goal for the minimum wage; administration officials like Wirtz and Humphrey revealed their support for MW increases as the administration bill was being drafted.[73] But Johnson's economic advisers continued to be wary of labor's demands. The President, when he finally sent up his Labor Message on May 18, "came up with a hedge."[74] The 1964 coverage and double-time bills were resubmitted in strengthened form, but it was declared that the time had not yet come for a shortening of the work week "except with respect to excessive overtime." As for the minimum wage, the President said, the question was not whether it should be increased "but when and by how much." It was a question, nonetheless, which the President declined to answer:

> The Congress should consider carefully the effects of higher minimum wage rates on the incomes of those employed, and also on costs and prices, and on job opportunities—particularly for the flood of teenagers now entering the labor force.[75]

Organized labor, as seen in Chapter 4, was occupied on a number of legislative fronts when the administration's FLSA amendments were introduced. Moreover, the bill for the most part affected workers who were not unionized; from the standpoint of most members of the AFL-CIO, one lobbyist pointed out, "the minimum wage is 'public interest' legislation." But there were AFL-CIO affiliates who did have a direct stake, and four of the most prominent of these—the Textile Workers of America; United Hatters, Cap, and Millinery Workers; International Ladies' Garment Workers; and Amalgamated Clothing Workers of America—had established effective patterns of cooperation as early as 1955. In addition, there were representatives in the AFL-CIO's Washington office who had a strong interest in the FLSA and who assumed a role similar to that played by Stover within the VFW: "Hell," admitted one, "we even lobby ourselves." All this meant that the FLSA amendments were to receive a considerable share of organized labor's attention and effort during the 89th Congress.

It also meant, however, that the concern was likely to be greater in the area—increases in the minimum wage—where the interests of union members were most tangible. Even if the Labor Department had not been restrained by the CEA, its priorities probably would have been quite different. As one official put it:

> There was no question coverage was our main interest. Now that never is the labor movement's main interest. They'll always say they're for expanded coverage, but when you get right down to it and something has to be compromised, it's always the expanded coverage they're willing to see go first. . . . The workers not covered are usually not in unions. Union members are naturally more interested in wage increases.

In any case, labor representatives went to Congress not merely, as on UC and medicare, to defend the administration's formulation, but, as during the Eisenhower years, to stimulate reformulation and amendment.

In a sense, they succeeded too well. On August 4 the Roosevelt Subcommittee reported a bill raising the MW to $1.75 by 1968 and exceeding the administration bill's recommended coverage by 3.3 million on MW and 400,000 on overtime. "We liked their bill," one labor lobbyist recalled, "but we did wonder about it." Their apprehensions were fully justified. Labor Department officials, who had been negotiating with Roosevelt for a MW increase "which was more than a few pennies under $1.75," felt betrayed and angered. The full Education and Labor Committee voted its approval of the Roosevelt Bill on August 18; "This should show that we're not just a rubber stamp for the President," Powell said.[76] But when the leadership proved reluctant to take up the bill and produced evidence that barely 100 representatives would support it, the Committee decided to withhold the proposal. Meanwhile, Roosevelt left the House to accept a United Nations appointment. Representative John Dent fell heir to the chairmanship of the General Subcommittee on Labor and to the task of rewriting the legislation.

Dent saw himself as a broker between organized labor and the administration: "He told us he wouldn't move the bill until we reconciled our differences and came to some agreement." The CEA in early 1966 agreed to a $1.60 increase and, though the President maintained an official silence, Wirtz let it be known that this figure was acceptable.[77] But bargaining continued on the effective dates of the stairstep increases. Finally, on March 10 Powell announced that all parties had agreed on increases for presently covered workers to $1.40 by February, 1967, and to $1.60 a year later. Newly covered workers were to receive $1.00 immediately; stairstep increases would bring non-farm workers to the full MW by 1971 and agricultural workers to a permanent figure of $1.30 by 1969. Subcommittee and Committee approval came quickly. The new bill's coverage figures remained close to those of the Roosevelt Bill, though certain categories of restaurant and farm workers were excluded and an amendment adopted by the full committee provided full and immediate coverage for some 700,000 blue-collar federal employees. The administration's double-time recommendations, about which neither the unions nor the Labor Department had ever been very enthusiastic, were dropped entirely.

After a delay of two months, the Rules Committee cleared the bill, setting the stage for three stormy days of floor debate. Most attempts to cut back coverage were defeated, but the delicately engineered timetable for MW increases was revised: the $1.60 increase for presently covered workers was postponed one year further. Powell, who was feuding with labor leaders at the time, gave his support to the revision without notifying Floor Manager Dent or the leadership. It was this "flaw" which preoccupied labor and administration leaders as they turned their attention to the Senate.

Senate Action. McNamara had held nine days of hearings in mid-1965, but strategic considerations and his own failing health had prevented further action during the rise and fall of the Roosevelt Bill. Yarborough took the Labor Subcommittee chairmanship on June 1, 1966, six days after House passage of the Dent Bill. The AFL-CIO, which had enjoyed a cordial relationship with McNamara (himself a card-carrying member of the pipe-fitters union), had hoped that Morse would take the job. But apprehensions about Yarborough, according to one lobbyist, had more to do with "the fact that he was new" than with any more fundamental misgivings. Yarborough set out to pass the bill quickly; he resisted pressures for a second round of hearings, according to one staff man, because he was convinced that "the only reason they were wanted was so that the lobbyists could impress their clients that they were doing a job." The Subcommittee and full committee followed Yarborough's lead in restoring the 1968 effective date for the $1.60 minimum, the latter by an 11-3 vote, and both voted unanimously to report the bill. The committee draft left largely intact the House's proposed extensions of coverage to agricultural workers and to hotel, hospital, laundry, restaurant, and other small business employees. Some marginal modifications restricted (for nursing homes, livestock producers, seasonal agricultural and industrial processors) the coverage of the House Bill, but a larger number nullified House exemptions or otherwise expanded coverage (for automotive partsmen, transit system drivers, agricultural workers covered under the Sugar Act, small logging crews, and management trainees). The Senate Committee adopted a Morse amendment requiring "sheltered workshops" employing the handicapped to pay 50 percent of the MW immediately and the full rate by 1969 and, at Senator Randolph's instigation, liberalized the House bill to provide that tipped employees must be paid at least 50 (instead of 45) percent of the applicable minimum wage. The reported bill also contained a Javits-Williams amendment, derived from a bill developed in Williams' Migratory

Labor Subcommittee and passed by the Senate in 1961 and 1963, which prohibited the employment of children under sixteen in agricultural jobs found by the Secretary of Labor to be "particularly hazardous." But the Committee rejected additional amendments pertaining to the employment of children in agriculture and a minority amendment barring age discrimination in establishments required to pay the minimum wage.

The groups opposing FLSA extensions were similar and in some cases identical to those that simultaneously were fighting the packaging and UC bills. They included large national organizations like the USCC, the NAM, the National Retail Merchants Association, and the American Farm Bureau Federation, but often more conspicuous were the scores of small local businesses and organizations which made their voices heard—a fact which helped explain why the House, with its smaller constituencies and more locally oriented membership, was conservative relative to the Senate on all three measures. But certain aspects of the FLSA legislation made it, as one executive official observed, more like an "old-fashioned tariff bill" than were the other bills. The nature of the wage and hour "program" made specific exemptions far less problematic, administratively or politically, than they would have been in areas like packaging or UC. Nor were there strategic questions as to whether one should concentrate on the general or the particular: most industries could develop proof of their "unique" status, and there were ample precedents for seeking specific exemptions on that basis. One observer described the typical lobbying operation:

> A company might send up five or six representatives; they'll get off the plane, see five or six friendly congressmen, and go back the next day. Or they might have some of these downtown lawyers scurrying around. Like on that logging crew exemption: you just wouldn't believe the pressures that were generated on that.

Countervailing pressures generally came from the administration, the AFL-CIO and National Farmers Union, and, more rarely, the small and often weak groups of workers whose employers were resisting inclusion.

The Senate Committee's responsiveness to these pleas for exemption was low relative to the number of entreaties made, though the solicitude of Griffin, Javits, and Morse for food processors, of Fannin for livestock producers, and of Prouty for nursing homes was evident in the reported bill. Similar efforts made for three lively days of floor debate and twelve roll-call votes. To several qualifying amendments, including a deletion of the stairstep increases to the full MW for "sheltered workshops" and miscellaneous modifications of overtime coverage, Yarborough offered little resistance. He agreed to take to conference the minority amendment prohibiting discrimination on account of age and a nongermane Javits-Morse amendment directing the Secretary of Labor to report to Congress on the adequacy of emergency strike laws. But Yarborough successfully fought off other proposed exemptions and withstood the crossfire from those wishing to provide stairstep increases to the full MW (rather than stopping at $1.30) for farm workers and those wishing to remove them from coverage altogether.

Yarborough's main concern, of course, was to preserve the MW timetable contained in the committee draft. On the merits, the administration had no great objection to the House's postponement of the effective date, but, noted a labor representative, "they stuck to the agreement we had reached and worked to get the Senate to restore it." How hard they worked, however, was a matter of some debate. One Labor Department participant admitted feeling "pretty confident" about the Senate fight; "we didn't have to do too much. It wasn't like UC, where both the Secretary [of Labor] and the White House got into the act, trying to round up votes." Yarborough, in any case, felt that the administration, as well as the Senate leadership, were overly complacent (Majority Whip Long in fact voted against Yarborough several times):

> *I personally ran up and down the aisles asking senators to give me a live pair to save us from defeats . . . It was the hardest floor fight of my [career].*

Fannin's motion to accept the House timetable was defeated, but by a narrow vote of 40-42. On the question of small business coverage this balance was tipped. A Dirksen amendment to raise the sales volume cutoff (below which businesses would be exempt from the act's general coverage) from $250,000 to $500,000 was defeated on a tie vote, but when Prouty proposed a $350,000 ceiling, enough senators switched their votes to give him a 41-38 victory. But this was Yarborough's sole defeat. Final passage came easily on August 26, 57-17.

The House conferees, as in 1961, were considerably more liberal than their parent chamber. They therefore agreed to the MW timetable in the Senate bill, while the Senate conferees "sacrificed" the Prouty amendment in favor of the House bill's more liberal small business coverage. The administration and organized labor thus got the best of both proposals. Most of the Senate's other modifications, marginal as they were, were retained. The Senate minority's age discrimination amendment was converted into a directive to the Secretary of Labor to study the problem, and the Javits-Morse amendment ordering a review of emergency strike law was dropped. House members, who had passed the original bill by 210 votes, came within 20 votes of recommitting the conference report. The margin in the Senate shrank from 40 to 17, with LPW members Hill, Murphy, Prouty, and Dominick joining Fannin in opposition. But the bill had sufficient support to withstand such defections; on September 23 the President's signature made it law.

Summary and Conclusions. The enactment of the FLSA Amendments of 1966 displayed a number of historical continuities. The administration again took the lead in formulating, publicizing, information-gathering, and mobilizing, while Congress assumed prime responsibility for interest-aggregation and amendment. Organized labor, enjoying free access to the executive branch but by no means its unqualified support, instigated efforts in, and shared functions with, both branches. The Senate LPW Committee, as in the past, defended and generally liberalized the bill, while the House floor again represented its most perilous obstacle.

But the 1966 story had its own unique features. Unlike some past FLSA revisions and the UC bill which at that moment was languishing in the Ways and Means Committee, the administration bill fell considerably short of what labor wanted. The CEA's misgivings about substantial MW increases altered both the locus and the substance of formulation. Negotiation and adjustment were necessitated within the executive branch; formulation became a bargaining process, "political" as well as technical. Nor could labor entrust itself to its executive patrons as it had on UC. The administration was not responding to any great extent to the employer interests opposed to the bill—its misgivings had to do with the overall health of the economy and with the reception labor's original proposal was likely to receive in Congress—but labor nonetheless was forced to develop proposals and information independently and to seek alternative points of access.

This process was facilitated by a second novel aspect of the situation during the 89th Congress: the presence and the disposition of the Roosevelt Subcommittee. Many participants were inclined to view the Subcommittee's action, in retrospect, as something of a fiasco. It is true that the Roosevelt Bill's MW provisions were not feasible politically (or, many claimed, economically); the formulation process had to be begun anew in 1966, with the congressional committee this time ratifying an administration-labor agreement. But the coverage of the bill the President signed was derived in large part from the Roosevelt proposal. Both organized labor and the administration professed interest in expanded coverage, and both defended the terms of the Dent Bill. But the initiative for the original expansion of the administration bill's coverage, a revision so extensive as to approach reformulation, had come from the House Subcommittee in 1965.

The role of the Senate Committee was in most respects secondary, though its solid pro-labor sympathies were, no less than in 1949, 1955, and 1961, important in stabilizing support and in deterring attempts to weaken the bill. To a much greater extent than in previous years, LPW left formulation, publicizing, and information-gathering to the administration, the unions, and the House Committee, but considerable responsibility for mobilizing the Senate and for holding the line against deletions fell to Yarborough in the end. Various members, especially from the minority side, undertook the aggregation of additional employer interests, but the activities of their House counterparts in this regard were much more extensive. Some additional employee groups were also accommodated on the Senate side, but these adjustments likewise appeared as marginal alongside the expansions in coverage effected by Roosevelt. The only Senate amendments that could not be classed as attempts to accommodate specific interests or to restore the House bill's language were those pertaining to emergency strike law, age discrimination, and the employment of children in "particularly hazardous" occupations—the first of which was deleted, the second modified, and the third retained in conference.

The FLSA episode furnished further evidence of the activism of Javits and various LPW majority members, the ideological homogeneity of the LPW majority and heterogeneity of the minority, and Hill's willingness, as one observer put it, to "let things happen" even though he could not publicly identify himself with the action. There could be little doubt that the LPW environment was crowded with diverse and conflicting groups or that members often chose to champion local interests, but it was also evident that the Committee's overall response was selective and that most groups found other points of access more promising. These and other committee characteristics became more evident when LPW was compared to its House counterpart—a committee that was often more uncritically responsive to both organized labor and local businesses, had much more erratic and divided leadership, and suffered far more serious integrative and adaptive disabilities. But perhaps the most striking aspect of the FLSA episode, particularly in comparison to the three bills previously discussed, was the small number of substantial policy initiatives that could be credited to the Senate Committee and its members. Liberalism and a desire for policy alterations could under certain circumstances lead not so much to independent initiatives as to the defense or ratification of the moves of others.

THE ECONOMIC OPPORTUNITY AMENDMENTS OF 1966

An Auspicious Beginning. A fifth major bill processed by the LPW Committee during the 89th Congress, and one involving the fifth of its major subcommittees, was the 1966 extension and revision of the Economic Opportunity Act. This bill contained a series of congressionally-initiated modifications of a program which in its inception provided a classic example of "executive legislation."[78] The instigation of the 1964 Act involved the Council of Economic Advisers, but in a far different role from that assumed during the FLSA battle two years later. CEA Chairman Walter Heller and President Kennedy had both been impressed with Michael Harrington's *The Other America* and other studies[79] publicizing the plight of America's "invisible poor." In mid-1963, as the work of the Council on the administration's tax cut neared completion, Heller was asked to explore the possibility of a legislative attack on poverty. At the time of Kennedy's assassination, the CEA and the Budget Bureau were reviewing various departmental proposals with an eye to the President's 1964 legislative program. One of President Johnson's first official acts was to endorse the nascent proposal as "my kind of program" and to order Heller "full speed ahead."[80]

A number of the program's CEA and BOB formulators were less interested in the proposals suggested by the departments than in the concept of "community action" that was gaining currency in certain academic and foundation circles and, most importantly, among the staff members of the President's Commission on Juvenile Delinquency in the Justice Department. The preliminary reports of Heller's task force thus projected a series of grants to local agencies and groups with few strings attached; the idea was to institutionalize innovation and flexibility, to maximize local initiative and involvement, and to cut through obstructive procedures and bureaucracies. A number of agency heads, of which Secretary Wirtz was the most outspoken, felt that their own suggestions had been ignored and that their own bailiwicks were threatened. The task of conciliating these various partisans and fashioning a specific legislative proposal fell to Peace Corps Director Sargent Shriver, named by the President on February 1, 1964, as architect and future administrator of the "War on Poverty." Shriver assembled a task force consisting of personal friends and associates, departmental representatives, and legal and academic experts; a "partial list" of 137 names was later released to demonstrate the number of group and community leaders Shriver had "consulted." Many of the earlier departmental suggestions were reviewed and accepted, but, partly because Attorney General Robert Kennedy championed the ideas of the Juvenile Delinquency Commission staff members within his department, the community action program (CAP) advocated by the CEA-BOB group was also retained.

Few of the programs proposed were as innovative as CAP. One title simply expanded and liberalized existing loan programs for small businessmen, while another enlarged upon a "Work Experience" program, requested by President Kennedy and authorized in 1962, whereby the federal government shared in the cost of training programs for unemployed men whose families were on the welfare rolls. Some of the proposals pertaining to rural poverty—grants and loans to farmers for agricultural and non-agricultural enterprises, loans to cooperatives assisting poor families, and a program to help farm development corporations resell land at reduced prices—represented more significant departures from existing policy. They were largely the work of James Sundquist, who before becoming Deputy Undersecretary of Agriculture had served as Senator Clark's Administrative

Assistant. Other provisions had discernible executive and congressional roots. A program of part-time work for needy college students had been among Kennedy's unsuccessful 1963 higher education proposals, developed and promoted independently on Capitol Hill by Senator Hartke. A domestic version of the Peace Corps—later called VISTA (Volunteers in Service to America)—had been proposed by a cabinet-level study group in 1962 and authorized by the LPW Committee and the Senate in 1963. Proposals for a "Job Corps" to provide training for youths in residential camps and a "Neighborhood Youth Corps" to provide training and part-time employment for young people in local projects drew on New Deal precedents. Senator Humphrey, over the opposition of the Eisenhower administration, had secured Senate approval of a program of the "Job Corps" type in 1959. Kennedy had requested both programs in 1961 and 1963; Senate action had been favorable, but the House Rules Committee had proved obstructive.

An even more sensitive task than the culling and reworking of agency proposals was the assignment of administrative responsibilities. Shriver was anxious to give his Office of Economic Opportunity a broad operational role; thus the Job Corps, CAP, and VISTA were put under direct OEO administration. It was anticipated that some of the other programs would be farmed out to the agencies—Youth Corps to Labor, for example, and Work Experience and Work-Study to HEW—but here, too, OEO would retain the functions of coordination and oversight. Shriver also realized that strong presidential support would be necessary if the new agency was to maintain its authority. He understood what the cigarette labeling episode also demonstrated: that agency "independence" often meant isolation and weakness. Thus the task force chose the administratively unorthodox scheme of placing the OEO, an operating agency, within the Executive Office of the President.

Congressional modifications were for the most part marginal, though the rural programs were cut back substantially and the House Education and Labor Committee added literacy training for adults and various services for migrant workers to the package. The adult education proposal was one which the President had requested, the House Committee had reported, and the Rules Committee had blocked in both the 87th and 88th Congresses. The migrant labor proposal was more exclusively congressional in its origins. In 1959, Harrison Williams, a freshman senator looking for issues, had secured appointment by Hill as Chairman of a Special Subcommittee on Migratory Labor. This subcommittee, made "standing" in 1961, held hearings around the country and quickly developed a number of proposals. Some of these, prohibiting child labor in agriculture and providing MW coverage for farm workers, broke ground for the FLSA Amendments of 1966; others, introduced by Williams as early as 1960, would have made funds available to private and public agencies to develop education, sanitation, housing, and day-care programs for migrants and their families. The Eisenhower administration was cool to the proposals; Kennedy and Johnson endorsed most of them but gave them low priority. Williams secured Senate passage of education and sanitation bills in 1961, but the Rules Committee delayed House action. These two measures, plus a day-care bill, were again approved by the Senate in 1963 and were thus pending on the calendar of the Education and Labor Committee when it began processing the poverty bill.

If Congress thus provided for the germination of a number of the Economic Opportunity Act's provisions, made minor changes in virtually every section, and even did some "combinatorial" work of its own, its primary role remained that of ratification. It was the administration that was creating and publicizing the issue, certainly not in advance of the need, but in advance of an "articulated public demand" or extensive exertions of group pressure.[81] Information-gathering and publicizing had begun in the private sector, much as they had on traffic safety and campaign finance, but the administration accelerated these processes. The Heller and Shriver task forces aggregated agency interests, stimulated some groups and accommodated others, and wrote the bill. Though the advice of legislative leaders was sometimes solicited and the congressional calendar scanned for ideas, Congress was looked upon mainly as a body to be mobilized, an obstacle to be overcome. Congressional interference, it was hoped, would be minimal and passage would be smooth. That the sessions of 1964 and 1965 largely lived up to these expectations was due in part to the cordial reception the bill received in both the Education and Labor and LPW Committees.

Powell appointed an Ad Hoc Subcommittee on Poverty in 1964 with himself as Chairman; the bill was given friendly hearings and reported with authorizations intact. The Senate bill was not reported as quickly, but it was acted on first because of the delaying tactics of the House Rules Committee. Hill declined to associate himself with the bill for political reasons, but he facilitated its consideration by appointing a Select Subcommittee on Poverty consisting of all LPW members except himself, with McNamara as Chairman. Here, too, the bill was given cordial hearings; it was reported with an authorization figure only $15 million under the administration's requested $962.5 million and, except for the cutting back of the agricultural programs, was preserved largely intact on the floor. Opposition was stronger and more partisan in character on the House floor, partly because of the bitter wrangling that had gone on within the Education and Labor Committee (the entire minority, as compared to two LPW Republicans, voted against reporting the bill). But the mobilizing efforts of party and President were sufficient to prevent serious cuts.

The congressional majorities provided by the 1964 elections gave the backers of the program a chance to consolidate their gains in 1965. The President raised his authorization request by 56 percent, asking for $1.5

billion, and proposed a continuation of existing authority for 90 percent federal financing of most OEO programs. Congress gave him this, and more. Powell complained publicly about political patronage, administrative mismanagement, and a failure to provide, as the CAP title specified, for the "maximum feasible participation" of the poor. But the Education and Labor Committee reported a bill which increased the President's authorization figure by $400 million and softened the congressional modifications of 1964 which had required a loyalty oath of Job Corps enrollees and had given Governors the right to veto Job Corps, CAP, Youth Corps, and VISTA projects in their states. The House passed the bill by 87 votes, compared to 41 the year before, but Republican opposition was still virtually monolithic. The majority was less generous but the minority less adamant on the Senate side. The LPW Committee's authorization was also over the President's request, but only by $150 million; an amendment sponsored by Senator Nelson earmarked this increase for CAP programs involving unemployed adults in community betterment or conservation projects. Yarborough, infuriated over Texas Governor John Connally's veto of a Youth Corps project, led a successful fight to strengthen the House Committee's partial repeal of the veto. LPW Republicans fought Yarborough in committee and on the floor, but they were conciliated by the approval (later dropped in conference) of a Prouty Amendment prohibiting political activity on the part of VISTA volunteers and CAP agency employees. Only Dominick and Fannin voted against reporting the poverty bill, and nine Republicans voted "yes" as the Senate approved it, 61-29.

The Honeymoon Ends. If the first and second sessions of the 89th Congress were "completely different" as far as the administration's willingness to expand its education programs was concerned, the disparity was magnified in the case of the War on Poverty, "the first domestic casualty of the war in Vietnam."[82] The preliminary budget requests of OEO were in the neighborhood of $2.5 billion. Although the President's State of the Union Message pledged "not only to continue, but to speed up" the program, the final authorization request approved by the Budget Bureau, $1.75 billion, was hardly sufficient to maintain the projects for which OEO was already obligated. OEO officials, formerly backed by the President in their quarrels with the agencies, now felt betrayed and were tempted to go underground to their congressional allies. Nor was this the only fissure that appeared in the coalition that had inaugurated and supported the program. The disaffection of the left was revealed as members of Citizens' Crusade against Poverty hooted Shriver from the rostrum and free-lance community organizer Saul Alinsky derided the poverty program as "a feeding trough for the welfare industry" and a "war against the poor."[83] Powell's criticisms increasingly partook of this rhetoric, though Harlem political wars also helped explain his hostility. Republican and Southern

Democratic critics, meanwhile, were encouraged in their efforts to dismantle the program by the disillusionment and controversy it had stirred and by the conservative reaction in Congress that was also threatening bills like UC. It seemed clear that the 1966 authorization battle would not be a repeat of past performances.

Powell's Ad Hoc Subcommittee began hearings in early March. The Republicans, never fond of the program and increasingly resentful of their treatment within the Committee, were more hostile than ever. Powell's disposition, though often unpredictable, was generally critical, and Democrats responsive to the administration—after some maneuvers that "had the look of a White House effort at persuasion"[84]—were in no mood to match the program increases they had voted in 1965. Thus the full committee reported a bill which authorized the exact amount requested by the President but allocated it quite differently. The most marked increase— from $300 million to $496 million for the Neighborhood Youth Corps—reflected the concern of Powell and other urban representatives for the provision of jobs. The most serious cuts were in CAP, which, one Committee Democrat acknowledged, had posed serious threats to "the political establishment."[85] And the Committee went on to specify how all but $323 million of the $805.5 million CAP authorization was to be spent.

Such specifications were not wholly unprecedented. In 1965, when Senator Nelson was interested in seeing the Youth Corps idea expanded to include unemployed adults and to benefit rural areas, the device he chose was to earmark community action funds. OEO officials generally opposed earmarking as a threat to the flexibility and latitude of CAP, though program chiefs were not always above encouraging congressional allies to set aside funds on their behalf. That such tactics were by no means the monopoly of OEO critics was demonstrated anew by the 1966 House bill. The earmarking of $352 million for Operation Head Start, a popular preschool education program, had virtually unanimous support on the House Committee. The earmarking of funds for narcotic rehabilitation programs and for small emergency loans to poor families represented the efforts of liberal members to push CAP in certain directions and to implement their own policy interests. The most noteworthy such attempt was made by Representative James Scheuer, who secured the adoption of an amendment earmarking $88 million for the development of "subprofessional" jobs for unemployed adults.

The House bill was reported on June 1, but floor consideration was delayed by a series of controversies in which Powell became involved: he refused to testify before the Rules Committee, postponed debate further in an apparent attempt to influence certain OEO administrative decisions, and finally became the target of a committee revolt which substantially reduced his powers. Meanwhile, Senate hearings got underway. The cast of characters had shifted somewhat: McNamara had died and the functions of the Select Subcommittee on Poverty had been absorbed by Senator Clark's Subcommittee on Employment and Manpower. But Clark and his subcommittee—which included Nelson, Javits, Prouty, Yarborough, and (after Clark recruited Robert Kennedy in mid-1966) both Kennedys—were no strangers to the poverty program. Clark had come to the Senate in 1957 acquainted with urban problems (as Mayor of Philadelphia) and anxious to assume an active policy role; his involvement had been facilitated by the policy gaps left by the Eisenhower administration and the unique permissiveness of the LPW Committee. Hill appointed him Chairman of a Special Subcommittee on Employment and Manpower, and Clark, aided by Sundquist, developed a manpower training bill which subsequently served as a model for President Kennedy's successful 1962 legislation. Employment and Manpower became a standing subcommittee in 1961 and soon became involved in extensive studies of national manpower policy—surely one of the most impressive examples of congressional information-gathering on record. But adding the poverty program to his jurisdiction appealed to Clark as a means of renewing and broadening his policy involvement, and Hill preferred that alternative to the naming of a new subcommittee. Thus was "and Poverty" added to the name of the Subcommittee on Employment and Manpower, "very nearly becoming," as one member put it, "the tail that wagged the dog."

Administration witnesses Shriver, Gardner, and Wirtz faithfully defended the administration's 1966 requests as a "budget for troubled times," though Wirtz locked himself in by defending the overall cutbacks and then supporting the increases provided by the House for his department's own Youth Corps. "I must admit being a bit surprised," Clark responded,

> [that] you didn't think the program could usefully spend any more money than the President recommended, particularly in light of the fact that you are supporting an increase in the part of the program which you administer. The House gave you these funds at the expense of cutting back some of the other programs.[86]

The most serious argument the Subcommittee heard against earmarking came not from administration witnesses but from Mitchell Sviridoff, president of a new national association of community action directors:

> In the absence of increased appropriations under [CAP], these limitations severely restrict the innovative capacity of community action agencies and tend to bureaucratize them.[87]

But OEO officials nonetheless went to work to loosen House restrictions on CAP funds and, somewhat less conspicuously, to encourage increases in the overall authorization. Prouty, in an effort reminiscent of his "House of Lords" speech on the education bill, portrayed the process in melodramatic terms:

The ubiquitous poverty officials . . . with a shrug of the shoulders and a quick little grin left with the Committee what might very well have been an intended impression that yes, poverty would like very much to have any amount for whatever purpose is the Committee's pleasure, without regard to the old Simon Legree of our melodrama, the Bureau of the Budget. . . . This administration would be well advised to get its own house in order and learn beforehand just to what extent officials of the OEO are responsible to it when they conduct a fund drive out of hearing of the public in the normally sacrosanct privacy of a Senate committee.[88]

This was to underestimate the constraints OEO officials felt; their programs were too conspicuous and their positions too vulnerable to permit underground operations comparable to those of NIH. But they did push for increases in CAP versatile funds, and—given the determination of several Committee members to institutionalize pet programs and earmark funds for them—this in effect meant acquiescing in overall authorization increases.

The Senate Committee did not allocate funds with as much rigidity as the House. "The specific statutory earmarking of community action funds and the imposition of funding ceilings" was avoided, the report stated, to preserve "flexibility and versatility of funding."[89] But the reported bill contained several new programs of its own, and the report contained quite specific funding suggestions. The Committee did not follow the House in writing explicit figures for legal services and Head Start into the bill, but the report indicated that authorizations had been granted with the intention of doubling the administration's projected expenditures for the former and increasing those for the latter by $200 million. The House's narcotic rehabilitation and emergency loan programs were dropped, but the Scheuer Amendment was revised and retained. The House Committee had combined the Scheuer and Nelson programs and authorized $88 million for both. Nelson, however, was anxious to preserve the rural and conservation-oriented character of his program, while senators like Clark, Javits, and the Kennedys saw the new program mainly in terms of its provision of jobs in urban areas. Thus the LPW Committee kept the programs distinct and indicated that $75 million was to be spent for each.

The Senate Committee's two original contributions came from the brothers Kennedy. Both were interested in carving out areas of policy leadership for themselves and, more specifically, in developing "Kennedy Amendments" to the poverty bill. The Massachusetts senator had become interested in health policy, though Hill's involvement meant that, for the moment, that area was less open than many others. Kennedy was impressed with the performance of a community health center operating in Boston under a CAP demonstration grant, and subcommittee counsel Arnold Nemore was enthused over a similar project in Denver. Dave Burke, Kennedy's Administrative Assistant, picked up the idea and developed an amendment specifically authorizing the use of CAP funds for this purpose. Some OEO officials directly involved with the health centers program, like those working with legal services and Head Start, were rather unsuccessful in masking their enthusiasm for earmarking, but their superiors were not generally sympathetic and cooperated only to the extent of devising workable language. The fact that Shriver was Kennedy's brother-in-law had little apparent effect, though it perhaps muted some opposition at the top levels of the agency. The senator's early success in gaining the sympathy of Surgeon General Stewart was important in defusing executive opposition and in gaining Hill's support. No substantial objections were raised to the health centers proposal in committee; it was specified that $100 million in CAP funds should be used for such projects.

Robert Kennedy's amendment stirred more controversy. His Legislative Assistant, Adam Walinsky, had been working on a proposal similar to the Scheuer amendment; when preempted by the House Committee, he hurriedly devised an alternative proposal aimed mainly at providing funds for the physical rehabilitation of slum neighborhoods. The proposal was ill-defined and Kennedy presented it ineffectively in subcommittee; Javits, spurred by Minority Counsel Kurzman, attacked its feasibility and blocked approval. For weeks Walinsky and Kurzman wrangled over compromise proposals; it was not until Kennedy himself intervened and Clark began referring hopefully to the "Kennedy-Javits" amendment that an agreement was reached. Thus a new "Special Impact" program for urban areas was approved by the full committee, but with an emphasis on job training programs involving private industry. The executive agencies did not object: the apprehensions of OEO were removed when the Special Impact program was made independent of CAP, and the Labor Department correctly anticipated that it would receive the new program and the funds and administrative authority that came with it.

The Senate Committee thus struck its own balance between the rigidities of the House bill and the flexibility desired by OEO. Authorization figures told a similar story: administration requests cut by the House were restored, while the authorizations the House had increased were retained. In each case, the larger figure proposed for a given program was accepted, and in several instances it was boosted further. The result was an overall authorization that exceeded the administration-House figure by 43 percent. "The measure proposed by the administration," the report began, "will not suffice, even to maintain the status quo. . . . In the judgment of the committee these funding levels are commensurate with the minimum needs and reasonable expectations of the nation's poor."[90] Clark had no illusions about the ease of getting a $2.5 billion authorization approved on the Senate floor or in conference, but he saw no other means of accommodating Committee members with special interests and at the same time preserving CAP flexibility: "We simply had to jazz up the entire authorization." His and Nemore's OEO collaborators expressed their approval:

> *I was very happy to see them authorize all that extra money, not so much because we thought we could ever get it as because it would give us something to bargain with in conference and get rid of those House amendments.*

The reported bill revealed a number of additional senatorial concerns. Clark had taken Shriver to task for OEO's restrictive guidelines regarding the provision of contraceptive devices to unmarried women; the Senate bill thus directed that the terms of such assistance be left to local community action agencies.[91] Another Clark amendment, this one responsive to problems that had arisen in Philadelphia, authorized the payment of allowances to low-income individuals serving on local community action councils. Other Committee members, notably Nelson and Yarborough, felt that OEO had ignored congressional directives to distribute CAP funds "equitably" between urban and rural areas; the bill thus required the Director to make contracts with independent agencies in rural areas where the establishment of community action agencies was not feasible. Senator Edward Kennedy had been impressed by an Aging Committee study which suggested that a 1965 amendment requiring special attention to the elderly poor had been ignored; the bill thus provided for the appointment of an Assistant Director for the elderly poor and required OEO to undertake additional studies and program development. OEO did not make an issue of these amendments, though it was generally assumed that Shriver was largely responsible for the agency's conservative birth control policy and one close observer confirmed that Shriver was "really opposed" to Kennedy's proposal for an Assistant Director.

Amendments sponsored by the minority were as diverse as the members themselves; there was a least-common-denominator minority report, but four Republican members felt compelled to supplement it with "Individual Views." Javits offered a proposal developed by Kurzman to authorize experimental projects combining Job Corps and Youth Corps approaches, providing residential facilities and programs of on-the-job training. More predictable in terms of past performance were several Javits attempts to establish inter-agency coordination and the participation of private industry by fiat; a Murphy-Javits amendment limiting the salaries of poverty workers; and a series of Murphy amendments purporting to guarantee the "stringent enforcement" of standards of conduct in Job Corps camps, to institute effective screening and follow-up procedures for the Job Corps, and to limit the political activities of CAP employees. Most of the minority amendments had their counterparts in the House bill, and both House and Senate bills contained many of the administration's original recommendations—raising limits on loans to rural families, providing the Director with more specific authority to prescribe CAP criteria, granting a moratorium on the repayment of student loans for VISTA volunteers, and authorizing OEO grants to organizations operating their own volunteer service programs. The Senate Committee rejected the House's proposed transfer of the small business loan program to the Small Business Administration but omitted authorizations for adult education in anticipation of committee action on a separate bill which would transfer that program to HEW.

Clark's Strategy Fails. The House finally passed the Economic Opportunity Amendments on September 29, adding several restrictions and specifications to those already adopted by the Education and Labor Committee but generally refusing to lower authorizations or to dismantle OEO further. The LPW Committee reported its bill on the same day, with only Dominick and Fannin voting "nay" but only Javits among the other Republicans registering a positive vote. There was, as in 1964, a notable lack of interest-group activity. The Citizens' Crusade against Poverty, whose organizers had hoped it could assume a publicizing and mobilizing role similar to that of the NCSC in the medicare struggle, suffered from chronic instability and could not offer its members either the incentives to active support or the leadership that a large-scale legislative campaign would have required. Large business and labor groups were preoccupied with legislation which affected their interests more directly. There was, however, another set of partisans calling for an accommodation of their interests and providing Congress with problems of aggregation—the executive agencies. The Labor Department, having been well provided for by both Houses, was interested in conserving its gains but had no clear preference for either bill; OEO officials naturally favored the more generous and more flexible Senate version. But President Johnson, Senator Dirksen reported after a White House meeting, was fulminating "like Hurricane Inez over what we were doing to his budget."[92] There was no question as Senate debate began who had the inside track. While OEO General Counsel Don Baker and his colleagues sat helplessly in the galleries, the Majority and Minority Leaders consulted with White House officials concerning cutbacks in the LPW authorization.

The crucial vote came on October 4 as Mansfield proposed that authorizations be reduced to $2.1 billion. Javits endorsed the Majority Leader's move, saying it offered the only hope of forestalling more drastic cuts; Clark and Morse disagreed, scoring the administration for abandoning the poor in the face of Vietnam. But the debate was rendered moot as Dirksen offered an amendment to the amendment which reduced the authorization to the administration-House figure of $1.5 billion. Mansfield denied that the "establishment" was conspiring to wreck the bill and voted against

Dirksen to prove it. But Dirksen easily prevailed, 45-27. A group of staff members devised a scheme whereby the amendments would be offered in reverse order, but Clark, weary and irritated, dismissed their efforts. An OEO participant was equally fatalistic: "There was nothing Clark could have done, and a change in the order of the offering of amendments would have meant nothing."

Clark lost two less crucial fights as well; Senator Harry Byrd, Jr., successfully proposed the cutting off of OEO funds to workers or program participants who incited riots or belonged to "subversive organizations," and a Prouty amendment earmarked 36 percent of CAP funds for Head Start. Both amendments brought the bill closer into line with the House version. Final passage came on October 4 by a vote of 49-20, with only Fannin, Dominick, and Hill among LPW members recorded in opposition.

"Adam Clayton Powell hurt us in many ways in 1966," ruminated one OEO official, "but the worst blow of all was probably the *delay*. The bill came up when everyone was tired and wanted to go home. In conference we lost a lot of what we could have gotten otherwise. We had already lost a lot of our bargaining power by what happened on the Senate floor, and then to that was added the press of time." Clark had already lost his battle for more funds, and in conference he lost the battle for flexibility as well; specific authorizations were made for the Nelson and Scheuer programs (which, however, remained separate, as in the Senate bill), emergency loans, Head Start, legal services, and health services-narcotic rehabilitation (now combined). Versatile CAP funds were returned to the House figure of $323 million. This represented a severe defeat for OEO, but it was a testimony to the breakdown of the executive's community of interest that the other executive participants viewed the conference outcome quite differently. The BOB had had its main concerns alleviated in House Committee and on the Senate floor. And the Labor Department could even claim a victory of sorts: its share of the poverty budget had been increased, and the conferees made the Department's responsibility for the various new work programs more explicit.

Senate conferees were placated—and for some the desire to safeguard CAP versatile funds was dampened—by the acceptance of the Special Impact and health services programs, Kennedy's proposal for an Assistant Director for the elderly, the Yarborough-Nelson amendment pertaining to rural agencies, and the Clark proposals regarding birth control and allowances for CAP council members. Amendments offered by LPW Republicans, most of which had House counterparts, were also generally approved, as was Byrd's antiriot rider. Several additional House restrictions were accepted, though the one that was rejected—a Powell proposal limiting the number of OEO civil service "supergrades"—threatened to deadlock the conference and jeopardized House approval. The conferees accepted the House's transfer of the small business loan program to SBA and omitted authorizations for adult education as the Senate had done, anticipating that that program would be transferred out of OEO as well. In short, the conference agreement was one in which most features of *both* bills were accepted—the opposite of a least-common-denominator settlement in some respects, but similar to it in its frequent indication of extreme haste (recall the contrasting cases of fair packaging and foreign investment, both end of session conferences). In the case of the poverty bill, this procedure benefitted the House, since it was the Senate whose bill contained fewer specific earmarkings and restrictions and changed the original statute least. Both houses approved the conference report during the final week of the 89th Congress, and the President signed the bill on November 8.

In a sense, the Economic Opportunity Amendments of 1966 represented simply another stage in the congressional ratification and modification of a program initiated, developed, and administered by the executive branch. The gathering and dissemination of information had become one of OEO's prime functions, and the fact that the administration had at stake the extension of a program to which it was publicly and politically committed made basic congressional efforts to instigate, to publicize, or even to mobilize unnecessary. Taken as an entity unto itself, however, the 1966 episode represented an independent expression of congressional policy interests, a substantial "reassertion of prerogatives."[93] The administration's suggested program revisions themselves appeared distinctly marginal alongside many of the congressionally-initiated modifications, and executive advocacy of an unearmarked authorization of $1.75 million became a defensive operation in the face of congressional innovations. This shift in role was in part attributable to a growth of interest and assertiveness on Capitol Hill among members as diverse as Powell, Javits, Murphy, Clark, and the Kennedys. But the trend was reinforced by the administration's reactions to the mounting costs of the Vietnam War. The aggregation of agency interests was shifted from OEO to the Budget Bureau, and the mode of aggregation became less coordination and promotion than control and restriction. Thus were congressional committees stimulated to undertake aggregation of a more positive sort. But the weakening of the OEO's position within the administration, as well as the difficulties into which some of its programs had fallen, strengthened the hand of its congressional detractors as well. Increased levels of formulation and interest-aggregation in Congress thus led to a great diversity in the intent and content of new proposals.

As it turned out, however, this diversity was not fully visible in the bill the President signed. Many of the provisions established restrictions and limitations which a unified executive had fought off the year before. The earmarking amendments were more difficult to categorize; they were the work of the friends as well as the enemies of OEO. But the distinctly friendly amendments expanding authorizations and increasing CAP flexibility failed; the bill in its final form did not give a "balanced" picture of congressional disposition and sentiment. Did certain characteristics of the LPW Committee help explain the failure of Clark and the liberal majority to get their share? The Committee again deviated from the parent chamber in its liberalism and activism, but such characteristics in this case led not to a "vanguard" role but to rejection and reversal. Once again a subcommittee chairman enjoyed great freedom and wrote his own legislative ticket, but in this case he found not only his independence but also his vulnerability increased. Some thought that with a different strategy Clark could have cut his losses. Equally interesting is the possibility that Hill's intervention—cutting back subcommittee authorizations at the full committee stage (as he did on the 1966 ESEA Amendments) or taking over floor management (recall Magnuson's handling of Neuberger and Hart)— might have had the same effect. At any rate, the 1966 poverty episode found the liberalism and decentralization of the LPW Committee, far from pushing the parent chamber to the limits legislatively, instead provoking a reaction that a more "moderate" committee might have avoided. The freedom to formulate and instigate was offset by an incapacity to mobilize.

Earlier pictures of the Committee have been complemented in other ways as well. The list of members interested in making a legislative name for themselves has more than doubled. No other episode has demonstrated more conclusively the minority's diversity and Javits' anxiety to develop Republican alternatives. In no case study has the importance of staff capacities and orientations to the program of an activist senator or committee been more obvious. And yet another pattern of committee-agency relationships has been uncovered. If 1966 showed that the EMP Subcommittee and OEO could not duplicate the performance of the Health Subcommittee and NIH, it also displayed a pattern of cooperation which presented both subcommittee and agency with policy-making potentialities.

HILL'S "CONDOMINIUM"

"You know how peculiarly Hill runs his committee," a USOE official remarked in early 1967; "it's a sort of condominium arrangement." The case studies in Chapter 6 thus focused less on the full Labor and Public Welfare Committee than on its five principal subcommittees; it was for this reason, among others, that the Committee was found in a series of legislative roles that far exceeded those of either Commerce or Finance in range and diversity. If Commerce and Finance could be described in terms of relatively uniform and contrasting patterns of legislative behavior, what was more interesting about LPW was the variety of roles displayed—initiating and promoting the cold war bill, ratifying but doing little else to the administration's FLSA bill, instigating new departures in education policy, and approving but reshaping the executive's medical complexes and poverty proposals. This variety, however, did not hide some striking points of comparison and contrast, particularly with respect to Finance, a committee whose subject matter resembled that of LPW in scope, complexity, and the extent of executive involvement. Some reasons for the difference, such as the constitutional restrictions under which the Finance Committee was operating, were fairly obvious. Others were less so. Did, for example, contrasting membership and recruitment patterns help explain differences in legislative role? How much could be attributed to differences in leadership and organization? How much could be explained in terms of group, agency, and House relationships? How important were staff capacities and orientations? It will be the purpose of the present chapter to explore these and similar questions.

Liberalism and Activism. The Labor and Public Welfare Committee, as is shown in Figure 5 and Table 4, was an unusually liberal group—or, as a minority member put it, "a stacked committee if I ever saw one." The average member's ADA score was 63, compared to the average senator's

FIGURE 5.   Distribution of members, Senate Committee on Labor and Public Welfare, according to the ratings given them by the Americans for Democratic Action, 1965.[1]

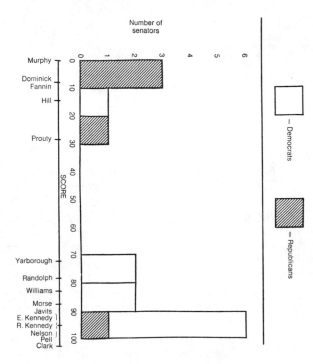

50. With Hill's deceptively low score (12) removed from computation, LPW Democrats displayed a remarkably high mean score (88); the abnormally high Republican average (27), while skewed by Javits' performance, was nonetheless, given Javits' position, reflective of the thrust of minority policy efforts. What explained this predominance of liberal sentiment? It was mainly a matter of self-selection. On the House side, where committee assignments were much more centrally controlled, Republicans often chose their most business-oriented and Democrats their most labor-oriented members for Education and Labor—thus insuring a polarized committee and frequently a negative minority role.[2] On the Senate side there was much less gatekeeping. The more senior and more conservative senators generally sought to defend their interests on Finance or Appropriations, thus leaving LPW seats relatively uncontested. Organized labor often made representations to the party leadership regarding appointments and urged friendly senators to seek LPW seats. But urban-state and other liberals had their own reasons for seeking membership. Hill, like

TABLE 4. Ratings given to Senators by the Americans for Democratic Action, 1965: Mean scores and standard deviations for selected Senate Committees.[3]

	Mean Score	Standard Deviation from Mean
Commerce Committee	55	30.1
Democrats	72 (76 without Lausche)	17.2 (11.7 without Lausche)
Republicans	22	20.9
Finance Committee	44	33.4
Democrats	64 (69 without Talmadge)	24.6 (19.1 without Talmadge)
Republicans	8	1.4
LPW Committee	63	38.0
Democrats	81 (88 without Hill)	24.5 (9.2 without Hill)
Republicans	27	34.9

Magnuson, chose to exert little control, though because of his subject-matter he ended up with a far different segment of the Senate under his tutelage than did Magnuson—a fact, one suspected, about which he had few regrets:

> Other committee chairmen make a lot more effort to see who goes on their committee than I do. [Agreeing:] Byrd was one example. I leave it pretty much to the Committee on Committees. We don't have a single southerner on there except Yarborough, and he's no conservative. It's a liberal committee all right.

Republican members, of course, were more diverse. Fannin, and to a lesser extent Murphy and Dominick, were staunch conservatives who came to the Committee with business backing and with the intention of opposing much that was going on there. But minority recruitment was less rigid than it was on the House Committee, and relatively liberal members —like Javits and Prouty and, before them, Ives, Smith, Aiken, Cooper, and Case—often sought and gained membership.

The LPW Committee was thus a good testing ground for the linkage, provisionally accepted in earlier chapters, between liberalism and activism; the behavior of most of its members was such as to confirm the relationship. The 89th Congress saw Edward Kennedy venturing into health affairs and the problems of the aged, as well as Judiciary Committee battles on reapportionment and civil rights. Clark continued to develop manpower legislation and assumed responsibility for accelerating the poverty program. Yarborough's legislative interests included, besides the cold war bill and FLSA extensions, bilingual education programs and miscellaneous extensions of veterans' readjustment and rehabilitation assistance. Robert Kennedy's Special Impact poverty amendment was part of a larger effort to develop an independent approach to urban problems; bills dealing with narcotic rehabilitation and the care of the aged bore his name as well. Morse introduced a long list of his own education and labor bills. Nelson continued to champion the idea of a National Teacher Corps (a proposal, like tire safety, which he was instrumental in developing but for which he got little credit after it was taken up by others) and to promote rural poverty programs. Pell secured the passage of bills to establish a National Foundation on the Arts and Humanities and to authorize federal assistance to "sea grant" colleges for oceanographic research. Williams added to his usual spate of migrant labor bills proposals to create a VISTA for senior citizens, to set safety standards for medical devices, and to establish a nationwide network of diagnostic centers utilizing computer technology. The calendar of the LPW Committee, in short, was much more crowded than that of either Commerce or Finance with proposals formulated or independently championed by its members. These bills reflected a wide variety of policy interests and a general desire for new or accelerated federal activity in almost every area of LPW jurisdiction.

If the minority displayed much less accord on the desirability of change, the behavior of its ranking members tended to confirm further the correlation between liberalism and activism. It was significant that the Finance Committee Republican who explained his colleagues' inaction by noting that "you don't develop an alternative to something you totally disagree with" went on to acknowledge a fundamental disagreement with Javits' mode of operation; "We are totally opposed on these things. I don't share his views." Nor did Cotton's staff-inspired efforts to refine Commerce Committee proposals offer a point of comparison. "Javits," as one aide put it, "is almost compulsive about offering 'alternatives,' and Prouty is, too, to some extent." No Senator had more bills before the Committee than did the ranking minority member; Javits kept score meticulously, issuing a report at the end of each session documenting the minority's "contributions" to the major bills processed by the Committee.[4] As Chapter 6 suggested, minority efforts were generally most intense in poverty and labor and least intense in health and veterans' affairs, with education falling somewhere in between. "Education and health are often bipartisan," one member explained, "but it's important for us to have alternatives in these other areas—in labor because the whole area of labor-management relations is so complex and controversial and in poverty because of the political nature of the program." Javits' efforts obviously were not motivated simply by the policy goals he shared with the majority. But his liberalism did encourage the activist strategies of "consequential constructive opposition," "innovation," and "cooperation."[5]

The point should not be overstated. In some cases a senator's place on the ADA spectrum seemed largely irrelevant to his legislative moves; Hill's felt necessity to compile a conservative voting record did not preclude his taking substantial initiatives in the health field and "letting things happen" in other areas as well. Recall also the "reform" battles in which Williams joined Douglas and Gore, and the efforts of various other senators on behalf of their pet industries. In some cases, conservatism, not liberalism, was linked with policy initiatives. The poverty proposals of Education and Labor Republicans, for example, while not always "constructive," were nonetheless substantial undertakings; recall also Dirksen's reapportionment and school prayer bills and the later efforts of Robert Griffin and others to legislate against "busing" as a means to school integration. But in general it was liberals and moderates who were most interested in developing new legislation or in formulating alternatives to administration requests; a more typical conservative role was to oppose or attempt to "weaken" a proposal that came from elsewhere. Table 5, while neces-

TABLE 5.   Grouping of members of the Senate Commerce, Finance, and Labor and Public Welfare Committees according to ADA rankings and modes of legislative activity. Senators by whose name an asterisk (*) appears are included in the activist category only because of projects undertaken in Congresses other than the 89th or on committees other than the three mentioned.[6]

Legislative	ADA SCORES		
activity in-	High (80–100)	Moderate (20–80)	Low (0–20)
cluded the	13	13	4
development of substantial new policy departures.	Clark, Douglas,* Hart, Javits, E. Kennedy, R. Kennedy, McCarthy,* Morse, Nelson, Pastore,* Pell, Ribicoff, H. Williams	Anderson, Bartlett, Fulbright,* Gore,* Hartke, Long, Magnuson, Monroney,* Neuberger, Prouty, Randolph,* Smathers,* Yarborough	Cotton, Dirksen,* Hill, J. Williams*
Legislative	2	4	9
activity largely limited to the proposal of deletions or marginal alterations.	Brewster, Metcalf	Bass, Cannon, Lausche, Scott	Bennett, Carlson, Curtis, Dominick, Fannin, Morton, Murphy, Pearson, Talmadge

sarily imprecise in its categorizations, nonetheless builds on previous chapters and further documents the point. This helps explain why most of the large-scale proposals coming from the LPW minority bore Javits' stamp, although Javits' control of staff resources and of the other prerogatives of leadership were obviously also important. At any rate, the efforts of LPW conservatives Murphy, Dominick, and Fannin rarely matched even those mounted by Ayres, Goodell, Quie, and Ashbrook, on the House side. Their typical move was rather to join with Javits in the proposals they could accept, to express their discontents individually or collectively in "supplemental views," and occasionally to take their own amendments haplessly to the floor.

If ADA scores help explain the impulses toward activism found on LPW, standard deviations from the mean score suggest a refinement in understanding. The majority, with Hill's score removed from computation, showed a standard deviation of only 9.2, much lower than comparable figures for Commerce and Finance. The minority, on the other hand, displayed a figure of 34.9. Roll call data supplemented these findings nicely: the majority's index of cohesion on LPW bills during the 89th Congress was an extraordinarily high 81, while the comparable score for LPW Republicans was only 54.[7] This meant that Democratic senators wishing to undertake legislative projects were ordinarily reinforced by a liberal and cohesive voting bloc. On the minority side, the wide ideological scattering betrayed the absence of the incentives a cohesive and supportive bloc might have provided.

But a major problem of interpretation remains. Table 5 groups "activists" together, Magnusons and Harts alike, over against those whose legislative efforts were more limited. But is liberalism uniformly related to various *aspects* of the legislative task?[8] Might it, in fact, be *negatively* related to the capacity to mobilize, as opposed to the propensity to formulate and publicize? It was perhaps no accident that senators who were frequently found assuming a successful mobilizing role—Magnuson, Anderson, Hill, and even Long—all displayed a "middling" ideological stance; their flexibility and moderation probably increased their capacities to mediate and persuade. But neither was it any accident that these were senior senators with high positions of formal authority. If their moderation and their ability to mobilize were related to one another, *both* were probably linked to the type of constituency they represented and the degree of seniority they had attained. And what of those members like Ribicoff, Hart, Clark, Neuberger, and Nelson, notable for their activism in the early legislative stages but often dependent on others in the later stages? Their liberalism probably bore some independent responsibility, reducing their flexibility and perhaps encouraging harmful deviations from Senate "folkways" as well. But here, too, a complex of factors was involved, a situation that will be discussed in more detail in Chapter 8.[9] Liberal, activistic senators were largely drawn from large and/or urban states that displayed a high degree of party competition. If this stimulated a "public" style, it also meant that these senators were electorally vulnerable and hence less likely to attain the seniority, occupy the positions, or accumulate the credits needed for maximum legislative leverage.

Again, it is important to avoid overstatement. The initiatory efforts of many LPW members were by no means mere exercises in futility. Most of them at the close of the 89th Congress could boast of bills passed as well as bills introduced. This was in part the result of the cohesiveness of the LPW Committee itself. A uniformity of policy outlook by no means made for complete harmony; members often reported that one or another of their colleagues compromised his effectiveness through impatience, irritability, pretentiousness, rudeness, ineptitude, laziness, or "nit-picking." Since these negative characterizations were given by persons who agreed with one another on most policy questions, they perhaps had a degree of credibility that the characterizations given by Finance Committee members lacked. But they were coupled with accounts of committee leaders who were able to unite the group in a common cause. Hill was universally respected as a "Senator's Senator" and a gentleman; "whenever he tells me to get cosponsors on something," one aide reported, "it usually takes all of ten minutes to get every member of the Committee, both parties." Morse also had his way smoothed by a reputation for honesty, hard work, and fairness. Even when a member was credited with traits that made him ineffective or disruptive, they could rarely be linked to specific committee defeats. When linkages were given, they were generally used to account for failures on the floor, where hostility could often have been expected on policy grounds alone. On the Finance Committee personal factors were often used to explain why a member did not succeed among "us"; on the LPW Committee, the reference was more often to "them." Personality factors did not seriously disrupt, and sometimes they promoted, the Committee's natural tendency to close ranks behind its members' proposals.

If the composition of their committee enabled LPW members to avoid the isolation that often confronted liberal activists in the early stages, it by no means always solved the problem of mobilizing the parent chamber. The FLSA and poverty episodes of 1966 suggested that the Committee's proposals were often too rich for the Senate's tastes. There were also reports of "folkways" violations and otherwise abrasive behavior which supposedly reduced the effectiveness of Javits, Clark, and other members. Nor did Hill often intervene after Magnuson's fashion, doing the bargaining and persuading for his members that they could not do for themselves. But LPW members, liberal and "pushy" as they were, could nonetheless claim in many instances to have mobilized the Senate. Most of the bills they reported came down to the left of what the average senator would have preferred, and many—recall the cold war and health complexes bills, the ESEA amendments of 1966, and the 1965 poverty bill—were passed in that form. If this suggested the persistence of one of the oldest folkways of all—deference to committee decisions—in the face of certain strains, it also suggested that some of these strains themselves might be relaxing. The Senate, in short, had become more liberal, and a certain tolerance had developed for senatorial activism and a "public" style. Circumspection and deference still had their rewards, but as crowning virtues they were definitely on the wane. As Edward Kennedy, who played the game meticulously his freshman term, remarked:

> *At first I was very reluctant to move and to push anything. But when I did, I had no problems. I think I could have done it much earlier.*

It was, in a way, the obverse of the role transformation Magnuson was undergoing. While the committee chairman and congressional politician *par excellence* was, under electoral constraints, turning his attention to the generation and publicizing of ideas, the LPW Democrats who had long specialized in that phase of the operation were discovering that they could indeed go further. The telescoping of roles and capacities was far from complete, but the trends revealed a great deal about what was to come in electoral and congressional politics.

"A Democratic Committee."[10] The most distinctive characteristic of the LPW Committee, and one of great importance in explaining its legislative role, was its extreme decentralization. "Other committees have subcommittees," Senator Morse remarked, "but not like this." Table 6 permits a comparison of the activities of LPW and Commerce subcommittees. Both Hill and Magnuson delegated a substantial amount of work and were willing to appoint special subcommittees to enable members to carry out legislative or information-gathering projects, But Hill carried the process much further. Subcommittees held all but five days—97 percent, compared to 44 percent for Commerce—of the Committee's legislative hearings during the 89th Congress. Every majority member except freshman Senator Robert Kennedy possessed at least one chairmanship. There was little control from the top: the seven standing subcommittees largely determined their own schedules, put out their own press releases, and controlled their own staff hiring. General Counsel John Forsythe coordinated activities and looked out for Hill's interests, but his was the only professional appointment at the full committee level. The situation was made to order for activists like Morse, Clark, Yarborough, and Williams, who, as Chapter 6 showed, were enabled to undertake major legislative projects by virtue of the independence and resources their chairmanships afforded.

Committee decentralization became even more pronounced after Hill's retirement, as Yarborough (91st Congress) and then Williams succeeded

TABLE 6. Days of hearings held before the full Committees and Subcommittees on Commerce and Labor and Public Welfare, 89th Congress. Chairmen's names are in parentheses. Hearings for nominations and private bills are excluded.[11]

COMMERCE COMMITTEE	DAYS	LPW COMMITTEE	DAYS
Full committee (Magnuson)	116	Full committee (Hill)	5
Standing subcommittees	(86)	Standing subcommittees	(138)
MMF (Magnuson, Bartlett)	35	Health (Hill)	13
Communications (Pastore)	11	Labor (McNamara, Yarborough)	24
Aviation (Monroney)	15	Education (Morse)	31
Surface Transport. (Lausche)	23	Veterans' Affairs (Yarborough,	
Consumer (Magnuson)	2	Randolph)	13
		EMP (Clark)	47
		Migratory Labor (Williams)	7
		Railroad Retirement (Pell)	3
Special subcommittees	(6)	Special subcommittees	(21)
Automobile Marketing		Poverty (McNamara)	2
Practices (Monroney)	0	Arts and Humanities (Pell)	7
Freight Car Shortages		Aging (McNamara, E. Kennedy)	3
(Magnuson)	6	Food, Drug, and Cosmetic Act	
Textile Industry (Pastore)	0	Amendments (Williams)	1
Transportation on Great		Captioned Films for the Deaf	
Lakes (Lausche)	0	Amendments (Pell)	1
		Utilization of Scientific	
		Manpower (Nelson)	3
		Sea Grant Colleges (Pell)	4
Total	208	Total	164

to the chairmanship. Predictably, pressures for the formation of new subcommittees and for staff expansion became quite intense. The new chairmen did not share Hill's aversion to being identified with (or getting the credit for) what the Committee produced, but the gaining of such identification through techniques of preemption and control of the sort Magnuson used was never a live option. "That simply would have been impossible," one staff man reflected. "Things had gone too far in the opposite direction under Hill. If Yarborough had tried anything like that he would have had a real revolt on his hands." Forsythe continued to inform himself and Yarborough as to what was going on in the far reaches of the Committee and to provide some coordination, but the man who succeeded him in 1971 was not equipped by experience or stature to play that role—nor was there any sign that the new Chairman wanted him to. Under Williams a new standing Subcommittee on Children and Youth was added and the Special Committees on Aging and on Alcoholism and Narcotics were made standing committees—under the leadership, respectively, of Walter Mondale (who had come to LPW in 1968), Thomas Eagleton (1969), and

Harold Hughes (1969). By 1971, then, *every* majority member chaired a *standing* subcommittee, and five chaired special subcommittees as well.

There were, however, differences among the subcommittees, and some of these suggested variations in policy role. Not all subcommittees, for example, were considered equally desirable by LPW members. The size of the group was one indicator of the demand for seats: during the 89th Congress, Education, Labor, and EMP each had nine or ten members; Veterans' Affairs and Health were slightly smaller; and Migratory Labor and Railroad Retirement had only six members each. Seniority figures told roughly the same story: the average member of the Education Subcommittee at the beginning of 1965 had been on LPW 6.6 years; the Health Subcommittee boasted the next highest seniority figure, 6.0 years (4.2 with Hill excluded); Labor and EMP were tied at 4.4; while the other subcommittees lagged far behind.[12] Did these preferences reflect calculations as to the relative fertility of various areas, or the relative openness of various subcommittees? A positive evaluation of policy-making possibilities frequently appeared to be a factor in the choice of Education or EMP. Railroad retirement, on the other hand, was too narrow in its jurisdiction to offer such incentives, and Migratory Labor, though it provided Williams and later Mondale with a fruitful and politically profitable field of operation, suffered from the same disability.

The other cases were more complex. Yarborough had come to the Veterans' Affairs chairmanship with one major project in mind; after the cold war bill was passed, he was ready to move on. Edward Kennedy was offered the chairmanship but refused it. Randolph, whose main legislative interests were on the Public Works Committee, which he chaired, accepted the Subcommittee "because Hill asked me to" and because he thought it might assist him in his pending reelection campaign; he certainly had "no big project like the cold war bill" in mind. Nor, for that matter, did Yarborough himself take the Labor Subcommittee chairmanship, according to one of his aides, "the way he went to Veterans' Affairs, with a particular project or program in mind." And both Clark and Morse, it will be recalled, refused to take the Labor Subcommittee.[13] Why? What explained the relatively low appeal of Labor and Veterans' Affairs? The remarks of two aides suggested a partial answer: "Labor is an area the executive pretty well has covered. There aren't any obvious gaps." And again: "You wonder sometimes—what else can we do for veterans?" The Labor Subcommittee maintained its place as one of the more sought after, partly because both labor and business organizations urged their friends to seek a voice in its affairs. Williams in fact took the Labor Subcommittee chairmanship in 1969 and retained it after he became full committee chairman, because organized labor was wary of Pell, who was next in line. But the Subcommittee's appeal, at least while a Democrat was in the White House, was reduced by the absence of conspicuous policy gaps.

The remaining subcommittee, Health, raises questions about the extent of the Chairman's permissiveness. Most members could recall instances when they or their colleagues had found it necessary to walk circumspectly to avoid implicating Hill or harming him politically. During the late fifties, when education policy was charged with racial implications and the Education Subcommittee Chairman, James Murray, was becoming senile, Hill controlled the Subcommittee's operations to an unusual degree. During the 1962 campaign, Committee operations were curtailed extensively across the board. But such situations were exceptional. The usual pattern was one of extreme permissiveness. If subcommittee recommendations were debated or altered at the full committee level, it was ordinarily because of objections raised by minority members not on the subcommittee in question. Hill himself rarely intervened. The alterations he made in the Education Subcommittee's 1966 ESEA Amendments were a means of forestalling more drastic cuts on the floor; his working relationship with Morse was, in fact, unusually cordial and mutually deferential. But Hill was equally reluctant to interfere with the operations of other subcommittee chairmen, even in controversial areas like labor standards and poverty. "He doesn't try to control Clark's subcommittee any more than he does any of the others," reported one counsel; "If you don't bother him he won't bother you," echoed another. Similar testimony came from the Chairman of one of the more controversial subcommittees:

> Hill gives me almost completely free rein. Of course I try to be considerate and clear things with him, but I never have to "trim my sails." Right now, as a matter of fact, we're handling a kind of touchy situation: my subcommittee is reporting out a [bill touching on civil rights], and we need to bring it before the full committee. Now Lister will waltz around a little on that to please his southern colleagues and his constituents, but we will get it out.

"Hill has never interfered with my operations at all," added another Chairman. "There's never been a ripple."

If Hill was uniformly generous with his subcommittee chairmen, however, he was probably less permissive than any of them in the way that he ran his own subcommittee. His rule was by no means autocratic; Edward Kennedy, in fact, came to the Subcommittee precisely because of the initiatives he felt he could take there, and both he and Williams developed a number of proposals in the health field. But their proposals fared better when they were handled by other subcommittees (e.g. Kennedy's Health Centers proposal and Williams' bill to provide health services for migrants). The Health Subcommittee held hearings only on bills sponsored by Hill during the 89th Congress, and Subcommittee aide Robert Barclay reserved most of his efforts for the Chairman. Senators who felt, as one of them put it, that "the Health Subcommittee hasn't really done much new lately" and attempted to do something about it rarely confronted outright obstructions, but neither did they receive much encouragement or assistance. Hill and Barclay were generally viewed as gatekeepers from whom clearance must be gained if one was to venture into the area. On many health matters, as the medical complexes bill demonstrated, Hill had largely preempted the field. "I wouldn't venture into that Hill-Burton [hospital construction] area," admitted one Subcommittee member not otherwise known for his deference. This of course affected Republicans as well as Democrats; "Hill and the Health Subcommittee are much less eager [than Morse] to accommodate us," testified one minority staff member. "They don't seek out our views much, and I tend to get in on things at a much later stage over there." A majority counsel verified the point:

> The Republicans have a problem in that health area. Javits has almost got to be different and come up with some things of his own. But Hill really has the area controlled. He can usually get cosponsors, and his opponents usually fold. So it's hard for Javits—and Ted Kennedy has the same problem—to do anything. Sometimes they do come up with proposals though, have hearings, and carry them through.[14]

If Hill's handling of health matters bore striking resemblances to Magnuson's guardianship of merchant marine and fisheries, he remained much less involved in his committee's other areas of jurisdiction than did the Commerce Committee Chairman. One staff member confirmed:

> There's none of this business of trying to get the subcommittee to trim its sails in order to take a united committee to the floor. Hill doesn't care about that, except on his health bills. His attitude would be to let Clark make a fool of himself if he wanted to.

What was the impact of this mode of leadership on the quantity and quality of the Committee's legislative output? How did it affect the Committee's capacity to marshall support on the floor? It was concluded in Chapter 3 that Magnuson's tendency occasionally to pull in the reins on his members or to take over their legislative projects, while it might have discouraged certain efforts at instigation or formulation, sometimes increased the Committee's capacity to mobilize. Similar conclusions for the LPW Committee were suggested by the 1966 education and poverty episodes. Hill's trimming of the Education Subcommittee's ESEA Amendments probably forestalled more drastic cuts on the floor, but more typical was his refusal to interfere in the poverty fight. Dirksen's attempts to cut authorizations to "administration levels" failed in the former case but succeeded in the latter. Hill's detachment, it might be argued, gave Clark and the Kennedys the freedom to develop a strong proposal but, in the long run, resulted in a defeat more severe than might have occurred had the Chairman taken over the bill or exercised a restraining influence. But it is difficult to generalize. Hill's members, much more than Magnuson's, would have resisted restraints and preemptions from the chair. Magnuson's behavior not only conciliated the parent chamber but often consolidated his committee as well. Had Hill assumed a similar role, he might have pacified Republican members at the price of the disaffection and disintegration of the liberal majority. As it was, he left formulation and instigation untrammeled and thus facilitated the consolidation of his committee around the norms and goals associated with the traditional "vanguard" role of the liberal major- ity. And that was a role which, if it had led to certain adaptive failures, had also, on balance, had a stimulative effect on congressional output over the years.

Organizational variables pertaining to the Republican third of the Com- mittee had a different policy impact than those pertaining to the Committee as a whole, mainly because of the interests and orientations of the sena- tors involved. The diversity of the minority made tight control impossible and resulted in widely scattered legislative efforts. But Javits nonetheless dominated Republican operations to a large extent. He was a member of all four major subcommittees—something Hill did not permit on the major- ity side—and, most important, he controlled the minority staff. If he could not prevent his more conservative colleagues from proposing their amend- ments and deletions, he could and did determine the shape of collective minority efforts in most areas under LPW jurisdiction. Had Javits decen- tralized his operations as Hill had his, the substantive policy impact might well have been the reverse of that witnessed on the full committee: the minority role in certain areas would have become more obstructive and the scorecard of "minority contributions" would undoubtedly have been shortened as well as altered in content.

As in previous chapters, the impact of personality and organizational variables may be summarized in terms of a structure of incentives. It was no accident that the LPW Committee, which had more subcommittees and a wider distribution of powers and functions than either Finance or Com- merce, had a stronger and more positive incentive structure than either. Senator Hill's permissiveness provided members with the opportunity and the machinery to pursue legislative projects. It also contributed to an "ethos" which sanctioned and supported such efforts. Leadership, of course, was not the entire story. The fact that the Committee contained a disproportionate number of liberals with an activist orientation made for a supportive atmosphere. The subject matter of the Finance Committee was comparable in its scope and import, but the identifications, ideologies, and self-images of that committee's membership often stimulated little more than a desire to veto or amend. To LPW liberals, however, the breadth of Committee jurisdiction represented a temptation to more ex- tensive lawmaking efforts, and committee norms sanctioned policy entre- preneurship as an appropriate response.

These positive stimuli were offset, but by no means nullified, by some significant disincentives. As Chapter 6 showed, the ability of certain groups to stimulate legislative efforts tended to reach a point of diminishing returns; the persistence and insatiability of labor and veterans' groups actually led certain senators to avoid becoming their legislative champions. The extensive involvement of the executive branch, while it made possible the launching of projects which senators could hardly have managed alone, also restricted congressional maneuverability and preempted certain lines of action. The extent of group and executive activity meant that in many areas LPW members could not find the sort of policy gaps that had stimulated their Commerce Committee colleagues in oceanography and consumer affairs. The incentives provided to activist senators by the presence of a supportive committee majority were sometimes tempered by a recognition of the adaptive problems this "vanguard" faced. And even Hill's leadership had its negative side. There were taboos against venturing into areas that might prove "embarrassing" to the Chairman, and more substantial difficulties faced those who would venture into health affairs, Hill's special bailiwick.

Integration and Adaptation. The LPW Committee's capacities for adaptation and integration were best appreciated when compared with those of a committee, like Finance, whose jurisdiction was similar in its scope and its potential for controversy. The Senate generally gave neither committee overwhelming margins of approval; the chamber's index of cohesion on LPW votes was 28, compared to 32 for Finance.[15] But the Senate failed to pass only one bill reported by LPW during the 89th Congress (the filibustered 14[b] repeal), while rejecting five of those reported by Finance. And LPW displayed greater internal solidarity; the Committee's index of cohesion on its bills was 45, while Finance's score on its bills was only 38. LPW Democrats, with an index of cohesion of 81, surpassed their Finance (57) and equalled their Commerce (81) counterparts.

It is hardly surprising that the LPW Committee, dealing with more controversial subject matter and deviating considerably from the Senate's ideological midpoint, could not match the Commerce Committee's successes at adaptation. More interesting, however, is the fact of internal cohesion—together with the evidence that this characteristic of the Committee, which Finance could not match, did "make a difference," however slight, in LPW's adaptive capacities. "This is a very happy committee," testified a senior Democratic member; "it was that way even when Barry Goldwater was ranking Republican." Most members expressed great satisfaction with the way the Committee was run, and not one sought a transfer as the 90th Congress began. Some of the more conservative Republicans, as might be expected, gave a less benign picture. One went so far as to call LPW a "constant headache": "You feel like you've got a hairshirt on the whole time you're in there." One Republican compared LPW unfavorably with Commerce in terms of harmony and pleasantness. Other minority members complained at their exclusion from the health field and singled out Clark and Yarborough as particularly difficult to work with. But there were also many reports of cooperation and collaboration and few indications of the kind of disaffection expressed by Republican members of Senate Finance or of House Education and Labor.[16]

Committee stability, often regarded as both cause and effect of integration, was hardly a hallmark of LPW. The Committee was indeed becoming more sought after: an examination of membership changes reveals that, while more senators transferred off than on LPW during 1947–1956, the reverse was true for 1957–1966; it rose from eleventh to eighth place among Senate committees according to this index of "desirability." The mean seniority of members at appointment stood at 0.6 years for the period 1961–1965, up from the 1947–1956 figure of 0.2. But LPW still ranked considerably below Finance and Commerce on both counts. Twelve new appointments were made to the Committee between 1961 and 1965, compared to ten for Commerce and three for Finance. And the average term of service of a LPW member at the beginning of the 89th Congress was only 4.9 years, lower than figures for Commerce (5.4) and Finance (8.5) or the figure computed for LPW itself in 1955.[17] The increasing stability of the Committee's membership—no Democrat transferred off the Committee between 1965 and 1972 (though the electoral vulnerability of the group was convincingly demonstrated by the defeat of Morse, Clark, and Yarborough)—augured well for its future integrative capacities, but the degree of cohesiveness it achieved during the 89th Congress was best explained by other factors.

Of great importance, for LPW as for Commerce, was the role of the Chairman. Hill was liked and respected for his fairness, his permissiveness, and his capacity for "social leadership." He was trusted by both liberals and conservatives and was viewed, as one minority member put it, as "pretty much a bipartisan figure. He often bridges the gap." The decentralization of the Committee was also, on balance, a positive factor. The reason was not so much that an efficient division of labor was thereby achieved[18]—most members belonged to several subcommittees and avoided strict specialization—as that members were given a chance to be active and productive. Decentralization, it is true, contributed to the disaffection of some Republicans by encouraging a more "radical" policy output and elevating relatively nonsolicitous Democrats to power. But for most members, decentralization meant freedom of movement and a high degree of satisfaction with the legislative possibilities of their committee posts.

The Committee's subject matter, a third variable bearing on its integrative capacities, resembled that of the Finance Committee in the money it

involved, the groups it touched, and the ideological and partisan controversies it raised. Its impact on the internal life of the Committee was softened, however, by a fourth factor, the nature of the LPW membership.
Most members, liberal and activist in outlook, found in their subject matter, as in committee decentralization, an incentive to involvement and
cooperation. Their uniformity of ideology and policy objectives muted
division and controversy. As noted above, they frequently described one
another as difficult to live with, but—in contrast to the Finance Committee
—these descriptions were generally used to explain adaptive, not integrative, difficulties; personal antipathies rarely prevented alliances between
like-minded members.

The Republicans obviously had their own integration problems. In contrast to their majority colleagues, four Republicans left the Committee
between 1965 and 1972. Their ideological diversity during the 89th Congress (see Figure 5) was mirrored in an index of cohesion of 54
on LPW-reported bills, compared to the Finance Committee minority's
score of 64 on bills of similar scope. The bills discussed in Chapter 6
involved 36 roll calls; the minority voted as a bloc on only six of these, and
15 (42 percent) of them displayed a "down-the-middle" (3–2, 3–3, or 4–2)
split. Some members indicated, with justification, that these figures did not
tell the whole story. "We get together when we can," reported one conservative. "Javits isn't as opposed to our things as much as you might
think—and even when he disagrees, he is very fair and cooperative." A
less benign attitude was often evident when specific amendments or such
intra-party matters as staff hiring were mentioned. But in any case, diversity on the minority side, far from threatening the integration of the Committee as a whole, probably promoted it. If LPW had had a more conservative and more cohesive minority, as did Senate Finance (ADA score = 8)
or House Education and Labor (19), the result would have been a polarized
committee and less "constructive" Republican participation. But with a
diversified minority membership (average ADA score = 27; standard deviation = 34.9) led by Javits, whose ADA ranking of 94 was higher than
the average Democratic score, LPW was spared some of the partisanship
and division its subject matter might otherwise have stimulated.[19]

The LPW Committee, then, did not enjoy the integration that a more
moderate membership or a less controversial jurisdiction might have given
it, but compared to other committees similarly situated, it was relatively
harmonious. How did this affect its performance as a legislative unit? The
integration of the LPW Committee, like that of Commerce, encouraged and
buttressed most of its members in their legislative endeavors. In one
respect, its impact was probably less ambiguous than was the case with
Commerce: the integration of LPW involved less sail-trimming and preemption on the part of the Chairman and hence brought with it fewer
disincentives to formulation and publicizing. Hill did, of course, occasion-

ally find it necessary to block or qualify a proposal, and the integration of the Committee—an important ingredient of which was deference to the Chairman—greatly increased his ability to work his will. One observer recalled the membership's reaction to the Committee's slowdown during the 1962 campaign:

> *The members understood. I remember when one got pretty impatient: he got the idea of circulating a petition to have more meetings. One of the first ones he went to was McNamara, and McNamara told him in no uncertain terms to shove it. So that was the end of that.*

But Hill did not ordinarily block, alter, preempt, or take over his members' proposals. Under the circumstances, this mode of leadership probably not only promoted group integration but also avoided some of the disincentives to activism that a more paternalistic kind of leadership might have produced. By the same token, however, the LPW Committee's mode of integration was less conducive than that of Commerce to the involvement of conservative members.

Certain additional considerations must qualify any assessment of the marginal effect of LPW integration on Committee output. In the first place, LPW senators were probably less likely than their Commerce counterparts to have their course of action determined by conditions within the Committee. They were more liberal, more activistic in orientation, more geared to the media and a "public" style, and perhaps less pragmatic and less governed by strategic calculations. They might have instigated, formulated, and publicized in any case—as did their counterparts on the much less harmonious or supportive House Education and Labor Committee. And what of the later legislative stages? Committee cohesion and homogeneity, as suggested above, represented an aid, and hence an incentive, to mobilization. But here, too, interpretation must be cautious. The case was in some ways analogous to that of the Finance Committee under Byrd: both committees were integrated around norms and goals considerably deviant from those of the parent chamber. In many instances committee integration permitted a withstanding of floor attacks, but in other cases —recall the medicare battle of 1964 and the 1966 poverty episode—solidarity at the committee level discouraged precautions which might have prevented an all-or-nothing floor defeat. The relationship between integration and adaptation, in other words, like that between integration and activism, could seldom be assessed in unequivocal terms.

A Representative Institution. The environment of the LPW Committee, like that of Finance, furnished a contrast to the setting of the Commerce Committee by virture of the prominence of organized labor and other inclusive groups seeking or opposing measures of a redistributive character and/or considerable scope. As was the case with the Finance Committee,

LPW often found its capacities for effective and independent response lessened by the information resources needed to deal with these measures, the bureaucratic operations they assumed or anticipated, and the imperviousness to the demands of ancillary groups they required. But the education episode suggested (and here there were interesting parallels to the situation confronting formulators of sugar policy) that the executive also had decided advantages in a situation where large and powerful national groups found themselves in *competition* over a policy which all of them wanted implemented in some form but which each of them was only able to *block* as long as their arena of operation remained the decentralized and bargaining Congress. Congress found it far easier to "cumulate" discrete distributive demands than it did effectively to "balance" competing demands, distributive or otherwise, and enforce a workable compromise.[20]

If such factors—and they will be discussed more fully in the final chapter—help explain the extent to which the LPW Committee in most areas found it necessary or helpful to share legislative responsibility with executive agencies, the character of the groups themselves and the identifications and legislative orientations of committee members still had an important impact on specific instances and patterns of responsiveness. The AMA, for example, virtually invited LPW to ignore its objections to the medical complexes bill, once again proving ideologically rigid and deficient in the art of compromise. Some small businesses, on the other hand, fared better on FLSA than they had during the Senate phase of packaging or UC, partly because the nature of the issue virtually forced upon them a strategy of seeking specific and piecemeal concessions. Yarborough's struggle to enact a cold war bill over the opposition of the major veterans' groups demonstrated in a negative fashion what sugar, shipping, and other veterans' bills often demonstrated more positively— how groups with self-aware and relatively narrowly based constituencies seeking tangible distributive benefits could obtain a secure niche in the policy process (but usually develop some debilitating rigidities at the same time). The cold war bill also demonstrated, however, as did various health, migratory labor, and poverty proposals, that interests which were weakly organized or otherwise failed to meet Mancur Olson's criteria of "strength" could nonetheless have their needs met by virtue of the entrepreneurial efforts of politicians who elected to appeal over the heads of the groups applying "pressure" in a given policy area. It is no denigration of the efforts and ingenuity of a Mary Lasker or a Ralph Nader to note that their success presupposed such an entrepreneurial orientation and a certain set of political goals on the part of the politicians whom they influenced.

The liberal and activistic predilections of most LPW members suggested not only that such policy entrepreneurship would be unusually common down through the ranks of the committee but also that the responses of members to the groups lobbying them would be quite selective. The predominantly urban New England and Middle Atlantic states claimed 44 percent of the Committee's membership. The average member's Chamber of Commerce rating was 33 (Democrats = 16, Republicans = 66), considerably below the Senate mean of 41. The average AFL-CIO score (Democrats = 88, Republicans = 22, entire committee = 64), on the other hand, was considerably above the Senate norm (51).[21] Such figures helped explain why business and other groups opposing social welfare legislation frequently were given short shrift. The FLSA episode displayed clearly that many LPW members were willing to champion marginal deletions or amendments on behalf of home-state interests. But LPW displayed a lesser tendency than Finance or even Commerce to formulate or to approve business-oriented policy modifications. It was not that the groups petitioning LPW were weaker or less skillfull: what generally made the difference was the predispositions of the members themselves. In areas where ideological considerations were less relevant, however, the contrasts between LPW and Finance were less marked: recall, for example, the education, FLSA, and social security amendments which benefited various classes of handicapped persons. And both committees, while often losing (frequently willingly) the "race" for the representation of larger and more inclusive interests, many times opened a second front of interest-aggregation for the more narrowly based or opposition groups with which the executive had failed to deal.

The independence and distinctiveness of the representative role of LPW depended in part on the nature of the House committee with whom jurisdiction was being shared on the bill in question. On the medical complexes bill, for example, it was apparent that Hill was collaborating with many of the same interests that were getting the upper hand in the executive branch; it was left to the House Commerce Committee to accommodate the AMA. The widely divergent mean ADA scores of LPW and House Commerce— 63 and 36 respectively—suggested that their responses to the various groups inhabiting the health field might frequently be quite different. The cold war bill pointed up a similar situation in veterans' affairs. The Veterans Administration suffered from certain disabilities in both interest aggregation and policy formulation, but both the VA and the House Veterans' Affairs Committee were largely responsive to the American Legion and VFW and to the old-guard contingents within those organizations which were more interested in pensions and disability compensation than in more broadly-based readjustment programs. The LPW Committee, more oriented to social-welfare issues and having no jurisdiction over pension and disability programs, was more responsive to the progressive wing of the VFW and the smaller, more liberal veterans' organizations.

Differences between LPW and House Education and Labor were less marked. The ADA and AFL-CIO gave them equally high, and the USCC equally low ratings. Opponents of administration bills often could not open an effective second front with either committee. The case studies, however, suggested slight divergences in patterns of aggregation. The Roosevelt Subcommittee was apparently more willing than LPW to do labor's bidding; an LPW counsel confirmed that more House Committee members were "willing to do down the line with labor all the way."

> Their constituencies are smaller, and some of them have heavy labor constituencies. Also, they have shorter terms. I think the six-year term gives senators more independence. For example, [Representative Frank] Thompson is holding hearings now on some pretty far-reaching amendments to the National Labor Relations Act. I can't imagine labor coming to the Senate with a bill like that.

But the final outcomes in both FLSA and poverty also suggested that a larger number of groups wishing to qualify and limit the legislation had sought and found access on the House side. Why? Minority influence was perhaps a partial answer: Education and Labor Republicans were more conservative and business-oriented than their LPW counterparts[22] and more united in their attempts to translate their sentiments into policy modifications. But House Republicans were *less* integrated into committee operations than the LPW minority, and a number of the Education and Labor amendments in question had majority sponsorship. The fact is that the average House member, regardless of party or ideology, probably surpassed his Senate counterpart in sensitivity to local agencies and interests—labor, business, and sometimes both—unless, as on the Ways and Means and Appropriations Committees, countervailing norms were in effect.[23]

Committees and Agencies. The environment of the Commerce Committee displayed a generally low and uncoordinated level of executive activity, together with two often subordinate House units. Finance was very nearly an opposite case: House committees were dominant, and executive agencies often had extensive and well-coordinated legislative operations. With LPW, however, such generalizations were not possible—which was another major reason for the variety of policy roles discovered in Chapter 6. Patterns of coordination and adjustment with other "islands of decision" were diverse, as were their legislative effects.

The agencies with which LPW was dealing displayed great variations, first of all, in their legislative energies and capacities. Chapter 6 pointed up the political as well as the technical capabilities of the Labor Department and showed how new leadership and changed orientations had increased the capacity of USOE for interest aggregation and policy formulation. NIH and OEO, whatever their weaknesses within the executive hierarchy, nonetheless were conspicuous for their brokerage skills and for their comparatively strong orientation toward program expansion and innovation. The capacities of the VA, on the other hand, were reduced by the constraints imposed on the agency from above, by its bureaucratic and "service" orientation, and by the distance which its quasi-judicial and budget-guarding functions introduced into its relationships with client groups.

Patterns of inter-agency coordination also varied widely. Chapter 6 revealed many disagreements among the agencies with which LPW was dealing—between BOB and USOE on education authorizations in 1966, between CEA and the Labor Department on minimum wage increases, and between certain VA officials and their colleagues in BOB and the Defense Department on "peacetime" benefits. In none of these cases, however, were the disputes and differences available for congressional exploitation. There were divergencies, in other words, but no serious failures of coordination; in all three cases a single "executive position" was developed, and the overruled officials were constrained, in the USOE official's words, to "play by the rules." But the executive was not always this way, as NIH and OEO demonstrated. Of primary importance to the independence of these agencies were their bases of support in Congress. Both, in addition, occupied a place in the executive structure that freed them from strict accountability or oversight. Both operated programs which, from the BOB's overall perspective, were of relatively low salience. Their constituency relationships and the orientations of their leaders also contributed to the maintenance of an active and independent policy role. NIH took the role much further: OEO was subject to more extensive White House checks, had no patrons comparable to Mrs. Lasker and her congressional allies, and received much more severe public and congressional criticism. But both agencies had the incentives and the means to resist executive coordination and to secure independent alliances.

If the executive agencies with which LPW was dealing showed great variations in capacity and coordination, so did the various House committees. Education and Labor matched LPW in its liberalism and activism, but it was much less cohesive or predictable in its policy-making operations. Its members displayed greater "extremes" in ideology and in responsiveness to business and labor groups and, like Senate Finance, it contained several members whose views were highly individualistic, defying placement on an ideological continuum but nonetheless frequently resulting in policy initiatives. As a Labor Department official put it:

> The Senate Committee is more likely to "take charge" on an issue and develop things in a coherent way. The main reason is the greater reliance on the staff. On the House side you have all the individual members getting involved, and they often go off in all directions.

A USOE official elaborated the point, likewise mentioning the erratic nature of House activity and the importance of the staff in stabilizing Senate operations:

> Work with the House Committee is more detailed, more politically charged, more ulcer-provoking. Our philosophy is more compatible with the Senate committee; on the House side you've always got a bunch of Quie and Green amendments which reflect a directly opposed philosophy. Another thing, on the House side you've got much less staff and much less dependence on them.

These factors, of course, contributed to the House Committee's failures of integration and adaptation as well as to its incessant activity.

The other committees with which LPW was working were more peaceful and predictable than Education and Labor—but far more divergent from LPW in their overall policy orientations. House Commerce was more conservative and less activistic; House Veterans' Affairs was often disinterested in readjustment legislation, the area over which (until 1971) LPW had jurisdiction. But House Veterans' Affairs nonetheless enjoyed a general preeminence in the field, a dominance reinforced by the breadth of its jurisdiction, the orientation of its membership, the interests and access-patterns of the major veterans' groups, the deference of the Senate Finance Committee, and the incapacities of the VA.

In education and labor, then, the areas where the bulk of LPW's legislative activity took place, the Committee found the field crowded with active but relatively like-minded units. Executive energy and unity did not, of course, automatically spell congressional impotence; Morse in 1965 again disproved the zero-sum proposition and demonstrated that he could increase his own leverage as a member of Keppel's team. But there was rarely room for the sort of parametric policy moves that Williams, for example, made in the migrant labor field. And such moves certainly lacked viability when they were made in opposition to executive interests, as Roosevelt's 1965 FLSA proposal and Morse's 1964 and 1966 education bills demonstrated. The poverty area was somewhat, but not entirely, different, thanks to the relative independence of OEO. The cooperative relationships that developed during the first two years of the poverty program provided executive and congressional advocates alike with maximum policy leverage. And once executive unity had broken down, the degree of independence which OEO was able to maintain and the liaison it established with LPW enabled both agency and Committee to avoid the isolation and impotence that otherwise would have come as the administration ordered program cutbacks. Interestingly enough, these officials found themselves similarly undermined in turn: lower-level OEO chiefs secured alliances with congressmen who wished to earmark funds and safeguard specific programs.

The relationship of LPW with Education and Labor was for the most part a cooperative one. The case studies suggested no patterns of domination, either in the initiation of policy or in the securing of inter-house agreement.[24] Overall figures revealed, however, that of the 32 bills reported to the Senate on which the two committees shared jurisdiction, 27 had originated in the House. This perhaps reflected a preoccupation with policy generation on the part of Powell and some of his members, but, as the 1965 education and labor episodes suggested, it was often the result of decisions made elsewhere: administration and congressional strategists, with the entire battle plan in view, wished to surmount the most formidable obstacle first. Paradoxically enough, the House Education and Labor Committee, precisely *because* of its individualism, unpredictability, and difficulties with the parent chamber, often received the advantages that derived from formulation and prior commitment. But because of the community of interest between the two committees and the activistic bent of many LPW members, the Senate Committee's policy impact was not thereby eclipsed.

In the area of health, LPW operated in a more parametric fashion. The executive branch, at least from the perspective of NIH and Senator Hill, appeared sometimes timid, sometimes obstructive. The orientations and weaknesses of PHS, the Institutes' parent agency, made it an uncertain advocate at best, and NIH was then subject to further checks at the HEW and BOB levels. Nor did the House Commerce Committee fill the breach. Health affairs, like sugar for the Finance Committee, was relatively unrelated to the House Committee's other concerns and operations; its members' interest, sympathy, and expertise, as well as their leverage with other decision-making units, were thereby reduced. And their orientation was decidedly conservative. Hill's advocacy thus represented in part the filling of a policy gap and in part a countering of viewpoints which he feared might otherwise prevail. But he by no means operated in complete isolation. Of primary importance was his own position as Chairman of the Subcommittee on Labor-HEW Appropriations. This left him virtually in control of health legislation in the Senate and, as with Magnuson and the Independent Offices, increased his bargaining powers tremendously. And his ties with Fogarty's House Appropriations Subcommittee, NIH, and the Lasker group were such as to multiply the resources and increase the powers of each.

The area of veterans' affairs displayed yet another pattern. Here, too, LPW's liberalism and activism made it a force to be reckoned with, and the cooperative ties it established with readjustment-oriented elements in the VA and among the veterans' organizations facilitated its policy role. But its resources and its impact were reduced by the narrowness of its jurisdiction, the absence of cracks in the administration facade, and the patterns of group and agency access that made the House Veterans' Affairs

Committee the "core group" in the field. The cold war bill, in fact, was the only LPW-reported bill in this area to reach the House floor during the 89th Congress. LPW reported six veterans bills of its own (in addition to 15 bearing House numbers), but five of them were rejected by the House Committee (the House Commerce Committee, by comparison, completely rejected only one LPW bill, and Education and Labor, two). If the perspectives and limitations of the VA and the Finance and Veterans' Affairs Committees frequently spurred Yarborough and his colleagues to action, their resources and their unity often doomed such efforts to failure.

Staff Capacities and Roles. The decentralization of the LPW Committee was nowhere more apparent than in its staff operations. General Counsel John Forsythe protected Hill's interests and otherwise involved himself in education and labor legislation, but all other majority legislative aides were located at the subcommittee level, with subcommittee chairmen possessing the powers of appointment. Under Hill the staffs remained small— most subcommittees had only one majority counsel; but under Yarborough and Williams they grew rapidly. LPW counsels were seldom hired according to the purely "professional" standards claimed by the Finance Committee, but neither were they primarily "political" or patronage appointments. Standards of "second-level" expertise were generally high, and lateral movement to and from government agencies and policy-oriented private groups was frequent. Samuel Merrick and Don Baker, whom we found leading the Labor Department and OEO through major legislative battles, were both former Labor Subcommittee counsels, as was Edward Friedman, Deputy Solicitor of the Labor Department. The 89th Congress saw Charles Johnston going from the Veterans' Affairs Subcommittee to the VA and Arnold Nemore from the EMP Subcommittee to the National Manpower Policy Task Force. But this movement took place at varying rates: Charles Lee of the Education Subcommittee and Robert Barclay of the Health Subcommittee had served five and six years respectively by the end of 1966, while turnover on the Labor, Veterans' Affairs, and EMP Subcommittee staffs had been more rapid.

The minority staff was smaller and more centralized. One of Prouty's aides was on the Committee payroll, but Chief Counsel Stephen Kurzman, who involved himself particularly in EMP affairs, and Roy Millenson, who covered education, health, and veterans' affairs, were Javits men. Their competence generally matched that of their majority colleagues, but they were spread even more thinly. And they were new on the job, appointed after what was frequently termed the post-Goldwater "housecleaning." One of the more conservative members described the process:

> They fired them all. By "they" I mean Javits. He has complete control over the staff. One by one the Goldwater people left—like Mike Bernstein, the best man up here on labor [who, significantly, became

Minority Counsel for House Education and Labor]. If they weren't fired, it was made so uncomfortable for them that they had to go. We fought it, but it was no use.

Minority aides, too, were hardly purely "professional" appointees.

Appointment practices naturally influenced staff accessibility. The chief beneficiaries of majority practice were the subcommittee chairmen; Morse, Yarborough, Clark, and Williams found their staff resources indispensable to their legislative efforts. Junior members also reported generally good access, though Barclay's operations on Hill's Health Subcommittee represented a partial exception to the rule. But staff resources were still thinly spread, and less senior and more active members, notably the Kennedys, frequently relied heavily on their personal staffs; recall the roles of Burke and Walinsky in the poverty episode. Accessibility was considerably more restricted on the minority side. Here, too, it was partly a matter of limited manpower, but divergencies in loyalties and objectives played a larger role. "Javits specifically instructed us to serve all the members," one minority aide asserted, "and we make an honest effort to do that." But such offers of assistance, if proffered, were frequently not perceived or acknowledged by some of the more conservative members. "Right now," said one, "I can't get the time of day from the staff." Personal staffs were often utilized: Dominick reported that the LPW man in his office was greatly overworked, and Fannin had taken on one of Goldwater's former LPW aides as Legislative Assistant. "When Fannin popped up with those industry amendments [on FLSA]," one minority Committee aide admitted, "it was news to us." The minority staff was thus linked to Javits, and to a lesser extent to Prouty; their patterns of loyalty and accessibility hardly facilitated the legislative participation of the more conservative Republicans.

Javits' "housecleaning" resulted in reduced partisanship at the staff level, or at least in a different kind of partisanship. "We work well with the minority staff, in general," said a majority counsel, "and there's often not much dispute." "The relation of the majority and minority staffs has changed," Kurzman agreed. "There used to be almost no contact, and a lot of hostility and competition. We're more toward the middle of the spectrum [in partisanship] now." But the middle of the spectrum still was a considerable distance from full cooperation. Barclay's preemption of the health field on Hill's behalf continued to frustrate Millenson and his mentors. The Kurzman-Walinsky impasse on what eventually became the Kennedy-Javits poverty amendment demonstrated that substantial policy agreement did not always mute personal and partisan conflicts. But the important point is that this gap between majority and minority operations was one which Javits and his aides did their part to maintain. In fact, in their way they *increased* the partisanship of the minority: Javits strove to develop a Republican program which, far more than anything Goldwater had envisioned, matched majority proposals in scope. "Javits places great

value on being ahead of the pack, on beating the administration to ideas,"
said one aide, "and he keeps the staff busy thinking up and testing out
new proposals." Kurzman, for example, could and did claim a major part
of the credit for devising and developing no less than 25 amendments,
some of them broad in scope and many of them ultimately successful, to
the 1965 and 1966 poverty authorizations.[25] Thus was partisan competition
simply transferred to another plane; if the staff became less negative and
isolated, its personal loyalties and partisan identifications became even
more important as a stimulus and a focus for constructive effort. New policy
goals gave the minority staff additional flexibility, allowing them to develop
cooperative relationships and to have a greater hand in shaping policy
outcomes, but the farthest thing from Javits' mind was the "neutral" professionalism of which the Finance Committee boasted.

Majority staff operations varied considerably from subcommittee to subcommittee. Arnold Nemore of EMP was conspicuous in 1966 for his instigative efforts and his brokerage role vis-à-vis other activists, many of
them "entrepreneurs" on the members' personal staffs. James Sundquist,
Clark's Administrative Assistant when the EMP Subcommittee was formed,
played a major entrepreneurial role in his own right, leaving his stamp on
manpower legislation. Sundquist left Capitol Hill somewhat disillusioned
with the role left to congressional activists when a liberal Democrat was in
the White House, but he remembered the Senate of the Eisenhower and
early Kennedy years as "absolutely unparalleled as a point at which a
staff type could exercise personal influence and leverage." A staff man
who professed still to find such a role open to him in the mid-sixties was
Charles Lee, the Education Subcommittee's Professional Staff Member.
Lee was often constrained to assume a role not unlike that of Commerce's
Zapple and Beeks: Capitol Hill "expert" on a large and complex policy
area, and a processor of executive proposals. But Lee served Morse and
a number of other senators on and off the Subcommittee as a source of
ideas and as a liaison with and advocate for various groups with particular
education needs.

Staff members on the other subcommittees had fewer opportunities and
incentives for legislative instigation. Hill's well-established role and somewhat stereotyped interests in the health field, as well as his preference for
doing business personally, often left Barclay in the role of technician. But
Barclay's technical competence was accompanied by little of that "neutrality" to which Finance Committee aids aspired. He rather guarded Hill's
domain faithfully—rendering only minimal assistance to potential inno-
vators in the field, devising and revising proposals in line with Hill's long-
standing concerns, but rarely instigating new policy departures on his own.
The role of "expert" was transcended to a lesser degree yet on the
Labor and Veterans' Affairs Subcommittees. Johnston was able to assume
a somewhat innovative role during the formative years of the cold war
bill, with Yarborough's encouragement but in spite of Yarborough's passion

for detail and his inability to delegate responsibility. But in both labor and veterans' affairs certain long-range factors were at work—the absence of policy gaps, the dominance of administration and House units, the strength and activism of interest groups—which, besides leaving congressional aides with little time for independent, large-scale policy projections, also left them little space. The same factors, in short, that discouraged senatorial initiative in these areas discouraged staff instigation as well. The Labor Subcommittee was by far the more challenging of the two, and it became a much more important source of policy initiatives after the Democrats lost the White House. But during the sixties, Labor, like Veterans' Affairs, was staffed by young men who moved on rather quickly. They were usually capable enough, but they seemed to value their position more for the opportunity it gave them to learn and to advance than as an outlet for their creative talents.

Even with respect to the more innovative among LPW staff members, however, it must be acknowledged that none were as distinctive and discernible in either role or impact as were Grinstein and his coterie on the Commerce Committee. Accordingly, while the LPW case suggests that staff "entrepreneurship" is not an isolated phenomenon, it also warns against stereotyping the orientation or overstressing the independence of its impact on committee output in every case. That independence seemed manifest on the Commerce Committee, by virtue of the "self-steering" character of staff operations and the transitional and often uncertain character of Magnuson's legislative role. Magnuson's soporific appearance could be deceptive; but he *was* being "pushed," though usually not unwittingly, and his aides were unusually free to implement their own policy preferences and strategies. The same degree of "slack" was present on neither LPW nor Finance, with the result that the independent effect of staff orientations was less apparent; aides seemed to be taking more cues from their bosses than they were giving.[26] LPW members were unusually ambitious legislatively and were more firmly entrenched in their policy-making roles and preferences than was Magnuson. This, when added to the fact the majority staff was decentralized and hired at the subcommittee level, made for both a greater variety of staff performances and fewer overt signs of "manipulation." Some activist senators, while desiring anything but "neutrality" in their staffs, did not encourage much in the way of "policy entrepreneurship" either—Hill and Yarborough being prime examples. Other members —Clark, Javits, Williams, Morse—had aides whose orientations and operations more nearly resembled those of the Commerce Committee staff. That staff men like Lee and Kurzman stimulated their bosses and made their own distinctive contributions to the Committee's legislative undertakings was not to be doubted, but their impact was best explained not so much by their own strategies and the "slack" they were left as by the way their goals coincided with those of their mentors and their orientations proved serviceable in the realization of those goals.

THIRTEEN BILLS AND THREE COMMITTEES: THE CHARACTER AND THE CONDITIONS OF LEGISLATIVE RESPONSIBILITY

The distribution of legislative responsibility on each of the bills analyzed in previous chapters is shown in summary form in Table 7. At the very least, it confirms the doubt voiced in Chapter 1 as to the possibility of speaking simply of "legislative initiative" or of pigeonholing major bills as "executive" or "congressional" products. Responsibility for the development and passage of a bill takes many forms and is inevitably shared, not only because the committees and agencies are in competition and conflict, but because of the prerogatives and resources each lacks: they need one another. In short, both the senator who claimed autonomy for the legislature and the political scientist who relegated Congress to "delay and amendment"[1] fell considerably short of the truth. The case studies will have performed a considerable service if they have reduced such stereotypes, complicating our view of what in reality is a complex and cooperative process.

In this complexity, however, certain patterns do appear. It will be the task of the present chapter to explore these patterns with some care, examining the distributions of lawmaking roles and capacities which have been found and discussing the adequacy and appropriateness of various ways of explaining them. Previous chapters have provided something approximating a legislative history of the 89th Congress in certain major areas of domestic policy, with a focus on the operations of three Senate committees. What follows is an attempt to bring together the conclusions suggested by this material as to who was responsible for this prodigious output—and why.

THIRTEEN BILLS: NOTES ON THE COMPARATIVE STUDY OF POLICY FORMATION

Recent years have left little doubt either that there is a renewal of interest among political scientists in public policy and its formation or that students

TABLE 7.   Distributions of Legislative Responsibility on

Bill	Function Formulation	Instigation-Publicizing	Information-Gathering
Fair Packaging	Hart, then Commerce Committee staff, consulting with Commerce Department officials	Hart, Commerce Committee staff; later Magnuson, then President	Committee and agency staffs
Cigarette Labeling	Neuberger, FTC, cigarette industry in response	Neuberger, PHS, FTC	Public Health Service
Traffic Safety	Nader, Commerce Department officials, Commerce Committee and staff	Nader, Nelson, Ribicoff, then President	Nader "translated" executive and private studies
Oceanography	NASCO, various House members, Commerce Committee staff	Scientists, congressional hearings	NASCO, later LRS
Medicare	Executive officials, AFL-CIO; alternatives from Javits, Aging Committee, lobbies	Executive officials & Congressional allies, AFL-CIO, NCSC, Democratic Presidents	Social Security Administration; Senate Aging Committee staff
Sugar	Industry, Departments of State and Agriculture, House Committee	Industry, Presidential message	Executive departments, lobbies
Unemployment Insurance	AFL-CIO and Congressional allies; then Labor Department, House Committee	Organized labor, Presidential message	Labor Department
Foreign Investors Tax	Treasury Department	Presidential task force and message	Treasury Department, JCIRT staff
Campaign Finance (rider to Foreign Investors Tax Act)	Long and JCIRT staff, little reliance on others' proposals	Long drew on interest created by President's bill	Private scholars, Congressional committees, later Treasury
Elementary and Secondary Education	USOE, consulting with NEA & USCC, drawing on task force, Morse, earlier admin. ideas	President, interest groups	USOE
Medical Complexes	Presidential task force, HEW officials	Lasker group, Presidential message	Task force, HEW
Cold War GI	Yarborough revised WW II-Korean statute	Yarborough, Senate hearings	Yarborough and staff, VA
Fair Labor Standards	AFL-CIO and Labor Dept., House Subcommittee	Organized labor, Presidential message	Labor Dept., Council of Economic Advisers
Poverty Amendments	Executive request; Committees worked independently, consulting with OEO	Presidential request, independent OEO & congressional efforts	OEO and Labor Department, private scholars, local sources

Thirteen Major Bills, 89th Congress

Interest-Aggregation	Mobilization	Modification
Congressional committees; House accommodations more extensive	Magnuson in Senate; White House in House	Congressional committees; more serious deletions in House
Congressional committees	Industry and its congressional spokesmen. Magnuson pushed his compromise.	Senate Committee combined House (industry) and Magnuson bills
Congressional committees; Senate staff in brokerage role	Committee Chairmen, assisted by continued publicizing and presidential commitment	Congressional committees
Senate Committee activated groups; House Committee concentrated on agencies	Magnuson in Senate; Subcommittee Chairman Lennon in House	Chairmen in control; Magnuson developed combination bill
HEW and Congressional committees	White House, committee and party leadership, lobbies	Congressional committees; House revisions more extensive
Executive departments, House Committee	Lobbies, Long with administration help in Senate; Cooley dominant in House	House Committee rewrote foreign quotas; Senate Committee work largely restorative
Labor Department and Congressional committees	Mills in House; administration, party, and Committee leadership in Senate	Congressional committees; Senate work partly restorative
Task force, Congressional committees	Committee leadership, with executive backing	House Committee rewrote bill; Senate used it as vehicle for non-germane tax riders
Senate Rules, House Administration Committees (re President's bill)	Long, with executive backing	Marginal changes by Finance Committee
USOE for NEA and U.S. Catholic Conference, Congress for others	White House, committee and party leadership, lobbies	Congressional committees
Task force, HEW, Congressional committees	Hill in Senate; White House pushed Committee leadership in House	Congressional committees; serious cuts in House Committee
Congressional committees; House Committee for large veterans' groups	Yarborough, finally House Comm. Chm. Teague, with administration acquiescence	House Committee
Labor Department and Congressional committees	Committee leadership, with administration help	Congressional committees and parent chambers
Congressional committees	Committee leadership, with administration help in House, sometimes at cross purposes in Senate	Congressional committees, sometimes in league with OEO; Senate Chamber, with White House blessing

of policy-making are moving toward a level of analysis that transcends the individual case history. Diagnostic and prescriptive essays as to the "state of the art" of policy study and its future course abound,[2] while case material is increasingly being developed, as in the present study, in a comparative framework with an eye to generalization and synthesis.[3] There remains, however, often within single volumes of essays, a curious disjuncture between calls for theory and proposals of elaborate analytical frameworks on the one hand, and studies of specific cases on the other. The present section represents an attempt partially to close this gap. In the first place, the six-fold functional breakdown of the lawmaking process will be used to sort out and summarize our findings regarding executive and congressional roles, and some further reflections will be offered on the utility and limitations of such schemes as analytical devices. Secondly, certain factors will be pointed up that commonly have a bearing on the speed and ease with which these functions are performed and proposals are developed. Finally, however, it will be suggested that attentiveness to concrete cases can also offer some clues as to why the phenomenon of "policy-making" remains so singularly resistant to generalization and theory-building; this will necessitate a renewed consideration of the peculiarly creative and purposive character of "policy entrepreneurship" and of the modes of explanation that are appropriate to it.

Six Functions Revisited: The Division of Labor. The six-fold categorization of the facets of legislative responsibility presented in Chapter 1 served reasonably well to isolate the actors and the moves crucial to the development and passage of the thirteen bills under consideration. "Legislative initiative" can thus be broken down into its component parts and a more refined account developed of how lawmaking roles and capacities are distributed within and between the executive and legislative branches. Table 7 suggests, however, that such generalizations are rather difficult to come by, particularly if the unit of analysis remains the entire executive or legislative establishment. Legislative initiatives are diverse and scattered phenomena; while various policymakers hardly find themselves possessed of equal incentives and resources, the system does display considerable "slack." Differences between individuals, committees, and agencies sometimes display fixed patterns attributable to "external" determinants. But the freedom of individuals and decision-making units to determine their own legislative roles is often considerable. This means, in particular, that many of the assertions commonly made concerning the necessary "decline" of Congress' policy-making preeminence must be adjudged premature or overdrawn. More important for our immediate purposes is the implication that fixed and determinate "causal" factors may be of only limited utility in explaining the diverse and seemingly inconsistent patterns of institutional behavior that in fact appear.

It is nonetheless true that two of the legislative "stages," information-gathering and modification, are frequently dominated by the executive and Congress respectively—thus confirming that in most policy areas the bureaus have a firm anchorage and definite advantages in the legislative process and that Congress has developed a patterned response of "delay and amendment" to legislative initiatives, whatever their source. The executive monopoly of information-gathering is most complete in areas where extensive governmental programs are underway and large-scale efforts at data collection and analysis are necessary. The case studies demonstrated that there still was room for the Senate Aging Committee to recast and highlight information on health insurance and for the Yarborough Subcommittee and the DeBakey Commission to do the same on GI benefits and health care. In areas less thoroughly "covered," the efforts of private citizens and congressional staffs to gather and interpret information on their own terms were more significant yet—recall the oceanography, traffic safety, poverty, and campaign finance episodes. Yet even here potential legislative instigators were often constrained by the availability and quality of executive resources and, more subtly, by the way bureaus had approached their information-gathering tasks and the questions they had deemed it appropriate to ask.

The congressional impulse to modify—or to "perfect" legislation, as the phrase goes—is most obvious in cases where the executive branch has dominated the earlier stages. Generally this involves accommodating interests left out of the executive calculus (FLSA, sugar, UC, medicare, ESEA); it also frequently involves "strengthening" or "weakening" a bill, clarifying or shifting its purposes, or making technical adjustments—sometimes with revisions so extensive as to constitute a virtual reformulation (recall traffic safety and the foreign investors tax measure). Similarly, there is little reluctance to modify measures sent over from the "other body," as House action on the cold war and consumer bills and Finance Committee operations in general demonstrated; such action is in fact often encouraged by a jealousy of one's own chamber's prerogatives and by negative perceptions of those making decisions in the "other body" —e.g. as uninformed, fiscally irresponsible, hostile to or controlled by certain interests.[4] But the two chambers differ markedly in their willingness to entertain floor amendments to bills reported by their *own* committees. The presumption against such action is strong in the House, particularly when the committee in question is a high-prestige one such as Ways and Means, while in the Senate attempts at floor amendments are much more common and accepted. Still, only 5 of the 13 bills examined were amended extensively on the Senate floor, and in only one instance (poverty) could the amendments not be termed marginal. Modification remains predominantly the function of congressional committees.

It is a partial measure of the continuing autonomy of Congress that executive participation in the modification process, regardless of where the bill in question originates, remains rather limited. It is also a measure, of course, of the extent to which the executive is involved in formulation and mobilization, thus rendering its posture at the modification stage of many bills largely defensive; amendments are at best "accepted," rarely "supported." But even on congressionally formulated bills, executive officials are rarely able to dominate the process of refinement—although anticipation of what the executive will accept sometimes exerts a restraining influence on those processing the legislation. The administration's attempts to reduce the education and poverty authorizations of 1966 demonstrated that the executive could seek modifications when the stakes were deemed sufficient, but more typical were the numerous instances where congressional modifications or even reformulations of executive-drafted bills—traffic safety, medicare, foreign investors tax, medical complexes, fair labor standards—provoked little executive opposition. Some of these changes doubtless represented genuine improvements from the administration's point of view, while others accommodated interests which the executive found it helpful for Congress to handle. But there were, in addition, norms and constraints which rendered it imprudent and difficult for executive officials to become deeply involved in the processes of legislative refinement except on matters of extraordinary concern.

The remaining four legislative functions can be assigned much less exclusively to one branch or another, though some generalizations are possible as to how and when responsibility is assumed. Publicizing and other modes of instigation were found scattered through both branches and the private sector as well. The resources of the President and executive officials are in many respects distinctly superior: better and more readily available information, superior media coverage, and a set of congressional and public expectations that anticipate presidential leadership and place great stock in presidential expressions of priorities. But Congress, and particularly the Senate, has some advantages of its own. One of these is its pluralistic structure: if this means that Congress can rarely highlight any one problem or proposal as successfully as can the President, it also means that a single senator or committee can often publicize an issue on which the administration, constrained to speak with a single voice, must conserve its energy for the sake of problems higher on its priority list. A related advantage derives from congressional permeability. Senators and their aides on most committees often have an easier time getting their ideas "floated" than do their counterparts in the more hierarchical executive branch—recall the suppressed desires of the consumer office on packaging, PHS on tobacco, ESSA on oceanography, certain VA officials on the cold war bill, and, on numerous occasions, NIH and OEO. Such executive "tightness" and inertia not only give legislators and their staffs an incentive to assume the instigator-publicizer role; they also encourage would-be instigators in the private sector and in the bureaus themselves to seek congressional alliances.

Formulation, like instigation and publicizing, is a widely shared function which actors in both branches often have (or can develop) considerable freedom to assume. The executive has obvious advantages in highly complex policy areas that involve or anticipate massive bureaucratic operations (recall the difficulties and dependencies of Senate liberals in the fifties in formulating medicare, UC, and education programs). Indeed, there are few policy areas where congressional formulators can proceed without agency consultation. In many areas, however, executive formulators fail to bring congressional participants into their deliberations, or at least to anticipate their concerns, only at their own peril. And congressional formulators have some advantages of their own; in the early legislative stages (and sometimes in the later), legislative partisans, more than their executive counterparts, often enjoy a freedom to float "trial balloons," to develop admittedly "one-sided," provisional proposals which nonetheless serve to get an issue on the agenda and to set the framework within which future discussion and adjustment will take place.

Interest-aggregation is an important component of the legislative process in both branches, but the cases suggest that it generally takes place in different ways and under different conditions in the two arenas. The executive frequently accommodates large national groups with a stake in large federal programs, sometimes balancing their interests (ESEA, sugar) and sometimes championing one "peak association" over its opposition (recall the Johnson Administration's relation to organized labor on UC and medicare). The evidence suggests that the congressional champions of these groups welcomed executive attempts at interest-aggregation and in fact often attempted to deflect or avoid the incessant demands of groups like labor and the veterans' associations. But there was also conclusive evidence that Congress in most areas finds it politically necessary, and often profitable, to undertake interest-aggregation on its own terms. On bills formulated in the executive branch this may mean tampering with a particular balance or level of accommodation that has been reached (e.g. House committee action on FLSA and sugar in 1964), giving a hearing to opposition groups, or accommodating the particular interests of smaller or local groups desiring marginal exemptions or increases in benefits. Congressional formulations likewise often reveal a response to—or an "entrepreneurial" attempt to stimulate and gain support from—a group ignored or slighted by other policy-makers. Legislators and committees differ greatly among themselves, of course, in their principles of selectivity, and Commerce Committee behavior demonstrated the ways in which ideology and political intent could decisively alter the degree to which the natural "strengths" of distributive and narrowly-based groups were translated into policy output. But Lowi is correct in finding within the legislative branch a general responsiveness to distributive demands—a responsiveness facilitated by the legislature's domination of the modification process and reinforced by notions that legislation should be "balanced" and "fair," that broad (particularly executive) formulations responsive to "major" groups often do not do justice to particular situations, and that legislators should generally honor one another's judgments as to what constitutes equity with respect to groups under their special care.

The fallacy of the zero-sum assumption with respect to the relative legislative involvement of the two branches becomes most obvious when we turn to mobilization. The case studies showed a supposedly strong-arm President and high-powered White House staff in fact to be highly dependent on the congressional leadership—and on committee chairmen in particular. The majority leadership (as on medicare) and even the minority leadership (recall Dirksen's attempts to trim the 1966 poverty and education authorizations to presidential specifications) were sometimes crucial, but the knowledge and leverage the chairmen enjoyed, in committee and then as floor managers and arbiters of attempts at modification, made their cooperation virtually indispensable. Nor was the administration as efficient and effective as might have been supposed; recall Yarborough's frustrations with the FLSA fight and the aborted dealings with Mills on UC. But congressional activists frequently found their own leverage limited, particularly with respect to the "other body"; the administration could therefore be essential to their own mobilization efforts, sometimes with respect to their own committee or chamber (as on Long's "grab bag") but more often with respect to the opposite house (as on both the "grab bag" and fair packaging).

An overview of the cases examined thus points up the variety of legislative tasks, the potential of participants in various institutional settings to undertake them, and the frequent interdependence of the actors. It is appropriate at this point to recall Theodore Lowi's hypotheses as to the types of issues Congress and the President, respectively, will be best able to resolve.[5] Our findings meet Lowi's expectations in some respects, in other ways suggest refinements, and, in general, warn against premature portrayals of determinate institutional roles and capacities. Our description of congressional interest-aggregation and of the legislature's domination of the modification process squares nicely with Lowi's picture of "the distributive game that Congress plays at every opportunity." The executive's frequent accommodation of "peak associations" and its mobilization of public and congressional support on measures such as medicare and unemployment insurance likewise meet his expectations. Lowi helps us understand the deadlocks that arose in Congress over redistributive questions during the fifties and the subsequent "removal of decision-making from Congress" on certain welfare-state issues. But the subdivision of the legislative process developed above makes possible increased precision regarding the legislature's abilities and disabilities and the shifts in responsibility that have actually taken place. In fact, the Senate and certain of its committees served, not only during the Eisenhower years but also during the administrations of Kennedy and Johnson, as an alternative (or supplementary) access-point for "peak associations" and as a center for the *formulation* and *publicizing* of major new "redistributive" proposals. Congressional initiators often had difficulty following through, undoubtedly for many of the reasons Lowi suggests, but a functional breakdown of the legislative process clarifies the ways in which their efforts complemented (and stimulated) administration efforts.

Lowi's tendency to oversimplify characteristic patterns of political interaction and to underemphasize the "slack" enjoyed by potential policy makers is most evident in his treatment of "regulatory" policy, the type whose boundaries are least clear. One need only examine the initiatives taken by the Senate Commerce Committee in the area of consumer affairs —clearly within the "regulatory" realm—to recognize the inadequacy of Lowi's claim that this is the "pluralistic" arena *par excellence,* in which the typical congressional action is an equilibrating of the interests of contending groups. In fact, one might argue that to conceptualize this arena in terms of a pluralistic "balance" is inadequate both normatively and descriptively; "consumer" interests are *more* inclusive than those with which they must contend, while they are often *less* amply financed and organized. Their accommodation, when it occurs, generally assumes the form not of an equilibration of contending groups but rather of an appeal over the heads of these groups to a politically potent, but rarely vocal or mobilized, public. During the 89th Congress this mode of political leadership in the consumer area was conspicuously missing in the executive branch; it was the Chairman, several members, and eventually a majority of the Senate Commerce Committee who were *more* willing than their counterparts either in House committees or in executive bureaus to base their positions on the presumed interests of the "whole public" and to cut short the process of group accommodation. Senators like Magnuson and Hart were acting as policy entrepreneurs, stimulating more than they were responding to fledgling consumer groups and creating a certain distance between themselves and the dominant groups in the field. It is important, then, not to overgeneralize as to what kind of balances must be struck and who will have the capacity to strike them in a given policy area. At the same time, it must be acknowledged that the interest-aggregating and modifying activities undertaken by the House Commerce Committee on various consumer measures *did* tend to meet Lowi's expectations, displaying Congress in its "classic" accommodating role. And as Lowi had shown elsewhere,[6] the intrusion of pluralism into the administrative process could and frequently did superimpose additional compromises upon those Congress had already struck.

The Nixon Years: A Postscript. One naturally asks to what extent the distributions of legislative responsibility described above were peculiar to the period most closely examined, during which liberal Democrats controlled both branches. The 89th Congress was chosen in part because it presumably put the thesis that "the President is now the motor in the system [while] Congress applies the brakes" in its strongest light; surely it revealed that generalization to be a dubious one, at least when applied to domestic policy. The inadequacy of the thesis becomes even more evident when one examines the Eisenhower and Nixon years, though of perhaps greater interest are the more subtle shifts to be found in the performance of the six discrete legislative functions. The way medicare, aid-to-education, and unemployment insurance were handled during the fifties strongly suggests that an analysis of major domestic bills processed during Eisenhower's presidency would find formulation and instigation-publicizing more often dominated by Congress than in 1965–66. Congressional advocates often controlled mobilization as well, even on bills the administration nominally supported; if this increased their "independence," it also increased their isolation and vulnerability. Interest-aggregation was undertaken by the executive with systematically different concrete results during the fifties, though this was probably due more to the *kind* of large national groups that were accommodated (e.g. the AMA rather than the AFL-CIO) rather than to any marked difference between the two administrations in responsiveness to local or distributive demands. Party differences and the challenges of Democratic activists such as Anderson, Clark, Humphrey, Morse, and Hill furthermore guaranteed that the Eisenhower administration would be much more likely than those of Kennedy and Johnson to undertake counter-mobilizations and to seek involvement in the modification process.

A significant fact about the first three years of Richard Nixon's presidency is that there has been nothing like a complete recurrence of the Eisenhower pattern. Senate liberals, for one thing, have been deprived of medicare, aid-to-education, and many of the other issues around which they rallied during the fifties. Nor have they shown a great deal of imagination in pushing beyond the traditional liberal agenda, in publicizing new issues or mobilizing new constituencies. This failure is attributable partly to the low-key styles and presidential campaign preoccupations of potential legislative leaders like George McGovern and Edmund Muskie and partly to the increasing tendency of the media to ignore questions of domestic policy and activist senators like Yarborough, Mondale, and Hart who are not presidential hopefuls. Edward Kennedy, who successfully sought the job of Democratic Whip in 1969 with apparent policy-making ambitions, suffered an eclipse in influence and motivation after his suspicious accident at Chappaquidick in mid-1969. He subsequently began to reassert himself in national health insurance and other policy areas, but in 1971 lost the post of Whip to conservative Robert Byrd, a man preoccupied with the internal politics and amenities of the Senate and a leader not at all interested in assembling and coordinating an innovative majority "program."[7]

Neither, of course, has the executive branch returned to the fifties. Despite Nixon's campaign rhetoric, "no Great Society program of any magnitude, either substantive or symbolic, perished" after he took office. This was the result in part of inertia and the "general slackness of purpose" with which Nixon proceeded in domestic affairs, in part of the ability of advisors favoring program continuity intermittently to gain the President's ear.[8] But less transitory factors were at work as well. The Johnson presidency left a legacy of public expectations, intra-governmental roles and relationships, ongoing programs with supportive constituencies, and bureaucratic vested interests that represented serious obstacles and disincentives to any thoroughgoing effort to dismantle. In terms of the balance of policy-making responsibility between the branches, the historical importance of the early Johnson years may lie here—not so much in the precedents that were set regarding the use of the presidential office as in the number of policy areas that were transferred from the realm of legislative craftsmanship, in which Congress inevitably shares, to that of the renewal and marginal alteration of ongoing programs, which the executive generally dominates. Once a problem is established as an area of federal responsibility, the administering agency generally develops a strong interest in the program's continuation, becomes a prime access-point for interested groups, and institutes mechanisms of intelligence and evaluation which issue in proposals for program expansions and alterations. The continuity the Nixon administration has maintained and the program renewals and adjustments it has requested can largely be understood in these terms.

The differences between the Nixon and Johnson administrations' proposed new departures in domestic policy likewise have not been as great as one might have predicted. The first two Nixon years saw the floating of some tax reform proposals (but only after Ways and Means had already seized the initiative) and a much-touted plan for federalizing the welfare system which never seemed to have the administration's full support and which, drawing fire from liberals and conservatives alike, at one point could muster only one vote on the Finance Committee. After a disappointing mid-term election, however, and considerable "self-criticism and self-analysis" within the administration's inner councils, Nixon presented the 92nd Congress with a much more ambitious legislative program than he had the 91st.[9] The five main legislative goals—welfare reform, revenue sharing, government reorganization, a compromise health insurance plan relying on private carriers, and several environmental "initiatives"—tended to be formalistic and to avoid redistributive questions, though Nixon, claiming to have opened "the way to a New American Revolution," managed to match his predecessors' exaggerated rhetoric and projection of inflated expectations.[10] A more significant new departure came in mid-1971 as, in face of continuing inflation, the President invoked authority voted by Congress in 1970 (and opposed by him at the time) to freeze wages, prices, and rents for three months and to provide for their continued control in a post-freeze "Phase Two." He also proposed a major series of tax cuts which both houses approved before the end of the year. Here, too, the legacy of the sixties was evident: the concept of a "weak presidency" with which Eisenhower had flirted was found wanting in light of public, congressional, and bureaucratic expectations, in face of the country's economic difficulties, and in consideration of where the mechanisms for relatively direct and effective action lay.

The fact remains, however, that Nixon's domestic legislative agenda is far less ambitious than those characteristic of the Johnson administration, at least during the 89th Congress, and that certain differences in priorities are discernible as well. How has this affected congressional roles and operations? Generalizations are hazardous to make, but some brief impressionistic observations may be ventured as to the effect of the shift in administrations on the policy-making activities of our three committees. It is the Commerce Committee whose legislative endeavors have probably been least affected. Executive caution and apathy in consumer, environmental, and oceanographic affairs were complained of and capitalized upon during the Johnson years; the committee's counter-moves became more partisan in character but little changed in substance during the Nixon administration. "Our relations with the administration are cool but not really problematic," an aide reflected in 1971. "In fact, in a way it helps to have an administration you can openly attack." On Finance, a more complex set of trends is in evidence. On the one hand, staff increases and Long's "loosening" of committee operations have resulted in some scattering of legislative initiatives. Finance has also become much more independent and sophisticated in its perusal of administration and House recommendations, sometimes undertaking reformulations of the sort formerly attempted only by Ways and Means. On the other hand, the Committee's membership has shifted slightly in the conservative direction, and the absence of Democratic White House pressures (along with Long's defeat for the Whip's post) have made for a certain retrenchment on the part of the Chairman and members like Talmadge and Fulbright. This has been evident not only in the treatment of administration proposals like welfare reform but also, for example, in the 1970 decision to accede to the House's 1966 position on the "Democratic" issue of UC standards and financing. The community of interest and patterns of consultation that were developing between the Committee and executive agencies have by no means broken down, but Finance has become considerably more critical, and sometimes obstructive, in its processing of administration requests. Meanwhile, its proclivity for interest-aggregation and modification shows no signs of abatement.

It is on LPW, however, that the differences between the Johnson and Nixon patterns is most evident—just as it is in the Labor-HEW area that Nixon's altered priorities have been made clearest. Four of Nixon's 12 vetoes during his first three years in office were of LPW authorizations (hospital construction, manpower training and public service employment, medical training for general practitioners, OEO extensions with day-care and other "child development" amendments), two were of appropriations in the same area (Labor-HEW-OEO for fiscal 1970, Office of Education for fiscal 1971), and two were in related domestic areas (HUD-Independent Agencies appropriations for fiscal 1970, public works-area redevelopment authorization).[11] It is in the LPW area that it has become clearest that it *does* make a difference to have a Republican President and that the Eisenhower patterns of executive-congressional initiative and response have come closest to being reestablished. Though LPW does not have jurisdiction over health insurance, Kennedy's formulating and publicizing ventures in the area have constrained the administration to develop a compromise proposal. The Health and virtually every other LPW Subcommittee have systematically stepped up the administration's authorization figures, reformulated requests and shifted program emphases, and decried the low level of funding of programs which, while they were being formally "continued," were being allowed to shrink to the dimensions of pilot projects. New legislation has also been generated—in alcoholic and narcotic rehabilitation, for example, cancer research, child care and development, job safety—often, as in the latter two cases, with administration opposition, and rarely with full-fledged cooperation and support. The role of the activist has not been an easy one to assume: the agenda is not nearly as "obvious" as it was in the fifties, the executive is far more ubiquitous, and the public mood seems uncertain and pessimistic. Under such circumstances, demands on congressional leaders are high: to develop and effectively to publicize a pointed critique of funding priorities and program administration, and to shape a new progressive agenda, focusing on new issues, constituencies, and legislative formulations. If Mr. Nixon's congressional opposition cannot, in general, be given superlative marks on this score, the LPW "vanguard," as previously, is surely ahead of the pack.

The Conditions of Success. The processing of any major piece of legislation will surely entail substantial efforts falling under each of the "functional" rubrics—formulation, publicizing, and the rest. But the performance of these discrete tasks differs widely from bill to bill. Conspicuous examples of failure and near-failure have been described (e.g. of publicizing on fair packaging and of mobilization on UC), while a spectacular publicizing effort on traffic safety was found to simplify the tasks (and reduce the vulnerability) of those assuming responsibility for the legislation at a later point. The concern in this section, however, is not primarily with the variations in these activities that are attributable to the strength or weakness of those who undertake them. The complexity and difficulty of the legislative functions in a given case, in fact, are conditions over which those who assume them have little control. A legislator comes to a project with his work, to a large extent, "cut out for him." Whatever may be his skills at this or that legislative activity, he is largely at the mercy of the antecedent conditions that set the terms of success. Information-gathering, publicizing, and mobilization will not always be equally formidable. Any *explanation,* therefore, of why a bill appears on the scene and flourishes must concentrate not merely on who chooses to do these jobs but also on the conditions which make their undertakings feasible.

When the tasks requisite to a bill's passage appear to be within the capacity of its advocates, it is often described as "ripe" for enactment. The attempt here will be to draw on the case material for hints as to the components of "ripeness," the conditions which give practicability to the kind of legislative undertakings that have been our central concern. A surprising number of analysts have laid heavy emphasis simply on the passage of time, often pointing to the "germination" process momentous proposals have undergone in Congress or elsewhere prior to their final enactment.[12] This mode of analysis has its convincing aspects, especially with regard to bills like medicare. The fact that the bill had been around in one form or another for over fifty years helped reduce the tasks of formulation, publicizing, information-gathering, and even mobilization to marginal dimensions in 1965. But *fifty years*—and for aid to education, nearly twice as long! The Traffic Safety Act, on the other hand, was on the statute books a bare six months after its initial introduction and less than two years after Nader and Ribicoff began to agitate the issue. Surely the shortness or length of the "germination" period is of limited value as an explanation for why a bill emerges when and at the pace it does.

This is not to say that the "maturity" of a piece of legislation is of no importance. A closer look at the thirteen bills considered suggests that the background factors which determined the character and the magnitude of their advocates' tasks were in fact of two rather distinct types:

(1) In the first place, there is the question of the status of the various legislative tasks at the time the bill was introduced or re-introduced in the 89th Congress. How much remained to be done in documenting the severity of a given problem, devising a workable legislative remedy, securing the support or acquiescence of affected groups, committees, and agencies, and prompting a public sense of need and readiness? The advocates of medicare, for example, had their way smoothed by the compromises struck in previous Congresses with various insurance and hospital interests. The

tasks of information-gatherers on cigarette labeling, traffic safety, campaign finance, and unemployment insurance were reduced greatly by the availability of previous private and governmental studies. The presence of an on-going program, as the sugar and fair labor standards amendments showed, could reduce the legislative efforts necessary at virtually every stage, as could the presence of legislative models and precedents (though the fate of Labor and Public Welfare's 1966 poverty amendments, and the difficulties encountered by oceanography and cold war GI bills in the early sixties, demonstrated that considerable obstacles could remain). The proximity of a related legislative effort could reduce the tasks of formulators, information-gatherers, publicizers, and mobilizers; the manner in which the Tire Safety Act broke ground for vehicle regulation is a case in point.

Had these bills not been helped along toward "maturity" in these ways, their passage might have been far more difficult. It is possible and helpful to specify the factors—not simply the existence of an extensive legislative history, but also the kinds of programs and precedents that exist in an area, the state of available information, and so forth—which have a bearing on the speed and character of the germination process. But two observations come to mind. In the first place, the case studies show that the past can burden as well as aid the advocates of a new policy departure. Advocates of new poverty efforts in 1966, for example, must have often felt that it would have been easier to introduce new bills than to attempt to expand and diversify an existing program that was becoming increasingly controversial. Education aid provides another example: some one hundred years of "germination," if they made for growing public acceptance and the collection of extensive information, also produced sufficient group polarization and conflict to make fresh starts in formulation and interest-aggregation necessary in 1964–65. In the second place, even where the impact of the "maturation" variables was generally positive, they seldom provided anything approaching a definitive explanation for why a bill's proponents succeeded when they did. Hence the need to focus on a second set of background factors which determined the difficulty and the magnitude of "what was to be done"—factors which affected what might be termed a bill's "viability."

(2) The massiveness of the 89th Congress' legislative output has often been commented upon; what, in addition, is particularly striking from our point of view is that major bills were passed which varied from one year to one hundred in their period of maturation. Moreover, an examination of the backgrounds of the landmark statutes which several of these bills amended (e.g. the Social Security Act, Sugar Act, Fair Labor Standards Act) reveals that a similar period of congressional productivity—likewise involving proposals that had "germinated" for varying periods in different arenas—occurred in the years immediately following the Depression. The kinds of

congressional majorities and presidential leadership that make possible such spates of productivity may be accounted for in terms of historical occurrences such as the Depression or the Goldwater candidacy, though there may well be an independent cyclical movement in a substantial portion of the electorate between the advocacy of domestic policy "activism" and retrenchment.[13] In any case, it is possible to specify various determinants of a bill's viability, some of which may be peculiar to the issue involved but others of which may affect various issues similarly at a given point in time. Here the focus is not on the state of the various legislative tasks themselves but on the contextual factors that have a bearing on the likelihood of successful performance.

One such factor is the existence of a crisis or a sense of need in a relevant sector. Nothing in 1965–66 could approach the impact of the Depression in this respect, though the polls did show a heightened public feeling that action was needed in the areas of education and health care. Mounting traffic deaths, rising campaign costs, bulging sugar warehouses, the dollar drain, the return of more and more disadvantaged Vietnam veterans—all served to condition Congress and the public favorably and to stimulate governmental action. The impact of such situations was of course dependent in large part on those who interpreted and publicized them, but various publics and politicians found them independently compelling: the deepening of the war, for example, did for Senator Yarborough's cold war bill what seven years of strenuous effort on his part had not been able to accomplish. Additional determinants of viability include the complexion of group support and opposition and the inclinations of relevant governmental units. The willingness of formerly deadlocked education groups in 1965 to accept a compromise proposal, for example, altered the dimensions of the tasks that confronted aid proponents enormously, while shifts in the dispositions of House Committees and executive bureaus handling the cold war and fair packaging bills did the same for their Senate champions. And finally there is the matter of partisan alignment. It is difficult to escape the conclusion that the single most important factor in explaining the successes of legislative activists in both branches during the 89th Congress—of initiators working at various "stages," in disparate areas, and on proposals of varying "maturity"—was the size of the liberal Democratic majority they could rely upon.[14]

Certain caveats are again in order: it should be evident, for example, that in certain cases, not the presence of a crisis or widespread public concern but instead their absence could increase a bill's viability, reducing the need for interest-aggregation and mobilization and allowing a proposal to "slip through"—as dozens of "distributive" bills demonstrate every session. Similarly, one could trace out in much greater detail the ways in which various patterns of group opposition and support, apathy and involvement, might shape the tasks confronting a bill's proponents.

But the *kind* of factors one would examine and the way their relevance might be explored should be evident. The prospects of one who undertakes any of the six legislative tasks—and hence his incentives to undertake them in the first place—will be dependent in large part on their present state (i.e. the bill's "maturity") and, more importantly, on the contextual factors which determine the likelihood of responsiveness and support (i.e. the bill's "viability"). It follows that any comparative analysis of why some proposals make it, others do not, and others are so greatly refracted in the process, will pay considerable attention to such matters.

The assumption thus far has been that central to the "explanation" of the emergence of a given policy must generally be the initiatives undertaken at various stages by individuals and groups interested in its enactment. The determinants of a measure's "maturity" and "viability" have been conceptualized as aids or obstacles to such action. But another set of enabling and constraining conditions is often of equal importance, those determining the opportunities and resources available to the would-be initiator. Those pertaining to his institutional setting and to the congressional committee in particular have been assessed above and will be discussed further below. The role assumed by an activist senator may depend, for example, on both formal and informal aspects of his committee's "organization"—on whether he enjoys the prerequisites and independence that come with a subcommittee chairmanship, and on the norms, incentives, and role-patterns which structure the expectations and responses of his fellow-members. Similar factors shape the roles and determine the influence of actors within the executive branch—their own and their bureaus' positions and resources within larger organizational units, the accessibility of information and communication channels, the availability of congressional and group alliances, and so forth. Nor are they irrelevant to understanding the roles assumed by group spokesmen and other actors in the private sector. The case of a "loner" like Ralph Nader, however, points up what is in fact true for all policy entrepreneurs regardless of their institutional location: alongside those obstacles or advantages provided by the work setting, and sometimes surpassing them in importance, are those stemming from the individual's own skills and resources. It is true that questions regarding the source of such resources or their utility will often take us back to the institution—a senator's "skills," for example, will often be dependent on the way the committee's staff is dispersed, while the advantages that he might gain through the possession of technical knowledge or certain personal traits will be dependent on the norms and traditions of the group—but those resources are often self-generated and individually and independently held. Thus both Commerce Chairman Magnuson's "social leadership" skills and Senator Ribicoff's ability to command a nationwide audience are relevant to an understanding of how and why the auto safety bill emerged as it did (and why, however they may have felt about it at the time, the two senators in this case needed each other. Here, too, the utility of breaking down legislative initiative into its component parts is evident, for the resources, skills, or style that facilitate the performance of one function may be decidedly less appropriate to another.[15]

Thus one has the beginnings of a paradigm whereby the conditions might be ordered and evaluated which contribute to the success or failure or deflection of one or another entrepreneurial effort and which help form the expectations and incentives that encourage such initiatives in the first place. Such a move succeeds when its initiators possess appropriate resources and skills and are favored with a "congenial" institutional setting; the success of the various initiatives which typically go into a legislative proposal is in turn dependent on the "maturity" and "viability" of the measure itself, on those factors which determine "what is to be done" at each legislative stage and how difficult it will be of accomplishment. Thus can one "explain" the passage of the Traffic Safety Act in terms of the skills of its champions, the deference enjoyed by the Senate Commerce Committee, the quick "maturation" provided by Nader's book and the tire safety episode, and the "viability" provided by favorable public opinion and a comfortable majority of liberal Democrats in Congress, with some idea as to the relative impact of these and similar factors and their interrelationships. It follows that one can develop generalizations of the form, "When such-and-such conditions prevail, then such-and-such sorts of policy initiatives will be likely to succeed." Obviously, the blanks of such statements will generally be filled in an enormously complicated fashion, but an attempt to answer the questions the paradigm raises promises to yield a fuller understanding of the fates of individual measures, the factors influencing legislative productivity in various arenas and policy areas, and the determinants of the "cycles" of activism and retrenchment which seem to cut across institutions and areas. It will not, however, produce a *comprehensive* explanation of why any measure developed as it did, let alone a comprehensive "theory" of policy development. Why this is so must now be considered.

The Irreducibility of Legislative Initiative. Putting forth and promoting a new policy departure is above all political "action"—intentional behavior directed by its agent to one or a series of ends. Some analysts have recently argued that this element of "subjective intentionality" is what distinguishes human behavior proper, and that understanding men's actions in these terms either excludes or makes irrelevant the "external" and deterministic modes of explanation utilized in the natural sciences.[16] It is adequate, however, to note that the explanations one adduces by reference to a subject's goals and intentions do not permit of *reduction* to the regularities and generalities of "external" cause-effect relationships. Charles Taylor explicates the point:

> *The distinction between action and non-action hangs not just on the presence or absence of the corresponding intention or purpose, but on this intention or purpose having or not having a role in bringing about the behaviour. . . . Thus to call something an action, while not to subsume the behaviour under any law, does involve ruling out certain rival accounts, those incompatible with the implied claim that the intention brought about the behaviour. Now a rival account must be one according to which changing the intention, other things being equal, would have no effect on the behaviour; that is, a rival account of some behaviour event B would be an account according to which B would occur on this antecedent condition, whether or not the agent intended to do B. Thus, if a given piece of behaviour is rightly classified as an action, then we cannot account for it by some causal antecedent, where the law linking antecedent (E) to behaviour (B) is not itself conditional on some law or rule governing the intention or purpose. For if the law linking E to B were not dependent on some law linking E and the intention or purpose, I, to do B, then E—B would hold whether or not E—I held. But then B would occur on E whether the corresponding intention was present or not. And then, even when it is present, it cannot be said to bring about the behaviour, so long as this is done by E. Thus to account for B in terms of E would be to offer a rival account, to disqualify B as an action.*[17]

Other analysts stress that legitimate accounts of human nature and behavior cannot violate the common-sense assumption and experience of purposive behavior that is both "free" and causally efficient,[18] that social science must do justice to the phenomenologist's (and ordinary agent's) awareness of the dialectical relationship between the "intentional consciousness" and the determinative regularities of the social world,[19] and that history, were it to remove the uniqueness and particularity of its subjects' purposes and motivations by subsuming them under general "covering laws," would be reduced to trivial or inappropriate explanations.[20] But all are agreed that the explanation of behavior in terms of "the prospective movement of the intentional self"[21] cannot be reduced to the form of lawlike relationships between psychological states or social forces.

This is not to say that behavior, or even intentions, are impervious to the impact of "external" contingencies. It is to say, however, that an actor's "inner" desires and intentions and the behavior that flows from them cannot be accounted for or predicted solely in terms of such factors.[22] This is not merely a matter of lacking adequate data; there is a fundamental conceptual distinction between "action" and "movements," though most behavioral sequences may be viewed legitimately (if partially) from either perspective. "Action" is defined by its conscious, willing character, as an implementation of the subject's desires and purposes, while "movement," whether conscious or not, is a response to forces and necessities impinging from without this intentional realm. These views of behavior, distinct in our ordinary usage and understanding, must remain distinct in the analysis of a given performance, but, as R. S. Peters suggests, they may complement one another. Purposive action cannot be reduced to a definitive series of "movements" or accounted for in terms of the antecedents of such movements, but the *necessary* (as opposed to sufficient) conditions of successful performance can be stipuated.[23] These may refer, one assumes, to conditions in the environment as well as in the actor himself; they will shape, but not "determine," the character and efficacy of his purposive efforts.

An attempt has already been made to specify certain conditions of this sort as they impinge upon the policy entrepreneur.[24] But it cannot be supposed that Senator Yarborough's (finally successful) efforts on behalf of the cold war veteran have been "explained" when it is simply noted that he was unusually persistent and had strong staff backing, that he was blessed with a permissive chairman who let him use the subcommittee machinery to his own ends, that ground had been broken by previous GI bills and by telling VA and HEW figures on the status of cold war veterans, or that the stepping up of the Vietnam War altered the views of the major veterans' organizations. Indeed, some of the factors that encouraged him and influenced his strategy and a great many of those that determined the final impact of his efforts can thus be understood. But to "explain" the initiatives of Yarborough and others who contributed to the bill's passage one must examine their motivations and purposes themselves, the intentions each had as a "self-steering" being setting out to formulate or publicize or modify a cold war statute. Each individual will demonstrate his own set of purposes, and in no case will their behavioral result be reducible to "movement," i.e. to the predictable outcome of the forces and stimuli impinging on the subject from "without." If this limits the extent to which a given policy output can be explained in terms of such "external" variables as those previously discussed, it clearly also limits the possibilities of generalization and prediction regarding the "causes" and conditions of policy emergence.[25] Variables that are not convincing or conclusive as an explanation for a single sequence of policy initiatives will hardly be more so when applied across a universe of cases. Human purposiveness and creativity cannot be reduced to determinate regularities; here the distinctions of everyday speech serve better than does the celebrated search of various social scientists for "inclusive" theories and "general" explanation.

To assert that purposive behavior is in an important sense "free" and undetermined, however, is not to portray it as arbitrary and capricious. We have already seen that the perception of various sorts of contingencies and necessities may shape the actor's priorities and strategies. It is also true, of course, that other "external" factors, particularly those to which the psychologist would point, might influence both the subject's purposes and his behavior in ways of which he is imperfectly aware—as is sometimes testified to in everyday speech by distinctions between *his* reason and *the* reason for a subject's actions.[26] It might, for example, be concluded that Yarborough's desire to generate socially beneficial legislation stems in part from psychological factors giving him an extraordinary need to be loved and recognized. But surely there is no obvious reason why such a desire, whatever its causal antecedents or its intensity, should lead one into politics or, once one is a senator, to undertake specific actions in favor of a disadvantaged group. Yarborough's response to his "needs" is predictable only in terms of his own particular perceptions and intentions. This does not, however, leave the analyst at sea as much as might be expected. The realm of purpose and action, as complex as its relationship to the realm of externals may be, is itself often highly structured, even routinized. Thus does Peter Winch, one of the analysts most concerned to point up the gulf between the external and internal views of behavior, place equal stress on the rule-governed and conventional character of "meaningful" action.[27] A man's intentional actions will, it is true, operate within bounds created by his own "needs" and various environmental constraints, but even more crucial to their understanding will often be the social and ideational context in which they occur. "Man is a rule-following animal," notes R. S. Peters. "His actions are not simply directed towards ends; they also conform to social standards and conventions, and unlike a calculating machine he acts because of his knowledge of rules and objectives. . . .[In fact] norms enter into and often entirely define the end."[28]

If an understanding of a society's or an institution's norms and conventions is essential to understanding the character and the proximate goals of its members' purposive behavior, so may one, as Charles Taylor suggests, also obtain a partial explanation of the shape purposive behavior assumes by objectively examining the "state of the system," i.e. the actions that are demonstrably linked to the attainment of a given end. "The particular form which [action] takes in any situation can be accounted for in part . . . by what the situation requires given the goal in question."[29] In a similar vein, William Dray acknowledges that "reasons for acting" as well as "conditions for predicting" have "a kind of generality or universality";[30] the implication is that by examining an agent's situation and assuming a certain consistency of values and purposes on his part, the analyst can discern "good reasons" for, and hence provisionally predict, certain courses of action.

A legislator who devises or publicizes a piece of legislation is no doubt pursuing many purposes simultaneously, but in this as in most of his actions it can safely be assumed that attracting the attention and support of a sizable number of voters normally enjoys a rather high priority among the ends in view. It is obvious, however, that just as this aim results in vastly different voting patterns for congressmen with differing constituencies, so does it issue in widely varying patterns of legislative initiative. And those who choose the activist role in the social-welfare area often show a striking similarity in their electoral situation; it seems reasonable to assume that an innovative style is perceived as consonant with "what the situation requires, given the goal in question," while for senators dissimilarly situated there might be few positive incentives and even certain disincentives to playing the activist role. The activist senator normally has a large and diverse constituency, with sizable urban centers and/or minority group concentrations. His electoral situation is usually a highly competitive one. The increasing role of the media in determining his constituents' political perceptions (and sometimes his own ambition for higher office) makes the cultivation of an "image" an important concern. That such a similarity in "situation" applied to the senators who had sought a seat on LPW and who, once obtaining it, were concerned to develop legislative programs was obvious in looking down the 1965–66 roster: Clark, Pell, Nelson, Javits, Williams (N.J.), Yarborough, and both Kennedys. Even more striking was the case of Commerce Committee Chairman Magnuson— whose "situation" in Washington state was found to be in transition. Before his near-defeat of 1962 Magnuson had concentrated his legislative energies in large part on the servicing of home-state industries, particularly fishing, shipping and aviation. But the growth of the state and the increasing role of television made necessary a new kind of appeal: hence the emergence of Magnuson as champion of the consumer and of the Commerce Committee as a center for the development of various consumer protection bills.

The elements which comprise the "situations" of activist senators will be discussed in more detail below, as will the norms and conventions which structure their intentions and suggest "approved" means of implementation. For now, the important point is that any realistic explanation of a specific assumption of legislative responsibility, or of patterns of initiative obtaining on a committee, must *combine* the specification of limiting or enabling conditions which have a determinate impact on the options and capacities of political actors with an analysis of those actors' intentions and goals in their own right. The two modes of explanation will frequently converge; the external conditions determining what has been termed the "maturity" and "viability" of a given legislative project, for example, will generally influence the strategies and even the basic intentions of legislators interested in the matter. But to suppose that the legislative behavior of a person or group can be accounted for solely in terms of the "causal" impact of external contingencies is to ignore the "slack" the system displays and the wide variations in behavior that actually occur and, more fundamentally, to misconceive the modes of explanation that are appropriate to political leadership in general and to the assumption of legislative responsibility in particular.

Our comparative analysis of thirteen bills has thus permitted the decomposition of policy entrepreneurship into the forms it typically assumes in legislative settings, certain generalizations as to the propensities and capacities of congressional and executive actors to assume legislative responsibility of one form or another, and the isolation of some of the factors that commonly facilitate or constrain such action and define the terms of success. It is now appropriate to focus more selectively on the three committees that handled the bills—to relate their specific legislative undertakings to more general patterns of action and to examine the aspects of the committee setting most directly related to the legislative roles assumed. It is important to note, however, another function—perhaps more valuable, though less anticipated—that the case studies have performed: they have clearly exposed the limitations of "causal" explanations of policy outcomes and "general" theories of policy development. The assumption of legislative responsibility can be fully understood only in its particularity, as a species of political action attributable to the subject's own goals and intentions. This has obvious implications for our understanding of the legislative initiatives of Senate committees and of the factors relevant to their explanation. In short, particular attention must be paid to the declared and demonstrated purposes of legislators, to the elements of their situation which shape or deflect those purposes, and to the norms and conventions which determine the legitimacy of their goals and prescribe means for their implementation.

THREE COMMITTEES: LEGISLATIVE ACTIVISM AND ITS ENVIRONMENT

Our case studies and interviews make possible certain provisional generalizations regarding the inclinations of several House and Senate committees to undertake one type of legislative activity or another. Such generalizations, summarized in Table 8, are risky, but certain patterns do seem to cut across various bills and areas of jurisdiction. Any inclination to "type" committees as activistic or otherwise, however, is dispelled once legislative responsibility is broken down into its constituent functions and it is recognized that committees (like individuals) active and efficacious at one stage are not necessarily so at another. The temptation is considerably stronger, in fact, to posit two *modes* of activism, in one or neither (but rarely both) of which committees tend to specialize: the one involving the formulation and publicizing of legislation, and the second, the "maturing"

TABLE 8.   Observed legislative "strengths" and/or frequently assumed roles, selected congressional committees, 89th Congress.

FUNCTION:	Formulation	Instigation-Publicizing	Information-gathering	Interest-aggregation	Mobilization	Modification
COMMITTEE:						
HOUSE						
Commerce				X		X
Agriculture	X			X	X	X
Veterans' Affairs	X			X	X	X
Ways and Means—JCIRT	X[31]		X	X	X	X
Education and Labor	X	X		X		X
SENATE						
Government Operations		X	X			
Commerce	X			X	X	X
Finance				X		X
LPW (by subcommittee)						
Education	X			X	X	X
Labor				X		X
Health	X			X	X	X
EMP	X	X	X			X
Veterans' Affairs	X	X	X	X		X
Migratory Labor	X	X	X	X		

and compromising of proposals with an eye to eventual mobilization. Several LPW subcommittees approximate the first pattern, while Commerce resembles the second. But such oversimplifications of the behavior of either group perhaps obscure as much as they clarify. Certain aspects of Commerce's situation (the "slack" left by executive and House units, staff orientations) made it appear even more suitable for "early" initiatives than LPW, while the record of LPW and trends within the Senate also suggested that the "vanguard" role was becoming less limited than it once had been.

If neat typologies are thus difficult to come by, the consistent patterns of activity demonstrated by the committees over a universe of cases nonetheless bear out our initial supposition that discrete legislative initiatives might profitably be viewed in their institutional settings. For it is in committee that a legislator has his attention focused, his degree of independence and the extent of his resources largely determined, and his ambitions and style tempered by group scrutiny and control. His legislative leverage comes to depend, not only on his own ability to fit into the group's ongoing life, but also on the prestige and power of the group itself in the broader policy-making environment. Because the individual's legislative initiatives are to such a large degree shaped and their efficacy determined by his committee situation, and because most successful assumptions of responsibility are in the end translated into committee action, the committee tends to mold individual initiatives into characteristic patterns of group action. Hence the possibility of describing "strengths" and roles peculiar to various committees as a whole and, more importantly, of focusing on the characteristics of the groups and their environments to help explain the individual and collective assumptions of responsibility that are found. The remainder of this chapter will summarize the results of our examination of the Senate Commerce, Finance, and LPW Committees in light of the six complementary "images" developed in Chapter 1 and the set of questions each suggested. The result will be a fuller notion of the sorts of forces and conditions that stimulate, shape, and constrain legislative activism in the congressional setting.

"Situations," Norms, and Legislative Responsibility. The necessity of combining an analysis of subjective goals and intentions with that of "external" structuring, incentive-producing, and constraining factors becomes clear when an attempt is made to relate the policy output of a congressional committee to "personality" and organizational variables. One recognizes, in the first place, the wisdom implicit in the commonplace assertion[32] that an understanding of committee behavior, or at least of policy initiatives, must begin with an understanding of the *people* involved—or, more precisely, of their desires and purposes as legislators entrusted with the oversight of sizable areas of public policy. These intentions, and the individual, committee, and chamber action to which they may lead, will not be predictable or understandable in terms of extraneous factors; much less can it be assumed that certain external conditions will regularly or uniformly stimulate a given sequence of purposive actions. But the intentions themselves, while calling for "internal" understanding and explanation, nonetheless lend themselves to generalized description and analysis. We have done this in terms of the "orientations" of legislators, as reflected in the testimony of the men themselves and in the kind of legislative activity they undertook. Those orientations may now be explored further, in relation to the "situations" they reflect and the normative settings that channel their expression.

It has already been noted that the "situations" of social-welfare activists adopting a public style—a type of senator in the majority on LPW, less conspicuous on Commerce, and rarer yet on Finance—contained certain common elements which bore a clear relation to the legislative propensities and capacities of the committees as a whole. The interrelationships of these elements are represented in diagrammatic form in Figure 6. The diagram shows the way "situational" analyses of the sort suggested by Taylor may be combined with the specification of limiting conditions which

FIGURE 6. **Diagrammatic representation of the interdependence of conditions and orientations relevant to the legislative roles and capacities of "activist" senators in the social-welfare area.**[33]

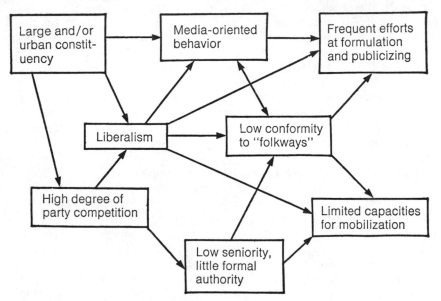

have a more classically deterministic impact on an actor's options and capacities. Factors that operate at one level to put a premium on innovative behavior (e.g. a competitive urban constituency) may operate at another level (e.g. by making for reduced seniority or formal authority) to reduce the actor's resources or magnify the dimensions of the tasks he faces. And here is yet another reason for breaking down legislative responsibility into its several facets: neither the incentives nor the constraints which a given "situation" offers will always apply equally or even similarly to each component of the policy-maker's task. Figure 6 suggests how the "situations" of LPW liberals foster in their Committee a propensity to formulate and publicize. At the same time, they may help explain some of the Committee's lingering difficulties with mobilization, though we have found the debilitating effects of low seniority and ostensible "folkways" violations to be definitely on the wane.

Another mode of "situational" analysis might concentrate on the circumstances that confront a senator inclined to legislative activism as he surveys and becomes involved in his various potential fields of action. He must take account of the character and involvement of groups and agencies with related or opposing intentions, of the informational and political resources needed to cope with a problem, and so forth. Some of these factors will be dealt with below as the committee's relationship to its policy-making environment is more fully discussed. For now it should simply be noted that, like the electoral-institutional setting represented in Figure 6, the environmental situation that gives rise to legislative action will rarely be a placid one. Policy initiatives feed on stress, and sometimes represent an attempt to create or increase it. Legislative responsibility is undertaken because change is regarded as desirable or profitable. But change must also appear *feasible* and nondestructive—which is to say that some kinds of situational stresses might repel or paralyze rather than attract the potential policy-maker. Recall the quite different situations confronting senators responsible for communications and labor policy. Communications policy normally involved neither intense public concern nor large-scale conflict between enduring factions; labor policy involved both. Yet in both instances senators—even those active in other areas and possessing considerable resources—rarely independently sought anything more than marginal policy changes. In the one instance the stresses seemed insufficient to stimulate involvement, while in the other they were so formidable as to appear threatening. More appealing to senators balancing political and programmatic goals and realistically assessing their personal and institutional capacities was apparently a more "balanced" situation— high (or potentially high) public or group interest in an area but without intense conflict; acutely felt but not intractable problems; precedents for federal involvement but relatively noncomprehensive and uncoordinated programs currently in operation. Certain analogies with the notion of "optimum stress"[34] developed in organization theory are apparent: legislative initiative is stimulated and channeled by certain tensions with the environment—a problem to be solved, a group to be cultivated, a political position to be strengthened, a federal program to be improved. Yet the tensions cannot be too great: legislative activity which offers few rewards, promises to stir up intense opposition, or threatens to touch off an escalation of expectations and demands will seldom be undertaken. Such situations, of course, are often peculiar to a circumscribed policy area and hence are often more pertinent to differences within than to those between congressional committees. But the incentives found directing senators and committees to areas like health, social security, and consumer affairs may readily be understood in these terms.

If intentional behavior can thus be related in its genesis and its efficacy to the "situations" of actors or groups of actors, so may Peters' suggestion that it proceeds in accordance with certain conventions and norms be pursued. It has already been seen how, during the sixties, the traditional Senate folkways of circumspection and deference became less pervasive —in part because of the altered "situations" of a number of senators, some of them, like Magnuson, in high positions of authority. As a result, the assumption of an active formulating and publicizing role by senior and junior

members alike has become a more familiar and accepted mode of behavior. But it is important to note that these shifts in norm and behavior
were not uniform from area to area or committee to committee *within* the
Senate. Junior members of the Finance, and to some extent even the
Commerce, Committees, to say nothing of oligarchies like Agriculture and
Armed Services, still had to cope with the fact that "pushy" behavior, even
if it served some of their purposes, might well have negative repercussions
for others. LPW members, on the other hand, had good reason to see
legislative initiatives as a *positive* means of entering into committee life
and living up to their colleagues' expectations. For as long as any of its
members could remember, LPW had had a disproportionate number of
members whose "situations" militated against strict obedience to the folkways, and the alternative norms that grew up in this context took on a life
of their own, providing members with "conventional" means of implementing their desires for visibility, constituent approval, programmatic
changes, or whatever. It will be recalled that virtually all Finance Committee members, liberals as well as conservatives, had offered *fewer* bills in
Finance than in their second committee, while virtually all LPW members,
conservatives as well as liberals, had introduced *more* bills and amendments in LPW than in their second committee. This indicates, one has
good reason to suspect, not simply that their intentions and incentives
differed from area to area but that certain purposes which remained constant were channeled into different modes of *expression* by virtue of the
norms and conventions prevailing in various committee settings.

It must be understood, however, that the assumption of legislative responsibility of one sort or another by a legislator or committee is not
subject to comprehensive explanation or prediction in terms of such contextual factors. They provide an additional, and important, dimension of
understanding. But the fact is that persons react to similar "situations,"
incentives, and norms in particular ways, in terms of private or less widely
shared perceptions and purposes. This, on the one hand, forces one to
acknowledge that in order to understand the legislative propensities of a
given committee he must appreciate the goals and ambitions of its members in their particularity (of which Long's obsession with campaign
financing was perhaps the most eccentric example). Perhaps more importantly, it leads one to perceive the "slack" that is present in most policy-
making situations. Legislators, unfortunately, are often only slightly less
likely than social scientists seeking "inclusive" explanations to concentrate on the regularities of the congressional "process" and on the constraints faced by one who would innovate within the system. It is important,
indeed, not to minimize the effect of such constraints, though it is equally
important not to accept all of them as "given." And another aspect of the
situation is deserving of emphasis: the extent to which innovative and
imaginative political actors can use their positions and resources as legis-

lators to implement their own ideals, to dramatize and explore social problems and needs, and to develop statutes and programs which speak to these problems and needs. The policy initiatives undertaken by LPW in health and manpower and by Commerce in consumer affairs are merely suggestive, one suspects, of the kinds of leadership and amelioration that might be forthcoming if legislators took their status and their potential as political actors seriously.

Personal and Organizational Resources. The present study, while vindicating certain common-sense assumptions as to the integrity and particularity of political action, has at the same time brought into question certain other facets of Capitol Hill's conventional wisdom about personality and politics—i.e. the assumption that personal traits and skills are the prime determinants of legislative effectiveness. There were, to be sure, cases where a reputation for ineptitude, uncooperativeness, or indifference to the sensibilities of his colleagues created a rather widespread negative inclination toward the legislative proposals of one senator or another. Such factors may even have affected the overall performance of two of our committees, for LPW had a collective reputation for "pushiness," while personal animosities and conflicts were particularly acute on Finance and breakdowns of mutual respect and support unusually frequent. In the case of LPW, the Chairman's skills and style served to militate against integrative and adaptive difficulties that might otherwise have developed, while Long did little to ease, and often made a substantial contribution to, the difficulties of the Finance Committee in this respect. But the independent effect of such personal aptitudes and attributes on individual or group performance is notoriously difficult to isolate, and it is instructive to note that senators rarely gave a negative personal assessment of a colleague with whom they did not have a prior policy disagreement. Nor could any instances be cited where such factors had reversed even a minor policy outcome from what might have been predicted on political and ideological grounds alone.

The evidence thus permits little more than the assertion that a diversity of skills and personal approaches can be serviceable for the would-be legislative activist; other factors will often be more determinative of the reception he gets. A sharp strategic sense, a thorough knowledge of the policy area in question, an accommodating and low-key style—all can be formidable resources. But the Senate is increasingly tolerant of those for whom the folkways are no longer crowning virtues, and there is much that an efficient staff and a coterie of supportive colleagues can do to blunt the impact of various personal deficiencies.

If it is difficult to be precise and definitive concerning the "personal" resources necessary to legislative success, the evidence is much more conclusive with respect to the organizational resources which facilitate a successful assumption of legislative responsibility. Committee "pluraliza-tion"—the number of "organizationally defined subunits"—was initially distinguished from the more general dispersal of prerogatives and re-sources within the group, with the realization, as in the case of the Senate Foreign Relations Committee, that the one was not always a perfect index of the other.[35] On LPW, Commerce, and Finance, however, which displayed high, moderate, and low degrees of pluralization respectively, subcommit-tee operations provided a generally reliable index of the extent of the Chairman's permissiveness and of the degree to which authority and re-sources were dispensed within the committee.

The patterns were not always consistent—recall Magnuson's and Hill's unusual jealousy of their prerogatives in their traditional MMF and health bailiwicks—nor were they always stable, as Magnuson's and Yarborough's later willingness to delegate responsibility in both areas demonstrated. But an examination of hearing and reporting procedures, patterns of bill spon-sorship and staff supervision, and the testimony of the members themselves tended to produce a consistent picture from committee to committee. And an examination of the assumption of legislative responsibility, particularly at the early stages, left little doubt that committee decentralization was often a vital stimulus to action and a prerequisite to success. If Finance Committee members were generally deterred from legislative activism by the norms of the group, the absence of subcommittees was a more tangible obstacle. Even the more independent and ambitious members lacked a forum to develop their views and gain publicity; they were thus limited to what little authority they could exercise and what few resources they could muster in the full committee setting. At the opposite extreme, LPW mem-bers found themselves in charge or very near the top of several subgroups that not only had the authority and the staff resources, but were also under something of a mandate in terms of the expectations of their colleagues, to take a creative and ameliorative approach to the policy areas under their care.

All this, of course, is very far from saying that decentralization stimulates or facilitates committee activism in every instance. Yarborough's Labor Subcommittee and Pastore's Communications Subcommittee again furnish prime examples; in neither area was the "situation" such as to stimulate large-scale legislative undertakings, though in both cases the subcom-mittee possessed the necessary leverage to undertake such projects. But re-flecting on the LPW experience poses a more intriguing possibility yet. Bar-ber and Wilson suggest, it will be recalled,[36] that pluralization at one level of an organization may actually result in fewer proposals, less radical in character, being adopted in the long run because of the veto, clearance, and bargaining procedures that will necessarily be instituted. That this expectation did not materialize on LPW could be attributed to the consen-sus on policy and the norms of activism and mutual assistance that prevailed there. But what of the fate of LPW measures on the floor? Clark's defeat on poverty in 1966—and Hill's unusual move the same year to salvage Morse's education authorization by trimming it—suggest that, once again, factors contributing to the successful assumption of one aspect of the legislative task might be counterproductive at another. Are there instances, as was suggested in Chapter 1, where even autocratic behavior by a chairman might enhance his committee's legislative potentiality? The study of the Commerce Committee furnishes strong affirmative evidence: both Hart and Neuberger felt that Magnuson, by "taking over" their projects, had in fact ensured the fruition of their early formulating and publicizing efforts. Furthermore, several members implied that, organizationally, the Commerce Committee had reached an "optimal" sort of balance—decentralized enough to permit the individual development and publicizing of projects, but controlled enough to trim the projects down to manageable dimensions and to put the full prestige of the Committee behind them.

Such conclusions, however, must be approached with great caution. Bartlett's situation demonstrated that the tightness of Magnuson's control over oceanography and MMF matters, while it may have increased the Commerce Committee's solidarity and leverage at certain points, also cut off a number of proposals at their source, dampening incentives and opportunities for legislative entrepreneurship. And there are questions as to whether the "balance" Magnuson maintained, optimal or not, would have been feasible in other committee settings. One might hypothesize that Hill could have improved LPW's batting average by inaugurating more extensive review proceedings at the full committee level and assuming more responsibility for the development of the proposals germinated in the far reaches of his committee, but one must also acknowledge that Hill was not in a position to play a role comparable to that of Magnuson, even had he possessed the inclination. Hill's credits with his members were considerable, but they hardly would have sustained interventions and preemptions of the sort Magnuson undertook. Hill's members had aspirations to a greater degree of policy-making independence than did most Commerce Committee members, and they had a greater interest in the publicity to be gained even from inefficacious legislative ventures. Many were perfectly satisfied with the laissez-faire mode of committee operations; certainly almost none would have expected to benefit from the "balanced" sort of control Magnuson managed to exercise.

While one can thus roughly specify the impact organizational variables have on a committee's legislative propensities and capacities, the selection of any degree of centralization as "optimal" will involve certain trade-offs. Nor will it necessarily be universally applicable to a set of committees whose members have widely varying orientations and preferred modes of operation. But it can hardly be questioned that tight centralization tends to dampen committee activism and that at least a modest dispersal of prerogatives and resources is necessary if legislative initiatives are to be undertaken and sustained down through the ranks. While committee decentralization may reach a point of diminishing returns in terms of the committee's potential to mobilize, without it few senators indeed would have the capacity to formulate, gather information, and publicize. And while junior members and subcommittee chairmen are perhaps the most obvious beneficiaries of decentralization, they are by no means the only ones. The chairmen, too, may gain legislative potential. Magnuson surely benefited in the end from the independent initiatives he permitted and encouraged in the lower ranks of his committee. The result was the development of a greater range of proposals than he ever could individually have conceived—proposals for which he and the Committee as a whole could then assume responsibility and claim credit. Similarly, one could argue that if Long were truly interested in developing the Finance Committee as an independent legislative force, one of his principal efforts should be to disperse resources and opportunities among those who share, or who with a changed "situation" and altered norms might come to share, an activist view of their policy-making role.

It should be noted, first, that general trends toward increasing decentralization have been visible in both the Finance and Commerce Committees since the 89th Congress, but, secondly, that there remain certain goals and supposed "necessities"—the preservation of their own legislative prerogatives and interests, the control of aberrant members or obstructive subcommittee chairmen (recall Lausche), the maintenance of the committee's reputation for prudence and the maximization of its capacity for mobilization—which constrain both Long and Magnuson to fall short of Hill's example. Surely, however, the maximization of the chairman's legislative potential or even of the committee's legislative "effectiveness" has its shortcomings as a prime goal of committee organization. It is difficult, in fact, to escape the conclusion that the vitality of Congress as a policy-making institution would be greatly enhanced by a loosening of oligarchical prerogatives so as to free creative energies both among junior committee members and at the top levels of party leadership. Congressional leadership is ill-served, on the whole, by the organizational dominance of men with the will and the power to squelch instigative efforts at the lower levels of the congressional hierarchy and to obstruct efforts at mobilization from the top. The continuing devolution of committee authority and resources to subcommittees and individual senators thus has much to recommend it; needed as a complement and a corrective, however, is a heightened concern for the comprehensiveness and quality of the congressional "program"—and increased mobilization efforts on its behalf—on the part of the majority leadership.[37]

All this, of course, must not be understood as an indictment of the "committee system" itself. That organization by committee often encourages and facilitates effective assumptions of legislative responsibility—by effecting a division of labor, focusing interest and developing expertise, dispersing authority and resources, and providing channels for collaboration with groups and agencies—seems obvious. It is equally certain that committees on occasion stifle potentially creative members, defy executives, and thwart popular and congressional majorities, but the present study has undermined some generalizations commonly made. Far from being "graveyards" for progressive legislation, committees can provide a setting and a stimulus for its development; norms of reciprocity and deference between committees can facilitate the development and passage as well as the bottling up and blocking of bills. More useful than praise or blame of the "committee system" in general is a recognition of how various modes of committee organization and operation may influence Congress' policy-making capacities. In that context, the case for pluralization and a wide dispersal of authority and resources within committees seems unusually strong.

When we turn from the question of centralization to that more elusive set of organizational variables associated with the committee's systemic functioning, the contextual conditions of legislative activism become much less evident. Negatively, it can at least be asserted that recent claims as to the supreme importance of integration to a committee's legislative effectiveness have been considerably overdrawn.[38] The relation of integration to legislative performance on the committees examined was in fact complex and often seemed contradictory. If the Finance Committee's integrative failings reduced its leverage in the 89th Congress, the tight cohesion of earlier years, around norms increasingly deviant from those of the parent chamber, had begun to have the same effect. And the internal divisions which in some ways reduced the committee's effectiveness were related to changes which promised to *increase* the Committee's legislative involvement!

Under certain circumstances, however, committee unity and stability can serve as an important source of encouragement and strength for potential activists. Commerce and LPW, though somewhat dissimilar in their modes of integration, both demonstrated such a positive relationship. On LPW, integration was related to the homogeneity of the members' policy outlooks, the compatibility of their respective legislative goals, and the Chairman's permissiveness and social leadership; the Committee thus provided a supportive setting for relatively bold policy moves. The group's cohesion was also generally a source of strength on the floor, though certain floor defeats raised the possibility that the very homogeneity of the Committee sometimes led to an imprudent neglect of *adaptive* concerns. The integration of Commerce, on the other hand, was fostered by norms of prudence and moderation, though the anticipation of promising "entrepreneurial" ventures and the Chairman's relative permissiveness in such matters also made their contribution. Commerce thus furnished a pleasant and productive place to work, while its adaptive strengths promised a high likelihood of ultimate success to anyone who used its machinery to develop a proposal. But here committee cohesion also represented a formidable obstacle to any attempt to challenge the Chairman's "low risk" mode of operation or the Committee's usual practices of sail-trimming and compromise.

A committee's systemic traits have a particularly important bearing on the legislative situation of its minority members, though of course the character of its minority contingent has a reciprocal impact on a committee's integrative capacities. Finance Committee Republicans, all of them conservative and several of them rigid and doctrinaire, did their part to keep the atmosphere of their Committee charged, but while the Committee's integrative failings gave them the occasional satisfaction of seeing the majority embarrassed on the floor, these failings also tended to relegate the minority to isolated and often unsuccessful attempts at modification or obstruction. "Minimal partisanship," on the other hand, was a working assumption on the Commerce Committee. Cotton and his colleagues contributed to the maintenance of that norm and in turn saw their legislative leverage greatly increased; their own proposals frequently received favorable treatment and they were able to participate in the development of legislation at the formative as well as the modification stages. To some extent the situation of Javits and Prouty on LPW was similar: they increased their own input through cooperation and "constructive opposition" and in turn helped the committee present a bipartisan front. But their conservative junior colleagues could take little comfort in the Committee's liberal, activist consensus, for it often relegated them to lonely and futile gestures of opposition.

The Committee in its Policy-Making Environment. Any assessment of the impact of groups and agencies on the policy-making incentives and opportunities of committee members must begin with a major caveat: the case studies have reinforced, and the analysis of legislative initiative as political action has given an added dimension to, the observations made in Chapter 1 concerning the independence and selectivity exercised by the legislator with respect to "external" entreaties. Among the groups interested in sugar policy, merchant marine subsidies, and veterans' pensions and compensation, patterns of legislative influence were found which approximated the classic "pressure group" model. But the characteristic relationship to sympathetic interest groups among legislative activists was "entrepreneurial"; the initiatives taken were best seen not as a response to group demands but as an anticipation or projection of group interests and a stimulation of their active concern. Such patterns characterized congressional dealings even with relatively narrowly-based groups concerned with special education programs, oceanography, and fishing, and they were even more conspicuous on broader "public-interest" questions— consumer affairs, health, poverty, veterans' readjustment. While the evidence thus confirms Mancur Olson's expectations as to the frequent inability of large, broadly-based groups to exert decisive pressures, it also suggests that legislators frequently find it possible and profitable to identify with and expand upon the aspirations of these groups.[39]

It is nonetheless not to be doubted that interest group operations constrain, stimulate, and shape committee behavior and that they differ considerably in the extent to which and the way in which they do so. Previous chapters have concentrated on the way the ideologies and identifications of committee members filter group demands and condition the committee's responsiveness to calls for marginal, often business-oriented, modifications of redistributive and regulatory measures.[40] Here the attempt will be rather to specify the impact of certain differences among groups themselves and among the policy areas in which they are operating on legislative initiative more broadly conceived. Again, Theodore Lowi's speculations serve as a convenient starting point. Lowi, it will be recalled, suggests that the nature of the subject matter being handled (i.e. whether its "impact on society" is distributive, regulatory, or redistributive) itself has a decisive impact on the patterns of initiative that characterize a given area. But he does not long sustain his discussion merely in terms of analytic distinctions between clusters of issues. To make use of his categories in explaining the propensity of Congress or the President to dominate policy-making in one area or another, Lowi must add to his basic typology further, though supposedly derivative, distinctions between the size and inclusiveness of the groups interested in each type of policy (e.g. "peak associations" for redistributive issues), the kinds of relationships that obtain among them ("mutual non-interference," "tangential relations," zero-sum conflict), and the nature of their constituencies ("classes" vs. discrete regions or economic groupings).[41] Though Lowi argues that his threefold categorization of policy-types helps one sort out and understand the characteristics of equally distinct "arenas of power," the fact is that his work raises the possibility that certain group characteristics might have an impact on the options and incentives of policy-makers independent of and distinct from the type of policy they are handling. And strangely enough, he at the same time ignores certain "subject matter" characteristics—e g the amount and complexity of information required by various types of proposals and the extent of the bureaucratic operations they presuppose or anticipate—which one would have expected his mode of analysis to suggest at an early point.

Our case material, in fact, shows the executive to have definite advantages in two kinds of policy "arenas," while closer analysis suggests that factors pertaining both to the nature of the subject matter and to the kinds of groups interested in it bear some responsibility. The first kind of arena, of which the medicare, UC, and FLSA episodes provided glimpses, is characterized by the presence of large, inclusive *"peak associations,"* seeking *mutually incompatible* policy goals in areas that are of considerable interest to *large numbers* of people. The second kind of situation, typified by the sugar and education cases, involved powerful *competing groups,* whose interests, if not in zero-sum conflict, nonetheless required authoritative *arbitration* and *adjustment.* In all of the instances cited, the information needs of those processing the proposals were considerable, as was the scale of the bureaucratic operations the proposals assumed or projected. And in all cases, congressional partisans who wished to assume legislative responsibility found themselves faced with critical disabilities. In some areas, indeed, the difficulties posed were so severe as to reduce the incentives for *initial* congressional involvement; recall the reluctance of LPW members to chair the Labor Subcommittee and the relief of Finance Committee members when differences within the sugar industry were resolved downtown.

Lowi is no doubt justified in the emphasis he places on the patterns of conflict that surround an issue in explaining such disincentives and difficulties. Congress is decentralized, regionally based, full of check-points, and governed by norms of reciprocity and compromise; a resolution in either the first sort of arena, which generally requires ignoring the opposition, or the second, which requires decisive and creative arbitration, is thus difficult to come by. More likely results are obstruction or deadlock. Lowi is misleading, however, when he attempts to account for these patterns of conflict in terms of the "redistributive" character of the issues the groups are handling. Lowi's paradigm cases are taken from the early New Deal, and his relating of patterns of conflict to opposing expectations of benefit and loss is most convincing in areas contested by labor and management. His notions also bear extension to areas like civil rights, if one is allowed to stretch the definition of "redistribution" to include apportionments of power and right that transcend the purely economic realm. But other areas of executive branch involvement, such as education and agriculture, are only with difficulty conceptualized as "redistributive," nor do they excite dualistic conflicts between opposing clusters of associations. Conflicts in these areas, which also may paralyze Congress and call for executive resolution, rather take place *within* a dominant cluster of interests that as a whole is often supportive of the program in question.

The patterns of conflict among the groups active in a given policy area will thus have some bearing on the capacity of congressional committees to undertake and sustain legislative initiatives. Obviously, the mere presence of conflict suggests that the groups involved perceive a threat or a promise in the "redistribution" of a given value between or among themselves, but this does not mean that the issue is redistributive with respect to the society as a whole. To amend Lowi's formulation in this manner, however, is to make necessary further qualifications. The executive branch was obviously not motivated or constrained to intervene in every group dispute over policy that found expression in Congress or elsewhere. Questions that stimulated executive involvement were ordinarily of considerable "scope" and "domain"[42] and they often arose within (or threatened) programs to which the administration already was committed. And if proposals, even those instigated elsewhere, presupposed or anticipated the information resources or bureaucratic machinery of the executive, this too created congressional disabilities and brought into play pressures and incentives for involvement on the part of the administration and its agencies —sometimes mainly in self-defense.

The case studies are too few in number to support definitive conclusions, but they do suggest that the variables listed above—the presence of large-scale and persisting group conflict in a major issue area, a need for complex and comprehensive information in order to deal with a problem or proposal, and a proposal's impingement upon or anticipation of bureaucratic structures and services—are each related to congressional difficulties in assuming legislative responsibilities, and hence to pressures for executive branch involvement. Lowi's observations regarding Congress' incapacities for "complex balancing on a very large scale" are thus generally borne out, though whether or not the issue is "redistributive" with respect to the society as a whole is hardly the only factor that bears on the kind of "balancing" that is required and the resources that are necessary to its achievement.[43] And what of those capacities which Lowi *does* attribute to Congress, i.e. "cumulation"? Lowi tends to treat policy-making in this mode as a patterned response to ubiquitous distributive demands. But here, too, congressional propensities and "strengths" may be only partially attributable to—and indeed coincide imperfectly with—the *type* of issues being considered.

Some years ago, Richard Neustadt concluded his account of the executive's growing involvement in legislative affairs with the perceptive observation that the institutionalization of the "President's program," while promising to step up the executive's policy-making input, at the same time necessarily *limits* the number of proposals that can be given "top priority" designation and effectively pushed by the administration. Massive, synoptic presentations tend to blur the impact of many particular items (recall the questions that arose as to whether the administration was *really* pushing fair packaging, UC, and FLSA), and the President's capacity to go "adventuring in controversial areas" is often impaired by virtue of the need to keep his priorities clear and not to jeopardize key elements of his program.[44] At the same time, the very role which the administration assumes in championing one or another "peak association," arbitrating differences between major groups, and defending or proposing large-scale bureaucratic operations, requires the ignoring or the slighting of ancillary groups which fit into the "big picture" only with some difficulty. Such groups often have a strong base in Congress by virtue of their regional character, while the fact that their wants can often be portrayed as "distributive" vis-à-vis the society as a whole further facilitates their accommodation through the processes of bargaining and "cumulation." But the advantages of Congress are not limited to such areas of marginal or distributive adjustment. The division of labor effected by the committee system and other incentives furnished by a legislator's "situation" may in fact make possible and profitable congressional initiatives demonstrating more single-mindedness and mobilizing more resources than all but the top few items on the President's agenda. It is true that congressional initiators will generally at some stage need executive assistance, particularly when extensive informational and organizational resources are called for or large-scale group conflict renders mobilization difficult. But the decentralization and permeability of Congress gives legislative ideas a visibility and viability there that they frequently would not have in the executive branch. Seen in this light, the congressional capacity to "cumulate" represents far more than a tendency to append a few distributive modifications onto major administration bills. If it suggests certain difficulties with "complex balancing," it also points up an enormous potential for focusing attention, gathering information, and developing ameliorative legislation in a number of diverse and scattered areas concurrently.

If such factors have much to do with the patterns of legislative responsibility (and neglect) that distinguish one issue area from another, the evidence suggests that they may have a cumulative impact on the options perceived and pursued by a committee over a range of policy areas. The Finance Committee, for example, was often confronted with redistributive proposals or others involving large-scale group conflict, its field was technically complex and "crowded" with bureaucratic operations, and executive priorities made certain Committee efforts appear superfluous. At the same time, the numerous and intense demands of groups desiring marginal exemptions and benefits were left to be "cumulated." All this surely encouraged certain patterns of legislative behavior which carried over into areas of Committee jurisdiction where the precise configurations of incentives and constraints varied considerably. Similarly, the fact that the Commerce Committee was dealing with relatively low-conflict questions, which had anything but the executive's undivided attention and were relatively undemanding in terms of bureaucratic resources, facilitated a general movement in Committee norms and practice toward a more independent and active role. And LPW, as usual, displayed greater variability: the executive's role was firm by virtue of its programmatic involvement in virtually every niche of the Committee's jurisdiction and its superior capacity to arbitrate conflict and accommodate dominant interests, particularly in the areas of labor and education. But the Committee was also found "cumulating" its own legislative program, championing the needs of groups (and agencies) disadvantaged by the aggregating of interests and ranking of priorities that took place in the executive branch.

Anything approximating a definitive analysis is complicated, however, by the fact that not only do Senate committees and their members frequently have their own reasons, apart from these environmental incentives and constraints, for acting as they do, but the behavior of groups, agencies, and House committees often displays a similar variability. Thus it proved necessary to examine patterns of group access and of House and agency initiative for the impact they, in their own right, had on Senate committee options.[45] First, group access: Mrs. Lasker's decision to take her heart disease-cancer-stroke proposal to the President was no accident, but it was a choice nonetheless, and it had an appreciable impact on the division of labor that eventually characterized the medical complexes effort. At other times Mrs. Lasker, like Ralph Nader and lobbyists for fishing, shipping, oceanographic research, special CAP projects, and veterans' readjustment, took advantage of the permeability and receptivity of the Senate and focused their efforts there; this in turn reinforced the legislative pre-eminence of the LPW and Commerce Committees. On the other hand, when labor, sugar, and education groups established cooperative ties with downtown agencies, they were undoubtedly attracted by the executive's superior resources for the arbitration of conflict, for information-gathering and program design, and for legislative mobilization—but they made their own contribution to the shift in legislative responsibility that came to characterize their areas of concern.

It was in the environment of the Commerce Committee that patterns of executive agency and House committee behavior most obviously encouraged and facilitated senatorial assumptions of responsibility. In a number of policy areas something approximating a situation of "optimum stress" seemed to obtain. There was, in the first place, a dearth of imaginative new proposals. This was in part a function of the President's "priority problem" discussed above, but with several decision-making units, such as FDA, the Commerce Department, and the House Commerce Committee, conservative ideological predispositions and interest-group influences played an independent dampening role. The disabilities of other agencies were variously associated with organizational isolation or weakness (PHS, FTC, BCF, the Consumer Office, ESSA) and the prevalence of bureaucratic and administrative orientations (FDA, Maritime Administration). Yet this vacuum was more promising than threatening to Senate Commerce members: many of the areas were ripe for profitable entrepreneurial development. While agency, group, and House opposition furnished some cause for alarm (and in some cases stimulated a desire to preempt), there was little danger that conflict would be bitter and sustained or that it would spread beyond a relatively narrowly circumscribed set of interests. More-over, within and among the executive agencies in the field were a number of promising opportunities for cooperation and alliance. Senate actors were able to avoid isolation and obtain needed resources through the working relationships they developed with like-minded individuals and offices within the executive establishment.

The situational "stresses" confronting Finance Committee members, involving as they did extensive and entrenched (and in some cases constitutionally prescribed) patterns of executive and House dominance, were far less conducive to independent and innovative legislative activity. Pressures and incentives for involvement were created, however, when Treasury, HEW, and Ways and Means chose to ignore the requests of various groups seeking tax and welfare "breaks," and several episodes during the 89th Congress suggested that new opportunities for legislative leverage through selective collaboration with the executive were developing. But it was on LPW that variations and shifts in environmental "stresses" were most apparent and intriguing. The agencies with which the Committee was dealing differed considerably in their legislative orientations, capacities, and independence: the Labor Department and USOE were equipped for large-scale legislative undertakings and were well integrated into the executive hierarchy, with all the strengths and limitations that entailed; NIH was ambitious and remarkably independent; OEO was ambitious and decreasingly independent; and the VA had legislative disabilities similar to those of the Maritime Administration. LPW, like Finance, was overshadowed by the House Veterans' Affairs Committee, but House Commerce offered little competition on health matters. In most areas, LPW shared jurisdiction with House Education and Labor, a committee equally active and liberal but one which sometimes excited LPW vigilance by its erratic mode of operations and its responsiveness to a range of interests, and which, moreover, was frequently forced to call on LPW for help by virtue of its adaptive failings vis-à-vis the House chamber.

These situations were by no means equally promising or productive. Hill's inclinations to enter the health field were reinforced by the executive's "priority problem" and by the lethargy of House Commerce, as well as by the prospects for fruitful cooperation with NIH, the Fogarty Subcommittee, and the Lasker organization. In the areas of labor and education, the presence of group conflict, bureaucratic complexity, and extensive administration efforts rendered LPW ventures alternatively perilous and superfluous. Ambitious senators, however, frequently found their leverage increased by the possibilities for cooperation, particularly with USOE, that their situation offered and, alternatively, were moved to independent but generally marginal efforts by administration or House negligence (or overindulgence) of certain problems or groups. Disagreements over the administration's funding priorities in education became more intense between 1965 and 1966;

the same period saw even greater shifts in the "stresses" pertaining to other areas of Committee jurisdiction. In veterans' affairs the effect of the shift of the House Committee and the major veterans' groups on the cold war question was notable for its impact not so much on Yarborough's remarkably independent and persistent legislative ambitions as on his prospects for success. On poverty, however, as on education, the situation became much *less* promising with the breakdowns of patterns of agreement and cooperation with the White House and, to some extent, the House Committee. That Morse, Clark, and others persisted as they did suggests that altered stresses may spur positive efforts as well as negative expectations and, more importantly, that legislative initiatives have a life and rationale of their own. But the patterns of opposition and possibilities for alliance present in a committee's field of action have a great deal to do with where, how, and with what success its members, individually and collectively, choose to do battle.

A Concluding Note: Information, Initiative, and the Potential of Congress. The last of the six "images" of the congressional committee developed in Chapter 1—that of the communications center—has led to an examination of committee staffs. Staff size, competence, and accessibility often demonstrably affect both the quality and the distribution of a committee's legislative endeavors; the increased sophistication of recent Finance Committee efforts in the areas of medicare and sugar policy and the difficulties of LPW conservatives after Javits came to control the minority staff represent striking cases in point. As anticipated, however, the additional factor of staff *orientation* emerges as particularly important when one searches for the roots of legislative initiative and creativity. What our examination of the staffs of three Senate committees has shown, in short, is that these aides, far from being "neutral and inferior instruments,"[46] are political actors in their own right. Their roles and their impact, as in the case of their mentors, are to be "explained" first of all in terms of their own goals and self-images.

Our investigations in fact revealed two relatively distinct staff "types"—the "policy entrepreneurs" found on Commerce and LPW and the "professionals" typical of Finance. They were by no means opposites in every respect. Both possessed considerable expertise, though both remained dependent on sources of information in the executive branch and the private sector. Both spent a great amount of time processing proposals that came from outside the committee and developing bills or amendments at the behest of various senators, and both felt some responsibility for remaining accessible to most committee members. But within these limits there were significant differences in the way tasks were interpreted and performed. For the "professional," expertise was the *summum bonum*, neutrality a basic norm, and the analysis of proposals coming from elsewhere his primary legislative task. He saw himself as an aid to the rationality of all committee members, though he saw the Chairman as having a particular need for expert guidance. The "policy entrepreneur," however, saw his job in a different light. He was committed to a continual "search" for policy gaps and opportunities. He was more willing to use his position to implement his own policy preferences and to let political considerations influence the role he assumed. He recognized the need to inform himself in the committee's policy areas and to hold his own preferences in abeyance in order to assist certain members, but in the end he valued creativity more than expertness and did not hesitate to establish a particular identification with the interests and ambitions of the chairman or (sometimes) other members.

While the "policy entrepreneur," then, was not a purely political aide or an old-style patronage appointee, he did differ from the "professional" in his activist notion of his job and in his partisanship. Partisanship, as the LPW case demonstrated, took various forms and had various effects among aides of this type. It was not a sufficient condition for the development of an activist role, as the operations of Hill's Health Subcommittee aide testified, and the activists themselves varied considerably in the depth and narrowness of their partisanship; Education Subcommittee aide Charles Lee, blessed with an abundance of activist senators, found it possible and profitable to work with and through a large sector of his membership. On the Commerce Committee the positive relationship was even more evident: partisan and personal ties obviously gave impetus and focus to staff efforts, while at the same time they made senators like Magnuson and Bartlett more willing to accept and respond to those efforts. That this partisanship could in certain respects become counterproductive—cutting off potentially active members, for example, or diverting staff attention from ideas which did not square with their mentors' needs and interests— should not obscure the basic point: a prerequisite to the assumption of the role of "policy entrepreneur" was normally an abandonment of the notion that staff members should remain neutral with respect to various senators and proposals or that their preferences should not "interfere" with their work.

Prescriptions as to "what Congress needs" in terms of information resources obviously depend on one's view of what Congress can and should be doing. Surely it is beyond dispute that the making of independent and rational policy judgments requires a higher level of staff competence and expertise and a more equitable distribution of staff resources than Congress has generally displayed in the past, though it is hardly feasible to contemplate a declaration of independence from executive sources. What the evidence suggests is that if, in addition, one values Congress as a "publicity machine"[47] and an independent *source* of policy, other staff characteristics assume added importance. The crucial variable is orientation: it is important that the aide give advice and present information in such a way as to point up policy needs and facilitate new departures. For this task he will find hard knowledge indispensable. But certain other components normally considered indispensable to "professionalism," notably neutrality and nonpartisanship, he may find inappropriate to the activist role.

We thus end our discussion of the factors shaping a committee's legislative role on a note similar to that on which we began, by pointing to the overriding importance of the goals and purposes of those who share in its life and work. The staff member, perhaps even to a greater extent than his mentors, will find his goals and orientations shaped and circumscribed by the norms and explicit prescriptions under which he works and by the demands, opportunities, and obstacles presented by external forces and circumstances. But the same situations that present legislators with considerable "slack" in terms of their own roles and responsibilities generally give staff members a comparable freedom to spur and shape their mentors' initiatives. For the aide no less than for the senator, therefore, it is appropriate to focus on political action in terms of its potential as well as on those factors which condition and constrain.

An overriding purpose of the present study, in fact, has been to demonstrate the past and continuing potential of the United States Congress as an arena for political action, a center for the examination and publicizing of pressing national needs and for the development of creative legislative responses. American liberals, of course, have been all too prone to overestimate the capacity of laws and programs to "solve" social dislocations and deprivations and to idealize the manner in which the "legislative process" grinds out a response. This book has done neither. The attempt has been rather to take a searching look at a period when executive and congressional attempts to deal legislatively with a range of domestic needs reached a high point, to assess institutional roles and the conditions fostering them, and to discern how much room for maneuver the system afforded. An adequate analysis of the potential for creative political action enjoyed by American policy-makers—or an adequate assessment of their specific responses in 1965–1966—would require a consideration of the ideological constraints within which American politics operates and a projection of what policy might and should look like in the several areas under consideration. This book, however, has largely (for the present) left such questions aside: the focus has rather been on the more immediate stimuli, constraints, and alternative courses of action facing the congressional policy-maker.

The conclusion, in short, is that the American legislator's role has been more prominent and diverse than is often supposed and—what is particularly important in the current period of reduced executive creativity and leadership—that the congressional "input" can and should become a more substantial and innovative one in the years ahead. Certain institutional advantages and disabilities have been found to transcend whatever failures of leadership or vision might characterize specific incumbents: particular attention has been paid to the President's "priority problems," the advantages of a decentralized and specialized Congress in publicizing a range of issues and developing and "cumulating" diverse proposals, the different means and mechanisms for interest-aggregation and conflict resolution that obtain in the two branches, and the executive's unique but limited publicizing, information-gathering, and mobilizing capacities. There is thus some truth in the familiar assertion that each branch is equipped to make its own "contribution" to the development of policy.

There is little reason to romanticize the process, however, as partisans of a "strong" Congress often seem particularly inclined to do. The Ways and Means Committee's performance on the foreign investors bill showed that a congressional capacity to "refine" legislation could be serviceable to all concerned, but UC demonstrated that "refinement" could become a euphemism for quite another type of operation. The same could be said for the often-touted "germination" function: if the medicare and aid-to-education ideas took root in Congress, they were also stifled there long after they had received public and party acceptance. On some bills Congress accommodated groups left out of the executive calculus, but in other cases such moves obstructed more than they complemented the administration's initiatives. How one evaluates congressional and executive "contributions" depends inevitably on the particular roles and substantive positions of those being evaluated. To recognize this is not to take refuge in the value-relativism which social scientists are all too prone to invoke; on the contrary, the policy roles of individuals and institutions in various policy areas can and should be concretely assessed. But there are limitations to the evaluations one can make, in once-and-for-all terms, of institutional roles and arrangements apart from particular policy-making situations. It must be acknowledged that a system of shared functions and prerogatives can produce deadlock as well as "due" deliberation, least-common-denominator settlements as well as "creative" new departures, loopholes and inequities as well as "appropriate" accommodations. If the system prompts the consideration of diverse viewpoints and imbues statutes with increased legitimacy, it often does so at considerable cost.

It is nonetheless instructive to find Congress, in the Johnson as well as the Eisenhower years, not only "checking" the President and "refining" his proposals but filling certain policy gaps on its own and stimulating, cajoling, and assisting the executive to fill others. Viewing this as a potentially fruitful role, we have laid particular stress on the ways congressional performance might be enhanced by increasing the congeniality to legislative endeavors of the committee setting—through wider dispersals of authority and resources, more creative and flexible modes of leadership, a more tolerant and supportive group ethos, the cementing of cooperative agency ties, and the development of entrepreneurial staff orientations. But it is equally important to recognize the degree of "slack," the potential for constructive legislative undertakings, that the situations of most congressmen, particularly senators, already display. The lawmaking roles assumed in the mid-sixties and subsequently by senators on LPW and Commerce represent, one suspects, a durable feature of the national policy-making landscape that may become even more prominent and important in the years ahead. And these initiatives provide only a hint as to the kinds of creativity and responsiveness that might result if legislators began to take full advantage of the resources and opportunities for leadership at their disposal.

NOTES

Chapter 1: WHO LEGISLATES?

1. *Congressional Record* (bound edition unless otherwise noted), January 25, 1967, p. 1558. Hereafter *CR.*

2. Robert A. Dahl, *Pluralist Democracy in the United States: Conflict and Consent* (Chicago: Rand McNally, 1967), p. 136.

3. Samuel P. Huntington, "Congressional Responses to the Twentieth Century," in David B. Truman, editor, *The Congress and America's Future* (Englewood Cliffs: Prentice-Hall, 1965), p. 23; cf. Harold P. Green and Alan Rosenthal, *Government of the Atom: The Integration of Powers* (New York: Atherton, 1963), pp. 21–23. But the remainder of Green's and Rosenthal's book portrays a significant exception to their generalizations; for additional dissenting views see Ralph K. Huitt, "Congress: The Durable Partner," in Elke Frank, editor, *Lawmakers in a Changing World* (Englewood Cliffs: Prentice-Hall, 1966), pp. 17–19; Frederic N. Cleaveland and associates, *Congress and Urban Problems* (Washington: Brookings, 1969), pp. 277–278, 348, 354–356; and Ronald C. Moe and Steven C. Teel, "Congress as Policy-Maker: A Necessary Reappraisal," *Political Science Quarterly,* LXXXV (September, 1970), pp. 443–470.

4. Quotations without citations are taken from interviews with 28 senators, 34 senatorial and committee aides, 16 executive branch personnel, and six lobbyists, conducted between June, 1966 and August, 1967, and in December, 1971. Senatorial interviews included nine from the Commerce Committee (six Democrats, three Republicans), ten from Finance (6–4), and eleven from Labor and Public Welfare (8–3). They varied in length from 20 minutes to 2½ hours. Extended, often multiple, interviews were also held with several staff members from each committee and a wide sampling of agency personnel working with them.

In general, the senatorial interviews attempted to get at the man's view of his job, his policy interests or lack of same, his feelings of efficacy and accomplishment, and the perceived and actual relationship of committee characteristics and resources and of his place in the group to his role. A schedule of open-ended questions was developed and used as time and circumstances dictated. Interviews with other respondents—aides, agency officials, and lobbyists—were more specific and less uniformly structured. Here the intent was ordinarily to get a description of the crucial actors and actions on a particular bill and then to move on to generalizations or comparisons as to the patterns of legislative behavior that generally characterized the committee or policy area in question.

A recording device was not used, nor were notes taken unless it was evident that doing so would not lessen rapport or hinder free exchange. A transcript, as nearly verbatim as possible, was prepared immediately after each interview; it is this from which the "quotations" in the text are taken.

5. Quoted in Wilfred E. Binkley, *President and Congress* (New York: Vintage, 1962), p. 238.

6. See Talcott Parsons, "*Voting* and the Equilibrium of the American Political System," in Eugene Burdick and Arthur J. Brodbeck, editors, *American Voting Behavior* (Glencoe: Free Press, 1959), ch. 4; and David Easton, "Categories for the Systems Analysis of Politics," in David Easton, editor, *Varieties of Political Theory* (Englewood Cliffs: Prentice-Hall, 1966), ch. 7. The idea that American political analysis has relied primarily on two paradigms, that of checked and balanced powers and that of the political system, is taken from Gabriel A. Almond, "Political Theory and Political Science," *American Political Science Review,* LX (December, 1966), pp. 871-877.

7. Talcott Parsons, "The Political Aspect of Social Structure and Process," in Easton, *Varieties,* pp. 72, 95.

8. Twenty percent of the bills were attributed to presidential influence, 30 percent to Congress and the President, 40 percent to Congress, and 10 percent to interest groups. There did appear to be an historical trend toward increased presidential influence, but Chamberlain warned against supposing prematurely that the role of Congress had become "definitely secondary." Lawrence H. Chamberlain, *The President, Congress, and Legislation* (New York: Columbia University Press, 1946), pp. 453, 462. For an attempt to update Chamberlain without, however, refining his concept of legislative initiative, see Moe and Teel, "Congress as Policy-Maker."

9. Chamberlain, *President, Congress, and Legislation,* p. 463; cf. Richard E. Neustadt, "Presidency and Legislation: Planning the President's Program," *APSR,* XLIX (December, 1955), p. 1015. Chamberlain's interest in Congress' creative role, observes Edward S. Corwin, led him to underemphasize the President's role as "catalyst" and the various factors that have converged to make presidential leadership an element of "ever in-

creasing indispensability" to the legislative process. *The President: Office and Powers* (New York: New York University Press, 1964), pp. 485-486.

10. Robert Dahl's *Who Governs?* poses similar problems. Dahl purports to isolate influential decision-makers in New Haven by determining who "initiated" specific proposals. By this he apparently means who first seriously suggested a course of action in a context where it could realistically be implemented; he thus telescopes criteria of origination and influence. Such an undifferentiated mode of analysis, problematic in any case, is clearly not applicable to major pieces of legislation in Congress. *Who Governs?* (New Haven: Yale Press, 1964), pp. 124, 151. On Dahl's concept of initiative, see David A. Baldwin, "Congressional Initiative in Foreign Policy," *Journal of Politics,* XXVIII (November, 1966), p. 759.

11. Harold D. Lasswell, "The Decision Process: Seven Categories of Functional Analysis," in Nelson W. Polsby *et al.,* editors, *Politics and Social Life* (Boston: Houghton Mifflin, 1963), p. 93.

12. The terms are taken from Harold D. Lasswell and Abraham Kaplan, *Power and Society* (New Haven: Yale Press, 1950), p. 73: "The *weight* of influence is the degree to which policies are affected; the *domain* of influence, the persons whose policies are affected; the *scope* of influence, the values implicated in the policies."

13. James A. Robinson, *Congress and Foreign Policy-Making: A Study in Legislative Influence and Initiative* (Homewood, Illinois: The Dorsey Press, 1962), pp. 14-15.

14. The use of the concept of "responsibility" is also appropriate, for reasons that will become clearer in Chapter 8, in light of the connotations it has in modern ethics. The term, notes Gibson Winter, came into prominence in the nineteenth century with the collapse of "cosmic or natural structures of obligation. . . . Responsibility was, in this sense, the ethical corollary of man as maker of history; placed in a world where he had to fashion his future, man identified himself as one who was answerable for that future." The term thus seems particularly appropriate to denote innovative or assertive political action. See Gibson Winter, *Elements for a Social Ethic* (New York: Macmillan, 1968), p. 255.

15. Kenneth J. Gergen, "Assessing the Leverage Points in the Process of Policy Formation," in Raymond A. Bauer and Kenneth J. Gergen, editors, *The Study of Policy Formation* (New York: Free Press, 1968), pp. 187-188.

16. Gabriel A. Almond, "A Functional Approach to Comparative Politics," in Gabriel A. Almond and James S. Coleman, editors, *The Politics of the Developing Areas* (Princeton: Princeton University Press, 1960), pp. 16-17, 26-28. Our six stages involve all four "input functions"—political socialization and recruitment, interest articulation, interest aggregation, and political communication—as well as the "output function" of rule-making.

17. Herbert Simon contends that a decision-making theory adequate to

political reality can never simply portray "the selection of an optimal course of action from among a set of specified alternative courses of action, on the basis of a criterion of preference." In particular, there is a need for focusing on "attention-directing" and "alternative-generating" processes. "Political Research: The Decision-Making Framework," in Easton, *Varieties,* pp. 18-20. See also Charles E. Lindblom, *The Policy-Making Process* (Englewood Cliffs: Prentice-Hall, 1968), p. 4.

18. Theodore J. Lowi, Editor's Introduction to *Legislative Politics USA* (Boston: Little, Brown, 1965), p. x.

19. Woodrow Wilson, *Congressional Government* (New York: Houghton Mifflin, 1913), pp. 44-45.

20. Various lines of historical development are traced in Binkley, *President and Congress*; Neustadt, "President's Program," pp. 980-1021, and "Presidency and Legislation: The Growth of Central Clearance," *APSR,* XLVIII (September, 1954), pp. 641-671; Harvey C. Mansfield, "The Congress and Economic Policy," in Truman, ed., *America's Future,* ch. 6; Abraham Holtzman, *Legislative Liaison: Executive Leadership in Congress* (Chicago: Rand McNally, 1970), pp. 1-17, 230-245; and Robert S. Gilmour, "Central Legislative Clearance: A Revised Perspective," *Public Administration Review,* XXXI (March-April, 1971), pp. 150-158.

21. Richard E. Neustadt, *Presidential Power* (New York: Signet, 1964), pp. 17-19.

22. See Lawrence H. Chamberlain, "The President as Legislator," *Annals of the American Academy of Political and Social Science,* CCLXXXIII (September, 1952), p. 95; Arthur N. Holcombe, *Our More Perfect Union* (Cambridge: Harvard University Press, 1950), pp. 240-262; Curtis Arthur Amlund, "Executive-Legislative Imbalance: Truman to Kennedy?" *Western Political Quarterly,* XVIII (September, 1965), pp. 640-645; and James L. Sundquist, *Politics and Policy: The Eisenhower, Kennedy, and Johnson Years* (Washington: Brookings, 1968), ch. 9, 11. Recall Theodore Lowi's hypothesis that innovation in party systems is likely to be a function of minority or opposition status. "Toward Functionalism in Political Science: The Case of Innovation in Party Systems," *APSR,* LVII (September, 1963), pp. 570-583.

23. Sundquist, *Politics and Policy,* p. 489.

24. William S. White, *Citadel: The Story of the U.S. Senate* (New York: Harper and Brothers, 1957), ch. 7; and Donald R. Matthews, *U.S. Senators and their World* (New York: Vintage, 1960), ch. 5.

25. See Nelson W. Polsby, *Congress and the Presidency* (Englewood Cliffs: Prentice-Hall, 1971), pp. 52-63; and Ralph K. Huitt, "The Outsider in the Senate; An Alternative Role," *APSR,* LV (September, 1961), pp. 566-575.

26. See Rowland Evans and Robert Novak, *Lyndon B. Johnson: The Exercise of Power* (New York: New American Library, 1966), pp. 69-76, 105-130; and Polsby, *Congress and the Presidency:* "Johnson sedulously

perpetuated the myth of the inner club while destroying its substance" (pp. 68-69).

27. Tom Wicker, "Winds of Change in the Senate," *New York Times Magazine,* September 12, 1965, p. 52. See also John Bibby and Roger Davidson, *On Capitol Hill: Studies in the Legislative Process* (New York: Holt, Rinehart, and Winston, 1967), pp. 146-153; Nelson W. Polsby, "Goodbye to the Inner Club," *Washington Monthly,* I (August, 1969), pp. 30-34; and Randall B. Ripley, *Power in the Senate* (New York: St. Martin's, 1969).

28. Dahl, *Pluralist Democracy,* pp. 139-142. For a dissenting view, see Alfred de Grazia, *Republic in Crisis: Congress against the Executive Force* (New York: Federal Legal Publications, 1965), ch. 7.

29. Wilson, *Congressional Government,* pp. 78-79. On the formative years of the committee system and its relationship to the roles of party and President, see James Sterling Young, *The Washington Community, 1800-1828* (New York: Columbia University Press, 1966), ch. 6-9.

30. David B. Truman, *The Governmental Process* (New York: Alfred A. Knopf, 1964), pp. 330-331. See also J. Leiper Freeman, *The Political Process: Executive Bureau-Legislative Committee Relations* (New York: Random House, 1965), ch. 2; Matthews, *U.S. Senators,* ch. 7; and Neil MacNeil, *Forge of Democracy: The House of Representatives* (New York: McKay, 1963), ch. 7. For an overview of "centrifugal" and "centripetal" forces currently at work, see Stephen K. Bailey, *Congress in the Seventies* (New York: St. Martin's, 1970), ch. 4-5.

31. See Richard F. Fenno, Jr., *The Power of the Purse: Appropriations Politics in Congress* (Boston: Little, Brown, 1966), p. xvi; and Ralph K. Huitt, "The Congressional Committee: A Case Study," *APSR,* XLVIII (June, 1954), pp. 340-341.

32. Recent studies attempting to isolate, relate, and explain various orientations among legislators include John C. Wahlke, Heinz Eulau, William Buchanan, and Leroy C. Ferguson, *The Legislative System* (New York: John Wiley, 1962); Roger H. Davidson, *The Role of the Congressman* (New York: Pegasus, 1969); and James D. Barber, *The Lawmakers* (New Haven: Yale University Press, 1965). While the notion of "role" has been widely utilized in the study of Congress, surprisingly few attempts have been made to link orientations to the legislative efforts individuals and committees do or do not undertake. Among the few partial exceptions are Warner R. Schilling, Paul Y. Hammond, and Glen H. Snyder, *Strategy, Politics, and Defense Budgets* (New York: Columbia University Press, 1962), ch. 3; and Huitt, "The Congressional Committee," pp. 340-365.

33. Wahlke *et al., Legislative System,* p. 246.

34. Raymond A. Bauer, Ithiel de Sola Pool and Lewis A. Dexter, *American Business and Public Policy* (New York: Atherton, 1964), p. 405.

35. Wahlke and his colleagues found some one-third of their state legislators articulating this "purposive role," often in combination with other

roles. *Legislative System,* pp. 254-256, 259-263. The figure for a random sample drawn from the U.S. House of Representatives during the 88th Congress was 31 per cent, though only seven percent listed the "inventor" role as their primary one. See Davidson, *Role of Congressman,* pp. 79-85.

36. Davidson finds "inventors" to be typically but not exclusively liberal. *Role of Congressman,* pp. 84-85, 91, 187. And Barber links the "lawmaker" orientation (large number of bills introduced, frequent speaking in committee and on floor, desire to pursue the legislative career) among freshmen state legislators with liberalism and a desire for policy changes. *Lawmakers,* pp. 207-211.

37. Donald Matthews found a liberal voting record and a willingness to defy Senate folkways (i.e., frequently speaking on the floor and refusing to adhere to norms of strict specialization) to be positively related to one another; each, in turn, was negatively related to "legislative effectiveness," defined as success in getting ones bills passed. One suspects, however, that the higher batting average of the conservatives and conformers could in large part be attributed to their lesser propensity to introduce bills, particularly as symbolic gestures, in the first place. See *U.S. Senators,* pp. 112-117, 287.

38. See William G. Scott, "Organization Theory: An Overview and an Appraisal," in Joseph A. Litterer, editor, *Organizations: Structure and Behavior* (New York: John Wiley, 1963), pp. 13-22; Chester I. Barnard, *The Functions of the Executive* (Cambridge: Harvard University Press, 1962), part III; and Mason Haire, editor, *Modern Organization Theory* (New York: John Wiley, 1959), ch. 1.

39. Incentives to legislative activism, it would follow, are of a different order than (and perhaps in conflict with) those maintaining group cohesion. Cf. the assertion of Leonard Sayles that the success of "innovating groups" within organizations *requires* that their system of goals and rewards be distinct from that motivating the organization as a whole. *Managerial Behavior* (New York: McGraw-Hill, 1964), p. 109.

40. Barnard, *Executive,* p. 139.

41. For treatments of the sources of innovation in organizations which stress the importance of the group "ethos," see Harold Guetzkow, "The Creative Person in Organizations," and Marvin Bower, "Nurturing Innovation in an Organization," in Gary A. Steiner, editor, *The Creative Organization* (Chicago: University of Chicago Press, 1965), ch. 2, 10.

42. James Q. Wilson, "Innovation in Organization: Notes toward a Theory" (mimeographed, 1963); and James D. Barber, "Some Consequences of Pluralization in Government" (mimeographed, 1965). The decentralization of Congress as a whole, suggests Lewis A. Froman, is indicative of its "highly differentiated social setting." "Organization Theory and the Explanation of Important Characteristics of Congress," *APSR,* LXII (June, 1968), pp. 521-525. This precondition for decentralization was

clearly present for all three committees now under consideration; yet they varied widely in their organizational diversity. Our intention is to view the latter as an independent variable and to explore its implications for the committees' legislative performance.

43. Cf. Peter G. Peterson, "Some Approaches to Innovation in Industry," in Steiner, ed., *Creative Organization,* ch. 11; and Anthony Downs, *Inside Bureaucracy* (Boston: Little, Brown, 1967), pp. 185, 203.

44. Cf. Charles E. Lindblom, *The Intelligence of Democracy* (New York: Free Press, 1965), pp. 325-326; Holbert N. Carroll, "The Congress and National Security Policy," in Truman, *America's Future,* p. 152; Nelson W. Polsby, "The Institutionalization of the U.S. House of Representatives," *APSR,* LXII (March, 1968), p. 166; and Young, *The Washington Community,* pp. 202-204.

45. See Charles O. Jones' description of the House Agriculture Committee: "The Role of the Congressional Subcommittee," *Midwest Journal of Political Science,* VI (November, 1962), pp. 327-344; and "The Agriculture Committee and the Problem of Representation," in Robert L. Peabody and Nelson W. Polsby, editors, *New Perspectives on the House of Representatives* (Chicago: Rand McNally, 1963), ch. 5.

46. See Wilson, "Innovation in Organization," p. 27.

47. Malcolm E. Jewell and Samuel C. Patterson, *The Legislative Process in the United States* (New York: Random House, 1966), p. 225.

48. Green and Rosenthal relate both the number and the power of the Joint Committee on Atomic Energy's subcommittees to the inventiveness and activism of the committee as a whole. *Government of the Atom,* pp. 51-52. Bibby and Davidson similarly relate the decentralization of the Senate Banking and Currency Committee in the area of housing— Subcommittee Chairman Sparkman enjoyed a generous budget, a sizable staff, and little interference from the full committee—to a high level of oversight activity. *On Capitol Hill,* pp. 179-181. Lowi, following a familiar theme in organization theory, associates organizational "permeability" with a tendency to innovative activity, and tight leadership with the opposite tendency. "Innovation in Party Systems," pp. 581-582; cf. Guetzkow, "Creative Person," pp. 37-40.

49. Robert K. Merton, *Social Theory and Social Structure* (London: Free Press, 1964), pp. 47-51.

50. Fenno, *Power of Purse,* p. xviii. Fenno's pioneer article, "The Appropriations Committee as a Political System" (1962), is reprinted in Peabody and Polsby, *New Perspectives,* ch. 4.

51. Fenno, *Power of Purse,* pp. 2, 191.

52. See Fenno, *Power of Purse,* ch. 3-5; Green and Rosenthal, *Government of Atom,* pp. 44-54; Jones, "Role of Subcommittee," pp. 328, 343; and John F. Manley, "The House Committee on Ways and Means: Conflict Management in a Congressional Committee," *APSR,* LIX (December,

1965), pp. 927-939. Note that many of the factors related to committee integration have their parallels in Matthews' list of Senate "folkways." *U.S. Senators,* ch. 5. Fenno observes that Senate Appropriations needs explicit norms and structures of integration to a much lesser extent than its House counterpart because of its lesser degree of differentiation from the parent chamber; committee members need only "behave like Senators." *Power of Purse,* p. 560.

53. See Easton, "Systems Analysis," p. 152; and Lewis A. Coser, *The Functions of Social Conflict* (Glencoe: Free Press, 1956), p. 157. Fenno discusses at length the role of the chairman, the place of subcommittees, committee goals and norms, the decision-making environment, incentives to committee membership and participation, recruitment practices and the traits of members—and it is instructive to note that, time after time, he simply talks past our concerns. One reason may be the peculiar nature of the Appropriations Committees; unlike Senate Commerce, Finance, and LPW, they are not responsible for substantive policy in a defined area. But they can and do alter and initiate policy in their own way. It seems clear that a treatment of the committee as a social system, with its "inward" focus and its concentration on "standardized" structures and processes, is unlikely to highlight the committee's policy role or the sources of innovation and initiative. See *Power of Purse,* p. 689; Merton, *Social Theory,* pp. 50-51.

54. Fenno, *Power of Purse,* p. 192.

55. *Ibid.,* p. 501. See Green and Rosenthal, *Government of Atom,* pp. 152-163, 194-197. Matthews develops indices of committee prestige (stability of membership, frequency of transfers on or off the committee), cohesiveness (tendency to vote together on the floor), and effectiveness (degree to which full Senate ratifies committee decisions); he finds positive relationships between all three factors. *U.S. Senators,* pp. 148-158, 166-169. On the negative side, Fenno finds a linkage between the House Education and Labor Committee's "classic incapacity as a consensus-building institution" and the frequent failure of aid-to-education bills. "The House of Representatives and Federal Aid to Education," in Peabody and Polsby, *New Perspectives,* ch. 8. And Bibby and Davidson report that integrative failures on the Banking and Currency Committee have made it "unable to present a united front to either the Senate or the administrative agencies it sought to influence, [thus limiting] its power. . . . This, in turn, has contributed to its general passivity toward this function." *On Capitol Hill,* pp. 190-195.

56. See Fenno, *Power of Purse,* p. 193; and Bibby and Davidson, *On Capitol Hill,* pp. 183-195.

57. See James D. Barber, *Power in Committees* (Chicago: Rand McNally, 1966), pp. 148, 155.

58. Recall Matthews' finding that conformity to Senate "folkways," while

increasing a legislator's "effectiveness," also involves a restriction of his legislative interests and activities. *U.S. Senators,* p. 115.

59. Truman, *Governmental Process,* p. 433.

60. Bauer *et al., American Business,* part V; Warren E. Miller and Donald E. Stokes, "Constituency Influence in Congress," *APSR,* LVII (March, 1963), pp. 45-56; and Warren E. Miller, "Majority Rule and the Representative System of Government," in Erik Allardt and Yrjo Littunen, editors, *Cleavages, Ideologies, and Party Systems* (Helsinki: Academic Bookstore, 1964), pp. 343-376.

61. E.g. de Grazia, *Republic in Crisis,* ch. 3; Willmoore Kendall, "The Two Majorities," *Midwest Journal of Political Science,* IV (November, 1960), pp. 317-345; and Theodore J. Lowi, "American Business, Public Policy, Case Studies, and Political Theory," *World Politics,* XVI (July, 1964), pp. 677-715. For an attempt to explain differences between House and Senate in comparable terms, see Lewis A. Froman, Jr., *Congressmen and their Constituencies* (Chicago: Rand McNally, 1963), ch. 6.

62. Lowi, "Case Studies and Political Theory," pp. 690-715. On the tendency of Lowi's independent and dependent variables to proliferate and become intermingled, see below, pp. 323-325. Further difficulties have to do with the boundaries and inclusiveness of his policy types themselves and with whether they are to be defined "objectively" or in terms of the perceptions of political actors. On the latter points, see Lewis A. Froman, "The Categorization of Policy Contents" and Robert H. Salisbury, "The Analysis of Public Policy: A Search for Theories and Roles," in Austin Ranney, ed., *Political Science and Public Policy* (Chicago: Markham, 1968), pp. 50-51, 157-159.

63. See pp. 296-297 below.

64. For arguments that the twentieth century's "organizational revolution" has made for a *general* decline in the representational capacity of Congress and a transferral to the executive of group entreaties and the policy moves they stimulate, see Huntington, "Congressional Responses," pp. 8-17; and Roger H. Davidson, "Congress and the Executive: The Race for Representation," in Alfred de Grazia, editor, *Congress: The First Branch of Government* (Garden City: Doubleday, 1967), pp. 365-402. Supportive evidence is provided by recent studies of lobbying: Lester Milbrath finds that 58 percent of the lobbyists willing to name a "predominant influence" in policy-making name the President or executive agencies. Only 10 percent name Congress—despite the fact that his sample is drawn exclusively from lobbyists registered under the Regulation of Lobbying Act (lobbyists not dealing in some way with Congress are not required to register). "Fully 77 percent of the lobbyists interviewed normally contact decision-makers in both legislative and executive branches." *The Washington Lobbyists* (Chicago: Rand McNally, 1963), pp. 22-23, 351-353, 397. Cf. the complementary findings of Paul W. Cherington and Ralph L. Gillen, *The*

Business Representative in Washington (Washington: The Brookings Institution, 1962), ch. 3-4. Our intention, of course, is to differentiate among our committees in terms of these general patterns.

65. Freeman, *Bureau-Committee Relations,* ch. 2-3. The rise of the congressional committee system after 1812, writes James S. Young, "brought cabinet members to the forefront of executive dealings with Congress . . . A subsystem of political relationships between department heads and their supervising congressional committees came to supplant, as the principal arena of confrontation between the executive and legislative establishments, the direct relationship between the President and his congressional party that Jefferson had enjoyed." *Washington Community,* pp. 204-205.

66. Lindblom, *Intelligence*, p. 9 and *passim.*

67. The term is borrowed from Herbert Kaufman, *Politics and Policies in State and Local Governments* (Englewood Cliffs: Prentice-Hall, 1964), p. 110.

68. Lindblom, *Intelligence,* ch. 3-5.

69. See Freeman, *Bureau-Committee Relations,* pp. 14-15; Lindblom, *Policy-Making Process,* pp. 30-32; and Neustadt, "President's Program," p. 1014. For pertinent case material see Morgan Thomas, *Atomic Energy and Congress* (Ann Arbor: University of Michigan Press, 1956), pp. 184, 232-234. Thus, incidentally, is borne out the appropriateness of Fenno's focus on adaptation as the mode of committee-agency relationships, although he concentrates on a different set of reasons which the committee has for "minimizing conflict and reducing uncertainty" and seeking a "stable relationship." See *Power of Purse,* p. 348.

70. Fenno, *Power of Purse,* pp. 507-511.

71. Important to the policy leadership of the JCAE, according to Green and Rosenthal, are the facts that (1) it is intercameral and thus not subject, like other committees, to direct checks from another group, and (2) it is an elite group containing senior members from other committees which, because of jurisdictional overlaps, might otherwise come into conflict with the JCAE. *Government of Atom,* pp. 26-34.

72. Ralph K. Huitt, "Congressional Organization and Operation in the Field of Money and Credit," in Commission on Money and Credit, *Fiscal and Debt Management Policies* (Englewood Cliffs: Prentice-Hall, 1963), p. 405. Cf. Freeman, *Bureau-Committee Relations,* p. 55; Truman, *Governmental Process,* pp. 404-415; and Richard F. Fenno, Jr., *The President's Cabinet* (New York: Vintage, 1959), ch. 6. Pertinent case studies include Arthur Maass, *Muddy Waters* (Cambridge: Harvard University Press, 1951); J. W. Anderson, *Eisenhower, Brownell, and the Congress* (University, Alabama: University of Alabama Press, 1964); and Theodore J. Lowi, *The End of Liberalism* (New York: W. W. Norton, 1969), ch. 4.

73. Lindblom, *Intelligence,* pp. 28-32, 126 131; cf. Downs, *Inside Bureaucracy,* pp. 198-200.

74. For a comparison of the policy-making incentives and advantages under conditions of committee-agency harmony with those obtaining under conflict, see Green and Rosenthal, *Government of Atom,* pp. 9-17. Particularly instructive is the way executive branch divisions contributed to Congress' successful "self-assertion" in 1947 in the form of the Taft-Hartley Act. Seymour Z. Mann, "Policy-Making in the Executive Branch: The Taft-Hartley Experience," in Lowi, ed., *Legislative Politics USA* (First edition, 1962), pp. 209-221. And it has often been observed that a more active congressional role in defense policy requires "more interservice squabbling." Lewis A. Dexter, "Congressmen and the Making of Military Policy," in Peabody and Polsby, eds., *New Perspectives,* pp. 317-319; and Raymond H. Dawson, "Innovation and Intervention in Defense Policy," in *Ibid.,* pp. 276, 284, 298.

75. Ernest S. Griffith, *Congress: Its Contemporary Role* (New York: New York University Press, 1961), p. 97; cf. Nelson W. Polsby, "Policy Analysis and Congress," *Public Policy,* XVIII (Fall, 1969), pp. 70-71. For a critical appraisal of such proposals, see Bertram M. Gross, *The Legislative Struggle* (New York: McGraw Hill, 1953), pp. 421-423; and Norman Meller, "Legislative Staff Services: Toxin, Specific, or Placebo for the Legislature's Ills," *Western Political Quarterly,* XX (June, 1967), pp. 381-389.

76. See Green and Rosenthal, *Government of Atom,* pp. 65-70, 89-103; Huitt, "Money and Credit," pp. 448-449; Alison Griffith, *The National Aeronautics and Space Act* (Washington: Public Affairs Press, 1962), ch. 5; and J. W. Finney, "Science Policy in the USA," *Discovery,* XXVI (December, 1965), p. 13.

77. James D. Cochrane, "Partisan Aspects of Congressional Committee Staffing," *Western Political Quarterly,* XVII (June, 1964), p. 345.

78. 2 USC 72a.

79. Max M. Kampelman, "The Legislative Bureaucracy: Its Response to Political Change, 1953," *Journal of Politics,* XVI (August, 1954), pp. 539-550; Cochrane, "Partisan Aspects," pp. 338-348; and Kenneth Kofmehl, *Professional Staffs of Congress* (Indianapolis: C. E. Pauley, 1962), ch. 4.

80. Downs, *Inside Bureaucracy,* pp. 2, 167-178.

81. Karl W. Deutsch, *The Nerves of Government: Models of Political Communication and Control* (New York: Free Press, 1966), p. 164.

82. See Warren H. Butler, "Administering Congress: The Role of the Staff," *Public Administration Review,* XXVI (March, 1966), p. 12; and Gross, *Legislative Struggle,* p. 422.

83. Studies dealing in a preliminary way with the legislative impact of staff orientations include Stephen K. Bailey, *Congress Makes a Law* (New York: Columbia University Press, 1950), ch. 3-4; Bibby and Davidson, *On

Capitol Hill, pp. 181-183; and Green and Rosenthal, *Government of Atom,* pp. 65-68.

Chapter 2: THE COMMERCE COMMITTEE IN ACTION

1. For an account of the fair packaging episode which focuses on Hart's role, see A. Q. Mowbray, *The Thumb on the Scale* (New York: Lippincott, 1967), especially ch. 4, 15. Fuller accounts of the present case study and of the twelve that follow may be found in David E. Price, "Who Makes the Laws? The Legislative Roles of Three Senate Committees" (Ph.D. dissertation, Yale University, 1969).

2. Committee on Commerce, United States Senate, 89th Congress, *Hearings* on S. 985, April 30, 1965, p. 225.

3. See Mowbray, *Thumb,* pp. 173-177.

4. *New York Times,* May 19, 1965, p. 19.

5. Committee on Commerce, USS, 89th Congress, *Report* to accompany S. 985, May 25, 1966, pp. 39, 44.

6. *CR,* June 1, 1966, p. 12012; June 2, 1966, p. 12093; June 8, 1966, p. 12678.

7. The State of the Union Message asked for efforts "to prevent the deception of the American consumer—requiring all packages to state clearly and truthfully their contents"; the Economic Message of January 27 endorsed "the fair packaging and labeling bill"; and the Consumer Protection Message of March 21 contained a more detailed endorsement of packaging as well as labeling regulation. Still, the President had neither sent up legislation himself nor endorsed any specific version of S. 985. See Congressional Quarterly *Almanac,* 1966, pp. 1208, 1227, 1261.

8. See Mowbray, *Thumb,* pp. 170, 177.

9. *CR,* October 19, 1966, p. 27603.

10. Mancur Olson, Jr., *The Logic of Collective Action* (New York: Schocken, 1965), ch. 1-2.

11. On the general disabilities of the NAM, USCC, and consumer groups alike, see *Ibid.,* pp. 128, 143-148, 166.

12. Cf. Richard Wagner's critique of Olson's "incomplete consideration of the institutions within which individuals interact." "The political entrepreneur's search for profit opportunities . . . provides the key to understanding why certain groups receive real income increasing favors while others do not; favor-seeking activity results from the operation of democratic decision processes and not from pressure groups *per se.*" "Pressure Groups and Political Entrepreneurs," *Papers on Non-Market Decision Making,* I (1966), pp. 161-170.

13. For a similar assessment, embedded in a study severely critical of the FTC, see Edward F. Cox, Robert C. Fellmeth, and John E. Schulz,

Nader's Raiders: Report on the Federal Trade Commission (New York: Grove Press, 1970), pp. x, 77-78.

14. The rule is reprinted in Committee on Commerce, USS, 89th Congress, *Hearings* on S. 559 and S. 547, March 29, 1965, p. 417. For an account of the cigarette labeling and advertising episode that concentrates on the role of the FTC, see A. Lee Fritschler, *Smoking and Politics: Policy-making and the Federal Bureaucracy* (New York: Appleton-Century-Crofts, 1969), especially ch. 2, 4, 7.

15. See Daniel S. Greenberg, "Tobacco and Health," *Science,* CXL (June 14, 1963), p. 1196, and "The Burning Question: Tobacco and Politics," *The Reporter,* XXX (January 30, 1964), pp. 34-35.

16. CQ *Almanac,* 1964, p. 249.

17. The exchange of letters is printed in the Senate *Hearings,* March 29, 1965, p. 429.

18. An accusation leveled at Representative Moss by Representative Cooley during the House debate, *NYT,* July 14, 1965, p. 23.

19. See Barber, *Lawmakers,* ch. 2.

20. Departmental reports are printed in the Senate *Hearings,* March 22, 1965, pp. 22-30.

21. *Ibid.,* pp. 34, 37.

22. See, for example, Senator Hartke's floor speech, *CR,* June 16, 1965, p. 13920.

23. Testimony of Bowman Gray, representing the major cigarette manufacturers, Senate *Hearings,* March 24, 1965, pp. 244-245.

24. Senate *Hearings,* March 29, 1965, p. 413. For the relevant statute, see 15 USC 45.

25. *Ibid.,* pp. 430, 460, 461.

26. E.g. Robert Kennedy: "Government . . . has not done enough to cope with this great public health problem . . . The only agency that has made a serious effort is the Federal Trade Commission." *Ibid.,* April 2, 1965, p. 986.

27. See the Council's testimony: *Ibid.,* March 22, 1965, pp. 103-141.

28. For accounts of interest group activity, see Elizabeth B. Drew, "The Quiet Victory of the Cigarette Lobby," *Atlantic Monthly,* CCXVI (September 1965), pp. 76-80; and Fritschler, *Smoking and Politics,* pp. 18-23, 116-128.

29. *NYT,* April 28, 1965, p. 30.

30. Committee on Commerce, USS, 89th Congress, *Report* to accompany S. 559, May 19, 1965, pp. 5-6.

31. The FTC reported annually on the mounting evidence of the health hazards of smoking and on the apparent inadequacy of the 1965 statute in terms of its impact on the consuming public. As the expiration of the moratorium approached, the FTC again announced its intention to require a health warning in printed advertising and the FCC proposed that cigarette

ads be prohibited on radio and television. In 1970 Senators Magnuson and Moss secured the enactment of a bill achieving the latter objective, strengthening the required warning label, and reducing the House's proposed six-year moratorium on further FTC regulations to 18 months. See Elizabeth B. Drew, "The Cigarette Companies Would Rather Fight than Switch," *New York Times Magazine,* May 4, 1969, pp. 36ff.; CQ *Almanac,* 1969, pp. 883-890, and 1970, pp. 145-146; and Susan Wagner, *Cigarette Country: Tobacco in American History and Politics* (New York: Praeger, 1971), ch. 13.

32. *CR,* June 16, 1965, p. 13893.

33. *Ibid.,* June 22, 1965, pp. 14413, 14417.

34. See Drew, "Quiet Victory," p. 80.

35. *NYT,* July 9, 1965, p. 28; July 14, 1965, p. 36; July 17, 1965, p. 26.

36. See *Ibid.,* February 13, 1966, IV, p. 2; February 14, 1966, p. 18.

37. See Ralph Nader, *Unsafe at any Speed* (New York: Grossman, 1965), p. 295-301.

38. Quoted in Elizabeth B. Drew, "The Politics of Auto Safety," *Atlantic Monthly,* CCXVIII (October, 1966), p. 98. On Nader's mode of operation and his activities subsequent to the automobile safety episode, see Patrick Anderson, "Ralph Nader, Crusader; Or, the Rise of a Self-Appointed Lobbyist," *New York Times Magazine,* October 29, 1967, pp. 25 ff.

39. Committee on Commerce, USS, 89th Congress, *Hearings* on S. 3005, April 4, 1966, p. 313.

40. See *Ibid.,* March 17-April 6, 1966, pp. 101, 110-132, 283-320, 598-600.

41. Drew, "Auto Safety," p. 96; Nader, *Unsafe,* p. 269-285.

42. Senate *Hearings,* March 16, 1966, pp. 35, 42.

43. *Ibid.,* March 17, 1966, pp. 94-95. Cf. Elinor Langer, "Auto Safety: Nader vs General Motors," *Science,* CLII (April 1, 1966), p. 49.

44. Senate *Hearings,* March 16, 1966, p. 79.

45. *Business Week,* April 9, 1966, p. 30. On the National Safety Council, the "hub" of the private "safety movement," see Nader, *Unsafe,* pp. 261-269.

46. Senate *Hearings,* April 5, 1966, pp. 396-400, 515, 436.

47. See Drew, "Auto Safety," p. 99.

48. *Ibid.,* p. 99.

49. *NYT,* May 5, 1966, p. 12.

50. Drew, "Auto Safety," p. 100.

51. Committee on Commerce, USS, 89th Congress, *Report* to accompany S. 3005, June 23, 1966, pp. 13, 32.

52. Senate *Hearings,* March 16, 1966, p. 73.

53. *CR,* June 24, 1966, p. 14238.

54. See Drew Pearson's *Washington Post* columns: June 1, 1966, p. D15; June 13, p. B13; June 24, p. B15; June 29, p. B13. I am indebted to Norman Dean for assistance in locating these references.

55. See, for example, *Business Week,* May 14, 1966, p. 38; and Pearson's *Washington Post* columns of June 24, 1966, p. B15, and August 8, 1966, p. C13.

56. *CR,* August 31, 1966, p. 21351.

57. See the publication of the Legislative Reference Service, Library of Congress, "Federal Legislation for Oceanography, 1956-65," January 9, 1967, p. 27.

58. See Don K. Price, *The Scientific Estate* (Cambridge, Belknap Press, 1965), ch. 7; and Gordon J. F. MacDonald, "Legislative History of Oceanography" (mimeographed, 1967), pp. 3-4.

59. "Federal Legislation," pp. 1, 16-17.

60. Price, *Scientific Estate,* p. 216.

61. See "Federal Legislation," pp. 2-4.

62. Price, *Scientific Estate,* p. 243.

63. A case study from an earlier decade finds the fishing industry complaining of inadequate representation in the executive branch but exerting relatively strong congressional influence. Bernard C. Cohen, *The Political Process and Foreign Policy: The Making of the Japanese Peace Settlement* (Princeton: Princeton University Press, 1957), ch. 12.

64. See Bartlett's and Magnuson's fulminations on the Senate floor, *CR,* August 12, 1964, pp. 19161-19163; and William S. Boesch, "The Commercial Fisheries Research and Development Act of 1964" (mimeographed, 1965), pp. 19-25.

65. See especially the testimony of Dr. John Calhoun, Committee on Commerce, USS, 89th Congress, *Hearings* on S. 944, March 16, 1965, pp. 75-79.

66. Committee on Merchant Marine and Fisheries, Subcommittee on Oceanography, U.S. House of Representatives, 89th Congress, *Hearings* on H. R. 921 and other bills, August 3, 1965, pp. 116-132.

67. Senate *Hearings,* February 19, 1965, pp. 10, 15, 23.

68. *Ibid.,* pp. 16-17. For the negative report of the Commerce Department, see p. 5.

69. *CR,* August 5, 1965, p. 19561.

70. House *Hearings,* August 10, 1965, p. 279; August 17, 1965, pp. 475, 484.

71. Senate *Hearings,* March 16, 1965, pp. 64, 71.

72. House *Hearings,* August 19, 1965, p. 611.

73. See *Science,* CLIII (July 22, 1966), pp. 391-392.

74. The final report of the Commission on Marine Science, Engineering and Resources, "Our Nation and the Sea," was issued on January 11, 1969. Subsequent legislation temporarily extended the life of the National Council on Marine Resources and Engineering Development, but it was allowed to expire in early 1971. The Commission's main organizational recommendation, for the formation of an independent National Oceanic and Atmospheric Agency, stimulated hearings but no final action in either

house; the President's Reorganization Plan No. 4 of 1970, however, consolidated ESSA, BCF, and other functions in a new National Oceanic and Atmospheric Administration within the Department of Commerce.

Chapter 3: THE COMMERCE COMMITTEE: AN OVERVIEW

1. Dan Cordtz, "The Senate's 'Maggie'," reprinted in *CR,* April 7, 1965, p. 7251.

2. Data taken from CQ *Weekly Report,* XXIV (February 25, 1966), p. 474. Committee roster taken from second session.

3. Data from Committee on Commerce, USS, 89th Congress, *Legislative Calendar,* December 31, 1966, pp. 17-88, 131-134, 147-153.

4. The term "prime sponsor" refers to instances when the senator was the sole sponsor, one of two sponsors, or listed out of alphabetical order at the head of a list of cosponsors.

5. See below, pp. 268-274.

6. On Lausche's obstructive role with respect to mass transit legislation, Magnuson's initial indifference, and the full committee's eventual overriding of the subcommittee on the question, see Royce Hanson, "Congress Copes with Mass Transit, 1960-1964," in Cleaveland *et al., Congress and Urban Problems.* The inhospitability of the Commerce Committee was a major factor in the shift of initiative on the issue to the Banking and Currency Committee and the lodging of administrative responsibility in the Housing and Home Finance Agency.

7. See Randall B. Ripley, "Congress Champions Aid to Airports, 1958-59," in *Ibid.*

8. Committee on Rules, USS, 89th Congress, "Investigations by the Committee on Commerce" (*Reports* to accompany S. Res. 76 and S. Res. 213), February 3, 1965, pp. 11-14, 20-25; February 9, 1966, pp. 9-12, 15-21.

9. "The prosperity of commerce is now perceived and acknowledged by all enlightened statesmen to be the most useful as well as the most productive source of national wealth, and has accordingly become a primary object of their political cares." Alexander Hamilton, *The Federalist,* no. 12.

10. The index of cohesion is defined as the difference between the percentage for and the percentage against a given motion. A unanimous vote thus gives an index of 100; a 50-50 split gives an index of zero. See Stuart A. Rice, *Quantitative Methods in Politics* (New York: Alfred A. Knopf, 1928), pp. 208-209; and Matthews, *U.S. Senators,* pp. 169, 281. Votes on nominations excluded.

11. Matthews, *U.S. Senators,* pp. 153, 156.

12. With the removal of the short-term appointments of Kenneth Keating and Glenn Beall from tabulation, the figure still showed a remarkable increase to 2.8 years, 2.7 for Democrats and 2.8 for Republicans.

Calculations made on the basis of data contained in Committee on Commerce, USS, *History, Membership, and Jurisdiction of the Senate Committee on Commerce,* June 24, 1966, pp. 57-61, *Calendar,* pp. 253-254; and relevant issues of the *Congressional Directory.*

13. See above, pp. 18-19.

14. Lowi, "Case Studies and Political Theory," p. 709.

15. Data taken from CQ *Weekly Report,* XXIV (February 25, 1966), pp. 472-474; and CQ *Almanac,* 1966, pp. 33-37. The five Senate Commerce members with business backgrounds, incidentally, were all critics of the Hart bill.

16. See p. 21 above.

17. On strategies available to the minority, see Charles O. Jones, "The Minority Party and Policy-Making in the House of Representatives," *APSR,* LXII (June, 1968), p. 482.

Chapter 4: THE FINANCE COMMITTEE IN ACTION

1. *CR* January 6, 1965, p. 180.

2. See Richard Harris, *A Sacred Trust* (Baltimore: Penguin, 1969), pp. 4-13; Edwin E. Witte, *The Development of the Social Security Act* (Madison: University of Wisconsin Press, 1962), pp. 94-95, 173-189; Edwin E. Witte, *Social Security Perspectives* (Madison: University of Wisconsin Press, 1962), pp. 314-321; and Chamberlain, *President, Congress, and Legislation,* p. 19.

3. Sundquist, *Politics and Policy,* p. 290. Richard Harris estimates that by 1905 the AMA and its allies had made outlays of over $50 million. *Sacred Trust,* p. 3.

4. Sundquist, *Politics and Policy,* pp. 290-296; Theodore R. Marmor, "The Congress: Medicare Politics and Policy," in Allan P. Sindler, editor, *American Political Institutions and Public Policy* (Boston: Little, Brown, 1969), pp. 13-20.

5. Sundquist, *Politics and Policy,* p. 297; cf. Harris, *Sacred Trust,* pp. 54-103.

6. See Witte, *Social Security Act,* pp. 100-104.

7. See in particular "Developments in Aging 1959 to 1963," February 11, 1963; "Medical Assistance for the Aged: the Kerr-Mills Program," October, 1963; and "Blue Cross and Private Health Insurance Coverage of Older Americans," July, 1964.

8. National Council of Senior Citizens, Legislative Memorandum, November 30, 1962.

9. Quoted in Sundquist, *Politics and Policy,* p. 306.

10. *Ibid.,* p. 314.

11. See p. 44 above and Harris, *Sacred Trust,* pp. 163-164.

12. *Ibid.,* p. 172.

13. CQ *Almanac,* 1964, p. 239.

14. *NYT,* January 10, 1965, IV, p. 6. President Johnson had been criticized by animal lovers for his habit of yanking his beagles by their ears.

15. Arlen J. Lange, "How Doctors Helped Expand Medicare," reprinted in *Medical Economics,* September 6, 1965, pp. 259-289.

16. Harold B. Myers, "Mr. Mills' Elder-medi-bettercare," *Fortune,* LXXI (June, 1965), p. 166.

17. *NYT,* April 11, 1965, p. 9.

18. *Ibid.,* January 12, 1965, p. 16.

19. Harris, *Sacred Trust,* p. 181.

20. See *Ibid.,* pp. 184-185.

21. *Ibid.,* p. 187.

22. *Ibid.,* pp. 190-191.

23. Committee on Finance, USS, 89th Congress, *Hearings* on H.R. 6675, April 29, 1965, pp. 182-185.

24. *NYT,* May 1, 1965, p. 11.

25. Senate *Hearings,* May 11, 1965, p. 602.

26. As for Long himself, more important than Cruikshank's Washington team was reportedly a Louisiana AFL-CIO leader who threatened "to block action on a tax-write-off bill on oil holdings that was then being considered by a committee of the state legislature and that had been written expressly for the Longs, whose money was largely in oil." The tax bill was to be released only if Long refrained from taking his amendments to the floor. But that did not mean that the amendments could not be offered by others, with Long's not-so-tacit support; they were, in fact, taken to the floor by Curtis and Ribicoff. See Harris, *Sacred Trust,* pp. 209-211.

27. *Ibid.,* p. 210.

28. A Hartke proposal to increase funds for public assistance programs in the Virgin Islands was rejected by voice vote.

29. Data are taken from Committee on Finance, USS, 89th Congress, *Legislative Calendar,* December 1, 1966, pp. 134-136, and from the relevant portions of the *Congressional Record,* July 7-9, 1965.

30. The fourth was Bennett's proposal on tips. Senators Javits and Kennedy of New York led an unsuccessful attempt on the floor, backed by the administration, to delete the committee amendment and substitute the House provision treating tips as regular income for social security purposes.

31. Harris, *Sacred Trust,* p. 211.

32. *CR,* July 8, 1965, pp. 15924-15927; July 9, 1965, p. 16119.

33. See the Finance Committee *Calendar,* pp. 136-138.

34. *CR,* July 27, 1965, pp. 18382-18383.

35. *Ibid.,* July 28, 1965, p. 18503.

36. See Harris, *Sacred Trust,* p. 213.

37. *Ibid.,* p. 4.

*38. See pp. 23-24 above.

39. See *Congress and the Nation* (Washington: Congressional Quarterly

Service, 1965), pp. 730-735, and, on pre-1934 sugar policy, Committee on Finance, USS, *History of the Committee on Finance,* March 5, 1970, pp. 59-61.

40. On the techniques and successes of Cuban interests in maintaining a healthy quota see Douglass Cater, *Power in Washington* (New York: Vintage, 1965), pp. 199-205.

41. The administration request came in response to a call from the Organization of American States for sanctions against the Dominican government, which had been implicated in an attempt to assassinate President Romulo Betancourt of Venezuela. The resistance of Cooley and his vice-chairman, W. R. Poage, to the request was widely attributed to their sympathies toward the Trujillo government.

42. CQ *Almanac,* 1960, p. 214.

43. *Ibid.,* 1963, p. 138.

44. Committee on Finance, USS, 89th Congress, *Report* to accompany H.R. 11135, October 18, 1965, pp. 4-5.

45. CQ *Almanac,* 1964, pp. 121-122.

46. Committee on Finance, USS, 89th Congress, *Hearings* on H.R. 11135 and S. 2567, October 14, 1965, pp. 177-179.

47. 48 *Stat.* 676 (1934); 50 *Stat.* 912 (1937).

48. CQ *Almanac,* 1962, p. 137.

49. *NYT,* August 18, 1965, p. 1.

50. Except for the Philippines, for whom a fixed tonnage had been set by a separate treaty.

51. Senate *Hearings,* October 14, 1965, pp. 58, 65.

52. See *CR,* September 22, 1965, pp. 24692-24695; October 12, 1965, pp. 26739, 26762-26763.

53. See "Sugar Stick-up," *The Nation,* CCI (October 4, 1965), p. 206.

54. *NYT,* October 15, 1965, p. 44.

55. Senate *Hearings,* October 14, 1965, pp. 90, 151-155.

56. *Ibid.,* pp. 118-119, 143-145.

57. Data are taken from CQ *Almanac,* 1965, p. 147.

58. *NYT,* October 16, 1965, p. 21.

59. See Senate *Hearings,* October 14, 1965, pp. 60-61, 178.

60. *CR,* October 20, 1965, p. 27527.

61. *CR,* October 19, 1965, p. 27372.

62. *NYT,* October 23, 1965, p. 28.

63. See above, p. 18.

64. Theodore Lowi, speaking of the administration of federal programs as well as of lawmaking, describes agriculture generally as "that field of American government where the distinction between public and private has come closest to being completely eliminated. This has been accomplished not by public expropriation of private domain—as would be true of the nationalization that Americans fear—but by private expropriation of public authority . . . The regulators are powerless without the consent

of the regulated." See *End of Liberalism,* pp. 102-115. On the "sugar subgovernment" in particular, see Cater, *Power in Washington,* pp. 17-20.

65. Lowi, "Case-Studies and Political Theory," p. 690.

66. See *Ibid.,* pp. 692-695. The House Agriculture Committee, as Charles Jones points out, is organized "to allow a maximum of constituency-oriented representation," with members ordinarily appointed to subcommittees dealing with commodities important to their districts. (Sugar, however, is handled at the full committee level). The subcommittees then often ratify one another's actions in full committee, though party loyalties and programs sometimes cause this system of reciprocity to break down. See Jones' two articles cited in fn. 45, p. 341, and the discussion on p. 14 above.

67. See above, pp. 35-36.

68. The machinations of lobbyists were in fact somewhat less in evidence as the House Committee wrote a bill extending the Act in 1971 under Poage's leadership—though one reason the committee could keep action at a low key was that the administration indicated its willingness to continue existing quota allotments. The list of countries whose quotas the House Committee increased in 1971 (CQ *Weekly Report,* XXIX [October 9, 1971], p. 2100) did not closely resemble the comparable 1965 list, though certain countries (e.g. Venezuela, Colombia, British Honduras) continued to be conspicuous beneficiaries. In 1971, the Senate Committee in fact made greater alterations in the existing quota system than did the House; a major reason was the continuing buildup of staff capacity. The Finance staff developed and applied a complex "objective" formula related to the countries' past performance. The Committees agreed in advance on a proportionately greater share of the domestic cane quota for mainland areas, but did not disturb the balance between domestic and foreign suppliers engineered in 1965.

69. Frank R. Breul, "Early History of Aid to the Unemployed in the United States," in Joseph M. Becker, editor, *In Aid of the Unemployed* (Baltimore: Johns Hopkins Press, 1965), ch. 1; Witte, *Social Security Act,* pp. 35, 79-143; and Witte, *Perspectives,* pp. 215-223, 235-256.

70. See *Congress and the Nation,* pp. 1289-1303; and Committee on Finance, USS, 89th Congress, "Data Relating to S. 1991," January 18, 1966, pp. 98, 103.

71. *CR,* May 18, 1965, p. 10795.

72. Committee on Finance, USS, 89th Congress, *Hearings* on H. R. 15119, July 15, 1966, p. 111.

73. *NYT,* May 13, 1966, p. 21.

74. See *NYT,* January 10, 1966, p. 9.

75. *Business Week,* June 4, 1966, p. 30.

76. See *NYT,* October 24, 1966, p. 35; CQ *Almanac,* 1966, p. 820. On the general waning of the President's influence in Congress see Evans and Novak, *Lyndon B. Johnson,* pp. 522-525, 584-588.

77. Senate *Hearings,* July 15, 1966, p. 113.

78. See John F. Manley, *The Politics of Finance: The House Committee on Ways and Means* (Boston: Little, Brown, 1970), ch. 4.

79. Senate *Hearings,* July 21, 1966, p. 415.

80. "The Senate marched up the hill last week," said Senator Williams before one such reversal, "and I think we ought to have a roll call to let the American people see how, when they were confronted with Walter Reuther, George Meany, and Jimmy Hoffa the Senate turned around and marched down the hill." *CR,* August 8, 1966, p. 18616.

81. *Ibid.,* p. 18594.

82. In 1970 a measure which closely resembled the 1966 House bill and on which President Nixon had put his imprimatur was approved. Coverage was extended to some 4.8 million employees of small businesses and state and non-profit institutions, though the Finance Committee failed in its attempt to secure in conference the coverage requested by the administration for farm workers. The President did no more than urge the states to adopt a 50% minimum benefit standard, nor did the Finance Committee return to its 1966 position. McCarthy's proposals to establish federal standards and to provide fully federal financing of the "triggered" extended benefits program failed in committee (Long and Fulbright backed off from the positions they had adopted under the Johnson administration's urging, but even if they had voted as they had in 1966, membership shifts would still have resulted in an 8-9 defeat) and on the floor (by 29-47 and 30-45 respectively). See CQ *Almanac,* 1970, pp. 289-293, 21-S.

83. CQ *Almanac,* 1963, p. 999.

84. See Mansfield, "Economic Policy," p. 138; and Huitt, "Operations in Money and Credit," p. 446.

85. On this point see Joseph A. Pechman, *Federal Tax Policy* (New York: Norton, 1971), pp. 36, 40; and Manley, *Politics of Finance,* pp. 342-346.

86. Committee on Finance, USS, 89th Congress, *Hearings* on H. R. 13103, August 8, 1966, p. 28.

87. *Ibid.,* p. 1.

88. *Ibid.,* p. 37.

89. *Ibid.,* pp. 51-52.

90. Cf. the testimony of Senator Bartlett, Joint Committee on the Organization of the Congress, 89th Congress, *Hearings* pursuant to S. Con Res. 2, August 3, 1965, pp. 1324-1329.

91. For summary accounts of federal activity in the area, see *Congress and the Nation,* pp. 1534-1535; Alexander Heard, *The Costs of Democracy* (Garden City: Doubleday, 1962), ch. 9, 13.

92. Heard, *Costs,* p. 421.

93. CQ *Almanac,* 1957, p. 189. Emphasis added.

94. "I would urge Congress," testified Adlai Stevenson, "to say to . . . the television industry: we reclaim for a few hours every four years the

public airwaves." Committee on Commerce, USS, 86th Congress, *Hearings* on S. 3171, May 16, 1960, p. 8.

95. See Richard L. Neuberger, *Adventures in Politics* (New York: Oxford University Press, 1954), ch. 10.

96. *NYT,* May 6, 1961, p. 14.

97. See President's Commission on Campaign Costs, *Financing Presidential Campaigns* (Washington: Government Printing Office, 1962), especially pp. 30-32.

98. See also Clark's remarks on Senate handling of the bill: *NYT,* August 5, 1966, p. 11; CQ *Almanac,* 1966, p. 485. Cf. the tone of finality in the *NYT* article of August 28, 1966, IV, p. 5.

99. Committee on Finance, USS, 89th Congress, *Hearings* on S. 3496 and other bills, August 18, 1966, p. 9. On the background of Long's bill and the story of its passage, see Herbert E. Alexander, "Financing Presidential Elections," in Gerhard Leibholz, editor, *Jahrbuch des Offentlichen Rechts der Gegenwart,* vol. XVII (Tübingen: J. C. B. Mohr, 1969), pp. 593-600.

100. CQ *Almanac,* 1962, p. 919.

101. Senate *Hearings,* August 18, 1966, p. 44.

102. *NYT,* October 5, 1966, p. 1.

103. *CR,* October 12, 1966, p. 26383.

104. *Ibid.,* p. 26401.

105. George Lardner, Jr., "The Day Congress Played Santa," *Washington Post,* December 25, 1966, p. 10.

106. *CR,* October 12, 1966, p. 16392.

107. Senator Ralph Yarborough, speaking in this instance for Texas bankers fearful of losing their Mexican deposits, proposed that the House amendments imposing estate and income taxes on foreign deposits in U.S. banks, the effective date of which the Senate Committee had deferred until 1972, be deleted altogether. Long announced that the administration was neutral on the amendment and suggested that the Senate might well approve it to strengthen its bargaining position in conference. This the Senate did by a twenty-vote margin, despite Williams' continuing protests that a "tax haven" was being created. The conference committee later accepted the House provisions, but with an effective date of 1973.

108. *CR,* October 13, 1966, pp. 26490-26491.

109. *Ibid.,* October 20, 1966, pp. 28245, 28251.

110. *NYT,* October 20, 1966, p. 1.

111. *CR,* October 22, 1966, pp. 28762-28763.

112. *Ibid.,* pp. 28760, 28787-28789.

113. Alexander, "Financing Presidential Elections," pp. 596-597. But the Campaign Fund Act was also destined to be one of the shortest-lived statutes on record. A rider attached to a tax bill in 1967, and debated for five weeks in the Senate, suspended the financing plan. See *Ibid.,* pp. 600-605. Long continued to nurture his bill, however, and in 1971, at the urging of

labor leaders and officials of the impoverished national Democratic Party, he attempted to resurrect it. This time Pastore was chosen to do the honors on the floor, and the Senate appended the provision to a tax cut bill that represented a keystone of President Nixon's New Economic Program. Mills, however, fearing House rejection and a presidential veto, declined to accept Long's checkoff plan in conference (a Senate provision for a tax deduction or credit for political contributions was, however, retained). See Don Oberdorfer's extended *Washington Post* coverage, reprinted in *CR,* December 16, 1971 (daily edition), pp. E13578-E13582. Meanwhile, a more orthodox reform proposal strengthening reporting requirements for federal candidates and limiting the amounts that could be spent for broadcasting and other advertising media finally cleared the four committees to which it had been referred and received the approval of both houses. Long decided at an early point *not* to append his proposal to this bill, which, as Morris Udall remarked, the President was "looking for an excuse to veto" (CQ *Weekly Report,* XXIX [December 4, 1971], p. 2485; Nixon had vetoed an earlier reform measure in 1970). The bill was signed into law on February 7, 1972.

114. Lardner, "Congress Played Santa," p. 10.

Chapter 5: FINANCE AND COMMERCE: COMPARISON AND CONTRAST

1. *Business Week,* February 19, 1966, p. 36.
2. See Table 3 below, p. 180.
3. Data taken from CQ *Weekly Report,* XXIV (February 25, 1966), p. 474. Committee roster taken from second session.
4. George Goodwin, Jr., *The Little Legislatures: Committees of Congress* (Amherst: University of Massachusetts Press, 1970), p. 60.
5. Finance Committee *Calendar,* pp. 107-100.
6. By the time the Senate began the 1967 debate that would eventuate in the suspension of the campaign fund plan, Finance Committee members Gore, McCarthy, and Metcalf had developed alternatives to Long's scheme. On the effect of the protracted battle on Long's prestige and leadership credits, see Norman C. Miller, "The Bayou Brawler Could Lose even while Winning," *Wall Street Journal,* May 2, 1967, p. 18.
7. Matthews, *U.S. Senators,* p. 149; Stephen Horn, *Unused Power: The Work of the Senate Committee on Appropriations* (Washington: Brookings, 1970), p. 11. The calculations below are based on data from Commerce Committee *Calendar,* pp. 253-254; Commerce Committee *History,* pp. 57-61; Finance Committee *History,* pp. 112-118; and relevant issues of the *Congressional Directory.*
3. Cf. above, p. 92; and Bibby and Davidson, *On Capitol Hill,* pp. 183-195.

9. The following passage from an autobiographical sketch written by Gore shows as much about the man's self-image as about the institution he is describing: "The Senate is not a club as so often said, but an arena filled with 99 strong-willed, independent, egotistical, and scrappy men. . . . What a lone Senator can do is stand by his principles, do his homework, know his people, attend to his committee meetings, and be prepared for his afternoons in the arena. . . . Several tags have been attached to me during my political career. One of these is 'maverick', and if one likes labels, this in some ways may be an apt description. It is apt in the sense that most Tennesseans are mavericks, since they are opposed to running thoughtlessly with the herd, feel no need to play follow the leader, and value their personal and social independence." Albert Gore, *The Eye of the Storm: A People's Politics for the Seventies* (New York: Herder and Herder, 1970), pp. 189-190.

10. See Green and Rosenthal, *Government of Atom,* pp. 51-53; and Fenno, *Power of Purse,* pp. 160-166, 191-192, 235-236.

11. CQ *Weekly Report,* XXIV (February 25, 1966), p. 474; CQ *Almanac,* 1966, pp. 33-34, 1411.

12. See above, p. 143.

13. CQ *Weekly Report,* XXIV (February 25, 1966), pp. 472-474; CQ *Almanac,* 1966, pp. 1411-1413.

14. Manley, *Politics of Finance,* p. 251; on patterns of interest-aggregation in Senate and House, see pp. 263-269. On House norms, see Fenno, *Power of Purse,* pp. 8-17, 99-108, 626-635.

15. The others were two amendments to the Bankruptcy Act proposed by Senators Ervin and Hruska which were eventually appended to a House-passed bill; Saltonstall's national debt proposal, included in the "grab bag"; and legislation implementing the International Coffee Agreement which the administration pushed in the Senate after the House balked. Data from Finance Committee *Calendar,* pp. 199-205; Commerce Committee *Calendar,* pp. 131-134.

16. Both Manley and Vogler, it should be noted, find the Finance Committee to fare better in conference encounters than one would infer from the present case studies or from the comments of members of both committees. Manley notes that the Senate's victories have been considerably less frequent in the area of social security than on matters of taxes and trade. See *Politics of Finance,* pp. 269-294; and David J. Vogler, *The Third House: Conference Committees in the United States Congress* (Evanston: Northwestern University Press, 1971), ch. IV. That Vogler finds both Ways and Means and Senate Commerce frequently to be bested in conference situations suggests that there might in some instances be an *inverse* relation between the advantages that comes with *initiation,* setting the initial parameters of a proposal, and "victory" at the conference stage. Recall Fenno's comparable finding for House Appropriations (*Power of Purse,* pp. 661-670). In any case, it is clear that conference outcomes considered in

isolation may be very misleading as an index to intercommittee "domi-nation."

17. "Presidential support" scores represent the percentage of roll-call votes on which a member voted in support of the President's announced position. Data taken from CQ *Almanac,* 1962, pp. 708-709, 714; 1964, pp. 731, 734-735; 1966, pp. 993, 996-997.

18. For evaluations of Stam's and Woodworth's roles see Rowland Evans, Jr., "The Invisible Men who Run Congress," *Saturday Evening Post,* CCXXXVI (June 8, 1963), pp. 13ff; and *Business Week,* June 11, 1966, pp. 106, 111. For a fuller discussion of the JCIRT, see John F. Manley, "Con-gressional Staff and Public Policy-Making: The Joint Committee on In-ternal Revenue Taxation," *Journal of Politics,* XXX (November, 1968), pp. 1046-1067.

19. Committee on Finance, USS, 91st Congress, "Medicare and Medic-aid—Problems, Issues, and Alternatives," February 9, 1970. For a recent profile of the staff, see Frank V. Fowlkes and Harry Lenhart, Jr., "Two Money Committees Wield Power Differently," *National Journal,* April 10, 1971, pp. 800-801.

20. *CR,* February 3, 1967, p. 2530.

21. Herbert Kaufman, "Emerging Conflicts in the Doctrines of Public Ad-ministration," *APSR,* L (December, 1956), p. 1060.

22. Polsby, "Policy Analysis and Congress," p. 63.

23. Manley, "Staff and Policy-Making," pp. 1062-1065.

Chapter 6: THE LABOR AND PUBLIC WELFARE COMMITTEE IN ACTION

1. Frank J. Munger and Richard F. Fenno, Jr., *National Politics and Federal Aid to Education* (Syracuse: Syracuse University Press, 1962), p. 140. For fuller accounts of the aid-to-education struggle prior to the 89th Congress see also Hugh Douglas Price, "Race, Religion, and the Rules Committee," in Alan F. Westin, editor, *The Uses of Power* (New York: Har-court, Brace, and World, 1962); Robert Bendiner, *Obstacle Course on Capitol Hill* (New York: McGraw-Hill, 1964); Eugene Eidenberg and Roy D. Morey, *An Act of Congress: The Legislative Process and the Making of Education Policy* (New York: W. W. Norton, 1969), ch. 2; Stephen K. Bailey and Edith K. Mosher, *ESEA: The Office of Education Administers a Law* (Syracuse: Syracuse University Press, 1968), ch. 1; Sundquist, *Politics and Policy,* ch. 5; and *Congress and the Nation,* pp. 1195-1205.

2. Munger and Fenno, *Politics and Aid,* p. 99.

3. Sundquist, *Politics and Policy,* p. 162.

4. *Ibid.,* p. 176.

5. Munger and Fenno, *Politics and Aid,* p. 104.

6. *Ibid.,* p. 131.

7. Sundquist, *Politics and Policy,* p. 188.

8. Munger and Fenno, *Politics and Aid,* p. 156.

9. Price, "Race, Religion, Rules Committee," pp. 62, 64.

10. See *Ibid.,* pp. 67-70; Munger and Fenno, *Politics and Aid,* pp. 170-185; Bendiner, *Obstacle Course,* ch. 9-10; Sundquist, *Politics and Policy,* pp. 193-195.

11. See Philip Meranto, *The Politics of Federal Aid to Education in 1965* (Syracuse: Syracuse University Press, 1967), pp. 42-50; and Frank J. Munger, "The Politics of Federal Aid to Education" (paper prepared for delivery at the 1965 Annual Meeting of the American Political Science Association), pp. 8-12.

12. Stephen K. Bailey, "The Office of Education and the Education Act of 1965" (Inter-University Case Program, no. 100; New York: Bobbs-Merrill, 1966), p. 4.

13. Cf. the accounts in Evans and Novak, *Lyndon B. Johnson,* p. 516; Bailey and Mosher, *ESEA,* pp. 26-30; and Eidenberg and Morey, *Act of Congress,* pp. 79, 90.

14. Message on Education, January 12, 1965. CQ *Almanac,* 1965, p. 1375.

15. Bailey, "Office of Education," p. 6.

16. Cf. the corroborating testimony of executive and House participants in Eidenberg and Morey, *Act of Congress,* pp. 76-77.

17. Committee on Labor and Public Welfare, Subcommittee on Education, USS, 89th Congress, *Hearings* on S. 370, January 26, 1965, p. 3.

18. The quotation is from Senator Cooper; see Sundquist, *Politics and Policy,* pp. 216-220.

19. For descriptions of the NEA and other groups involved in the federal aid struggle see Munger and Fenno, *Politics and Aid,* pp. 20-34, 56-72; Meranto, *Aid in 1965,* pp. 50-84; and Eidenberg and Morey, *Act of Congress,* pp. 59-69, 78-88.

20. Quoted from an NEA official by Eidenberg and Morey, *Act of Congress,* p. 64.

21. *NYT,* March 27, 1965, p. 1.

22. Senate *Hearings,* January 26, 1965, p. 888.

23. *Ibid.,* p. 101.

24. *CR,* April 7, 1965, p. 7317.

25. Committee on Labor and Public Welfare, USS, 89th Congress, *Report* to accompany H. R. 2362, April 6, 1965, pp. 15-16.

26. *CR,* April 7, 1965, pp. 7320-7321.

27. Senate *Report,* p. 82.

28. *Ibid.,* pp. 87-88.

29. *CR,* April 7, 1965, p. 7320; April 9, 1965, p. 7690.

30. Senate *Report,* pp. 83-84.

31. *CR,* April 8, 1965, p. 7537.

32. *NYT,* April 14, 1965, p. 24.

33. For further evidence on the usual patterns of group influence—and further support of Mancur Olson's contentions regarding the determinants of group strength—cf. the observation of Bailey and Mosher: "Although it forms the largest [education] lobby, NEA is not the most powerful interest group. The vocational education lobby, the audio-visual lobby, the publishers' lobby, and the library lobby have been, in their respective fields, more effective forces in shaping federal educational legislation than has NEA." *ESEA,* p. 15.

34. Data taken from *Congress and the Nation,* pp. 1125-1150; CQ *Almanac,* 1954, p. 165; 1965, p. 162.

35. Quoted in Elizabeth B. Drew, "The Health Syndicate: Washington's Noble Conspirators," *Atlantic Monthly,* CCXX (December, 1967), p. 79.

36. *Ibid.,* pp. 78-79.

37. *Ibid.,* p. 79.

38. See *Report of the Commission on Research* (Chicago: American Medical Association, 1967), p. 70.

39. Drew, "Health Syndicate," p. 79.

40. See The President's Commission on Heart Disease, Cancer, and Stroke, "Report to the President" (Washington: Government Printing Office, 1964), vol. I, pp. 29-35.

41. Committee on Labor and Public Welfare, Subcommittee on Health, USS, 89th Congress, *Hearings,* on S. 596, February 9, 1965, p. 59.

42. See Elinor Langer, "Presidential Medicine," *Science,* CXLII (March 20, 1964), pp. 1308-1309.

43. Senate *Hearings,* February 9, 1965, p. 68.

44. *Ibid.,* p. 28.

45. *Ibid.,* pp. 62-63.

46. *Ibid.,* February 10, 1965, pp. 142, 144; see Elinor Langer, "Heart Disease, Cancer, and Stroke," *Science* CXLVIII (May 14, 1965), p. 932.

47. Senate *Hearings,* February 10, 1965, p. 123.

48. Committee on Labor and Public Welfare, USS, 89th Congress, *Report* to accompany S. 596, June 24, 1965, p. 12.

49. Senate *Hearings,* February 9-10, 1965, pp. 79, 158.

50. Committee on Interstate and Foreign Commerce, U.S. House of Representatives, 89th Congress, *Hearings* on H. R. 3140, July 21-28, 1965, pp. 114, 187, 388-389.

51. *CR,* June 25, 1965, pp. 14823-14838.

52. *NYT,* September 20, 1965, p. 3.

53. *CR,* September 24, 1965, p. 24126.

54. House *Hearings,* July 27, 1965, p. 301.

55. The establishment of the next major new research program—in 1971, for cancer—revealed significant shifts in this coalition. A Lasker-oriented panel established by Senate resolution in 1970 to study the problem, Senate champions like Yarborough and Kennedy, and eventually the Nixon

Administration all came to favor the establishment of a cancer research agency funded and administered separately from NIH. See Lucy Eisenberg, "The Politics of Cancer," *Harper's Magazine,* CCXLIII (November, 1971), pp. 100-105. In the end, Representative Paul Rogers and the House Commerce Committee were able to keep the program within NIH, but the episode demonstrated that the efficacy of NIH autonomy and administrative control, which had been a working assumption of Hill and his collaborators, was no longer taken for granted by partisans of stepped-up "applied" research. Behind this lay a perceived decline in the political clout and independence of NIH, attributed in part to the departure of Shannon and other energetic administrators and in part to the concomitant (and largely successful) efforts of HEW and BOB to reassert budgetary control. To leave the cancer program within NIH thus seemed to limit the scope and size of the program and to invite trade-offs between it and other research efforts.

56. See Finance Committee *History,* pp. 75-83; William P. Dillingham, *Federal Aid to Veterans, 1917-1941* (Gainesville: University of Florida Press, 1952); David Camelon, "I Saw the GI Bill Written," in Henry A. Turner, editor, *Politics in the United States* (New York: McGraw-Hill, 1955); and *Congress and the Nation,* pp. 1335-1348.

57. Testimony of Francis W. Stover before the Subcommittee on Veterans' Affairs (press copies), March 22, 1957, p. 1; April 21, 1959, p. 2.

58. Committee on Labor and Public Welfare, Subcommittee on Veterans' Affairs, USS, 89th Congress, *Hearings* on S. 9, February 19, 1965, pp. 167, 173.

59. Committee on Veterans' Affairs, U.S. House of Representatives, 89th Congress, *Hearings* on S. 9 and other bills, September 2, 1965, pp. 2972-2974.

60. Senate *Hearings,* February 26, 1965, pp. 253-258.

61. *Ibid.,* pp. 222-237.

62. "I do not think you ought to come up here as a flunky for the Defense Department," Yarborough told Farmer during hearings on proposed liberalizations of the cold war program in 1968. "But I recognize that you have [your] orders . . ." "We are acting in concert with the Armed Forces," Farmer acknowledged, ". . . we are part of the executive together, you know." Committee on Labor and Public Welfare, Subcommittee on Veterans' Affairs, USS, 90th Congress, *Hearings* on S. 2985 and other bills, July 1, 1968, pp. 145, 160.

63. See above, pp. 66-67.

64. *CR,* July 19, 1965, p. 17348.

65. House *Hearings,* August 31, 1965, p. 2914.

66. *Ibid.,* September 1, 1965, pp. 2944, 2952.

67. *NYT,* March 4, 1966, p. 4.

68. On the background and passage of the FLSA see Orme W. Phelps,

"The Legislative Background of the Fair Labor Standards Act," *Studies in Business Administration,* IX (University of Chicago Press, 1939); John S. Forsythe, "Legislative History of the Fair Labor Standards Act," *Law and Contemporary Problems,* VI (Summer, 1939), pp. 464-490; and Jerry Voorhis, *Confessions of a Congressman* (Garden City: Doubleday, 1948), ch. 9.

69. CQ *Almanac,* 1960, p. 319. On postwar legislation see Gus Tyler, *A Legislative Campaign for a Federal Minimum Wage, 1955* (New York: McGraw-Hill, 1960); and *Congress and the Nation,* pp. 635-651.

70. The cycle continued in 1972, and past patterns of committee-chamber interaction were replicated as well. House Education and Labor reported a bill considerably more generous than that advocated by the administration. But its extension of coverage to 6 million additional workers was deleted on the House floor, and its proposed MW increase to $2.00 was altered to provide for an increase to $1.80 immediately and to $2.00 a year later. The bill reported by LPW retained the immediate increase to $2.00 and expanded coverage by some 8 million; the full Senate approved the LPW bill with few alterations on July 21.

71. See pp. 14, 203 above and Goodwin, *Little Legislatures,* p. 50.

72. See Munger and Fenno, *Politics and Aid,* ch. 5-6; and Fenno, "House and Federal Aid."

73. *NYT,* April 14, 1965, p. 29; April 16, 1965, p. 14; May 16, 1965, p. 71.

74. *Ibid.,* August 8, 1965, IV, p. 4.

75. CQ *Almanac,* 1965, p. 1412.

76. *NYT,* August 19, 1965, p. 31.

77. *Ibid.,* February 1, 1966, p. 17; February 24, 1966, p. 21.

78. See Bibby and Davidson, *On Capitol Hill,* ch. 7. On the formulation and passage of the 1964 act see also Sundquist, *Politics and Policy,* ch. 4; Davidson, "Race for Representation," pp. 392-393; John C. Donovan, *The Politics of Poverty* (New York: Pegasus, 1967), ch. 1-2; Douglass Cater, "The Politics of Poverty," *The Reporter,* XXX (February 13, 1964), pp. 16-20; Elinor Graham, "The Politics of Poverty," and "Poverty and the Legislative Process," and S. M. Miller and Martin Reim, "The War on Poverty: Perspectives and Prospects," in Ben B. Seligman, editor, *Poverty as a Public Issue* (New York: Free Press, 1965), pp. 231-320.

79. Michael Harrington, *The Other America* (New York: Macmillan, 1962); Leon Keyserling, *Poverty and Deprivation in the United States* (Washington: Conference on Economic Progress, 1962); and Dwight Macdonald, "Our Invisible Poor," *New Yorker,* January 19, 1963, pp. 82ff.

80. Bibby and Davidson, *On Capitol Hill,* p. 227.

81. See Graham, "Politics of Poverty," p. 244; Miller and Reim, "War on Poverty," p. 277; and Donovan, *Politics of Poverty,* pp. 73-74.

82. See above, pp. 213-214; and Donovan, *Politics of Poverty,* p. 64.

83. *NYT,* April 15, 1966, p. 1; April 20, 1966, p. 26.

84. *Ibid.,* May 12, 1966, p. 21.

85. *Ibid.,* April 28, 1966, p. 1.
86. Committee on Labor and Public Welfare, Subcommittee on Employment, Manpower, and Poverty, USS, 89th Congress, *Hearings* on S. 3164, June 21-23, 1966, pp. 44, 144-149, 214.
87. *Ibid.,* June 22, 1966, p. 155.
88. *CR,* October 3, 1966, p. 24793; cf. p. 212 above.
89. Committee on Labor and Public Welfare, USS, 89th Congress, *Report* to accompany S. 3164, September 29, 1966, p. 14.
90. *Ibid.,* pp. 3, 5.   ,
91. See Senate *Hearings,* June 21, 1966, pp. 96-98; *NYT,* June 22, 1966, p. 36; Senate *Report,* p. 17.
92. *NYT,* October 5, 1966, p. 1.
93. Donovan, *Politics of Poverty,* p. 73.

Chapter 7: HILL'S "CONDOMINIUM"

1. Data taken from CQ *Weekly Report,* XXIV (February 25, 1966), p. 474. Committee roster taken from second session. No scores available for Robert Griffin, who was appointed to the Senate upon McNamara's death and immediately took a seat on LPW.
2. See Munger and Fenno, *Politics and Aid,* pp. 113-115.
3. Data taken from *Ibid.* George Goodwin Jr. has compiled a similar "conservatism score" for Senate Committees, covering the period 1947-1968. He finds Finance to be the most conservative, LPW the most liberal, with Commerce squarely in the middle. *Little Legislatures,* pp. 112-113.
4. See Committee on Labor and Public Welfare, USS, 89th Congress, *Legislative Calendar,* December 1, 1966, pp. 212-213; and *CR,* October 22, 1965, pp. 28946-28947; October 22, 1966, pp. 29032-29034.
5. Jones, "Minority Party and Policy-Making," p. 482.
6. ADA scores taken from CQ *Weekly Report,* XXIV (February 25, 1966), p. 474. Estimations of legislative involvement made from committee calendars and personal interviews.
7. See fn. 10, p. 350, and the further discussion below, pp. 274, 276.
8. See above, pp. 11-12, 79-81.
9. See below, pp. 313-317, and especially Figure 6, p. 314.
10. See Morse's remarks during the 1967 debate on the Legislative Reorganization Act: *CR,* February 3, 1967, p. 2532.
11. Data taken from Commerce Committee *Calendar,* pp. 147-157; and LPW Committee *Calendar,* 89th Congress, pp. 250-266. The Special Textile Industry and Great Lakes Transportation Subcommittees held hearings during the 88th Congress and issued reports in 1963 and 1965 respectively. The Select Subcommittee on Poverty was discontinued after the first session, 89th Congress.

12. Data taken from Committee on Labor and Public Welfare, USS, 90th Congress, *Legislative Calendar,* December 1, 1968, pp. 305-306, and the relevant issues of the *Congressional Directory.*

13. See above, pp. 237, 242. Morse was reluctant to give up his policy role in education, but more personal factors entered into his decision as well. In 1961, when Morse had wanted the Labor Subcommittee, labor leaders, distrustful of him after he took an independent line on the Landrum-Griffin bill (as they were to be later in the 89th Congress on the emergency strike question), rejected him in favor of McNamara. Morse thus derived great satisfaction from ignoring their entreaties in 1965.

14. This situation naturally changed considerably with Hill's retirement. Yarborough, as LPW's Chairman and most senior member, chose Health as the Subcommittee he would chair, and Kennedy's patient tenure on the Subcommittee culminated in his succession to the Chairmanship after Yarborough's 1970 defeat. Hill had kept the Subcommittee small, and the exclusiveness of his control had represented something of a disincentive to membership. But soaring membership figures after 1968 revealed both the fertility and political attractiveness of the policy area and the fact that subsequent Subcommittee chairmen did not even approximate Hill's monopoly of the field. By 1971 major subcommittee rosters had been increased to 12 across the board, but exceptional membership pressures dictated that 14 slots be available on the health subunit.

15. By "LPW votes" is meant the 90 roll calls on bills reported by LPW during the 89th Congress. Cf. Table 3, p. 180 above.

16. Munger and Fenno frequently contrast LPW with Education and Labor to point up the latter's "classic incapacities as a consensus-building institution." *Politics and Aid,* pp. 107-124.

17. See Matthews, *U.S. Senators,* pp. 149-156; and Horn, *Unused Power,* p. 11. Data taken from LPW Committee *Calendar,* 90th Congress, pp. 305-306, and the relevant issues of the *Congressional Directory.*

18. See above, p. 17; and Green and Rosenthal, *Government of Atom,* pp. 51-53.

19. Data taken from CQ *Weekly Report,* XXIV (February 25, 1966), pp. 472-474.

20. See Lowi, "Case Studies and Political Theory," p. 715.

21. Data from CQ *Weekly Report,* XXIV (February 25, 1966), p. 474; and CQ *Almanac,* 1966, p. 1411.

22. ADA scores were 19 and 27 respectively; USCC scores were 83 and 66. Data from CQ *Weekly Report,* XXIV (February 25, 1966), pp. 472-474.

23. See above, pp. 187-188. The behavior of Education and Labor on the two bills in question could be attributed in part to less general factors; the members most influential in shaping them were unusually receptive to the idea of modification. Dent was among the Committee's more conservative Democrats (ADA score = 63), and, after the Roosevelt debacle, he

was preoccupied with the need for compromise. And Powell found that criticisms of OEO from the "new left" and from Harlem comported surprisingly well with some of the program modifications conservatives were advocating.

24. For Vogler's similar conclusion with respect to conference outcomes, see *Third House,* p. 69. The computations to follow are based on data from LPW Committee *Calendar,* 89th Congress, pp. 269-279.

25. See the *CR* listings of minority "contributions" cited in fn. 4 above.

26. Cf. Manley, "Staff and Policy-Making," p. 1067.

Chapter 8: THIRTEEN BILLS AND THREE COMMITTEES: THE CHARACTER AND THE CONDITIONS OF LEGISLATIVE RESPONSIBILITY

1. See p. 1 above.

2. Two recent collections are Ranney, ed., *Political Science and Public Policy,* and Bauer and Gergen, eds., *Study of Policy Formation.*

3. E.g. Sundquist, *Politics and Policy,* and Cleaveland et al., *Congress and Urban Problems.*

4. For an assessment of how such perceptions affect the interactions of the House and Senate Appropriations Committees, see Fenno, *Power of Purse,* pp. 626-641. On Finance and Ways and Means, see Manley, *Politics of Finance,* pp. 250-263, 269-272.

5. See above, pp. 18-19.

6. *End of Liberalism,* ch. 4. For a discussion of the way in which the growth of bureaucracy may have reduced, paradoxically, the capacity of the executive to have a redistributive impact, see Salisbury, "Analysis of Public Policy," pp. 169-170.

7. See Robert Sherrill, "The Embodiment of Poor White Power," *New York Times Magazine,* February 28, 1971, pp. 9ff.

8. See Rowland Evans, Jr., and Robert D. Novak, *Nixon in the White House: The Frustration of Power* (New York: Random House, 1971), pp. 37-43, 211-233.

9. *Ibid.,* pp. 351-353, 379-382.

10. The text of the 1971 State of the Union message is reprinted in CQ *Weekly Reports,* XXIX (January 29, 1971), pp. 263-266.

11. Three additional vetoes were of bills affecting federal employees and one quashed the initial congressional attempt to limit broadcast campaign spending. On the political background of the hospital construction and appropriations vetoes, see Evans and Novak, *Nixon,* pp. 122-129.

12. See Chamberlain, *President, Congress and Legislation,* pp. 453-463; Polsby, "Policy Analysis and Congress," pp. 65-67; and Sundquist, *Politics and Policy,* pp. 392-415, 493-495. Cf. Sundquist's discussions of "timeli-

ness" and of the general factors accounting for the legislative successes of 1963-1965, pp. 393, 481-489, 496-505.

13. See Sundquist, *Politics and Policy,* ch. 11.

14. For an argument that "the critical variable in Johnson's success was the increase in the number of Democrats in general and Northern Democrats in particular" (as opposed to his peculiar skills and strategies), see Joseph Cooper and Gary Bombardier, "Presidential Leadership and Party Success," *Journal of Politics,* XXX (November, 1968), pp. 1012-1027.

15. Cf. pp. 12 above and 313-316 below. Kenneth Gergen, while distinguishing "personal efficacy" from the other "resources" which enable one to exercise leverage in public decision-making, fails to note that the former as well as the latter may not be equally appropriate or helpful at each "sub-phase" of the policy-making process. Gergen, "Assessing Leverage Points," pp. 185-190.

16. See Peter Winch, *The Idea of Social Science* (London: Routledge and Kegan Paul, 1958) and the responses by Alasdair MacIntyre and D. R. Bell, "The Idea of a Social Science," *Proceedings of the Aristotelian Society,* XLI (1967), pp. 95-132. Recall the position of R. G. Collingwood: "For science, the event is discovered by perceiving it, and the further search for its cause is conducted by assigning it to its class and determining the relation between that class and others. For history, the object to be discovered is not the mere event, but the thought expressed in it. To discover that thought is already to understand it. After the historian has ascertained the facts, there is no further process of inquiring into their causes. When he knows what happened, he already knows why it happened. This does not mean that words like 'cause' are necessarily out of place in reference to history; it only means that they are used there in a special sense. When a scientist asks, 'Why did that piece of litmus paper turn pink?' he means 'On what kinds of occasions do pieces of litmus paper turn pink?' When an historian asks 'Why did Brutus stab Caesar?' he means 'What did Brutus think, which made him decide to stab Caesar?' The cause of the event, for him, means the thought in the mind of the person by whose agency the event came about: and this is not something other than the event, it is the inside of the event itself." *The Idea of History* (New York: Oxford University Press, 1956), pp. 214-215.

17. Charles Taylor, *The Explanation of Behaviour* (London: Routledge and Kegan Paul, 1964), pp. 33-35. Whether and in what sense explanation in terms of "I" can be termed "causal" is a matter of some debate. See *Ibid.,* p. 33; Donald Davidson, "Actions, Reasons, and Causes," in Norman S. Care and Charles Landesman, editors, *Readings in the Theory of Action* (Bloomington: Indiana University Press, 1968); Charles Landesman, "The New Dualism in the Philosophy of Mind," *Review of Metaphysics,* XIX (1965), pp. 329-345; and Richard Taylor, *Action and Purpose* (Englewood Cliffs: Prentice-Hall, 1966), ch. 10, 14, 16-17.

18. Taylor, *Action and Purpose,* ch. 4, 9.

19. Winter, *Elements for a Social Ethic,* ch. 2, 5.

20. William Dray, *Laws and Explanations in History* (New York: Oxford University Press, 1957), ch. 5.

21. Winter, *Elements for a Social Ethic,* p. 163. For an illuminating discussion of the relation between *verstehen* and "empirical generalization" see Samuel H. Beer, "Political Science and History," in Melvin Richter, ed., *Essays in Theory and History: An Approach to the Social Sciences* (Cambridge: Harvard University Press, 1970), pp. 46-57, 72-73.

22. See Taylor, *Explanation of Behaviour,* pp. 54-62.

23. R. S. Peters, *The Concept of Motivation* (London: Routledge and Kegan Paul, 1958), pp. 1-16; cf. Taylor, *Explanation of Behaviour,* pp. 25n, 54-56; MacIntyre, "Idea of a Social Science," pp. 104-105; Taylor, *Action and Purpose,* pp. 111-119, 204-223; and Dray, *Explanation in History,* ch. 2, 5.

24. Among the conditions discussed above it should be clear that some are the outgrowths of "action" in their own right. But for the policy initiator (and for one "explaining" *his* actions and their outcome) these contingencies, whatever their intrinsic character, represent "external" factors which can be classified and generalized about as to their likely impact on the subject's action. A related question has to do with how the *final* outcome, the "resultant" of discrete actions and reactions, is best conceptualized. A number of analysts, most notably Charles E. Lindblom in *The Intelligence of Democracy* and, less persuasively, various group theorists, have insisted that most policy "resolutions" cannot be understood in terms of any single or coherent purpose or rationale; they are in that sense "unintended" though not necessarily defective in terms of the *post hoc* criteria of rationality or efficacy an analyst might want to employ. The fact that the intentions of discrete policy-makers are rarely fully implemented, however, does not obviate their centrality to an understanding of the partisan "moves" that comprise the process.

25. Cf. Taylor, *Explanation of Behaviour,* pp. 44-45, 232, 242-243; MacIntyre, "Idea of a Social Science," pp. 111-114; Taylor, *Action and Purpose,* pp. 174-184, 218-220.

26. See Peters, *Concept of Motivation,* pp. 8-9; MacIntyre, "Idea of a Social Science," pp. 97-101.

27. *Idea of a Social Science,* ch. 2-3.

28. Peters, *Concept of Motivation,* p. 5.

29. Taylor, *Explanation of Behaviour,* pp. 9-10, 196. Peter shows that "his reason" explanations assume that the action in question is in fact an efficient means of attaining the end desired, which the subject will undertake on an appropriate occasion if he realizes this to be the case. *Concept of Motivation,* p. 4.

30. With the significant difference, however, that "if a negative instance

is found for a general empirical law, the law itself must be modified or rejected, since it states that people *do* behave in a certain way under certain circumstances. But if a negative instance if found for the sort of general statement which might be extracted out of a rational explanation, the latter would not necessarily be falsified . . . the explanatory value of the principle for those actions which *were* in accordance with it would remain." *Explanation in History,* p. 132.

31. Ways and Means' "formulations" were typically extensive reformulations of executive proposals; the same was often true of other "activist" committees operating in areas of strong presidential concern. Cf. Manley, *Politics of Finance,* ch. 7.

32. See above, p. 11.

33. Another orientation often taking its place in this pattern is a career perspective that looks beyond the Senate. Cf. Matthews, *U.S. Senators,* pp. 109-110. On the incentives party competition possibly gives for liberalism, see Samuel P. Huntington, "A Revised Theory of American Party Politics," *APSR,* XLIV (December, 1950), pp. 669-677.

34. The term is borrowed from Arnold Toynbee and applied to organizations by James March and Herbert Simon, *Organizations* (New York: John Wiley, 1964), p. 184. Cf. Deutsch's concept of the "promising instability." *Nerves of Government,* p. 147.

35. Cf. Bibby and Davidson's discussion of how Banking and Currency subcommittees, though formally equal in status, have in fact differed greatly in the prerogatives and resources they were granted and hence in their capacity to assume a vigorous oversight role. *On Capitol Hill,* pp. 173-183.

36. See above, pp. 14-15.

37. On the fallacy of regarding "individualism" and "centralization" as opposing modes of Senate organization, see David E. Price, Review of Randall B. Ripley, *Power In the Senate, APSR,* LXIV (June, 1970), pp. 630-631.

38. See above, pp. 16-18.

39. Olson's theory, it will be recalled, was useful as well in understanding the resources mustered and leverage exerted by smaller, more narrowly-based groups—some, like sugar and shipping, seeking distributive benefits, and others seeking marginal changes in social-welfare and consumer measures. But here too, an assessment of group "strengths" alone rarely enabled one to predict the way their demands would be mirrored and refracted in the final congressional product. See above, pp. 35-36, 136, 215.

40. See particularly pp. 185-189, 278-280 above and, on the business "bias" of the pressure system, E. E. Schattschneider, *The Semi-Sovereign People: A Realist's View of Democracy in America* (New York: Holt, Rinehart and Winston, 1960), ch. 2.

41. See above, pp. 18-19, and Lowi, "Case Studies and Political Theory," pp. 691, 713: *"Once one posits* the general tendency of these areas of policy or governmental activity to develop characteristic political structures, a number of hypotheses become compelling" (emphasis added).

42. Lasswell and Kaplan, *Power and Society,* p. 73.

43. See above, pp. 296-297, and Lowi, "Case Studies and Political Theory," p. 715.

44. Neustadt, "President's Program," pp. 1016-1017; cf. Holtzman, *Legislative Liaison,* pp. 259-264.

45. Cf. Richard Fenno's justification for his own description of the "environmental constraints" of House committees in terms of the goals and relative prominence of "interested outsiders"—party leaders, executive officials, clientele groups, and members of the parent chamber—rather than in terms of subject-matter characteristics. Richard F. Fenno, "Congressional Committees: A Comparative View" (Prepared for delivery at the 66th Annual Meeting of the American Political Science Association, 1970), p. 29. Fenno abstracts certain characteristics of these groups of outsiders —the intensity of their interest in committee affairs, the patterns of conflict, cooperation, and leadership that obtain between them, the leverage they possess with respect to committee members—thus developing a characterization of the "policy coalitions" that face various committees and some hypotheses as to how these coalitions "influence . . . committee behavior." The present study, focusing as it does on the assumption of legislative responsibility, has treated subject-matter, interest group, and "island of decision" characteristics as interrelated "situational" variables, while at the same time stressing the integrity and autonomy of legislative initiative, both in the Senate actors with which we are directly concerned and in the coordinate actors to whom they must relate and respond.

46. For a critique of the alleged tendency of organization theory in America to conceive of "staff" in such terms, see Robert T. Golembiewski, "Toward New Organization Theories: Some Notes on 'Staff'," *Midwest Journal of Political Science,* V (August, 1961), pp. 237-259.

47. Polsby, "Policy Analysis," p. 63. For a discussion of Polsby's view of staff operations in terms of the goals he sets for Congress, see David E. Price, "Professionals and 'Entrepreneurs': Staff Orientations and Policy-Making on Three Senate Committees," *Journal of Politics,* XXXIII (May, 1971), pp. 316-336.

INDEX

For the three committees and thirteen bills that are the primary object of this study, see the Table of Contents.